More Praise for *And*

> *"I am no longer perplexed by the chronic conflict and polarization I see in organizations and in the world."*

"To be able to make a difference in the world has always mattered to me. This book has supported me to break out of the constrictions of *Or* and into my expanding world of *And* which holds more possibilities for me. In the space of more possibilities, I am more aware of my increased capacity to love and to be connected. I am no longer perplexed by the chronic conflict and polarization I see in organizations and in the world. I feel I can access the energy flow between two wants and hold the whole. That is how I make a difference in my circle of influence, and it is my hope that in some small way I make a difference in the world. I am confident that others will benefit as much as I have."

Shareefah Sabur, MA, MNO, CDP, GPCC, BCC
Executive Director, Gestalt Institute of Cleveland

> *"Within equity, inclusion, and justice work, the Both/And lets us be honest about our privileges without descending into guilt or shame ..."*

"*Both/And* thinking allows for the recognition that two seemingly contradictory things can both be true at the same time. Within equity, inclusion, and justice work, the *Both/And* lets us be honest about our privileges without descending into guilt or shame, recognize urgency while understanding that growth takes time, and focus on the concerns of marginalized communities while uplifting our shared humanity."

Shelly Tochluk
Author, Witnessing Whiteness: The Need to Talk About Race
and How To Do It and Living in the Tension: The Quest for a
Spiritualized Racial Justice

> *"... it has made such a difference in the work I do with leaders at all levels ..."*

"Polarity Thinking is the most elegant approach to dealing with the critical issues that we wrestle with in institutions, organizations, and groups the world over. When we grasp the concepts and their application, we realize that we can truly make a difference in the world by seeing and making sense of both horns of knotty dilemmas. We can have our cake and eat it! Leaders at all levels too-readily see complex issues as problems to solve rather than polarities to leverage. Leaders thus make the issues more complex by invoking solutions that 'solve' only one pole of the issue. The shadow of these one-sided solutions eventually come to the foreground and thus cause downward spiraling and anguish for all involved. Barry's vision has energized and innovated my own work. I'm happy to endorse Polarity Thinking because it has made such a difference in the work I do with leaders at all levels and the design of programs and interventions with those leaders and their organizations."

David Magellan Horth
Director of Innovation Venturing and Partnerships / Senior
Fellow, Center for Creative Leadership

> *"... extremisms are driven by exclusionary Or–thinking. And ... builds an inclusionary paradigm ..."*

"*And*-thinking is critical in my work with one of the most difficult issues in the world – religious extremism. In Northeastern Nigeria, Muslim and Christian antagonism that goes back generations has paved the way for the brutal Islamic extremist group Boko Haram. In Sri Lanka and Myanmar it's Buddhist extremism, in India it's Hindu extremism, in Israel it's Jewish extremism, and in the United States it's Christian extremism. All these extremisms are driven by exclusionary *Or*-thinking. *And*: Volume One and *And*: Volume Two take us step by practical step to understand and dismantle the exclusionary paradigm that we are so used to, and builds an inclusionary paradigm with one simple tool, *And*."

Rev. Dr. Shanta Premawardhana
President, OMNIA Institute for Contextual Leadership

"Barry's book is both manifesto and a 'do-it-yourself' pragmatist's approach ..."

"Barry's book is both manifesto and a 'do-it-yourself' pragmatist's approach to leading ourselves, our communities, our organizations, and our global institutions. There is not a moment that goes by when I hear and then try to flip an *either/Or* into 'Did I just hear a polarity?' in my head. So much traction is gained when it happens, by me simply pointing to the upsides of each, and protecting (giving voice to) the downside fears."

Patrick Sweet, PhD
Co-Director of Geneva Leadership Alliance, Center for Creative
Leadership, Stockholm, Sweden / Geneva, Switzerland

"... helped countless public and private sector organizations get to the heart of what really matters in delivering results and delighting customers."

"Barry Johnson's groundbreaking thought leadership on polarity management has helped countless public and private sector organizations get to the heart of what really matters in delivering results and delighting customers. *And* builds on this incredible body of work to offer real-world applications to help you master your understanding of the power of polarities. I and my past organizations have benefitted greatly from the insights in this book, which provide a practical engagement map for a topic that has never been more important for individuals, for businesses, for the Nation and the world."

David Wennergren
CEO, ACT-IAC
Former Deputy CIO, United States Department of Defense

> *"Barry shows us in very practical terms how to break down barriers between people."*

"For those of us looking for a sensible way to approach strategy for large organizations, Barry's book is a must. His ideas changed the way thousands of people think and work more creatively. Barry shows us in very practical terms how to break down barriers between people and offers an approach to navigate the most difficult situations."

Barbara Singer
CEO, Executive Core
Professor of Leadership, University of Notre Dame

> *"[Barry] belongs with the enlightened few. In an age when values seem to be splitting and flying apart, we desperately need him."*

"Paradox, dilemma and polarity are at long last beginning to be recognised as having a logic of their own. They recently made it to the Harvard Business Review, but Barry was thirty years ahead and trod a once lonely path. For depth of insight he is hard to beat. He belongs with the enlightened few. In an age when values seem to be splitting and flying apart, we desperately need him."

Charles M. Hampden-Turner
Cambridge University
Author, Charting the Corporate Mind, Creating Corporate Culture, and The Seven Cultures of Capitalism

You can read More Praise for _And_ on page 325.

You can read Barry's breaking "Postscript Articles: A Polarity Lens On the COVID-19 Pandemic" on Page 291.

And

Making a Difference by Leveraging Polarity, Paradox or Dilemma

Volume One: Foundations

HRD PRESS

To Dana
Thank you, again

To the Editors
Thank you for helping me be as clear as possible.

Linda Mc Fadden

Kristin Dighe

Shalom Bruhn

David Wheeler

Jean Miller

For Layout, Graphics, and Cover Art
Thank you for making the graphics and text
as clean and understandable as possible.

Luke Massman-Johnson

To My Partners at Polarity Partnerships
Thank you for giving me the time and support to finish this book.

Leslie DePol

Cliff Kayser

Susan Dupre

Peter Dupre

Bob Tauber

Love and Gratitude

Table of Contents

Introduction to Volumes One and Two

I am in Brazil being warmly welcomed by a representative of Natura outside the front entrance to their main building. They know that I have written about polarities so they smile as they translate the Portuguese words carved deep and large into the wall: "Being Well *And*[1] Well Being." They explain that "Being Well" means that we must take care of Natura as a company. It must be financially sound and healthy. "Well Being" means that it is equally important to take care of those who work at Natura, the community, and the environment. (*from Chapter 6*)

This Book is the First of a Two-Volume Set.
Volume One – Foundations

Volume One is a resource for people who want to make a positive difference. How? By overcoming two obstacles: resistance to change and polarization. From a problem-solving perspective, either of these challenges could be overwhelming. From a Polarity Thinking™ perspective, both can be addressed by replacing *Or* with *And* when *And* is required.

For example, the question, "Am I going to hold on to my values *Or* accept the change proposed?" is likely to create resistance to the change. That resistance could be significantly reduced by replacing *Or* with *And*. "How am I going to hold on to my values *And* gain the benefits of the change proposed?" We can save the baby *And* throw out the bathwater. (*Section Three*)

The question, "Am I going to support the group that wants to decentralize *Or* the group that wants to centralize?" is likely to create polarization. That polarization could be significantly reduced by replacing *Or* with *And*. "How do we get the benefits of decentralization *And* the benefits of centralization?" Effective decentralization requires effective centralization. (*Chapter 5*)

"Am I going to support 'Black Lives Matter' *Or* 'All Lives Matter?'" This false choice is less polarizing if *Or* is replaced with *And*: "Black Lives Matter" *And* "All

---

[1] When the word "and" is used to connect two poles of a polarity, it will be capitalized and in italics: *And*. When the word "or" is used, incorrectly, to connect two poles of a polarity, it will also be capitalized and italic: *Or*.

Lives Matter." It is precisely because all lives matter that disproportionate attacks on and incarceration of black people matters. (*Chapter 7*)

Regardless of the size of the system that you want to change, this book guides you through a clear process:

1. **Seeing**: Is this an issue where *And* is required?
2. **Mapping**: How can I see a more complete picture and respect alternative views?
3. **Assessing**: How are we doing with this polarity?
4. **Learning**: What can we learn from our assessment results?
5. **Leveraging:** What action steps will we take to make a positive difference?

Reading this book will help you address resistance to your efforts to make a difference. Also, it will help you address chronic conflicts that become vicious cycles as both sides become more polarized.

You will learn when and how to bring *And* into your efforts to make a positive difference. When done well, supplementing *Or*-thinking with *And*-thinking will help you convert the wisdom of those resisting change into a resource to support a more effective change. *And*-thinking will help you join polarized groups and convert a vicious cycle into a benefit for all. The results will benefit both groups and the larger system of which they are a part.

Volume Two – Applications

Volume One is from my perspective with a lot of input and help from others. What is missing are important other voices. When considering groups with power and privilege which have dominance in the United States and those groups that have been marginalized by the dominant group, I am a member of the dominant group in every category. I am white, cis male[2], financially secure, college educated, raised in a hetero-normative all-white family, from a Christian tradition, without physical or mental disabilities. Having the power and privilege that comes by being in these groups does not make me a good person or a bad person. But membership in the dominant group does come with responsibility to learn from those who are marginalized. It also includes sharing power with them and interrupting the practices and policies of the dominant group that contribute to their marginalization. This marginalization is oppressive and dehumanizing for both the dominant and the marginalized groups. Some marginalized groups include Black, Indigenous, and People of Color (BIPOC), women, LGBTQI+[3] people, the poor, those from religious traditions other than Christian, and those with physical or mental disabilities.

Volume Two includes the voices of people from marginalized groups. Each author provides an example of how they have applied Polarity Thinking to make a difference in their life and work. The authors come from a variety of disciplines. They have worked inside organizations as founders and leaders. They have also worked

---

[2] Cis men are men assigned "male" at birth and feel that "man" and "male" accurately describe who they are.

[3] LGBTQI+ = Lesbian, Gay, Bisexual, Trans, Queer/Questioning, Intersex, plus other identities.

as external resources to organizations as coaches, trainers, organizers for justice and equity, consultants, and teachers. At least one author in each chapter has completed a Two-Year Polarity Mastery Program.

Their stories can be used and adapted to your unique situation. The variety of examples will expand your possibilities and help you avoid common pitfalls as you apply Polarity Thinking. These diverse examples demonstrate how you can succeed in making a difference by combining your life experience with Polarity Thinking and the Polarity Map®.

Start with the Chapter That Interests You Most.

Though Volume One is written in a logical sequence, I encourage you to find the chapter that seems most relevant to you and read it first. Which chapter connects to where you want to make a difference?

All Are Loved *And* Accountable – All Are Connected *And* Each is Unique.

This book begins and ends with two double-messages (polarities) that come to us from most religious traditions.

1. All of us are loved unconditionally, without exception, *And* we are all accountable for our actions and inactions, without exception. In our effort to make a difference, we need to hold ourselves and others accountable. At the same time, the context for our accountability is that we are loved unconditionally *(Section Four)*. When our message of accountability is combined with an often unstated message of unlovability, we generate a natural resistance from the self, family member, organization, or the country receiving the message of unlovability.
2. We are all connected in a unified whole *And* we are each unique. Neither our unity nor our uniqueness can be lost *(Section Two)*. We can make a difference by affirming the reality of our connectedness *And* our uniqueness. We need not struggle to make us connected *Or* to make us unique. We are already both.

Not recognizing these two polarities (*1 & 2 above*) undermines our efforts to make the positive differences we seek to make with our families, organizations, and countries. Not recognizing these and other polarities in this book has contributed to organizational dysfunction, gross inequity and the marginalization mentioned above. Recognizing and intentionally leveraging these polarities and others can make a difference in how well our organizations are run, how financially sound they are, and how effective they are at enhancing our quality of life on the planet for all of us. My hope is that <u>*And:*</u> Volume One and <u>*And:*</u> Volume Two will support you in making your difference in the world.

Barry Johnson (he, him) [4]

---

[4] In this book, I recognize diversity of identity and use she, her / they, them / he, him. For people I know well, and those identified in the public arena, like Dr. MLK, Jr., I use the pronouns they use for themselves.

SECTION ONE
The Basics
Why? What? How?

Special Request

Dear reader, before reading this first chapter, I have two requests:

1. If you have not read the brief introduction, please do so. It sets an important context in which to think about your making a difference and for reading this book.

2. I encourage you to choose any chapter in this book that seems most interesting and read it first. I would like to respond to your interest as soon as possible, and one way to do that is by having you read your chosen chapter first.

Thank you.

Chapter 1
Why?

Why Write This Book?

To support you in your ways of making a positive difference. To encourage you to join us in our mission at Polarity Partnerships:

Enhance Our Quality of Life On the Planet
by Supplementing *"Or"* Thinking With *"And"* Thinking.

Let's take a look at what this means.

Enhance our quality of life on the planet...

This desire is not unique to us. We assume that each of you has a similar desire to make a difference and enhance our quality of life on the planet. It is part of being: a parent wanting the best for your children; a worker, bringing us products or services; an elected representative, working for the common good; a teacher, expanding our horizons; a healthcare worker, caring for our wellness; a person in the justice system or military, doing your best to serve and protect; a community organizer addressing inequity, the marginalization of some of us to the detriment of all of us, poverty, racism, sexism, and the climate crisis; an artist, bringing us beauty and joy; a member of any of our religious traditions, affirming that we are loved unconditionally. We recognize that our individual quality of life is tied, inseparably, with the quality of life of everyone else. There are many ways you may choose to enhance your quality of life for yourselves, your families, and for the larger community. Supplementing *Or*-thinking with *And*-thinking can help.

...by supplementing *Or*-thinking with *And*-thinking.

Or-thinking is essential for learning and for solving problems.[R1,5] As a small child each of us learned to name things. When we name things we are solving the most basic of problems: "What is this?" Is it my elbow *Or* my foot *Or* my eye? Differentiating one thing from another is also the beginning of language. Our problem solving gets expanded as we learn mathematics, science and art. What is 4 plus 4? Is it 8

---

[5] As we go through this book, there will be an expanding number of polarity "realities" that come up. These realities include descriptions and principles that apply to all polarities. When they occur, they will be identified by a superscript; for example: [R1] or [R25]

Or some other number? If 8 is the correct answer, we have solved the problem and can move on to another problem. There are many problems to be solved in creating a smart phone. How does a manufacturer combine the functions of a phone, a camera, a computer, a GPS, and a clock? This involves a series of problems that must be solved. Without making a series of *Or* choices, we do not get a smart phone. Thus, *Or*-thinking and problem solving are essential to becoming effective in the world. It is also essential for passing one's language and culture from one generation to the next. Yet *Or*-thinking <u>alone</u> is not enough. There are a whole set of issues in life for which *Or*-thinking and problem-solving skills are not up to the job. These are issues for which *And*-thinking is required.

And-thinking is a supplement to *Or*-thinking, not a replacement.[R2] *And*-thinking is useful when you are dealing with issues for which *Or* is a false choice. As a parent, should I love my children unconditionally *Or* hold them accountable for their actions? As a leader, should I be Self Assured *Or* Humble? As an organization, should we Centralize for coordination *Or* Decentralize for responsiveness? As a nation, should we focus on Freedom *Or* Equality? As a humanity, should we Take Care of Ourselves *Or* Take Care of the Environment? In each case, the answer is, "Yes." In each case we must pay attention to both poles of an interdependent pair. In these situations, *Or*-thinking alone gets us into trouble. Adding *And*-thinking will help us out.

These interdependent pairs go by different names in the literature. We call them Polarities. They are also called Paradoxes, Dilemmas, Tensions, or Positive Opposites.[R3] No matter what they are called, they are unavoidable because we live in them and they live in us.[R4] They are also inherently unsolvable in that you cannot choose one pole of the pair as a "solution" to the neglect of the other pole and be successful over time.[R5]

There is a natural tension between the two poles of a polarity.[R6] If you treat a polarity as if it were a problem to solve, this natural tension becomes a vicious cycle leading to unnecessary dysfunction, pain and suffering.[R7] However, if you can see that an issue is a polarity, you can leverage that natural tension with *And*-thinking so it becomes a virtuous cycle lifting you and your organization to goals unattainable with *Or*-thinking alone.[R8]

In summary, I am writing this book to support you in your chosen ways of making your difference. Also, to join you in enhancing our quality of life on the planet by supplementing *Or*-thinking with *And*-thinking.

Why Read This Book?

- **To become more effective.** The ability to see and leverage polarities will support you in being effective in all these areas: at home, as a partner or parent; at work, as a leader, follower or team member; within your religious or spiritual community; and as a citizen of your community, your country, and our planet. The research is clear on this. Individuals and organizations that leverage polarities well outperform those that don't.[R9] This reality is supported, in part, by the Annotated Bibliography on page 321.

- **To address big, complex issues without being overwhelmed.** Sometimes, just taking care of our personal lives and the issues in our family can be overwhelming, let alone addressing international issues. Because the principles of how polarities work apply the same to individual issues as well as organizational and international issues, what you learn from applying *And*-thinking to your family or organization will apply directly to your efforts as a national and world citizen.[R10] The greater the complexity, the more useful it is to see underlying, predictable patterns. Polarities are just such a set of underlying, predictable patterns.[R11]

- **To increase the attainability, speed, and sustainability of change.**[R12] Whether we are talking about individual change or needed changes in our organization or our society, a polarity lens can help. The natural tension within all polarities is often experienced as resistance. Polarity thinking helps us leverage the wisdom within this resistance. It helps us convert resistance to change into a resource for stability *And* change.[R13]

- **To address chronic conflict and polarization.** Because polarities are unavoidable and unsolvable, we often experience them as chronic conflicts between polarized groups. If the polarization is over a polarity, not only are both sides "right," they both need each other's wisdom to be successful over time.[R14]

- **To increase your capacity to love.** "Seeing is loving."[6] When we can see any person, organization or country completely, love is a natural result. Polarity Thinking helps us see ourselves and our world more completely, thus increasing our capacity to love.[R15] Love is not naïvely ignoring our times of being cruel with each other. It is the compassion that comes from seeing our moments of inhumanity in the context of a larger reality. It is the capacity to see ourselves, our organizations, and our countries as more than our shortcomings. It is the Mercy pole of the polarity of Justice *And* Mercy. This polarity shows up, by different names, in all of our religious or spiritual traditions. It involves stopping the bullying *And* seeing the bully as more than a bully.

- **To access what, in 2020, is the most comprehensive description of polarities, how they work, and how to leverage them.** The phenomenon of polarities, like gravity and sunshine, is a free gift to all of us. No one owns the phenomenon of polarities any more than we own gravity or sunshine.[R16] Though free, the ability to leverage this gift to make a positive difference can be significantly enhanced. Since you have been living within polarities and polarities have been living within you for your whole life, you already have some tacit wisdom about them.[R17] This wisdom is already helping you get along in the world. What we bring to your tacit wisdom is:[R18]

---

[6] Jack Gibb is a mentor who shared this with me in 1983.

- A Polarity Map®[7] – a simple yet robust model providing a picture of how polarities look.

- Polarity Realities – an extensive set of descriptions and principles to explain how all polarities work.

- A polarity approach – a way to combine your tacit wisdom about polarities with our map and principles so you can see them more clearly and leverage them more effectively. As your tacit wisdom becomes explicit wisdom, you can more intentionally use this gift to Make a Difference *And* Enjoy Life.

Our Polarity Map, principles, and approach have been evolving since the first Polarity Map and set of "realities" were created in 1975. We assume they will continue to evolve with your help.[R19] As you apply this book to your work and life, we would appreciate hearing from you about how to improve on them.

Summary

In summary, I am writing this book to support you in making a difference. Also, to join you in enhancing our quality of life by supplementing *Or*-thinking with *And*-thinking.

Read this book to:

- Increase your effectiveness
- Address big, complex issues without being overwhelmed
- Increase the attainability, speed, and sustainability of change
- Address chronic conflict and polarization
- Increase your capacity to love
- Access what, at this point in time, is the most comprehensive description of polarities, how they work, and how to leverage them.

A List of Polarity "Realities" = "R1"

As we go through this book, there will be an expanding number of polarity "realities" that come up. These realities include descriptions and principles that apply to all polarities. When they occur, they will be identified by a superscript; for example: [R1] or [R15] The moment you determine that you are dealing with a polarity, you can be assured that all the realities of any polarity apply to it. You can know that it will function in predictable ways regardless of the complexity in which the polarity sits.

At the end of each chapter, I will list the realities that were identified in that chapter for the first time. Appendix C contains all of the Polarity Realities.

---

[7] The Polarity Map® is a registered trademark of Barry Johnson and Polarity Partnerships, LLC. Commercial use encouraged with permission.

Polarity Realities in Chapter 1

Reality 1	*Or*-thinking is essential for learning and for solving problems.
Reality 2	*And*-thinking is a supplement to *Or*-thinking, not a replacement.
Reality 3	Polarities are also known as interdependent pairs, Paradoxes, Dilemmas, Tensions, or Positive Opposites.
Reality 4	No matter what they are called, Polarities are unavoidable because we live in them and they live in us.
Reality 5	Polarities are inherently unsolvable in that you cannot choose one pole of the pair as a "solution" to the neglect of the other pole and be successful over time.
Reality 6	There is a natural tension between the two poles of a polarity.
Reality 7	If you treat a polarity as if it were a problem to solve, the natural tension between the poles becomes a negative, self-reinforcing loop or "vicious cycle" leading to unnecessary dysfunction, pain and suffering.
Reality 8	If you can see a polarity within an issue, you can leverage the natural tension between the poles so it becomes a positive, self-reinforcing loop or "virtuous cycle" lifting you and your organization to goals unattainable with *Or*-thinking, alone.
Reality 9	Individuals and organizations that leverage polarities well outperform those that don't. See the bibliography of books supporting this point.
Reality 10	Polarity principles are scalable. What applies to a polarity at the family level of system, applies at the "family of nations" level of system.
Reality 11	The greater the complexity, the more useful it is to see underlying, predictable patterns. Polarities are just such a set of underlying, predictable patterns.
Reality 12	Leveraging polarities will increase the attainability, speed, and sustainability of change.
Reality 13	The natural tension within all polarities is often experienced as resistance. Polarity thinking helps us leverage the wisdom within this resistance. It helps us convert resistance to change into a resource for Stability *And* Change.
Reality 14	Because polarities are unavoidable and unsolvable, we often experience them as chronic conflicts between polarized groups. If the polarization is over a polarity, not only are both sides "right," they both need each other's wisdom to be successful over time.

****

Reality 15   Polarity Thinking helps us see ourselves and our world more completely, thus increasing our capacity to love. This is built on Jack Gibb's insight that "Seeing is loving."

Reality 16   The phenomenon of polarities (paradoxes, dilemmas), like gravity and sunshine, is a free gift to all of us. No one owns the phenomenon of polarities any more than we own gravity or sunshine.

Reality 17   Since you have been living within polarities and polarities have been living within you for your whole life, you already have some tacit wisdom about them.

Reality 18   Your tacit wisdom is already helping you get along in the world. What we bring to your tacit wisdom are: A Polarity Map; Polarity Realities; and a polarity approach.

Reality 19   Our Polarity Map, principles, and approach have been evolving since the first Polarity Map and set of realities were created in 1975. We assume they will continue to evolve with your help.

Chapter 2
What?

What Are Polarities?

Polarities are interdependent pairs that need each other over time.[R20] They live in us and we live in them. They exist in every level of system from the inside of our brains to global issues. They are energy systems that we can leverage.[R21] They are unavoidable, unsolvable (in that you can't choose one pole as a sustainable solution), indestructible,[R22] and unstoppable.[R23] They are a gift of nature, a natural phenomenon like gravity and sunshine.

How Polarities Look and Work

There are many models available for describing the phenomena of polarities (paradoxes, tensions, dilemmas). Our constantly developing model is our best representation at this time. It is a base from which to understand how polarities work. I will use the simple metaphor of Activity *And* Rest to explain our model, including some principles of how all polarities work and how to leverage them. Each of us lives in this polarity all the time. We get out of bed, are active during the day, and return to bed to rest. We will have periods of activity and rest within the day as well. Whatever our rhythm, we will be engaged in *both* activity *And* rest over time. Below is how our model describes this natural process.

Activity *And*[8] Rest

In *Figure 1,* you can see the most basic form of our Polarity Map®. It contains two poles (Activity *And* Rest); the word "*And*" between them; and the infinity loop that represents the natural flow of energy within all polarities.

Figure 1

Each pole of a polarity has benefits – an "upside" that it brings to its relationship with the other pole. They are the positive results from focusing on that pole. The two upsides

---

8   When the word "and" is used to connect two poles of a polarity, it will be capitalized and in italics: *And*.

are represented with the (+) sign. Each pole also has its own limits or "downside," represented with the (-) sign.[R24]

Figure 2, highlights how the energy crosses in the middle between the poles, keeping them separate. The poles never merge to become one.

Figure 3 highlights how the energy also wraps around the outside of the two poles, holding them together as an interdependent pair. The two poles never separate into one without the other. They exist in nature as an interdependent pair.[R25]

Figure 2   *Figure 3*

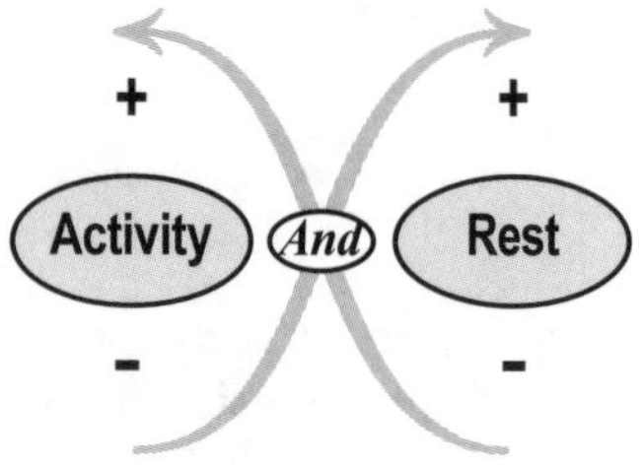

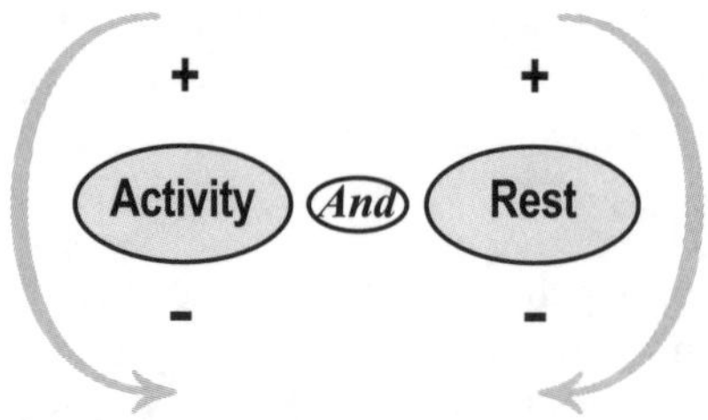

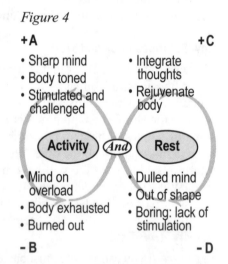

How Do They Work?

In *Figure 4* there is a natural flow of energy from (+A) to (-B) to (+C) to (-D) and back to (+A).[R26] You can start anywhere and move through the infinity loop. If we start in (+A), we see the positive results of being physically and mentally active: a sharp mind, a toned body, and being stimulated and challenged. There are many other positive results you could add to the list. These positive results are the reasons for being Active.

Though Activity is essential and has a long list of positive results, if we over-focus on Activity to the neglect of Rest, we find ourselves in (-B), the downside of Activity.[R27] As we move into this downside, our mind gets on overload, our body is exhausted and we feel burned out. The absolutely necessary benefits of Activity (+A) become a growing list of difficulties (-B).

Figure 4

+A   +C
• Sharp mind   • Integrate
• Body toned   thoughts
• Stimulated and   • Rejuvenate
  challenged   body

Activity *And* Rest

• Mind on   • Dulled mind
  overload   • Out of shape
• Body exhausted   • Boring: lack of
• Burned out   stimulation

- B   - D

When we find ourselves in the downside of one pole, the upside of the other pole is the natural, self-correction needed.[R28] In this case, we move from (-B) to (+C) to take a break, integrate our thoughts, rejuvenate our body, and relax. Notice how easy it is for us to see the downside of Activity (-B) as a "problem" and the upside of Rest (+C) as a "solution." It is true that being exhausted is problematic. It is also true that rejuvenation is just what is needed. At the same time, Rest alone is not a sustainable "solution".[R29]

If we pursue the upsides of Rest (+C) to the neglect of Activity, over time we will find ourselves in (-D), the downside of Rest. Without conversations with friends, reading, internet, TV, or other forms of mental stimulation, our minds would become dull. Without physical activity, we would get out of shape. And our lack of stimulation would lead to boredom. For those of you who have been over-focusing on the Activity pole recently, the upside of Rest (+C) could be so attractive that even the downside doesn't appear too bad!

However, the longer we focus on Rest to the neglect of any mental or physical activity, the more problematic it will become.[R30] A dramatic version of this occurred when my daughter, Shalom, was diagnosed with Polymyositis. She was 15 and the treatment, at the time, included large doses of Prednisone. This resulted in hairline fractures in her spine. She ended up in bed or a wheelchair with a back brace for a year. By the time the fractures had healed, she had so much muscle atrophy in her legs, it took her six months to be able to walk again.

Fortunately, most of us are not faced with this kind of forced, over-focus on Rest to the neglect of Activity. At the same time, we all know that Rest without Activity can be problematic. Here, again, it is easy to see the downside of Rest (-D) as a "problem" and the upside of Activity (+A) as a "solution." The upside of Activity (+A) is the necessary self-correction required and it, also, is not a sustainable "solution." When we get back to the upside of Activity (+A) we have completed one oscillation through the infinity loop. This natural oscillation occurs in all polarities.

A couple of other points about how polarities work:

1. The shorter the cycle time through the infinity loop, the more obvious it is that you are in a polarity.[R31] Since we move through Activity *And* Rest on a 24-hour cycle, it is clear that Activity *Or*[9] Rest is a false choice. We can't choose one to the neglect of the other. When the cycle time is longer, we are more likely to see the downside of one pole as the problem and the upside of the other pole as the solution. For example, in organizations it is easy to see Centralization as a "solution" to the silo "problem." It might take a few years before our Centralization "solution" is itself experienced as a "problem." It becomes a "fix that failed" and is called a "mistake." It wasn't a mistake. It wasn't a solution in the first place. We often call this the "swing of the pendulum" as it goes from Centralization to Decentralization and back again.

2. There is no place we can go to step outside of the Activity *And* Rest polarity and decide, "Do I want to be involved in Activity *And* Rest, or not?"[R32] We are living in this polarity. The same is true in our organizations addressing Centralization *And* Decentralization. We live inside this organizational polarity. In both cases, the question is not, "Will I deal with this polarity?" The question is, "How can we leverage this polarity to make a positive difference?"

---

[9] When the word "or" is used, incorrectly, to connect two poles of a polarity, it will be capitalized and italic: *Or*.

New Realities in Chapter 2

Reality 20   Polarities are interdependent pairs that need each other over time.

Reality 21   They are energy systems we can leverage.

Reality 22   They are indestructible. If there is life, polarities will be at play.

Reality 23   They are unstoppable. The only way to stop the flow of energy in any polarity is to destroy the system in which it is flowing.

Reality 24   Each pole of a polarity has a benefit or "upside" which it brings to its relationship with the other pole. They are the positive results from focusing on that pole. Each pole also has its own limits or "downside."

Reality 25   The energy flow within a polarity crosses in the middle between the poles, keeping them separate. It also wraps around the outside of the two poles, holding them together as an interdependent pair. The poles never become one *And* they never separate into one without the other. They exist in nature as an interdependent pair.

Reality 26   There is a natural flow of energy within a polarity that goes from the downside of one pole to the upside of the other followed by anticipating or experiencing the downside of the new pole, which drives the system back to the upside of the original pole.

Reality 27   If we over-focus on one pole to the neglect of its pole partner (the other pole), we will find ourselves in the downside of the pole on which we over-focus.

Reality 28   When we find ourselves in the downside of one pole, the upside of the other pole is the natural, self-correction needed.

Reality 29   When in the downside of one pole, it is easy to see that downside as a "problem" and the self-correcting upside of the other pole as the "solution." Though the upside of the other pole is the necessary self-correction, it is not a sustainable "solution."

Reality 30   The longer we focus on one pole to the neglect of the other, the more problematic it will become.

Reality 31   The shorter the cycle time through the infinity loop, the more obvious it is that you are in a polarity. The longer the cycle time, the more likely the polarity will be seen as a problem to solve.

Reality 32   Since we live in polarities and they live in our brain, there is no place we can go to step outside of the polarity and decide <u>if</u> we want to engage it.

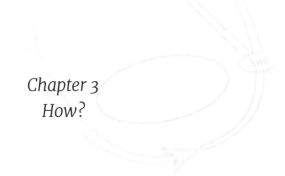

Chapter 3
How?

How Do You Leverage Polarities to Make a Difference?

Keeping with the metaphor of Activity *And* Rest, it is clear that we all find ourselves living within this polarity and we do it more or less well. But what if we want to run a marathon? This desire to do something special, to make a difference in our own capacity, leads to leveraging this polarity rather than just living within it.

How Do You Leverage Polarities?

Think **SMALL** to go big: **Seeing**, **Mapping**, **Assessing**, **Learning**, and **Leveraging** [R33]

Seeing – In one sense this is a problem to solve: How do I develop the capacity to run a marathon? The first thing we need to do is see that there is an underlying polarity to leverage in order to run a marathon. One underlying polarity is Activity *And* Rest. We can't just start running 26.2 miles. We will have to build a training regimen that intentionally leverages Activity *And* Rest.

Mapping – The Polarity Map®[10] is a wisdom organizer. The wisdom about the content often lies within the experience of the person or group creating the map.[R34] The map increases our clarity about what we need to pay attention to in order to leverage a polarity. In *Figure 1,* we can see the elements of a Polarity Map. We have the two poles, Activity *And* Rest, connected by "and," with the infinity loop oscillating between and around them. We also have clear upside

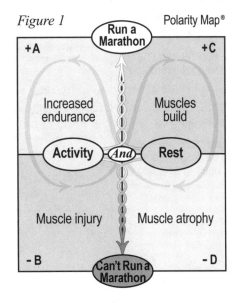

Figure 1

---

10 The Polarity Map® is a registered trademark of Barry Johnson and Polarity Partnerships, LLC. Commercial use encouraged with permission.

benefits from focusing on each pole. A positive result of Activity in reference to running a marathon is "Increased endurance (+A)." A positive result of Rest is that our "Muscles build (+C)." It is worth noting that muscles build on the Rest part of the cycle. The map also has clear downsides or limits to each pole. The negative result of Activity without Rest is "Muscle Injury (-B)", while Rest without Activity leads to "Muscle Atrophy (-D)."

Notice that the infinity loop goes high into the upside of the two upper quadrants and goes only slightly into the downside of the two lower quadrants. This distorted shape of the infinity loop reflects the desire, with all polarities, to maximize both upsides while minimizing both downsides.[R35] When this is done well, the natural tension between the two poles becomes a virtuous cycle, symbolized by the upward spiraling arrows[R36] lifting the runner toward the Greater Purpose Statement[R37] at the top of the map: "Run a Marathon."

If we over-focus on either pole to the neglect of the other, the natural tension between the poles becomes a vicious cycle, symbolized by the downward spiraling arrows[R38] leading to the Deeper Fear[R39] at the bottom of the map: "Can't Run a Marathon."

Assessing – Once we have this more complete picture of the polarity, we can assess how we have been doing with this polarity recently. See *Figure 2*.

Figure 2

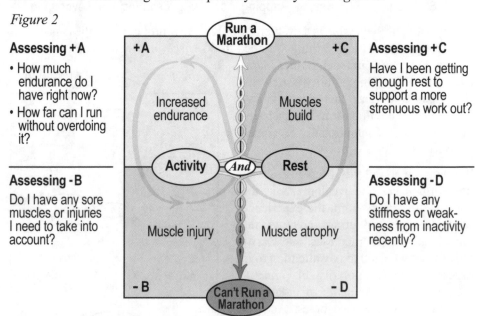

Assessing +A
- How much endurance do I have right now?
- How far can I run without overdoing it?

Assessing -B
Do I have any sore muscles or injuries I need to take into account?

Assessing +C
Have I been getting enough rest to support a more strenuous work out?

Assessing -D
Do I have any stiffness or weakness from inactivity recently?

How am I doing at maximizing each upside? For example, in Assessing (+A), I could ask: "How much endurance do I have right now? How far can I run without overdoing it?" In Assessing (+C), I could ask, "Have I been getting enough rest to support a more strenuous workout?"

How am I doing at minimizing each downside? For example, in Assessing (-B), I could ask: "Do I have any sore muscles or injuries I need to take into account?" In Assessing (-D), I could ask: "Do I have any stiffness or weakness from inactivity recently?"

The combination of the four quadrant assessments gives us an overall picture of how I am doing, at the present time, in moving up the middle of the map from "Can't Run a Marathon" to "Run a Marathon." How close am I to safely running 26.2 miles?

Learning – What can we learn from our assessment results? You could be coming off a serious case of the flu that had you in bed for the last week. Or, you could have been so busy the past few months that you haven't taken time to do any regular workouts so your endurance has been lowered. Whatever you learn from your assessment, it will give you a starting point from which to move into your final step in preparing to "Run a Marathon" = Leveraging.

Leveraging – The first four steps (Seeing, Mapping, Assessing and Learning) are about understanding our present situation. This final step is doing something about it. It is about using the energy within the polarity to make a difference.

This involves:

1. Action Steps to maximize each upside[R40]
2. Early Warnings to minimize each downside[R41]

In *Figure 3* you can see examples of these elements that you might build into a workout routine.

Figure 3

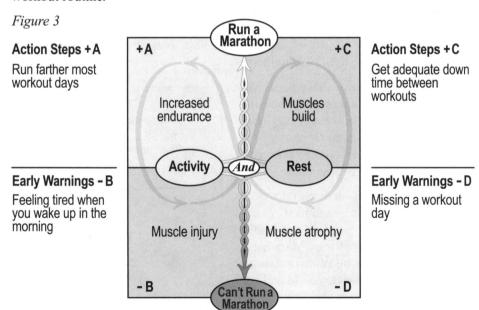

Action Steps +A

Run farther most workout days

Early Warnings - B

Feeling tired when you wake up in the morning

Action Steps +C

Get adequate down time between workouts

Early Warnings - D

Missing a workout day

1.   Action Steps Maximize each upside:

Action Steps (+A): Your schedule would include running farther most workout days. There will be exceptions when you need to hold at a certain distance or cut back a few days before the marathon. But the general process will be to gradually work up to 26.2 miles.

Actions Steps (+C): Because your muscles build on the Rest part of the cycle, you need to get adequate downtime between workouts.

2.   Early Warnings Minimize each downside:

Early Warnings (–B): How will you know, <u>early</u>, that you have over-focused on Activity to the neglect of Rest? One possible Early Warning is feeling tired when you wake up in the morning. Maybe you had to work late the evening before, so you didn't get your normal amount of sleep. Instead of running 15 miles that morning, you might cut back to 10 miles to avoid over-extending yourself and getting a muscle injury.

Early Warnings (–D): How will you know, <u>early,</u> that you have over-focused on Rest to the neglect of Activity? An example could be that you miss a workout day. For some reason, you had to get into work very early and had to skip your morning workout. Missing one workout is not a problem in the overall managing of your training. At the same time, it is an early warning that you can't continue to miss workouts or you will undermine the endurance you are working to build (+A).

Anyone preparing to run a marathon will do some version of these 5 Steps. They will know that preparation includes both Activity *And* Rest. They will not waste time arguing whether they should do Activity *Or* Rest. They will do both to get the benefits of each while minimizing the potential downsides of each. Though all of us live within the polarity of Activity *And* Rest, only those who intentionally leverage it will be able to run a marathon.

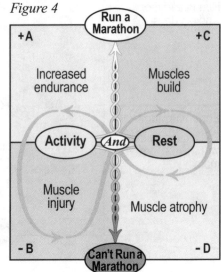

Figure 4

This reality will be true of all the polarities in this book. They are immediately available because we live in them or they live in us. If we see them as an *Or* choice, we are in trouble from that point forward. The *And* perspective is essential.

The marathon example demonstrates two more realities I have mentioned about polarities. My oldest son, Tim, has qualified five times for the Boston Marathon. But he has not run in all of them. Once, after qualifying for the Boston Marathon in the Detroit Marathon, he decided to significantly reduce his time from previous Boston Marathons. *Figure 4* summarizes what happened. In his enthusiasm to reduce his time, he over-focused on his endurance (+A) and did not pay adequate attention to down time for muscle build (+C). This resulted in shin fractures (-B). As mentioned earlier, when you over-focus on one pole to the neglect of the other, you always get the downside of the pole on which you over-focus.

There is a second reality that builds on the first. If you continue to over-focus on one pole to the neglect of the other, you get the downside of the other pole as well.[R42]

Getting the downside of both poles is pictured in *Figure 5*. First, Tim got the muscle injury (-B). Then, he was so limited from his injury that he found himself in the downside of Rest (-D) as well. Instead of running the Boston Marathon, he became the "couch potato" he wanted to avoid!

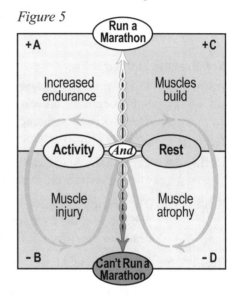

Figure 5

Some assume that if you focus on one pole, at least you get the benefits of that pole. We might think that getting these desired benefits make it worth tolerating the downside of the pole. Unfortunately, that is not how polarities work. The over-focus on one pole will eventually lead to your losing the very benefits you value about that pole. In Tim's case, his strong desire to increase endurance (+A) led to a situation of muscle injury (-B) and muscle atrophy (-D).

Summary

Though all of us live within the Activity *And* Rest polarity and have it available as an energy system to leverage, we can't all run a marathon. If we have a Greater Purpose to do something special, something out of the ordinary like Run a Marathon, it helps to be intentional about leveraging one or more key polarities. In this case, one key polarity for running a marathon is Activity *And* Rest. We can make a difference in our capacity to run a marathon by intentionally leveraging this polarity well.

This involves a 5-step (**SMALL**) process: **Seeing**, **Mapping**, **Assessing**, **Learning**, and **Leveraging**. This process is useful with all polarities.

A Polarity Map has the following elements:

1. Two poles connected by "*And*"
2. An infinity loop symbolizing an energy system that flows between and around the two poles
3. Two upside and two downside quadrants

4. A Greater Purpose Statement (GPS) at the top of the map
5. A Deeper Fear at the bottom of the map
6. A synergy arrow pointing upward toward the Greater Purpose Statement reflecting a positive reinforcing process between the poles called a Virtuous Cycle
7. A synergy arrow pointing downward toward the Greater Fear reflecting a negative reinforcing process between the two poles called a Vicious Cycle
8. Action Steps alongside both upsides supporting the effort to maximize both upsides
9. Early Warnings alongside both downsides supporting the effort to minimize both downsides

New Realities in Chapter 3

Reality 33   SMALL: Seeing, Mapping, Assessing, Learning, and Leveraging, is our process for leveraging (making a difference with) any polarity. This process is influenced significantly by Robert 'Jake' Jacob's work on Real Time Strategic Change (RTSC).[11]

Reality 34   The Polarity Map is a wisdom organizer. The wisdom about the content often lies within the experience of the person or group creating the map.

Reality 35   The distorted infinity loop going high into the two upper quadrants and dipping only slightly into the two lower quadrants reflects the desire to maximize both upsides and minimize both downsides.

Reality 36   When leveraged well, the natural tension between the two poles becomes a virtuous cycle, symbolized by the upward, spiraling arrows on the Polarity Map. The original idea of synergy arrows pointing upward came from Bob DeWit and Ron Meyer.[12]

Reality 37   The upward spiraling synergy arrows represent lifting the person or system toward the Greater Purpose Statement (GPS) at the top of the map. The Greater Purpose Statement answers the question, "Why bother to leverage this polarity?" John Scherer identified the need for a Greater Purpose and suggested using GPS to play on the familiar Global Positioning System.[13]

Reality 38   When not leveraged well, the natural tension between the two poles becomes a vicious cycle symbolized by the downward spiraling synergy arrows on the Polarity Map.

---

[11] Jacobs, Robert. *Real Time Strategic Change. How to Involve an Entire Organization in Fast and Far-Reaching Change.* Berrett-Koehler,1994.
[12] DeWit, Bob; Meyer, Ron. *Strategy Synthesis: Resolving Strategy Paradoxes to Create Competitive Advantage.* Thomson,1999.
[13] Scherer, John. *Work And The Human Spirit.* John Scherer and Associates,1993.

Reality 39   The downward spiraling synergy arrows represent dragging the person or system toward the Deeper Fear at the bottom of the map. The Deeper Fear is the opposite of the Greater Purpose Statement. The stronger one's desire to gain their Greater Purpose, the stronger the desire to avoid the Deeper Fear.

Reality 40   There are Action Steps alongside each upside of the map. These steps are to proactively gain or maintain the upside they are next to.

Reality 41   There are Early Warnings alongside each downside of the map. These are early indicators that you are getting into a downside so that you can self-correct as early as possible. While Action Steps are proactive, Early Warnings are responsive. Todd Johnson contributed the idea of Early Warnings out of the need to have something measurable relating to the two downside quadrants.

Reality 42   A persistent over-focus on one pole to the neglect of the other gets you into the downside of both poles. The fear of getting into the downside of the opposite pole leads to sustained over-focus on your preferred pole. This sustained over-focus leads first to the downside of the preferred pole, then to the downside of the very pole you were attempting to avoid. Paradoxically, you get what you are afraid of through your efforts to avoid it.

SECTION TWO
Part *And* Whole

God and the entire cosmos are about two things: differentiation [people and things becoming themselves] and communion [living in supportive coexistence]. [14] ~ Richard Rohr

Each of us is Unique *And* All of us are Connected. [R43]

We are born unique and our uniqueness increases with age. Each child or nation is "one of a kind," a unique Part of the Whole. We do not have to do anything to "become unique." As we have more experiences, we become more unique. Each experience cuts another facet in the diamond that reflects our lives.

At the same time, we are all connected within the Whole. We are born connected, a part of a world of interdependence. This interconnectedness becomes truer and more obvious as we grow through life. It has always been clear in our spiritual traditions and it is increasingly clear, globally, with the economy and the environment.

Section Two – Introduction

What does my two-year-old grandson Evan have in common with: a business unit in a Fortune 100 company; the Conscious Capitalism movement; [15] Targeted Universalism; [16] the Black Lives Matter movement; the historic tension between The Tea Party *And* Occupy Wall Street; the global struggle with the climate crisis; and the functions of the Right *And* Left Hemisphere of our brains? In each case, a fundamental energy system at play is the polarity of the Part *And* the Whole.

---

[14] Rohr, Richard. *Richard Rohr's Daily Meditations: Gender and Sexuality*. Center for Action and Contemplation, October 21, 2019.

[15] Mackey, John; Sisodia, Raj. *Conscious Capitalism: Liberating the Heroic Spirit of Business*. Harvard Business Review Press, 2014.

[16] Powell, John A. *Racing to Justice, Transforming Our Conceptions of Self and Other to Build an Inclusive Society*. Indiana University Press, 2012.

Chapter 4
Family as the Whole

It is winter in Detroit and I have just come back from a morning run through the home neighborhood of my daughter, Kristin, and her family. I am inside the back door on the landing where you choose to go down into the basement or into the kitchen. As I am leaning against the wall and doing a little post-run stretching, my two-year-old grandson, Evan, comes around the corner and looks up at me with a big grin.

He is wearing soft, flannel, winter pajamas with foot booties built into the bottom of the legs. His right hand is holding something which he proudly displays. "Grandpa!" he says with excitement in his voice. "I've got money!" He opens his little fist and I see a handful of Canadian coins.

The day before, I was working in Toronto. I had flown into Detroit too late to see Evan before he went to bed. I had put some Canadian change from my pocket on the nightstand by the bed. It looked like Evan had gone into the bedroom to find Grandpa and found the money instead. Evan knew that money was useful, so he was beaming.

I said, "Hey, Evan, you do have money. It looks like my money." Evan's smile changed to a frown and he looked down at his hand full of coins. He seemed to be looking at the money for a long time. I could no longer see his face so I was wondering what might be going on in his head. Then he slowly raised his head and looked at me with a face full of renewed excitement and possibility. "Shall we share?" he asked.

Now where did that come from? "Shall we share?" This two-year-old grandchild had learned something important from his parents. He had learned about sharing. It is a simple concept that all of us learned from our parents and, if we have children, we pass on to them.

Sometime in his young life, Evan had probably been playing with neighborhood friends and had gotten into an argument over some toys. At that point, Kristin or Krishna, Evan's dad, came into the room to see what the fuss was about. When his parent realized there was a fight over the toys, they saw a natural opportunity to teach Evan about sharing.

There is wisdom in this simple lesson about sharing. It is a way we teach our children about their interdependency with others and how to make it work. Evan was only 2, yet he was already learning about polarities. They could have said, "Evan, this is a polarity you can leverage." Instead, they just got to the heart of the matter and taught him to share. He is learning that through sharing, he can take care of himself *And* his friends and that this is one way to address a conflict.

Seeing, Mapping, Assessing, Learning, Leveraging (SMALL)
Seeing/Mapping

In *Figure 1,* we can see some key elements of "sharing" on a Polarity Map®. As we move through the two highs and two lows on the infinity loop (+A, -B, +C, and -D), we can follow the normal flow and understand the *And*-thinking behind teaching our children to share.

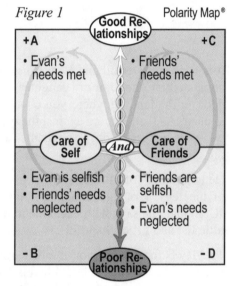

Figure 1   Polarity Map®

(+A) Kristin and Krishna want Evan to learn to take care of himself and to get his needs met. This desire shows up as the upside of "Care of Self."

(-B) They also know that if Evan over-focuses on Care of Self to the neglect of Care of Friends, he will be seen as selfish, his friends' needs will be neglected, and his relationship with his friends will be undermined. This is the downside of <u>only</u> focusing on Care of Self.

(+C) In order to minimize this downside, they want Evan to consider his friends so that their needs are also met. This flow from the downside of Care of Self (-B) to the upside of Care of Friends (+C) is the natural, self-correction that is needed.

(-D) At the same time, if Evan were to over-focus on Care of Friends to the neglect of taking Care of Self, he could see his friends as selfish and his needs being neglected. This new over-focus would lead to the downside of Care of Friends. In order to minimize this downside, the natural self-correction would be to return to (+A) and make sure that his needs are met. While Evan and his friends are alive, this is an energy system that he and they can leverage.

Evan can take care of himself *And* take care of his friends. Why bother? If he learns to share, the natural tension between the two poles will become a virtuous cycle leading to "Good Relationships." If he does not learn to share, the same natural tension will become a vicious cycle leading to "Poor Relationships."

Assessing/Learning

In doing a quick assessment of how well Evan and his friends are doing at sharing, Kristin and Krishna can check how things are going in each of the 4 quadrants of the map in the following *Figure 2*. "To what degree are Evan's needs being met? (+A)" "To what degree are Evan's friends' needs being met? (+C)"

The assessment continues by checking "Is Evan keeping all the toys for himself? (-B)" And also checking "Are Evan's friends keeping all the toys for themselves? (-D)"

Figure 2

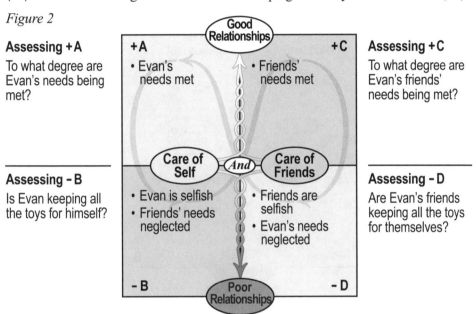

This is the simple assessment Kristin and Krishna would be paying attention to as they stepped into the dangerous zone of two-year-olds crying over the toys! This will inform what they do next. They know that it is not an *either/Or* situation in which *either* Evan has all the toys *Or* his friends have all the toys. This is a situation in which *Or*-thinking, alone, will lead to "Poor Relationships."

Leveraging – Action Steps and Early Warnings

The learning from the quick assessment leads directly into Evan's parents stepping into action. Again, the four quadrants of the map become resources for what to do. You may be thinking that this SMALL process and map structure is a bit much for intervening in an argument over toys by a few two-year-olds. You have a point! At the same time, I think it is worth looking at the process we go through when dealing with these simple conflicts. It's also important to appreciate that we have experience with leveraging polarities from an early age, and that this experience can be used as we deal with more complex issues in future chapters.

In *Figure 3*, on the following page, we can see a simple version of how Action Steps might be used to proactively seek to maximize both upsides. Action Steps for (+A) and (+C) could include seeing that Evan gets some of the toys he wants for part of the time *And* that Evan's friends get some of the toys they want part of the time. It might also include sharing some of the toys together part of the time. This would be what we call a high leverage action step because the same action step supports both upside quadrants. You can put an (HL) after the action step to remind yourself and others that it is High Leverage.[R44]

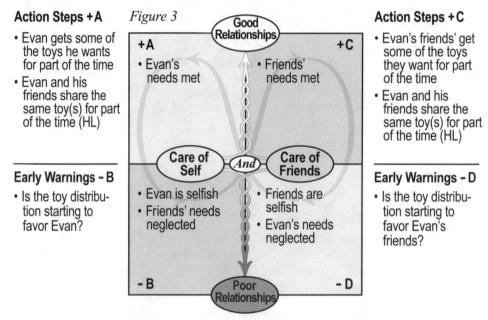

Action Steps +A
- Evan gets some of the toys he wants for part of the time
- Evan and his friends share the same toy(s) for part of the time (HL)

Early Warnings – B
- Is the toy distribution starting to favor Evan?

Figure 3

Good Relationships

+A
- Evan's needs met

+C
- Friends' needs met

Care of Self   *And*   Care of Friends

– Evan is selfish
- Friends' needs neglected

- Friends are selfish
- Evan's needs neglected

– B   Poor Relationships   – D

Action Steps +C
- Evan's friends' get some of the toys they want for part of the time
- Evan and his friends share the same toy(s) for part of the time (HL)

Early Warnings – D
- Is the toy distribution starting to favor Evan's friends?

Early Warnings are also worth considering so that we can know early if things are headed toward trouble. In this case, an Early Warning could be that the distribution of toys is starting to favor Evan (–B) or Evan's Friends (–D).

As I acknowledged earlier, the SMALL process seems a bit elaborate for a fight among two-year-olds. Yet I suggest that all the elements are at play in this simple example and will be at play when we get to a global fight within a Fortune 100 company in the next chapter. The map and SMALL process have become wisdom organizers. The wisdom in this case is in Kristin and Krishna.

Summary

Seeing – They know that it will not work to just take care of Evan *Or* his friends. They see that it is an issue requiring *And*-thinking.

Mapping – Though they may not be working with a Polarity Map, in their minds they do know that they want to attend to the needs of *both* Evan *And* His Friends (+A *And* +C). They know that if they support either to the neglect of the other there will be downside consequences (–B) and/or (–D). They also know that it is possible to share in a way that will help build "Good Relationships" (Greater Purpose) and if the kids don't learn to share it will lead to "Poor Relationships" (Deeper Fear).

Assessing – They will quickly assess what the situation is.

Learning – Interpreting the assessment results supports Evan's parents taking action.

Leveraging – They will act on behalf of both sides in the argument (Action Steps) and are likely to help the kids pay attention to ways they can keep from getting in the same fix 15 minutes later (Early Warnings).

A few more points about sharing to conclude this chapter:

- Sharing is a good example of how we have been learning about polarities (though not called polarities) since we were very little. I am not suggesting that you haven't been leveraging polarities before reading this book and might choose to do so when finished. I am suggesting something entirely different – that you have been engaged with polarities your whole life and learning to share is but one example.

- Sharing is a principle that applies to all polarities. In this chapter, the polarity is about Self *And* Other, which we will re-visit in *Section Six*. With a slight change in Pole names to Evan *And* Evan's play group (including Evan), we would have the Part *And* Whole polarity. Another version of Part *And* Whole at the family level of system is Individual *And* Family. We teach our children life is about them (Part) *And* it is about more than them – it is also about the family (Whole).

- Polarities are also about energy and power. In order to create a virtuous cycle with the tension within any polarity, you must empower both poles.[R45] This power sharing within polarities is not a zero-sum game. In other words, empowering one pole a certain amount does not require you to disempower the other pole by the same amount. On the contrary, with a polarity it is possible to empower both poles in a way that the polarity becomes a power generator with both poles being increasingly powerful *And* the system in which the polarity sits will increase in power.[R46]

New Realities in Chapter 4

Reality 43   Each of us is unique and all of us are connected.

Reality 44   High Leverage Action Steps are valuable because they simultaneously support both upsides of a polarity. You get double the benefit from one action. They are shown by just putting the same action step alongside both upsides. You can put an (HL) after the action step to remind yourself and others that it is High Leverage.

Reality 45   Polarities are about energy and power. In order to create a virtuous cycle with the tension within any polarity, you must empower both poles.

Reality 46   With a polarity, it is possible to empower both poles in a way that the polarity becomes a power generator with both poles being increasingly powerful *And* the system in which the polarity sits will increase in power.

Chapter 5
Organization as the Whole

I am on a phone call with three people from a multi-national company located in 46 countries. Those on the call are the Chief Operating Officer, the Chief Learning Officer, and the head of a design team preparing for a four-day leadership development program for their top 200 people. They want to spend one of the four days applying Polarity Thinking. The call is intended to help me understand the company and the design of the four days. I want them to experience Polarity Thinking as useful: that it will make a difference.

Leading Through Values

One of the first things they let me know is their program theme: "Leading Through Values." My response is that this is a terrific theme for learning Polarity Thinking because values come in pairs. They show up in the two upsides or the two poles of a Polarity Map®.[R47] The COO asks, "You're saying that values come in pairs?"

I respond, "Yes sir.[17] I think so. When I work with an organization in developing their values, I encourage them to put them as pairs. If they already have a list of values, I look through their list with them to see if one value on the list might have its value partner somewhere else on the list. If so, I encourage them to put them together as an interdependent pair. If one or more of the values does not have its pair on their list, I encourage them to identify its value pair and add it to their list. As a simplistic example, if they had "Activity" as a value, I would look for something like 'Rest' as another value somewhere on the list. If Rest is not on their value list, I would suggest that they add it – not because I have anything against Activity. I just know that Activity without Rest is not sustainable. It will lead to burn out and injury."

The COO anxiously responds, "Wait a minute. If you are going to be messing with our values in front of our top 200 people, I want to know what you would do with them." They immediately send the organization's list of values. One value on their list is "Autonomous Business Units." It makes sense that they would value Autonomy for their Business Units, especially when they are in 46 countries. What

---

[17] This conversation took place before I was aware of the use and value of inclusive pronouns.

I immediately look for is an interdependent value within their list that would provide the necessary balance to "Autonomous Business Units."

If you were in my place on the phone, what would you be looking for as a pole partner on their list? Without reading ahead, write down, below, a couple of words or phrases that would provide some balance and help keep the company from getting into trouble from an over-focus on Autonomous Business Units alone.

_____ , _____ , _____

You probably came up with something like centralized or coordinated or integrated. There is not one right word or set of words we would be looking for. There is a general category of words that would work as a dynamic balance to Autonomy for the Business Units.

The reason you were able to come up with possible names for the other pole is that you have been living within this polarity as long as you have been working within any organization. Organizations will decentralize to give their "Parts" the freedom to do what they are uniquely qualified to do and to take initiative to quickly respond to situations they encounter. Over time, the "swing of the pendulum" will occur and the organization will self-correct by centralizing in order to take care of all the "Parts" *And* have them work as a coordinated or integrated "Whole."

In other words, you have been through some form of this infinity loop many times in your life. Your experience with this polarity, combined with your own intuition, will help you "take my place" on the phone.

The Generic Part *And* Whole Polarity Map

Your ability to help this organization will increase significantly when you combine your experience and intuition with a Polarity Map and our increasing list of polarity realities. Each section of this book has a generic Polarity Map which is a starting point for building a more specific map that will be a custom fit for a person or organization. The generic Part *And* Whole Polarity Map is the basis for all the chapters in this section.

Building a Polarity Map is always a values and language clarification process.[R48] The content of the map needs to make sense for the person or group using it or the map will not be useful to them. If any of the maps in this book do not make sense to you because you would use different words, just change the map so it works for you or your group. The map content just needs to follow certain guidelines:

1. Both poles need to be either neutral or positive.[R49] If one pole is seen as negative and the other as positive, the map will tend to favor the pole that is seen as positive. This is likely to lead to an over-focus on the pole with a positive value. For example, with the polarity of Activity *And* Rest, it would be a setup to have the pole names be: Burned Out *And* Rejuvenated. When the pole names are both neutral or positive, it is easier to identify the upside and downside of each pole.

2. The content of each upper quadrant needs to be the "positive results" from focusing on that pole. They will be "positive" based on the key stakeholders' definition of "positive."

3. The content of each lower quadrant needs to be "negative results" from an over-focus on that pole to the neglect of its pole partner.

4. There will be a Greater Purpose Statement at the top of the map that answers the question, "Why bother to leverage this polarity?" The answer becomes an integrative focus when agreed to by all stakeholders.

5. There will be a Deeper Fear at the bottom of the map which represents the opposite or loss of the Greater Purpose.

Hopefully, the content of the *Figure 1* map will work for you in terms of your language and values. If not, change as necessary. Just follow the above guidelines.

Let's look at the content in this map and I will identify a few more Polarity Realities. Then we can return to the conversation with the 3 people from the Fortune 100 company.

Figure 1 — Polarity Map®

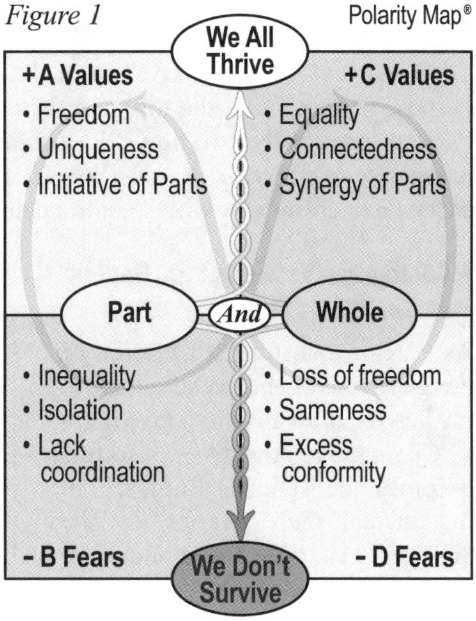

(+A) Whether the Part is an individual *And* the Whole is the Team, or the Part is a Business Unit *And* the Whole is a Company, or the Part is a Country *And* the Whole is the United Nations, the Part will value its Freedom, its Uniqueness and its ability to take Initiative without having to check with the Whole.

(+C) At the same time, those concerned about the Whole will value some basic Equality among the Parts, the Connectedness between the Parts and a Synergy between the Parts resulting in the Whole becoming more than the sum of the Parts (2+2=5).

(−B) In any human system, when we over-focus on Freedom, Uniqueness and Initiative by its Parts (+A) to the neglect of Equality, Connectedness, and Synergy between the Parts (+C), it leads to Inequality, Isolation of some Parts from others, and a Lack of coordination between the Parts.

(−D) Also, if we over-focus on Equality, Connectedness, and Synergy between the Parts (+C) to the neglect of Freedom, Uniqueness, and Initiative for the Parts (+A), it leads to Loss of Freedom, bland Sameness, and Excess Conformity (Group Think).

You will notice that each of the two upper quadrants have the word "Value" in them, and the two lower quadrants have "Fear" in them. This reminds us that the words in the two upper quadrants represent something that is valued about each pole. Thus, the two upsides of a polarity represent a values pair. The downside of the opposite pole represents the loss of that value which is a legitimate fear by those holding on to the diagonal upside value. Those who value Freedom (+A) will fear the loss of Freedom (-D). The stronger the value, the stronger the fear and the reverse.[R50]

A powerful value/fear diagonal when combined with *Or*-thinking gets us "hooked" by a false choice between the poles. We become blind to the other value/fear diagonal and over-tolerate the downside of our valued pole. We then get "stuck" there – unable to access the upside of the pole that is feared.[R51] For example, the strong value for Freedom (+A) and strong fear of its loss (-D) combined with *Or*-thinking, will make it difficult to access Equality (+C). For them, the false choice is, "Do I want Freedom (+A) *Or* do I want to lose Freedom (-D)?" They, of course, will choose Freedom every time. Their choice is within one diagonal (+A/-D) as if the other diagonal (-B\+C) does not exist.

The final two content pieces in the Polarity Map in *Figure 1* are the Greater Purpose Statement (at the top) and the Deeper Fear (at the bottom). The Greater Purpose answers the question, "Why bother to leverage this polarity?" My answer, in the case of *Figure 1*, is that "We All Thrive." The Deeper Fear is the opposite of the Greater Purpose which could be that "We Don't Survive".

A Customized Version of the Generic Part *And* Whole Map

As I create a customized version of the generic Part *And* Whole map in my head, I know I want to give them a "Competitive Advantage," so this becomes the "Higher Purpose" in my mental map, *Figure 2*. The "Deeper Fear" at the bottom is, "Can't Compete."

Seeing – With the generic Part *And* Whole map, *Figure 1*, as a reference, I think of a Business Unit as a Part *And* the Company as the Whole. I wanted to use their exact language for the left pole and use parallel language for the right pole. Thus, in

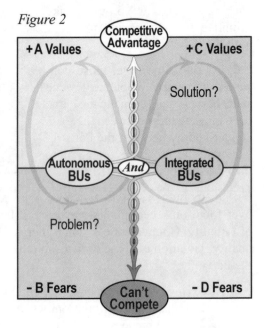

Figure 2

Figure 2, my customized mental map was Autonomous Business Units *And* Integrated Business Units.

They do not have "Integrated Business Units" or any reference to centralizing or coordination on their values list. This means they are likely to over-focus on Autonomous Business Units (+A) to the relative neglect of Integrated Business Units (+C). With this over-focus, they will find themselves in the downside of Autonomous Business Units (-B).

Without reading ahead, but using *Figure 1* if you would like, think of some words that would work for you to describe the content for (-B). What difficulties is this company likely to experience if they over-focus on Autonomous BU's to the neglect of Integrated BU's? Write a few words or phrases that come to mind:

_____ , _____ , _____

Now, think of some words that would work for you to describe the content of (+C). What is this company likely to decide they need to do to address the difficulties in (-B)? This content will be the positive results from focusing on Integrated BU's. Write a few words or phrases:

_____ , _____ , _____

Back to the Phone Call

The COO asks me what I think of their values list. I say, "It's a great list. I notice that you have Autonomous Business Units as a value but there is no value about Business Unit Integration or Coordination." He agrees that they are absent and asks me what I think of that. I respond, "From a polarity perspective, your organization is likely to experience: silos and isolation of some of the business units; excess competition between the units; inequality within the units with resentment toward those that appear to have "preferred" status; and, redundancies that are costly."

Your listed words or phrases for (-B) would probably be different than mine but they are likely to have a lot of overlap. We are not looking for a few "correct words" but for a general set of issues that are likely to occur when you over-focus on Autonomy of Business Units to the neglect of Integration.

I continue on the phone to suggest, "At some point, these issues are going to be identified as a 'problem.' You will bring your Business Unit Heads together with your executive team to address them. When you meet, you will agree to do a number of things to 'solve' these issues. You will agree to move from Silos to Integration; from excess competition to collaboration and mutual support; from inequality to equality; and from redundancies to coordinated efficiency."

Again, your list for (+C), though probably different from mine, would fit into the same general cluster of things they would decide to do to centralize and coordinate their organization.

Not Walking Their Talk

The following *Figure 3* shows the next phase of the conversation. After suggesting what problems are likely from their not having a pole partner for Autonomous Business Units (-B) and what they will agree to do to solve those problems (+C), I suggest that they are not likely to move toward (+C) in spite of their agreement to do so.

There is silence on the other end of the phone. After a few seconds, I say, "Hello?" The COO speaks with an angry tone and says, "Who have you been talking to?!"

I respond that I have not been talking to anyone. I just understand how values work and how polarities work so the results are predictable.

The COO responds by saying, "Wait a minute. I understand how our Value of Autonomous Business Units without adequate attention to Integrated Business Units would lead to your "Problem" list (-B). It is also clear how you would identify what we would agree to do as a "Solution (+C)." But did I hear you correctly that we were not likely to walk our talk and do the very things we agreed to do?"

My response is, "Yes sir."

The COO continues, "I want to know how you knew that, because I held that meeting you described two years ago. We agreed, to the person, to make those corrections and we have hardly made any progress. It is costing us millions of dollars. I want to know how you knew this would happen and what can be done about it."

This became the focus of the leadership day I spent with them. I knew they were likely to see the issue as a problem to solve and frame it from a "Gap Analysis" perspective. *Figure 3* is how it might look. Gap Analysis has 3 parts:

1. The present state, with its limits = the Problem (-B).
2. The preferred future state, with is possibilities = the Solution (+C),
3. A strategy to bridge the Gap between the limited present state and the preferred future state.

You will recall that when a system is in the downside of one pole, it is easy to see the upside of the other pole as a

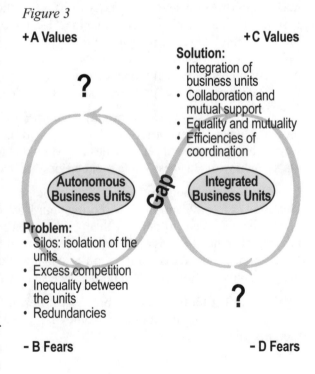

Figure 3

+A Values

?

+C Values

Solution:
- Integration of business units
- Collaboration and mutual support
- Equality and mutuality
- Efficiencies of coordination

Autonomous Business Units   Gap   Integrated Business Units

Problem:
- Silos: isolation of the units
- Excess competition
- Inequality between the units
- Redundancies

?

- B Fears   - D Fears

solution. It was the combination of a problem solving, gap analysis frame and an *Or*-mindset that undermined their ability to walk their talk.

Since some form of gap analysis is used in virtually all change efforts and since problem solving is our natural response to dealing with difficulties, there was a strong possibility that these two would be combined to address their issues.

When we look at their values from a polarity perspective, we quickly see what is missing. The problem solving, gap analysis frame, gives us two parts of the underlying Part *And* Whole Polarity Map and assumes that we have everything we need: A problem (-B), a solution (+C), and a strategy to gain the solution. The strategy would show up as Action Steps to gain the upsides of Integrated Business Units (+C). These two, diagonal parts of the map are important and accurate, they are just incomplete. When we get into trouble with polarities, the reason is not that our problem-solving perceptions are inaccurate, it is that they are incomplete.[R52]

What is missing in the gap analysis is the upside Value of Autonomous Business Units (+A) and the downside Fear of Integrated Business Units (-D). We know we can get "hooked" by a strong Value/Fear diagonal combined with *Or*-thinking. We then get "stuck" in the downside of our valued pole and are unable to access the upside of the pole that is feared.

All we need to do is fill in the missing parts of the map to see what this company values so strongly (+A) and what it will fear with its loss with equal intensity (-D). This will tell us why they have had trouble getting to their agreed upon solution (+C).

With the support of the generic Part *And* Whole map, *Figure 1*, combined with your life experience, you can create your own content for (+A) and (-D) in *Figure 3*. What would be the positive results of building in some autonomy for your business units, especially if you are in 46 countries? Your answers, below, will help us appreciate why they put Autonomous Business Units in their values list in the first place. What words would you put in (+A) of *Figure 3?* Write below:

—————————— , —————————— , ——————————

Given whatever you have written above, the exact opposite would go in (-D) of *Figure 3*. The real opposites in a Polarity Map are the diagonals. The poles are interdependent but not always what we might call opposites.[R53] As a culture, the company that values your (+A) words, above, will be afraid of losing that which is valued. What "opposite of (+A)" words come to mind for you for (-D) in *Figure 3?*

—————————— , —————————— , ——————————

In *Figure 4*, on the following page, we can see a more complete map that I had in mind when looking at the companies values list. Your content above for (+A) and (-D) will be different than mine but, hopefully, there is overlap and we are thinking about the same general cluster of words that would fit in those two quadrants. They are not the same words as in the generic Part *And* Whole map, *Figure 1*, but you can see how *Figure 1* would help you think of the general type of content that would show up in *Figure 4*.

Notice what a solid list of items shows up in (+A). This great list does not show up within gap analysis. This list of values is the heart of the company on the phone. They love this so much that, not only did they have "Autonomous BUs" as a value, they did not have anything like "Integrated" or "coordinated" in their values.

Notice the items that show up in (-D). This also is a rich list that does not show up with gap analysis. There is a powerful fear, at the gut level, in this culture, of these downsides. This value/fear (+A/-D) diagonal will get in the way of doing what the COO and everyone else at the head level saw as the logical "Solution" (+C) to their "Problem" (-B).

It is not that they could not come up with content for (+A) and (-D) if they were asked. The gap analysis framework just doesn't ask for those two quadrants. The wisdom is in the company. The Polarity Map asks for more of that wisdom than does the gap analysis frame.

Figure 4

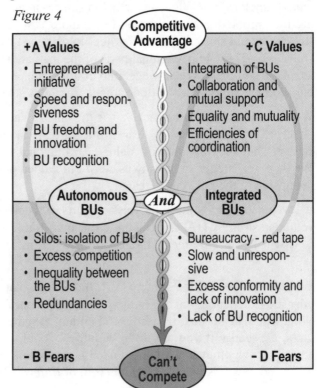

+A Values
- Entrepreneurial initiative
- Speed and responsiveness
- BU freedom and innovation
- BU recognition

Competitive Advantage

+C Values
- Integration of BUs
- Collaboration and mutual support
- Equality and mutuality
- Efficiencies of coordination

Autonomous BUs *And* Integrated BUs

- Silos: isolation of BUs
- Excess competition
- Inequality between the BUs
- Redundancies

- Bureaucracy - red tape
- Slow and unresponsive
- Excess conformity and lack of innovation
- Lack of BU recognition

- B Fears

Can't Compete

- D Fears

Engage Key Stakeholders in Each Step of the SMALL Process.[R54]

I have talked about a Polarity Map being a wisdom organizer. I have also talked about building a map being a values and language clarification process. The combination of these two realities supports the engagement of key stakeholders in each step of the SMALL process. What I mean by key stakeholders are those people who are influenced by or could influence the process for which you are building the map. The wisdom you are organizing within the map will be wiser and less vulnerable to "blind spots" when key stakeholders are involved. Also, if the values and language of the map do not work for some key stakeholders, their support will not be there to help you leverage the polarity.

Below is a quick summary of why and how the practice of including key stakeholders was useful in the leadership session we were preparing for on the phone call.

Seeing – Perceptions about an organization's reality are different in different parts of the system. In order to have a more accurate "Seeing," it is helpful to get a view from different parts of the system: different levels, locations, and areas of focus. One way to do that is to get as representative a group as possible of key stakeholders to help identify the most important polarities at play for the organization and to name the poles. In this case, the top 200 represented all geographical areas and areas of business. There were representatives from the Business Units (Part) *And* representatives from the executive, corporate offices (Whole). Key stakeholders from lower levels of the system were missing. You can always build a map without some key stakeholders present. We often do. The vulnerabilities of doing so are reduced if their interests and perceptions are kept in mind as you go through the process.

We agreed on Autonomous Business Unites (BU's) *And* Integrated Business Units (BU's) as the two pole names for the leadership day on Polarity Thinking.

Mapping – At the gathering, we had table groups of six, all filling out the four quadrants of the Autonomous BU's *And* Integrated BU's map. We consolidated the highly overlapping content into a map that worked for them. We did our best to make sure the map would work for those stakeholders not present. When building a map for yourself and people not present, it is helpful to think of the initial map as a "draft." Keep some flexibility to edit the map to incorporate the wisdom and points of view of others as you share the draft map with them.

Assessing – They recognized that they were in the downside of Autonomous BU's (-B) and needed to self-correct to the upside of Integrated BU's (+C). Here again, having key stakeholders involved in the assessment will increase the trust-worthiness of the assessment. It will be more trustworthy to the degree the stake-holders involved do represent the variety of perspectives in the company (and outside the company, if that is desired.)

Learning – This step involves giving your own meaning to the assessment results. What have we learned from our process so far? How do we understand and interpret the results? What contributed to the results, whether positive or negative? Key stakeholders' presence can enhance the richness of this step. What you learn from this step supports the actions you take in the next one.

Leveraging – This step involves identifying what "Actions Steps" the company was already doing and could start doing to maximize the upside of each pole. Also, what would be "Early Warnings" that would be measurable, early indicators that they are getting into the downside of one pole or the other. This would help them self-correct without getting caught in the downside of a pole. Here, again, having key stakeholders present will improve the quality and quantity of the Action Steps and Early Warnings.

In summary, with groups and organizations, it is helpful to include key stake-holders in every step of the SMALL process.

Coaching – When doing one-on-one coaching, the process is easier. The map you create together only has to fit with the values and language of the person you are coaching. If it works for them, you are good to go.

> **Important Acknowledgement**
>
> *Over the last 20 years, Robert 'Jake' Jacobs has been a friend, coach and founding partner of Polarity Partnerships, LLC. Jake is the author of <u>Real Time Strategic Change</u> (RTSC).*[18]
>
> *In our years together, Jake has significantly influenced how we think about and work toward fast, sustainable change within Polarity Partnerships, LLC. His RTSC principles and his processes for engaging key stakeholders are built into our Polarity Approach to Continuity And Transformation (PACT). Polarity Thinking and RTSC have influenced each other significantly over the years. This mutual influence is summarized in Jake's chapter in our applications book.*

Paradoxical Shift in Poles – A Return to the One-Day Workshop with the 200

In the process of creating Action Steps for each upside, we started with the Action Steps for the upside of Autonomous BU's first (+A). The reason we started with Autonomous BU's was to counter the fear that we would focus on Integrated BU's to the neglect of Autonomous BU's (-D). To assure everyone that we were not neglecting Autonomous BU's (AKA "Throwing the baby out with the bathwater"), we <u>started</u> by identifying things we will continue to do and new things we will start doing to maximize Autonomous BU's. After everyone was assured that we were committed to Autonomous BU's, then, and only then, did we shift to focus on Action Steps for Integrated BU's (+C). This fits with our paradoxical orientation toward moving from one pole to the other: If you want people holding on to the present pole to support movement toward the other pole, first guarantee, with Action Steps, support for the present pole.[R55]

It is also helpful to acknowledge, with Early Warnings, the legitimate fears of the downside of the pole we are moving toward (-D) before creating Early Warnings for the downside of the pole we are moving from (-B).[R56] The message to those holding those fears is that they have a point and that we can identify measurable, early ways to let us know when we are starting to get into this predictable downside. Those warnings will help us self-correct to keep from getting "stuck" in that downside. When we have gotten early warnings for the pole we are moving toward (-D), we can create early warnings for the present pole as well (-B).

---

[18] Jacobs, Robert. *Real Time Strategic Change. How to Involve an Entire Organization in Fast and Far Reaching Change.* Berrett-Koehler,1994.

The leadership found this perspective and process very useful. They now know that this is a polarity that they will be living within as long as their company exists. They know that there is a natural tension between the two poles that can be leveraged. And, if they can leverage it well, they will outperform any competition that sees one pole or the other as a "solution" to a problem. They made a difference for themselves using a polarity map and the SMALL process.

Summary

Looking at values in pairs, as a polarity, can strengthen an organization's value platform. Not identifying the pole partner of a value will make an organization vulnerable to what is missing. Adding the value partner does not diminish the original value. On the contrary, it contributes to the sustainability of the original value and the sustainability of the company. This is true because a polarity is indestructible while one pole of a polarity is inherently unsustainable. For a story of a Brazilian company, Natura, converting its original values list to a list of values in pairs, see the chapter, "Values Come in Pairs at Natura" in *And: Volume Two*.

The generic Part *And* Whole polarity is useful as a starting point for seeing various versions of this polarity in our organizations. Since building a Polarity Map is always a values and language clarification process, we need to make sure the map we create is one that works with key stakeholders. When building a map, keep open to having it modified as you share it with others. For it to work for them, you may need to create a modified map with words and values that will work for you and them.

When an organization treats a polarity as if it were a problem to solve, it will reduce the attainability, speed, and sustainability of the "solution" they are trying to accomplish. When an organization can see a key underlying polarity within a difficulty or set of difficulties, it will increase the attainability, speed, and sustainability of the desired outcome.

A lack of "Power" or lack of "Alignment" were not the problem. In this change effort, those with the power in the organization were serious about wanting to make the change. So was everyone else. They were all "aligned" to move from the "problem," as they saw it, to their collective "solution." This is important to recognize. The "resistance" to this move was coming from the very people who were supporting it. They were not being dishonest and would not see themselves as saboteurs. At the same time, their values for the upside of Autonomous Business Units and equally strong fears of the downside of Integrated Business Units combined with *Or*-thinking was keeping them from getting to the upside of Integrated Business Units: their "Solution."

This is a very important reality to be aware of when trying to make a difference from either inside or outside of a system. Sometimes leaders and others in the organization may be flat out lying when they say they are committed to a change you are trying to make. I think this is seldom the case. It is much more likely that in their heads it seems reasonable and they do support it. They will even invest considerable time and money working in support of the change. Yet the change does not happen! There is an alternative explanation which I believe is much more common than lying about their support.

The alternative explanation is that everyone supporting the change has misdiagnosed the context. They have seen it as a problem to solve when it is, more accurately, seen as a polarity with a much-needed move from the downside of an over-focused pole to the upside of a neglected pole. Everyone in this company agreed to go from the downside of Autonomous Business Unites to the upside of Integrated Business Units. They had the power of leadership support, the power of employee alignment, and the reality that the change had significant financial benefits, yet they were still unable to walk their talk! This is the power of our unconscious bias for *Or*-thinking.

At an unconscious level, even the strongest advocates for the change, those who really wanted to make a difference in company performance, were undermining the effort. Their undermining was coming from an unconscious framing of a false choice in which their support of the benefits of Integrated Business Units would result in their losing the benefits of Autonomous Business Units. This would lead to being caught in the downside of Integrated Business Units. The stronger the value, the stronger the fear. The stronger the fear of the downside of a pole, the more difficult it is to access the upside of that pole, especially when approaching it from an *Or* perspective. This is very important in organizational change efforts as in this case. It is equally important in social change efforts and political change efforts, locally, nationally, and internationally.

New Realities in Chapter 5

Reality 47   Values come in pairs. They show up in the two upsides or the two poles of a Polarity Map.

Reality 48   Building a Polarity Map is always a values and language clarification process.

Reality 49   Both poles need to be either neutral or positive.

Reality 50   The downside of one pole represents the fear of losing the value in the upside of the other pole. The stronger the value, the stronger the fear and the reverse.

Reality 51   A powerful value/fear diagonal when combined with *Or*-thinking gets us "hooked" by a false choice between the poles. We become blind to the other value/fear diagonal and over-tolerate the downside of our valued pole. We then get "stuck" there – unable to access the upside of the pole that is feared. Cliff Kayser was the first to describe this process as getting "hooked" leading to getting "stuck."

Reality 52   When we get into trouble with polarities, the reason is not that our problem-solving perceptions are inaccurate; it is that they are incomplete.

Reality 53   The real opposites in a Polarity Map are the diagonals. The poles are interdependent but not always what we might call opposites.

Reality 54   It is helpful to engage key stakeholders in each step of the SMALL process. Based on Robert 'Jake' Jacob's Real Time Strategic Change (RTSC).

Reality 55   Our paradoxical orientation toward change – that if you want people holding on to the present pole to support movement toward the other pole, first guarantee support, with Action Steps, for the upside of the present pole. Based on Gestalt psychology described by Arnold R. Beisser in Gestalt Therapy Now.[19]

Reality 56   It is helpful to acknowledge with Early Warnings the legitimate fears of the downside of the pole we are moving toward before creating Early Warnings for the downside of the pole we are moving from. This is based on the same paradoxical orientation in Reality 55.

---

[19] Shepherd, Irma Lee; Fagan, Joen. *Gestalt Therapy Now*. Gestalt Journal Press, 2008.

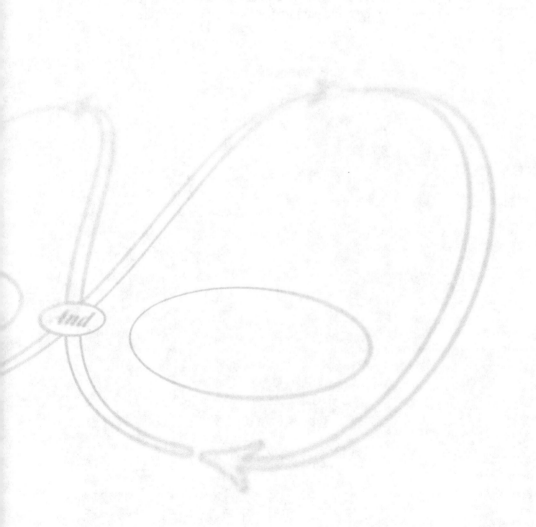

Chapter 6
Organization as the Part

I am in Brazil being warmly welcomed by a representative of Natura outside the front entrance to their main building. They know that I have written about polarities, so they smile as they translate the Portuguese words carved deep and large into the wall: "Being Well *And* Well Being." They explain that "Being Well" means that we must take care of Natura, as a company. It must be financially sound and healthy. "Well Being" means that it is equally important to take care of those who work at Natura, the community, and the environment.

They are beaming. "Looks like we know something about polarities, right?" "Absolutely!" I reply. I am smiling, inside and out. This wonderful company is making a positive difference at many levels and, by happy coincidence, they are contributing to the mission of Polarity Partnerships. They are enhancing our quality of life on the planet by supplementing *Or*-thinking with *And*-thinking. They know you need to take care of the employees (Part) *And* take care of Natura (Whole). Also, you need to take care of Natura (Part) *And* the community/ environment (Whole). With this motto carved in their wall, it is no accident that Natura is continually identified as one of the best companies to work for in Brazil.

In this one summary carved on the wall, they have captured the essence of *Chapter 5* in which the company was the Whole, and this chapter in which the company is the Part.

In *Chapter 4*, we noted that my grandson, Evan, had learned at two that life was about him (Part) *And* it was also about his group of playmates (Whole). Sharing was a good way to care for both. In *Chapter 5*, we looked at the Business Unit as the Part *And* the Organization as the Whole. In this chapter, we will look at the Organization as the Part *And* the rest of the World as the Whole. When the Whole becomes a Part, or the reverse, the Value focus shifts while the generic polarity remains the same.[R57]

The basic elements of *Figure 1* on the next page are at play as we move to larger and larger Wholes. As an individual member of a team (+A), I want the Freedom to express my Uniqueness and make my contribution. I also want to be able to take some Initiative without having to check with the leader or my Whole team. When I get promoted to the team leader with responsibilities for the team as a Whole, I will shift my primary focus to (+C). I will pay attention to making sure that each member of the team feels like they are being treated fairly in comparison to other team members – Equality. I will want all the team members to feel Connected to each other and the team's goals. I will also want the team to work together in a coordinated way, so they become more than a collection of individuals. The "team" then performs in exceptional ways not available without team Synergy.

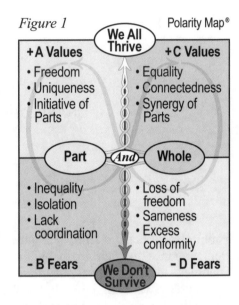

Figure 1   Polarity Map®

As a team leader, when I go to a meeting of all the teams in my department, I shift my primary focus back to the Part pole. Now, my team becomes the Part *And* the department becomes the Whole. What do I want for my team as a Part of the department? The Freedom to express the Unique capabilities of the team and, as a team leader, to be able to take Initiative without always having to check with the department leader or the other teams in the department (+A).

As I move up in the organization, the Part I am responsible for gets larger and so does the Whole in which that Part sits. No matter what Part I am paying attention to, in the long run it will be beneficial for the Part *And* the Whole for me to take care of both. This is because, regardless of size, it is always in the long-term interest of each pole of a polarity to take care of both poles.[R58] When this reality is applied to the Part *And* Whole polarity, it is stated: It is always in the long-term interest of a Part to take care of itself *And* the Whole it is within. Also, it is always in the long-term interest of the Whole to take care of itself *And* the Parts within. For example, at Natura they knew it was in the long-term interests of Natura as a Whole to take care of the Parts within, i.e., their employees. They also knew it was in the long-term interests of Natura to take care of the community (Whole) *And* environment (Whole) of which they are a Part.

Conscious Capitalism

In the book <u>Firms of Endearment</u>,[20] the authors were researching to identify criteria for smart investing, especially in the long run. What they discovered is that companies, like Natura, that focused on taking care of their company's interests (Part) *And* were dedicated to taking care of more than their company (the Whole), offered

---

[20] Sisodia, Rajendra S.; Wolfe, David B.; Sheth, Jagdish N. *Firms of Endearment, How Companies Profit from Passion and Purpose*. Wharton School Publishing, 2007.

the best return on investment. This research-based insight is at the heart of the movement called Conscious Capitalism and the book by the same name.

The point of the research is that there are companies all over the world who are taking care of their shareholders by taking care of other stakeholders as well. They know that it is smart to be caring *And* it is caring to be smart.

Being a Team Player *And* Being a Team Leader

All of us have been a part of many groups, including our family. Most of us have been a leader of a group. When we have been a leader of a group, we have experienced the value of the upside of the Whole pole in the Part *And* Whole polarity. We also know the value of the upside of the Part pole from being a member of a team. Having an appreciation for both poles allows us to empathize with the interests of the Part when we are representing the Whole and to empathize with the interests of the Whole when we are representing the Part. This awareness combined with a Part *And* Whole Polarity Map® will serve us well as a member or leader of a family, a team, an organization, a nation, or the United Nations. It will support us in being world citizens.

Summary

A thriving organization as a Whole will take care of the Parts within: the Business Units, the Employees. As a Part, a thriving organization will take care of the Whole it is within: the community with its necessary services, the customers from the community, and the environment.

Anyone who has led a group of any size has the basis for understanding both poles of the generic Part *And* Whole polarity. This understanding is scalable and will serve all of us well when trying to make a difference with issues tied to the Part *And* Whole polarity no matter how big the Part or how big the Whole. It will serve us well when making a difference with 'Nation as the Whole' in *Chapter 7* and when looking at 'Nation as the Part' in *Chapter 8*.

New Realities in Chapter 6

Reality 57   When the Whole becomes a Part, or the reverse, the Value focus shifts while the generic polarity remains the same.

Reality 58   It is always in the long-term interest of each pole to take care of both poles.

Chapter 7
Nation as the Whole

All nations live within the Part *And* Whole polarity. One question for each country in relation to this polarity is, "How do we leverage the natural tension between the value of Freedom *And* the value of Equality?" These are at the top of the lists in the two upsides in *Figure 1*.

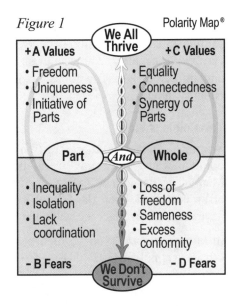

Figure 1

Polarity Map®

Attention to these two upsides has been clear since day one in the United States' Declaration of Independence, 1776.

"We hold these truths to be self-evident that all men are created **equal** (+C) *And* that they are endowed by their creator with certain unalienable rights and among these are life, **liberty** (+A) and the pursuit of happiness."

At the time the founders made this declaration, some of them owned slaves, were displacing Native Americans, and wouldn't let women vote. Other than that, they stood for Freedom *And* Equality?

Clearly, there was work to be done to bring the real closer to the ideal. And there is still work to be done. Yet, the idea of having *both* Freedom (+A) *And* Equality (+C) as a birthright is a solid polarity on which to build a nation and to support a thriving democracy.

Eighty-seven years later (1863), Lincoln re-visits this same polarity as a basis for challenging slavery during the civil war. His Gettysburg address begins: "Four score and seven years ago, our fathers brought forth on this continent a new nation conceived in **liberty** (+A) *And* dedicated to the proposition that all men are created **equal** (+C)."

One hundred years later (1963) Dr. King, at the Lincoln Memorial, joins Lincoln in harkening back to this same polarity. "I have a dream that one day this nation will rise up and live out the true meaning of its creed: 'We hold these truths to be self-evident, that all men are created **equal**.'" (+C) He then concludes his speech by quoting an old African American spiritual "**Free** at last, **Free** at last. Thank God almighty, I'm **Free** at last." (+A) That was my first civil rights demonstration.

In the name of Democracy, equity and enhanced quality of life, we need *both* Freedom *And* Equality. A polarity lens can help any nation move toward becoming a great place to live, work, and play for everyone. Creating a virtuous cycle with the natural tension between the Part (Freedom) *And* the Whole (Equality) will make a difference in that movement. It already has.

In the process of working for justice and inclusion, it is helpful to make a distinction between equality and equity. Equity is the greater purpose that results from leveraging the tension between Freedom *And* Equality. Equity is the result of combining equality, connectedness and synergy (+C) with freedom, uniqueness and initiative (+A). The focus on Equity recognizes the limits of focusing on equality, alone.

Two Points of View

Within all polarities, there are two equally valid, essential, and interdependent points of view. They show up as the value/fear diagonal quadrants of a Polarity Map®. The wisdom in each point of view is a combination of the value being affirmed (upside) and the fear of losing that value (diagonal downside).[R59] As I have said, the stronger the value the stronger the fear of its loss.

In *Figures 2 and 3*, you can see a simplified version of the two points of view as we break them out from within the generic Part *And* Whole Polarity Map.

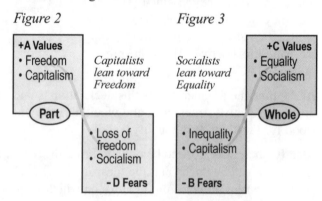

Figure 2   *Figure 3*

+A Values				+C Values
• Freedom	*Capitalists*	*Socialists*		• Equality
• Capitalism	*lean toward*	*lean toward*		• Socialism
	Freedom	*Equality*		

Part   **Whole**

• Loss of freedom	• Inequality
• Socialism	• Capitalism
– D Fears	– B Fears

Notice how the energy arrows toward Freedom and toward Equality are pulling the two apart. This reflects the polari-

zation process when an individual or group holds on to their value and assumes that they have to choose Freedom *Or* Equality. They pull apart from each other.

Those who are ardent supporters of Capitalism have a point of view leaning toward the Part pole with a strong value for Freedom (+A) and an equally strong fear of the Loss of that Freedom (–D). Those who are ardent supporters of Socialism have a point of view leaning toward the Whole pole with a strong value for Equality

(+C) and a proportional strong fear of Inequality (−B). Both points of view contain a powerful drive away from what is feared and toward what is valued. Each sees his/her/their value as the "solution" to the other, which, of course, they identify as the "problem."

Capitalists see Capitalism in the upside of the Part pole: Freedom, while Socialists see Capitalism in the downside of the Part pole: Inequality. Socialists see Socialism in the upside of the Whole pole: Equality, while Capitalists see Socialism in the downside of the Whole pole: Loss of freedom. When either affirms their values, it triggers the other's fears. The stronger and more absolutely one advocates for Equality, the greater the fear that will be generated in those with the alternate point of view who are concerned about losing Freedom. Also, the stronger and more absolutely one advocates for Freedom, the greater the fear that will be generated in those who are concerned about losing Equality.[R60]

As I have mentioned, building a polarity map is always a values and language clarification process. In *Figure 2,* the word "Socialism" is placed in a downside quadrant as something to fear. In *Figure 3,* the word "Socialism" is placed in an upside quadrant as something to value. "Socialism" could also be the name of the right pole, as something neutral with an upside and a downside. If there is a disagreement of where "Socialism" should go on a polarity map, we need to ask those who want it in an upper quadrant what it is they value about it (Equality in *Figure 3*). *And,* we need to ask those who want it in a lower quadrant what it is they fear about it (Loss of freedom in *Figure 2*). When we can recognize the values and fears associated with the word, we can take "Socialism" off the map and appreciate the legitimate values and fears involved and address them rather than the loaded word, "Socialism." The same can be done with "Capitalism" with its associated value of freedom and associated fear of inequality. When those values and fears can be recognized, we can take "Capitalism" off the map and appreciate the legitimate values and fears involved and address them rather than the loaded word, "Capitalism." This is how building a polarity map can be a values and language clarification process that respects the values and fears of both sides.

Substitute Communism for Socialism and you have the makings of a post WWII "Cold War." This is a good example of the natural tension between the two poles of Part *And* Whole becoming a vicious cycle.

The reason Capitalism versus Socialism is a chronic issue is that it lives within the Part *And* Whole polarity that is unavoidable, unsolvable, indestructible, and unstoppable. Regardless of the names we give the poles, we will be living inside some version of the Part *And* Whole polarity with our families, organizations, nations, and humanity as long as we have families, organizations, nations, and humanity.

Part *And* Whole Within the United States

In <u>Culture's Consequences</u>,[21] Geert Hofstede identifies the polarity of Individualism *And* Collectivism as an important dimension for distinguishing one national culture from another. Hofstede's research indicates that the United States has the strongest preference for Individualism of any country on the planet.

This strong value for "Rugged Individualism" had an early start: "Give me liberty or give me death!" (Patrick Henry, 1775). We value *both* Freedom *And* Equality in the U.S. At the same time, as a culture, given an *either/Or* choice between the two, we tend to choose Freedom. The question is, "For whom?"

In *Figure 4,* this pole preference makes us vulnerable to over-focusing on Freedom (+A) to the relative neglect of Equality (+C), which leads to Inequality (-B). We tend to be blind to the downside of our pole preference because we are "hooked" by its upside value (+A) and by our fear of losing this value (-D) combined with *Or*-thinking. This leads to an over-tolerance of and getting "stuck" in the downside of our preferred pole. In the U.S. this shows up with gross inequality and considerable tolerance for it. The grey infinity loop in the map reflects this vulnerability by looping primarily into the downside of the Part pole.

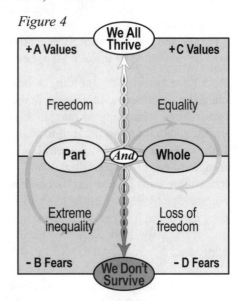

Figure 4

Our love of Freedom (+A) and natural fear of losing it (-D), combined with *Or*-thinking, makes it difficult for us as a culture to access the Equality (+C) we want and need. Just as the company in *Chapter 5* had trouble accessing the upside of the Whole pole because of their love of the upside of the Part and fear of the downside of the Whole, we have a similar difficulty at the national level in the U.S. The increase in wealth inequality is not just a U.S. issue. At the same time, the U.S. has the greatest wealth inequality by far.[22]

There is a parallel difficulty for those nations that have a strong leaning toward Equality (+C). Their love of Equality (+C) and natural fear of losing it (-B), combined with *Or*-thinking, makes it difficult for them, as a culture, to access the Freedom (+A) they want and need. This is a vulnerability of Socialist countries.

[21] Hofstede, Geert. *Culture's Consequences: Comparing Values, Behaviors, Institutions and Organizations Across Nations.* Sage Publications, 2001
[22] Sherman, Erik. *America is the Richest and Most Unequal Country.* Fortune, September 30, 2015.

The Wisdom of Both the Tea Party *And* Occupy Wall Street

One of the nice things about the Polarity Map and principles is that they have the capacity to include a very broad range of perceptions, values, and beliefs. This is especially helpful with significant polarization. There is room for everyone in a Polarity Map.

In *Figure 5,* we have a Part *And* Whole map that is slightly modified from the generic Part *And* Whole map in *Figure 1.* It contains a Tea Party (TP) point of view (+A/-D) *And* an Occupy Wall Street (OWS) point of view (-B\+C). Other groups who, like the Tea Party, tend to identify more strongly with the Part pole include Conservatives and Republicans. Those who, like Occupy Wall Street, tend to identify more strongly with the Whole pole include Liberals and Democrats. Feel free to substitute those named pairs for the two points of view in *Figure 5.*

Figure 5

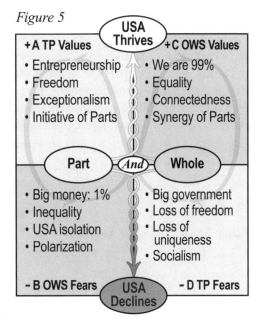

Looking at the two groups through a polarity lens with the map and our polarity realities in mind, the wisdom and contribution of each becomes clearer. Both the Tea Party and Occupy Wall Street saw themselves as standing proudly on U.S. tradition, and they are. The Tea Party supported Entrepreneurship while abhorring Big Government; stood for Freedom and were willing to fight its loss; proclaimed Exceptionalism/Uniqueness and wanting to avoid losing that Uniqueness (not wanting to be seen as the same as every other country); supported Initiative and saw Big Government and "Socialism" as against everything in which they believe.

Occupy Wall Street supported the "99%" while abhorring Big Money and the idea of "1%" running the country; stood for Equality and were willing to fight its loss; proclaimed our Connectedness with other countries in the community of nations and wanted to avoid our Isolation as a country and the increasing gap between the "Haves" and the "Have nots;" supported the synergy of all working together and saw our Polarization as a symptom of greedy "Capitalism."

Not only are they both right, they both need each other over time for the USA to thrive. It is easy to see how, in the natural tension between the two poles, each group would see themselves as "the solution" and the other group as "the problem." All of us in the U.S. lean toward one pole or the other.

The Tea Party *And* Occupy Wall Street, in a sense, represent all of us and our collective wisdom. They are just a little more strident and clearer about their values and fears. Both are accurate. Each is incomplete without the other.

The Recession of 2008 Contributing to President Obama's Election

Life is richer and more complicated than what can be summarized within a Polarity Map and set of polarity realities. At the same time, they can be useful to appreciate predictable, underlying patterns within complicated issues. For example, there were many issues at play within the recession of 2008 in the U.S. that had such a powerful impact on the U.S. and the global economy. One underlying dynamic was the tension within the generic Part and Whole polarity map of this chapter which I have modified in *Figure 6*. One element within the complex process was the assumption that Regulation is an *either/Or* choice.

You might put some different words in the quadrants. Feel free. The point is not about the exact words in the quadrants. It is about seeing that the Part *And* Whole polarity was one key dynamic in the process.

Figure 6

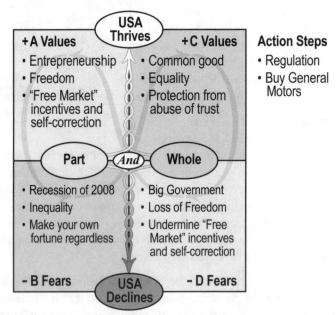

During the Clinton administration, there was considerable support for Deregulation. It can be seen as an Action Step in support of (+A). There were good reasons: it would encourage Entrepreneurship (+A) and minimize "Big government" getting in the way (-D). The "Free Market" (+A) would be allowed to work without undermining its incentives (-D).

This, combined with our cultural leaning toward Freedom and *Or*-thinking, led to an over-focus on Entrepreneurship (+A) to the relative neglect of the Common good (+C), which led to abuses and selfish efforts to make our individual fortunes regardless of the vulnerability of others. This selfishness eventually contributed to the Recession of 2008 (-B). As we follow the normal flow within a polarity, we know that there is a natural self-correction from the Recession of 2008 (-B), identified as a "Problem," to the Common good (+C) as the "Solution."

In the process of responding to the crisis, we took a couple of Action Steps to take care of the Common good and protect all of us from abuse of our trust (+C). One Action Step was to take a look at Regulation and tighten up. Another Action Step was to buy 60% of General Motors. Though this may be seen as a support of (+C), it understandably generated a concern by many that their fear of Big government (-D) had happened! The over-focus on Freedom (+A) to the relative neglect of Equality (+C), first, contributed to the Recession of 2008 (-B), and then to Big government as we bought General Motors (-D). It is not likely that those favoring Deregulation and Entrepreneurship (+A) will see how they contributed to the eventual purchase of General Motors and the Big government (-D) they wanted to avoid. That is because we are likely to see Deregulation (an Action Step for +A) as a solution to a problem rather than the necessary self-correction in an ongoing oscillation within the Part *And* Whole polarity. With polarities you get what you are afraid of by trying to avoid it.

President Trump Elected in 2016

In the 2016 election, it is easy to see, within *Figure* 6, the self-correcting oscillation back to Deregulation as a campaign promise by then candidate Trump. It is also easy to understand support for that Deregulation to allow Entrepreneurship, Freedom, and "Free Market" self-correction (+A).

I've mentioned that life is more complicated than these simple Polarity Maps would imply. We make it more complicated and dysfunctional by treating a polarity which needs leveraging as if it were a problem to solve. For example, to argue in Congress, on Wall Street, or on Main Street over whether we should regulate *Or* deregulate is worse than a waste of time. It is a false choice contributing to a vicious cycle that, in the long run, serves neither side of the argument and does not serve our nation or the world.

The good news is that it is possible to see this underlying polarity and intentionally leverage it to the benefit of both sides and to the service of the nation. How would this be done? We would reframe the issue for starters. We would respect the wisdom of those wanting to deregulate and those wanting to regulate. We would ask people who appreciate the complexities much better than I to create a dual strategy that gets both upsides while minimizing each downside. We need to deregulate to the maximum possible and regulate to the minimum required. One thing that is certain, seeing the underlying polarity and intentionally leveraging it will be more effective than seeing it as a problem to solve. Like all polarities, it is not going anywhere, so we have plenty of opportunity to leverage it better in the future.

Russian Revolution (1917) – Break-up of the Soviet Union (1991)

In 1993, I was presenting on Polarity Thinking to a sub-group within a large Organization Development conference. Just before our session started, one of the conference organizers let me know that a group of six people from Russia attended the conference and wanted to sit in on my session. They were at the conference because they were eager to learn about the field of Organization Development and how it might be useful to Russia in the Post-Soviet Union era.

I had been thinking about a polarity perspective on the Russian Revolution and the recent break-up of the Soviet Union. This seemed like a great learning opportunity for me and possibly them. The six Russian guests came in together just before the session started and I had a chance to shake their hands and greet them. They were warm and friendly and expressed an eagerness to soak up whatever they could in order to bring it back to Russia. At that moment, I decided to change my presentation. I began by welcoming everyone and gave a special welcome to the six guests from Russia sitting in the front row.

I then acknowledged that I am not an expert on Russia or the Soviet Union and that I had never had the privilege of visiting Russia. At the same time, their presence gave me an opportunity to check with them to see if a polarity lens might provide a useful way to appreciate what had just happened with the break-up of the Soviet Union. I looked at the six guests in the front row and said, "I would appreciate your letting me know, after my presentation, whether the polarity lens makes sense to you and whether you find it useful in looking at recent events in Russia." They nodded in agreement. I was both anxious and excited. Would this lens be useful to them? Time to find out.

In *Figure 7* a simple, generic Part *And* Whole map is close to what I created quickly on a flipchart to begin my presentation. I did not have a Greater Purpose and Deeper Fear at the top and bottom of the map at that time.

Figure 7

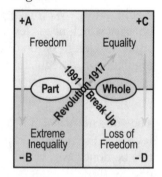

In the complex set of events that led to the Russian revolution in 1917, one of the underlying factors was the Freedom (+A) of the Tsar and others to concentrate power and wealth to the neglect of Equality leading to Extreme inequality (-B) and increasing resentment about it. A central thrust of the revolution of 1917 was to move toward the ideal of more Equality (+C) as the "solution" to the misery being experienced by so many (-B).

I pointed out that we tend to be blind to the downside of our pole preference because we are "hooked" by its upside values (+A) and by our fear of losing those values (-D). This, combined with *Or*-thinking, leads to an over-tolerance of and getting "stuck" in the downside of our preferred pole.

In this case, the Tsar and others with concentrated power and wealth (+A) were increasingly afraid of losing it (-D). This fear contributed to the decision to go to war with Germany and to repressive efforts to control protest activities at home; both of which increased the degree of suffering and the numbers of people suffering (-B). Their actions, out of fear of the revolution, led to them getting what they were afraid of – the revolution moving from (-B) to (+C).

The longer and more painfully we experience the downside of one pole (-B), the stronger the fear of that pole and the more we idealize the upside value of the opposite pole (+C).[R61] This perception is what revolutions are made of. It supports the willingness to encounter extreme suffering in order to gain the idealized upside of the other pole. It also creates, for the revolutionaries, their own strong fear\value diagonal (-B\+C). What we know about strong fear\value diagonals combined with *Or*-thinking is that they get us stuck in the downside of our preferred pole. Thus, we can anticipate that a successful Russian revolution would find itself stuck in the downside of the Whole pole (-D).

Once the revolution succeeded, the "solution" was achieved. Yet, from a polarity perspective, the upside of one pole is not a sustainable solution; it is a necessary self-correction in an ongoing oscillation between the two poles. Because of the powerful, historical pain under the Tsar (-B) and the powerful value of the dream of Equality (+C), it is easy to understand how there would be some blindness to and an over-tolerance for the Loss of Freedom which followed (-D). The response was something like, "This may not be so good (-D), but it is a lot better than what we experienced under the Tsar!" (-B)

It is worth noting that the revolution was experienced initially as both a move toward Equality and as a move toward Freedom from the oppressive circumstances under the Tsar. This is because the sustained effort by the Tsar and others to claim freedom for themselves to concentrate power and wealth with complete disregard to any effort toward equality, led to experiencing the downside of both poles. The very poor had neither Freedom nor Equality. In the process of the build-up and completion of the revolution, the most obvious "problem" was the gross inequality and suffering of most while a few were living in relative luxury. The "solution" was obvious and worth fighting for.

When we over-focus on a new pole as a "solution" to past "problems," we inevitably experience the limits or downside of the new pole. When we experience these downsides, the original "solution" (in this case, the move to Equality) gets identified as a "mistake." It was not a mistake. It was the natural and necessary self-correction in an ongoing polarity. The effort to shift poles gets called a mistake because it was misdiagnosed as a solution in the first place.[R62]

Over time, as the Soviet Union experienced more and more of the downsides of the Whole pole: Loss of Freedom (-D), and got farther and farther from the memories of the downside of the Part pole: Inequality (-B), the stronger the forces became to self-correct to the upside of the Part pole: Freedom (+A) as the new "solution".

Each Part of the Soviet Union increasingly pressured for their Freedom and independence – a move from (-D) to (+A). The breakup, allowing Freedom for the Parts, was won in 1991. This move to the upside of the Freedom pole completed one 74-year oscillation through the infinity loop of the Part *And* Whole polarity. The longer the cycle time, the less obvious it is that you are dealing with a polarity to leverage rather than a problem to solve.

When I finished describing the Russian Revolution and break-up of the Soviet Union from a polarity perspective, I noticed that the six Russian guests in the front row were all crying. I asked them what was happening. They said it was the first time in years that they had heard someone describe the dreams their grandparents had died for as something other than a "terrible mistake."

They said it made sense to them and was a helpful way to understand the struggles at the present time in Russia between those excited about the upside of the Part: Freedom (+A) and those afraid of the downside of the Part: Extreme inequality (-B). To see it as an ongoing tension and energy system that could be leveraged was both helpful and hopeful. It was one of those encouraging times, in the 45 years that I have been paying attention to polarities, that I thought, "This really can be useful!"

Abundance for Some *And* the Basics for All

Whenever there is a distribution issue with goods and services – food, education, healthcare, jobs, shelter, safety, and opportunities – the Part *And* Whole polarity is at play.[R63] The *Figure 8* version of the Part *And* Whole map provides a framework for looking at distribution issues.

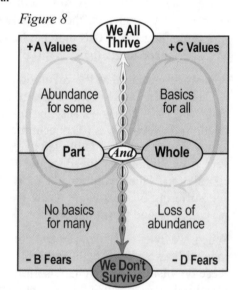

Figure 8

With the distribution of goods and services, there are some who, for a variety of reasons, will be able to access more goods and services than others. Some, like me, end up with Abundance (+A). Those who have abundance and value it strongly will have an equally strong resistance to their Loss of abundance (-D).

There is wisdom in this point of view (+A/-D). The value is worth holding and the feared outcome is worth avoiding. White U.S. Citizens with abundance can often point to the hard work, creativity, and sacrifice that got us there. With *And*-thinking, we can be justifiably proud of family accomplishments, past and present *And*, at the same time, can acknowledge unearned advantages from being born white in the U.S. *Or*-thinking gets in the way of our recognizing white privilege because it frames the false choice that *either* we can be proud of family accomplishments *Or* we can acknowledge white privilege. *And*-thinking allows us to do *both*. When we recognize and acknowledge white privilege, it need not diminish our pride of family accomplishments. We can keep it *And* increase our appreciation of similar accomplishments attained by those without the benefits of white privilege.

There is a second point of view (-B\+C). It is held by the many who are hungry or are called to feed the hungry; are naked or are called to cloth the naked; are concerned about the gap between the haves and the have nots; are concerned about white privilege and are attempting to interrupt it. With this point of view, it is easy to identify No basics for many (-B) as the "problem" and Basics for all (+C) as the "solution." As mentioned earlier, the longer and more painfully one experiences the downside of one pole: No basics for many (-B), the more idealized becomes the upside of the opposite pole: Basics for all (+C). And the more difficult it is to see any upside to the present pole: Abundance for some (+A), or any downside to the pole toward which you want to move: Loss of Abundance (-D).

We can have Abundance for some *And* provide the Basics for all. But it will only happen if the natural tension in the two points of view is seen as a polarity to leverage rather than seeing either upside as a solution to a problem. If it appears to either side of this tension that we are required to choose *either* Abundance for some *Or* Basics for all, this will remain a chronic source of pain, unnecessary suffering, and periodic revolutions.

Remember the story of the Fortune 100 company that could not walk its talk even though everyone agreed the present situation was painful and costing them considerable money? Leadership and followership were aligned to make the change; and all had agreed on plans for the change. This combination of realities did not lead to the desired change. There were no "bad actors" sabotaging the effort. No one was intentionally resisting the changes. The problem was using a combination of gap analysis and a problem solving (*Or*-thinking) framework when a polarity (*And*-thinking) framework was required to make the sustainable difference they wanted.

Whenever we are addressing this polarity of Abundance for Some *And* Basics for All, many of us with Abundance and many without abundance, may strongly believe in the need to provide Basics for all (+C) in our heads and our hearts but will not walk our talk. The conscious or unconscious fear in our gut of loss of abundance (-D) will radically undermine our efforts. Our unconscious bias for *Or*-thinking is getting in the way. To attribute the lack of "walking their talk" to a lack of integrity by those with abundance who are working for Basics for all is, in most cases, a serious misunderstanding of the dynamics at play and a very unreliable platform for self-righteous indignation. We are more likely to make a positive difference by reframing the issue as a polarity to leverage than by blaming people for not believing in what they are saying.

The Wisdom of "Bread for the World"

The Polarity Map® is a wisdom organizer. When invited to speak at a meeting of Bread for the World, I was given some literature on their mission and their work. I also had an opportunity to interview a member of their executive team. They are an example of tacit wisdom leading to leveraging a polarity without having heard about Polarity Thinking. They followed a version of our 5-step process: **Seeing** – They saw the natural tension in serious discussions about addressing world hunger. Rather than avoid the tension, they have a balance of Republicans *And* Democrats on their board rather than choose one *Or* the other. **Mapping** – They listened to two points of view and did their best to learn from and show respect for both. **Assessing** – They did their research and documented the present vulnerability of so many who are hungry. **Learning** – They learned about the forces at play in addressing this issue. **Leveraging** – They created Action Steps that respond to both points of view.

Figure 9 is the version of the generic Part *And* Whole polarity I shared with them. The content is from their literature and my interviews. I have just organized it within our Polarity Map with Action Steps and Early Warnings.

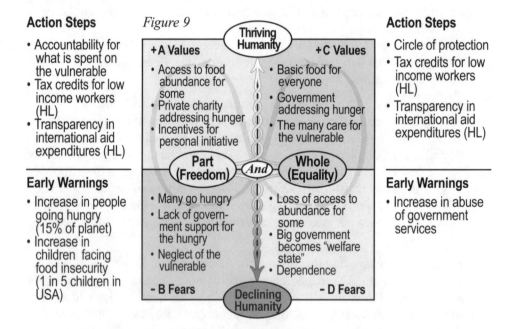

The over-focus on Freedom (+A) to the relative neglect of Equality (+C) in relation to food distribution results in Millions going hungry, a Lack of government support for the hungry, and Neglect of the vulnerable (−B). They documented that 15% of the planet is going hungry and one in five children in the U.S. is facing food insecurity (2013). These realities show up on the map as Early Warnings for the over-focus on Freedom to the neglect of Equality. These warnings might not be very "Early" but they are real and measurable.

They knew that their efforts to provide Basic food for everyone (+C) would meet with resistance from those in government who were afraid of becoming a "welfare state" and of fostering Dependence (-D). They recognized that Early Warnings of this potential downside would be an "increase in abuse of government services." They also point out that seriously measuring for such abuse indicates how rare it is.

Out of respect for the alternate point of view, they agreed on Action Steps to affirm the values of the Freedom pole (+A). These include: Accountability for what is spent on the vulnerable, Tax credits for low-income workers, and Transparency in international aid expenditures. Notice that the last two also show up as Action Steps for the upside of the Equality pole as well. They become high leverage (HL) action steps. By seeking out and respecting the values and fears of those who might resist their efforts to move toward Basic food for everyone (+C), they increased the possibility of collaboration with those with the alternate point of view.

Bread for the World provides hope, not only that more of our hungry will be fed but that it is possible to leverage the natural tension between two points of view and create a virtuous cycle that serves both those with abundance and those without the basics.

The Pattern

Within *Figure 10* (+A), I have written 'Abundant _____*' to indicate you can enter any of the items listed (*food, education, jobs, healthcare, shelter, and safety) and each will work as part of a pattern that applies to all these products or services. For example, you can put "food" in the blank space of each of the four quadrants and it would fit for the story I just told about Bread for the World.

No matter what word from the list you put in the blank space, we know there is a natural tension between the two upsides, (+A) and (+C),

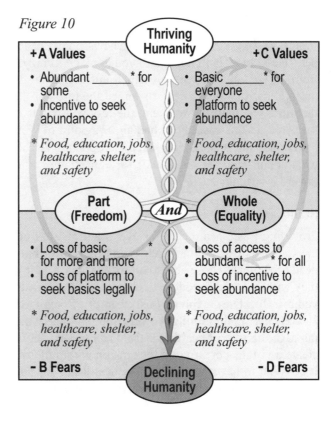

Figure 10

Thriving Humanity

+A Values

- Abundant _____* for some
- Incentive to seek abundance

* Food, education, jobs, healthcare, shelter, and safety

+C Values

- Basic _____* for everyone
- Platform to seek abundance

* Food, education, jobs, healthcare, shelter, and safety

Part (Freedom) —*And*— **Whole (Equality)**

- Loss of basic _____* for more and more
- Loss of platform to seek basics legally

* Food, education, jobs, healthcare, shelter, and safety

- Loss of access to abundant ____* for all
- Loss of incentive to seek abundance

* Food, education, jobs, healthcare, shelter, and safety

- B Fears

Declining Humanity

- D Fears

and that this tension can become a vicious cycle or a virtuous cycle depending on whether that tension is seen as a problem to solve (*Or*-thinking) or as a problem to solve *And* a polarity to leverage (*And*-thinking).

Education

When we provide Basic education for everyone (+C) we create a platform for them to get the basics of everything else. We also can support each person in maximizing their educational potential *And* their contribution to the community. Some will end up with an Abundant education at our best schools (+A). Their abundant education (MD, PhD, research, new science and technology) enhances the quality of the basic education for everyone. It also contributes to *both* upsides (+A) *And* (+C) for all the other elements in the quadrants. We, as a society, become better at creating and supplying food, jobs, healthcare, shelter, and safety. Our creating abundant education for some while also assuring a basic education for everyone can create a virtuous cycle that benefits each person *And* society as a Whole. For addressing polarities within education, read Unleashing the Positive Power of Differences, by Jane Kise.[23]

Jobs

In 1914, Henry Ford made a big announcement that shocked the country. He doubled his base pay for workers to $5.00 a day. It caused the financial editor at *The New York Times* to stagger into the newsroom and ask his staff in a stunned whisper, "He's crazy, isn't he? Don't you think he's crazy?" Henry Ford looked "crazy" from an *Or* point of view in which enhancing the basics for his workers would mean a loss of abundance for some at the top. For them, it was a zero-sum game: the more you paid the workers, the less you had to create the desired abundance for some. In this case, Ford had an *And* point of view in which paying workers a larger base amount (+C) increased their potential to buy the cars they were making, which contributed to abundance for himself *And* others (+A). He was contributing toward a virtuous cycle.

Healthcare

Providing Basic healthcare for everyone (+C) has been a source of contention in the U.S. The two points of view on this subject both are not only legitimate but need each other. Those able to afford the very best in healthcare are concerned that they will lose their Freedom of choice of doctors and access to the abundance they value (-D). They express their fear of "Socialized Medicine" and "Universal Healthcare," undermining the very foundations of our country. Here, again, looking at the service of healthcare from an *Or* perspective undermines the potential to create a virtuous cycle from the tension within the two points of view. Not only is it possible to have *both* Abundant healthcare for some *And* Basic healthcare for everyone, the two can support each other in mutually reinforcing ways to create a

---

[23] Kise, Jane. *Unleashing the Power of Differences: Polarity Thinking in Our Schools*. Corwin Publishers, 2013.

virtuous cycle that benefits *both* those with Abundance *And* those with the Basics. Leveraging this polarity is not easy. The alternative, to fight over the two points of view as if it were a problem to solve, makes a difficult task an impossible one. For addressing polarities within healthcare, read <u>Polarity Thinking in Healthcare: The Missing Logic to Transformation</u>, by Bonnie Wesorick.[24] She has also co-authored two of the five chapters with this same focus in <u>*And*: Volume Two – Applications</u>.

An Unconscious Bias for *Or*-thinking Alone Creates Unconscious Resistance

Figure 11 summarizes the point of view that generates resistance to "Basics for all" and gets us caught with "No basics for many." An unconscious bias for *Or* results in a simple question, "Are we going to have abundance *Or* lose abundance?" Our unconscious *Or* prioritizes that point of view and the other point of view fades into the background. I have put the text "No basics for many\Basics for all" point of view in light grey to reflect its lack of power relative to the unconscious fear of those of us concerned that we will lose abundance.

Figure 11

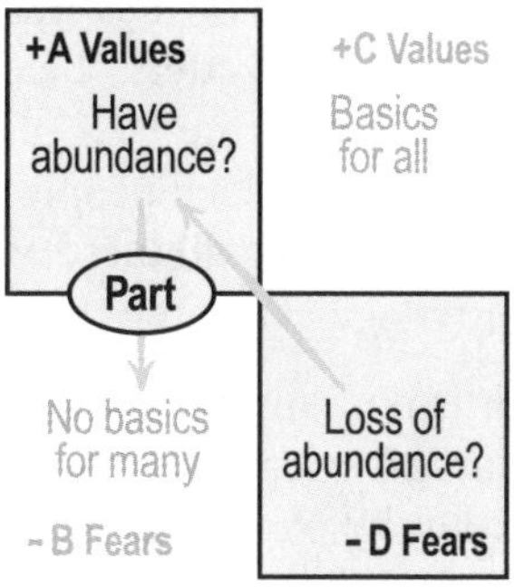

+A Values	+C Values
Have abundance?	Basics for all

Part

No basics for many	Loss of abundance?
– B Fears	– D Fears

This reality is a powerful resistance against any effort to address the basic needs of humanity. Until basic needs can be seen from a polarity perspective in which we organize ourselves to *both* have Abundance for some *And* have Basics for all, we will not be effective in making a sustainable difference in addressing any of our distribution issues including: food, education, fair paying jobs, healthcare, shelter, and safety.

An Unconscious Bias of a Dominant Part Toward Marginalized Parts, Creates Additional, Unconscious Resistance.

A second resistance to equality and equity within the U.S. (the Whole) is the unconscious bias of the dominant Part toward marginalized Parts. In the U.S., the dominant power Part is white, cis males like me.[25] Some marginalized groups include: Black, Indigenous, and People of Color (BIPOC), women, and the LGBTQI+ community. Those of us in this dominant power group are not somehow "bad" because we are white or because we are cis males. At the same time, we have a major responsibility for inequities in those systems and cultures in which we hold dominant power. The combination of the two types of resistance (*Or* bias and marginalized groups bias) results in gross inequities which fall disproportionately on those whom we have marginalized.

All polarities require the intentional maximizing of power of both poles so the issue of power is present within every polarity. As we move through the key

---

[24] Wesorick, Bonnie. *Polarity Thinking in Healthcare: the Missing Logic to Transformation.* HRD Press, 2016.
[25] A cis man is a man who identifies as male and was assigned a male sex at birth.

polarities within this book, there will be an important thread of power imbalance between a Part dominating the Whole and marginalized Parts within the Whole. In every case, it will be important to remember that each Part is Unique *And* Connected. Also, each Part is Accountable *And* Loved. This power imbalance is a focus in "Black Lives Matter", below, and again in *Chapters 22, 29* and *31*. It will also be addressed in section one of <u>*And*: Volume Two – Applications</u> where we look more deeply at polarities, power, and privilege from the perspective of members of marginalized groups. They are the ones writing this section about how they are making a difference by leveraging polarities.

Black Lives Matter *And* All Lives Matter

In every one of the "Basics" mentioned above: food, education, jobs, healthcare, shelter, and safety, black people in the U.S. are disproportionately negatively impacted by the lack of the basics.[26] Each area of inequity is a form of violence into which black people are born and with which they live. The cumulative effect of combining all these areas of inequity is a burden that those of us living in white privilege can barely imagine, let alone understand.

It is not only the inequity of goods and services that is oppressive. A deeper and more powerful level of oppression is the denial of human equality for people of color by our dominant white culture in the U.S. Human inequality is not the same as wealth inequality. It is more oppressive and more destructive to the human spirit.

The last item on the inequity list is safety. In late August, 1968, I was arrested in Chicago at the Democratic National Convention for participating in a non-violent sit-in organized by Clergy and Laity Concerned About Vietnam. That night, in the Cook County Jail, I shared a cell with three young black men who had been arrested for a city curfew violation the night Dr. King was killed in Memphis on April 4.

They had been in the Cook County Jail for five months for a curfew violation and were still waiting for their day in court! One of the most shameful and cowardly acts in my life was to accept bail from Clergy and Laity Concerned and to leave them behind the next morning. I could have refused to leave until they had their day in court. I could have used my white privilege to get them the attention and legal support they needed to end the injustice they were caught in. Neither option crossed my mind. All I did was report their situation to a movement newspaper. I am sharing this story to give others with white privilege one peek into the extreme difference between being black or white in Chicago at that time. Also, to help us appreciate the hesitancy of marginalized people to trust us from the dominant group who claim to want to be allies. Will we disappear when the going gets tough?

In that year, 1968, given the relative sizes of the black and white populations, in the name of "safety," we incarcerated, proportionally, 5.4 times as many black people as white people. Fifty years later, in 2018, the inequity had increased to

---

[26] Jones, Janelle; Schmitt, John; Wilson, Valerie. *50 years after the Kerner Commission.* Economic Policy Institute, February 26, 2018.

incarceration of 6.4 times as many black people as white people.[27] Though progress has been made in some areas of racial inequity, incarceration, over the past 50 years, is not one of them.

On top of all these historical and present inequities, the final straw that led to the founding of Black Lives Matter in 2013 was the acquittal of George Zimmerman for the killing of Trevon Martin.[28] This was not an isolated incident. It was part of a painful reality that black people are losing their lives in disproportionate numbers to vigilantes and to some of the police officers who are paid to keep us all safe. In 2018, a black person was 3 times (2.845) as likely to be killed by police as a white person.[29] It is in the context of this host of historical and present inequities experienced by black people, including the disproportionate loss of black lives, that a movement emerged with a simple claim: "Black Lives Matter."

Figure 12 shows this claim within the same Part *And* Whole map we have used throughout this chapter. I will follow the normal flow of energy through the four quadrants starting with (1) and ending with (5) in the downside of the Whole pole.

(1) Black lives don't matter. With all the inequities that disproportionately harm black people in the U.S., including killings, it is easy to understand how those aware of these inequities would assert that Black lives don't seem to matter.

(2) Black Lives Matter. *Figure 13* on the next page highlights a point of view from within Figure 12, which focuses on the natural move from (1) Black lives don't matter to the upside of the Part pole (2) Black Lives Matter. This message is more than just true. It is essential that every other "Part" of humanity support this

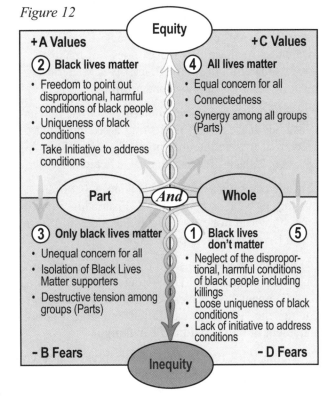

Figure 12

+A Values | Equity | +C Values

(2) **Black lives matter**
- Freedom to point out disproportional, harmful conditions of black people
- Uniqueness of black conditions
- Take Initiative to address conditions

(4) **All lives matter**
- Equal concern for all
- Connectedness
- Synergy among all groups (Parts)

Part *And* Whole

(3) **Only black lives matter**
- Unequal concern for all
- Isolation of Black Lives Matter supporters
- Destructive tension among groups (Parts)

(1) **Black lives don't matter** (5)
- Neglect of the disproportional, harmful conditions of black people including killings
- Loose uniqueness of black conditions
- Lack of initiative to address conditions

- B Fears | Inequity | - D Fears

27 Jones, Janelle. Ibid.
28 www.BlackLivesMatter.com/herstory.
29 *Number of people shot to death by the police in the United States from 2017 to 2019, by race.* Statista Research Department, October 30, 2019.

"Part." It is not an exceptional message. It is as natural as the messages: "My parents' lives matter;" or, "My children's lives matter." Black people are a part of our human family. Of course, Black Lives Matter!

The obviousness of the choice between the two quadrants within one point of view generates confusion and anger toward those who resist it. Those of us with the point of view represented in *Figure 13* are clear about how obvious and necessary it is to move to affirming that Black Lives Matter. So, where does the resistance come from to this essential message? It would be easy to attribute all the resistance to conscious and explicit racism. Though that is probably true of some resistors, the most powerful resistance is coming from people with (1), an implicit bias for *Or*-thinking combined with (2), an implicit bias (unconscious racism) toward black people. Lack of conscious awareness of these two biases does not make them any less undermining of the Black Lives Matter movement. It makes them more undermining.

Figure 13

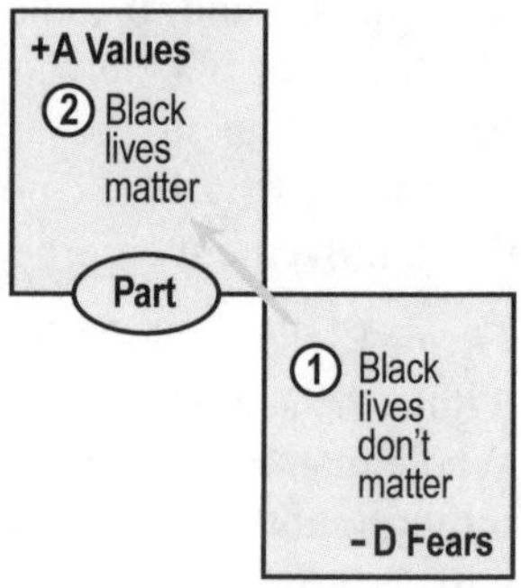

Figure 14 shows a second point of view. The two unconscious biases result in treating a second point of view as if it were the only point of view. When this happens, "Black Lives Matter" gets heard as...

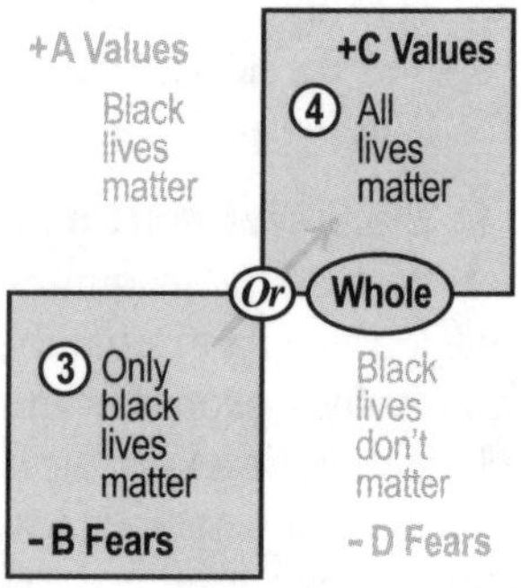

(3) Only black lives matter. This is not what is said – but this is what is being heard. From this point of view, they can honestly believe they need to inform Black Lives Matter supporters that...

(4) All Lives Matter. This can often be said with self-righteous indignation! The outrageousness of using the statement "All Lives Matter" as a platform to counter the "Black Lives Matter" movement is not obvious to those making the statement or they wouldn't be making it.

Figure 14

Of course, All Lives Matter. The problem is not with the statement. The problem is with using the true statement, "All Lives Matter" as a pushback against the equally true statement, "Black Lives Matter" as if one had to choose between the two statements. "All Lives Matter" is the fundamental basis for claiming that "Black Lives Matter" rather than an argument against it! "All Lives Matter" supports any group claiming that their lives matter. When the dominant group, in terms of power and privilege, ignores the inequitable conditions of groups we have marginalized, the implicit message is that the lives of those groups do not matter. When in response to these inequities, members of a marginalized group, with understandable anger, affirm "Our Lives Matter," imagine the shock of being told, in rebuttal, by members of the dominant group that "All Lives Matter!" If all lives really mattered to the dominant group, we would not have marginalized them in the first place and we would not be blaming them for their marginalization. We would be using our dominant group power and privilege to address the inequities we have created.

Why do many of us in the dominant group hear "Only black lives matter" when that was not said?

First, implicit *Or*-thinking: from an *Or*-thinking perspective, one must choose between All Lives Matter *Or* Black Lives Matter. If, in that false choice, you choose Black Lives Matter, you must be rejecting All Lives Matter. If you are rejecting All Lives Matter, you are saying "Only black lives matter." This is the first contributor to hearing "Only black lives matter" when it was not said. Second, implicit bias against black people in the U.S.: our unconscious racial bias increases the likelihood that the message "Black Lives Matter" will be heard as "Only black lives matter." The unconscious fear and mistrust of black people along with unconscious assumptions of superiority comes from being raised in the United States in which that fear, mistrust, and implicit superiority (unconscious racism) is present throughout the dominant culture.

Figure 15 summarizes how dominant culture tolerance for black inequities leaves the impression that (1) "Black lives don't matter," which leads those concerned about black inequities to remind us that (2) "Black Lives Matter," which gets heard as (3) "Only black lives matter," leading to the affirmation that (4) "All Lives Matter," which puts the Black Lives Matter movement back where they started in which the inequities experienced disproportionately by black people get dismissed. This reinforces the original concern that… **(5) Black lives don't matter!**

Figure 15

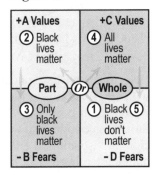

In this process, often well-intentioned members of the dominant group bring unconscious *Or* bias combined with unconscious Racial bias to how we hear and respond to "Black Lives Matter." It leads to powerful, often unconscious, resistance like using the reality that All Lives Matter as a platform against Black Lives Matter. A polarity perspective can help avoid a false choice shouting match between Black Lives Matter *Or* All Lives Matter.

When the response to "Black Lives Matter" is "All Lives Matter," the essence of a return message can be something like, "Yes, absolutely. As a matter of fact, it is exactly because All Lives Matter that Black Lives Matter, along with the lives of any other part of our humanity. Because Black Lives Matter, the unique concerns and inequities of black people need to be addressed." Explicitly switching from *Or* to *And* with this polarity and showing the Polarity Map can be helpful in addressing the unconscious bias for *Or*-thinking.

Figure 16 shows how those supporting Black Lives Matter can explicitly drive toward Equity by maximizing both upsides of this polarity. There is no opposition to "All Lives Matter." There is no opposition to "Black Lives Matter." Both are affirmed as essential in moving toward equity in the United States and around the world. It affirms that "Black Lives Matter *And* All Lives Matter." Switching from *Or* to *And* returns "All Lives Matter" to a platform for support of "Black Lives Matter," where it belongs, rather than allowing it to be used as a platform against the Black Lives Matter movement.

Figure 16

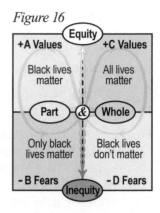

The second part of the resistance to Black Lives Matter is the unconscious bias against black people. This can be seen in the difference between the response to "Black Lives Matter" and the response to "Blue Lives Matter." Both were understandable statements coming from concern for the loss of innocent lives: black people and police officers. Yet there was no challenging response to "Blue Lives Matter" by asserting that "All Lives Matter." If the resistance to Black Lives Matter were only coming from an unconscious bias for *Or*-thinking, the "All Lives Matter" response would have also been given to "Blue Lives Matter." On the contrary, not only was "All Lives Matter" not given as an oppositional response to "Blue Lives Matter," bills have been passed at both the State and Federal levels declaring that "Blue Lives Matter."[30]

Here, again, we have one truth being used against another truth by connecting them with *Or*. What causes the polarization is still the unconscious bias for *Or* in which the question becomes, "Do Black Lives Matter *Or* Do Blue Lives Matter? This false choice combined with unconscious bias against black people results in suspicion and isolation of Black Lives Matter and praise for Blue Lives Matter by the dominant culture. The response to the claim that Blue Lives Matter needs to be: Police officers are a part of our humanity; of course Blue Lives Matter because as we agreed earlier, All Lives Matter. Given that Black Lives Matter *And* Blue Lives Matter, we must address the realities faced by each of these Parts of our humanity. How do we pay attention to the inequities experienced by black people *And* address the unique concerns of Police officers? Because Police officers already have support of the dominant culture, it is important to pay attention to the inequities of black people because they do not have the same amount of support from the dominant culture. The inequities uniquely experienced by being black are far greater than the unique challenges experienced by being a police officer, which does not even start until you are an adult. Another important reality is that one can remove their uniform but not the color of their skin. We are now back to the source of Black Lives Matter in the first place, which must not be lost when recognizing that Blue Lives Matter. Implying that we must choose between these two groups is a setup for perpetuating the marginalization of black people.

---

[30] Conlon, Kevin. *Louisiana Governor Signs 'Blue Lives Matter' Bill.* CNN, Friday, May 27, 2016.

It is understandable that the Blue culture, like the rest of us living in the dominant culture, will absorb some of the unconscious bias in the dominant culture against black people. This creates an additional challenge to the black police officer on top of an already demanding career. Think of the tension within the black officer when a false choice is asserted between Black Lives Matter *Or* Blue Lives Matter.

There are clear examples of explicit, conscious racism standing stridently against movements like Black Lives Matter. In the name of justice, it is essential to stand with Black Lives Matter against explicit racism. And, it is equally important to pay attention to unconscious sources of resistance and make them conscious. How much of the resistance to Black Lives Matter is coming from an unconscious bias for *Or*-thinking and how much from an unconscious bias against black people is unclear to me. It is easy to underestimate both and it is important to take both into account. They exist within all of us *And* within the culture in which we have been raised.[31]

Targeted Universalism

I highly recommend john a. powell's book, <u>Racing to Justice, Transforming Our Conceptions of Self and Other to Build an Inclusive Society</u>.[32] Dr. powell, who prefers his name in lowercase, focuses on our interdependence and identifies many interdependent pairs in his book, including Self *And* Other in his subtitle.

His first chapter focus on "targeted universalism" speaks eloquently to the Part *And* Whole polarity talked about in this chapter.

"One alternative is to learn a great deal about how to talk about race in ways that are not divisive. The second is to make sure our institutions do the work we want them to do. The latter is accomplished by adopting strategies that are both targeted and universal. A targeted universal strategy is inclusive of the needs of both dominant and marginalized groups, but pays particular attention to the situation of the marginalized group." (*Page 14*)

I hope that a polarity lens will be useful in talking about race in a way that is not divisive. And, I hope it is useful in adopting strategies that are *both* targeted *And* universal.

Figure 17 is one way to organize the "targeted universalism" wisdom from john a. powell. The Greater Purpose, Justice and an Inclusive Society, is from his book title. With all polarities, the objective is to maximize both upsides and minimize both downsides. "Targeted" is a very useful way to represent the upsides of the Part pole (+A). "Universalism" represents well the upside of the Whole pole (+C).

---

[31] This statement is focused on the United States but marginalization of communities of Black, Indigenous, People of Color, women and LGBTQI+ is not limited to the United States. The Black Lives Matter movement is global in its scope and advocates for marginalized groups everywhere.

[32] powell, john. *Racing to Justice: Transforming Our Conceptions of Self and Other to Build an Inclusive Society*. Indiana University Press, 2012.

In his explanation, Dr. powell quotes Aristotle on equality: *"It is just to treat those who are situated similarly the same, but it would be unjust to treat those who are situated differently the same."* This statement readily fits in the upside and downside of the Whole pole in *Figure 17*. Aristotle's point fits exactly with our understanding of how polarities work. If you focus only on Universalism as a solution without also being Targeted in your strategy, you will find yourself in a situation that Dr. powell calls "false universalism" (-D).

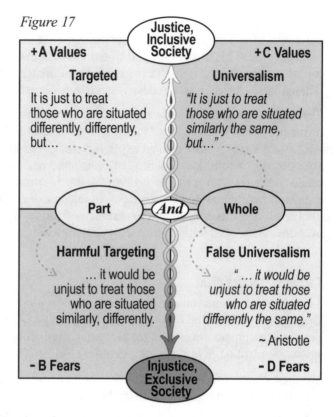

Figure 17

+A Values — Targeted

It is just to treat those who are situated differently, differently, but...

Justice, Inclusive Society

+C Values — Universalism

"It is just to treat those who are situated similarly the same, but..."

Part — And — Whole

Harmful Targeting

... it would be unjust to treat those who are situated similarly, differently.

False Universalism

" ... it would be unjust to treat those who are situated differently the same."

~ Aristotle

- B Fears   Injustice, Exclusive Society   - D Fears

The real opposites in a Polarity Map are the diagonals, so having Aristotle's quote filling (+C and -D) of the Whole pole, the opposites of those two elements of the quote would fit in the two quadrants of the Part pole. The opposite of (+C) is (-B). The opposite of (-D) is (+A). This provides a more complete picture of the map.

Notice how "targeted universalism" fits with our example of Black Lives Matter. Implicit bias and explicit bias against black people result in them experiencing both downsides of the map. As Dr. powell points out, even well intended Universal efforts (+C) that do not consider the fact that black people are situated differently (+A) are unjust (-D). That is why it is just to treat black people differently to the degree that they are situated differently (+A). Institutional practices and policies that have reduced access for black people to good education, jobs, healthcare, etc. need to be targeted (identified and changed). Those who have been disadvantaged by these institutional practices and policies need to be targeted in ways that support their access and experience of good education, jobs, and healthcare (+A). This is essential for Justice and an Inclusive Society (Greater Purpose).

In *Figure 17*, it is also possible to over-focus on Targeting to the neglect of Universalism, which leads to what I call "Harmful Targeting" (-B). Racial profiling is a good example. If a young white man and a young black man were each driving their car with a tail light out (situated similarly) it would be unjust for them to be treated differently (-B). The reality is that the young black man is more likely to be searched, to go to jail, to stay in jail longer and more likely to be killed while unarmed. He is also more likely to be stopped than a white young man if both cars are (situated similarly) with no observable problem. It is simply the vulnerability of driving while black in the U.S.

I do not have a clue of what it must be like to be afraid that my driving age grandson could be killed by an anxious police officer while driving home from a party. I could easily be that police officer. He, she, or they have a dangerous job and were raised in the same culture in which we absorbed our unconscious bias against black people that increases their vulnerability, particularly to those of us in the dominant group. I also do not have a clue of what it must be like to be afraid that a family member who is a police officer might be killed in the line of duty protecting all of us. Black Lives Matter and Blue Lives Matter because All Lives Matter.

Using "All Lives Matter" or "Blue Lives Matter" as a counter to "Black Lives Matter" or to detract from the reality that "Black Lives Matter" is a clear example of racism whether it is conscious or not. And its impact is to powerfully undermine our collective responsibility to join Dr. powell and the Black Lives Matter movement in pursuit of a just and inclusive society.

Beyond Goods and Services

Love, peace, joy, hope, and implicit power are not a "goods" or a service. They do not have the same limits of distribution as food or shelter. They are available to each of us and all of us in unlimited supply. I will explore this further in *Section Four* on Justice *And* Mercy and in *Section Six* on Self *And* Other. For now, I just want to acknowledge that focusing on the distribution of goods and services is important *And* there is more to life than the distribution of goods and services. Love, peace, joy, hope, and implicit power are the needed support when addressing the most oppressive of inequities; the denial of human equality.

Summary

The tension in each nation between Idealism *And* Realism continues. In my own country, the United States, this tension shows up in the contrast between the idealism of our Declaration of Independence and the realism of our gross inequities. Since polarities are unsolvable and indestructible if a system is alive, we can learn from our mistakes. When a nation finds itself in the downside of one pole or caught in a vicious cycle, as long as the nation exists, there is the possibility of creating a virtuous cycle with that same tension. There is hope for any nation that it can become a great place to live, work, and play for everyone. This hope is also true for us as a community of nations.

Abundance for Some *And* Basics for All. Whatever the distribution of goods or services, it is possible to provide the basics of those goods and services to everyone while allowing abundance for some. If we have an unconscious *Or* framework in which we must choose *either* abundance for some *Or* basics for all, we will have chronic inequities that will fall most harshly on marginalized groups. *Or*-thinking without *And*-thinking is not up to the challenge of making a difference with these inequities. It is a major cause of these inequities.

Black Lives Matter *And* All Lives Matter. Black people are one of the marginalized groups in the United States. "Black Lives Matter" is a natural and essential response to inequities being tolerated as if Black lives do not matter. An implicit bias for *Or*-thinking combined with an implicit bias against black people results in using "All Lives Matter" as a platform to undermine the Black Lives Matter movement. From a polarity perspective, "All Lives Matter" becomes an interdependent truth which requires us to affirm that Black Lives Matter. We must support both upsides of this polarity for the sake of *both* the dominant group *And* those groups that have been marginalized by the dominant group.

Targeted Universalism. Dr. john a. powell has identified the need for this dual strategy in building an inclusive society. It applies to every example in this chapter and is especially valuable in making a difference when Racing to Justice.

New Realities in Chapter 7

Reality 59   Within all polarities, there are two equally valid, essential, and inter-dependent points of view. They show up as the value/fear diagonal quadrants of a Polarity Map® (+A/-D) and (-B\+C). The wisdom in each point of view is a combination of the value being affirmed (up-side) and the fear of losing that value (diagonal downside).

Reality 60   The stronger and more absolutely one advocates for the value in their point of view (+A) or (+C), the greater the Fear that will be generated in those with the alternate point of view (-D) or (-B).

Reality 61   The longer and more painfully we experience the downside of one pole, the stronger the fear of that pole and the more we idealize the upside value of the opposite pole.

Reality 62   When we experience the downsides of the original "solution," it gets identified as a "mistake." It was not a mistake. It was the natural and necessary self-correction in an ongoing polarity. The effort to shift poles gets called a mistake because it was misdiagnosed as a solution in the first place.

Reality 63   Whenever there is a distribution issue with goods and services, such as food, education, healthcare, jobs, shelter, safety, and opportuni-ties, the Part *And* Whole polarity is at play.

Chapter 8
Nation as the Part

It is always in the national interest to pay attention to the "National interests" *And* to pay attention to "more than the National interests."

In 1997, the United States Senate unanimously passed by a vote of 95 – 0 the Byrd-Hagel Resolution, stating that it was not the sense of the Senate that the United States should be a signatory to the Kyoto Protocol on climate change. There were essentially two reasons stated for the resolution. One was that it was not mandated within the Kyoto Protocol that there be "new specific scheduled commitments to limit or reduce greenhouse gas emissions for Developing Country Parties within the same compliance period." The second was that the Kyoto Protocol "would result in serious harm to the economy of the United States."

The essential message of the second reason for not signing the Kyoto Protocol was that it was not in our national interest. This was also China's reason for not signing. The same argument was used 20 years later, on August 4, 2017, when the Trump Administration delivered an official notice to the United Nations that the U.S. intends to withdraw from the Paris Agreement as soon as it is legally eligible to do so. As it turns out, the legal eligibility to withdraw occurs the day after our next election. The timing could not be more precise in having the climate crisis be one, important referendum in the U.S. 2020 elections. The Paris Climate Agreement got support from 194 countries and the European Union, including both the United States and China, the two largest contributors to the climate crisis. Leaving or staying with the agreement is a problem to solve, yet the decision can be informed by a polarity lens.

The Climate Crisis Debate is a Problem to Solve with Underlying Polarities.

The question of whether the planet is warming or not is a problem to solve. Another problem to solve is the degree to which we humans are contributing to the warming, if it is happening. I believe, with the overwhelming and increasing majority of scientists studying this issue, that the planet is warming and that we humans are significant contributors. A decreasing minority believe that we are not warming beyond a normal cycle of warming. Often, this belief is combined with the belief that humans are not significant contributors to any warming that might be taking place.

So, what do we do with this disagreement about the "facts?" With these two questions, we can use research and scientific inquiry as a basis for arriving at a "solution." They are both problems to solve. Majority opinion does not make it so. The majority used to think the earth is flat. That did not make it so. The fact that some people still think the world is flat also does not make it so. It is a question of what our best and most recent research and science tell us. This is a case in which *Or*-thinking is useful. Are we warming beyond normal oscillations of warming and cooling *Or* are we not? Are humans major contributors to this claimed warming *Or* are we not?

When each of us looks at the research, our willingness to consider global warming and the climate crisis is significantly impacted by our perception of an underlying polarity. That polarity is some version of Part *And* Whole.

Figure 1 is a simple version of the generic Part *And* Whole Polarity Map® with the Nation as the Part. Within any country, it is a strong argument that the interests of that country must be respected (+A). Political leaders will use this argument to go to war; to sign agreements; to refuse to sign agreements, as in the case of the Kyoto Protocol; or to back out of an agreement, as in the case of President Trump and the Paris Climate Accord.

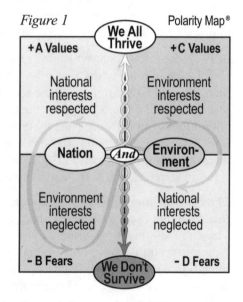

Figure 1   Polarity Map®

+A Values — We All Thrive — +C Values

National interests respected   Environment interests respected

Nation *And* Environment

Environment interests neglected   National interests neglected

- B Fears — We Don't Survive — - D Fears

From an *Or* perspective, the question becomes, "Are we going to protect our National interests (+A) *Or* are we going to neglect our National interests (-D)?" From that point of view, (+A/-D) the answer is obvious. We will vote to protect the National interests. Thus, the Byrd-Hagel Resolution was passed 95–0. Also, President Trump got significant support for backing out of the Paris Climate Accord.

But what if the National interests of any country were the "Part" of the Part *And* Whole polarity? From this perspective, there is an equally valid, essential, and interdependent point of view: (-B\+C). When seen from a polarity perspective, an over-focus on National interests (+A) to the neglect of Environment interests (+C) will result in the neglect of Environment interests (-B). This possibility is shown in *Figure 1* by the infinity loop dropping down into the lower left quadrant.

This is a case in which there is a problem to solve: "Do I vote for the Byrd-Hagel resolution *Or* not?" "Do we stay in the Paris Climate Accord *Or* not?" Yet there is an underlying polarity of National interests *And* Environment interests which provides a helpful context for the decision. The polarity context reminds us that if the decision is empowering one pole of a polarity, over time, we will need to empower the other pole as well.[R64] If we continue to vote only to empower one pole, first we will get the downside of the pole that we have been empowering, then we will get the downside of the other pole as well. In this case, continued decisions that empower the National interests without decisions that support Environment interests will undermine the United States' National interests.

For example, when we increase the temperature of the atmosphere, we increase the amount of water vapor the atmosphere can hold. The increased capacity to hold water vapor means the atmosphere can draw and withhold more water from some areas, increasing areas of drought, and drop more water in other areas, increasing the frequency and damage of flooding. Both drought and flooding create significant hardship for those nations experiencing one or both.

Costs to China[33]

China has been struck by an extreme weather paradox of severe drought in the north and severe flooding in the south, said the State Flood Control and Drought Relief Headquarters. ...

As of Tuesday, more than 50 million people from 28 provinces and regions were affected by flooding and more than 4 million people were relocated, while direct economic losses reached 108 billion yuan ($17.5 billion), according to the State Flood Control and Drought Relief Headquarters. ...

Northern China, however, has been hit by severe drought since June, with Henan suffering its worst drought in 63 years.

As of Tuesday, about 4.4 million hectares of farmland were hit by drought and about 2.4 million people are facing drinking water shortages, according to the headquarters.

"We must prepare for a worst-case scenario, with severe drought and flood to be fought at the same time," Su said.

Costs to United States[34]

Deadly storms Harvey, Irma, Maria, and Ophelia dominated the news in August, killing more than 150 people and causing more than $300 billion in damages in just the United States. ...

Wildfires devastated Northern California this October, with more than 245,000 acres burned and 14,000 homes destroyed. Insured losses in the region amounted to more than $3 billion, but danger does not end when the fires are extinguished. The remaining ash and debris (including hazardous waste, electronic waste, and heavy metal contamination) can be spread by wind and rain, posing even further health concerns to those nearby.

---

[33] Qian, Yang. *Droughts, floods pound nation*. China Daily, January 2, 2018.
[34] Ivanovich, Casey. *A look back at 2017: The year in weather disasters – and the connection to climate change.* Environmental Defense Fund, January 3, 2018.

These are just a few examples in China and the U.S. of how focusing on the "National interest" to the neglect of "Environmental interests" is not, in the long term, in the "National Interest."

How *Or*-thinking, Alone, Makes Us Unreceptive to the Possibility of the Climate Crisis.

Or-thinking does not allow us to choose *both* when we encounter a tension between two things. If I believe that to consider the reality of the climate crisis I must let go of doing what I think is best for my country, I am less likely to seriously consider that the climate crisis is happening. I will look for anything that might call the climate crisis into question out of my natural instinct to protect my country. "Do I deny my country what it needs to survive *Or* do I deny climate change?" This question might not be one we are aware of consciously, but it can be an unstated assumption of a choice I must make. Given that assumed choice, it is difficult to objectively consider the arguments for and against the reality of the climate crisis.

In a similar way, *Or*-thinking makes it difficult to consider the climate crisis if my business or industry is identified as contributing to global warming and the climate crisis. "Do I choose my livelihood *Or* do I buy this climate change stuff?"

As with all polarities, there is a natural tension between the poles. If we see the tension between National interests *And* Environment interests as a problem to solve in which we must choose one *Or* the other, we will create a vicious cycle that serves neither our country nor the environment. One reason to supplement *Or*-thinking with *And*-thinking is that it increases the likelihood that we will be able to sign and implement the agreements necessary to address the climate crisis.

Humanity as the Whole, Then Humanity as the Part

I want to briefly look at Humanity as the Whole and then Humanity as the Part in the context of the environment. Each of our nation states needs to look at our national Part in contributing to global warming and the climate crisis to the planet as a Whole. This was the focus of *Figure 1* on page 72, which looked at National interests *And* Environment interests.

What was skipped was *Figures 2* and *3*. In *Figure 2,* we have the Nation as the Part *And* Humanity as the Whole. In *Figure 3,* we have Humanity (Humans as a species) as the Part *And* the Environment as the Whole.

The reason each nation state on the planet should leverage this polarity well is not primarily for the sake of the environment; it is for the sake of our nations and us as a species (Part) within the environment (Whole). The environment (Whole) will continue with or without us humans (Part). The only way to take care of ourselves is to also take care of the rest of the environment. It is possible for us to make the planet uninhabitable for us or for a large portion of us.

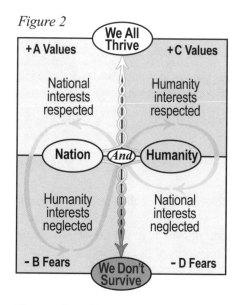

Figure 2

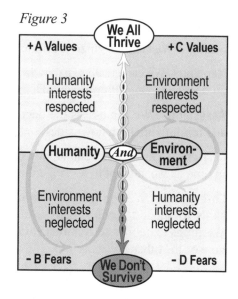

Figure 3

How vulnerable are we making ourselves by not addressing global warming and climate change more effectively as Nations and as Humanity? We are making ourselves very vulnerable. The evidence of global warming and its potential impact is increasing. Regardless of the degree to which we think global warming is happening or the degree to which we think humans are contributing, it is very clear that there is a natural tension between National interests *And* Environment interests. There is a similar tension between Humanity interests *And* Environment interests. In both cases it will be helpful to see these tensions as polarities to leverage rather than as an *either/Or* choice in which we must choose one *Or* the other. These tensions will exist as long as we have Nations and as long as we have people on the planet.

Hope for the future lies in recognizing that the natural tension within all polarities can be leveraged. We as Nations and as Humanity can create a virtuous cycle rather than a vicious cycle with this tension. We can take care of our National interests *And* Humanities interests by taking care of our Environment. This can best be done by supplementing *Or*-thinking with *And*-thinking. *Or*-thinking, alone, is not up to the job.

Summary

It is helpful for each of us to look at our country as a Part of our family of nations *And* as a Part of the Environment. When we address issues like global warming, the climate crisis, and the contribution of humans to what is happening, we are dealing with problems to solve and can look to the best research and science available. *And*-thinking can allow us more objectivity to consider the science. This is because there are underlying polarities at play as we look to solve the problems. One such underlying polarity is the Part *And* Whole. *Or*-thinking, alone, can create a false choice between: our Nation *Or* the Environment, our Nation *Or* Humanity, our Humanity *Or* the Environment.

The **SMALL** process will be useful in addressing these polarities:

Seeing – We can recognize the underlying Part *And* Whole polarity,

Mapping – We can create a map which indicates the upsides and downsides of each pole and a Greater Purpose and Deeper Fear associated with it.

Assessing – We can assess the degree to which we are maximizing both upsides and minimizing both downsides.

Learning – Our assessment supports our ability to make adjustments at this point in time as we attempt to leverage the polarity.

Leveraging – We can use the best of our research, science and problem-solving skills to support Action Steps to maximize both upsides and to identify Early Warnings to help us self-correct early as we find ourselves in the downside of one pole or the other.

Or-thinking alone is not up to the job. We need *Or*-thinking *And And*-thinking.

New Realities in Chapter 8

Reality 64   There are times when we have an *either/Or* choice to make which is a problem to solve, like voting for or against a proposal. Even in these times in which we have a problem to solve, it can be helpful to see the choice in the context of an underlying polarity. If the vote empowers one pole of a polarity, we can know that, over time, future votes will need to empower the other pole as well.

Chapter 9
Ethics and National Culture

"Your ethics are naïve!"

"At least we have ethics!"

In *Chapter 8*, I referred to the United States Senate passing the Byrd-Hagel Resolution with a vote of 95−0 to not sign the Kyoto Protocol because it was not in the national interest. The second reason was the protocol did not mandate that there be "new specific scheduled commitments to limit or reduce greenhouse gas emissions for Developing Country Parties within the same compliance period."

This argument, like concerns for the national interest, had a very strong and positive response in the United States Senate. They would see it as ethically sound. If we are asked to have specific scheduled commitments to limit or reduce greenhouse gas emissions within a certain compliance period, every country should have scheduled commitments within that same compliance period. This is the logic of normative ethics: what applies to one should apply to all. Therefore: "Holding some countries accountable and not holding all countries accountable is not fair. It's unethical!"

United States – Individualism (Part) *And* China – Collectivism (Whole)

In *Chapter 7*, I mentioned Geert Hofstede's work in distinguishing national cultures. Some countries lean toward Individualism *And* others toward Collectivism. The United States and Australia, for example, have a strong leaning toward Individualism. China and Guatemala lean strongly toward Collectivism.

The following *Figure 1* captures the close parallel between the USA's lean toward the benefits of Individualism and a preference for the Part pole with its value for Freedom and Flexibility for the Individual (+A). There is also a close parallel between China's lean toward the benefits of Collectivism and a preference for the Whole pole with its value for Equality and Responsibility to the collective (+C).

Seen from a polarity perspective, it is easy to understand the natural tension between the two cultures. It is also easy to see how dysfunctional it would be to treat this tension as a problem to solve with either upside being seen as a "solution." The question immediately becomes, "How do we leverage this natural tension in a way that creates a virtuous cycle moving upward toward both countries thriving?" Understanding how to see and leverage the Part *And* Whole polarity will serve us well in addressing the tension between countries that lean toward Individualism *And* those that lean toward Collectivism.

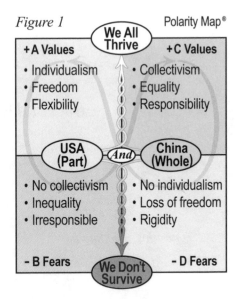

Figure 1

Ethics as a Balancing Dynamic for Individualism *And* Collectivism

From a polarity perspective, we can see the benefits to be gained from the interface between the two cultures and their preferred poles. But what is it within the Chinese culture that helps protect them from over-focusing on the Whole and what is it within U.S. culture that helps protect us from over-focusing on the Part? A partial answer is the ethics of each culture:

Normative Ethics (NE) Brings Accountability to the U.S. (*Figure 2*)

The essence of Normative ethics is that the "ethical" thing to do is dependent on guidelines that are consistent regardless of the context. Normative ethics brings equality and accountability to a decision (+C). "What applies to one applies to all." "No one is above the rules." You know how to behave "ethically" in every situation. Thus, Normative ethics brings many of the positive attributes of the Whole pole (+C). It is a useful balancing force with Individualism in Cultures, like the United States, that lean toward the Part pole (+A).

Figure 2

Contextual Ethics (CE) Brings Flexibility to China (*Figure 3*)

The essence of Contextual ethics is that the ethical thing to do is dependent upon the context at a given point in time. Contextual ethics brings Freedom and Flexibility to a decision (+A). Who is involved? What is unique about this situation that needs to be considered before taking action? Thus, Contextual ethics brings many of the positive attributes of the Part pole (+A). It is a useful balancing force with Collectivism in cultures, like China, that lean toward the Whole pole (+C).

Figure 3

In *Figure 2,* we can see how reliance on Normative ethics (+C) in the United States would be seen as "Naïve" and Rigid by the Chinese (-D). "How can you assume that what is 'ethical' in one situation would also be ethical in any other situation? This is too naïve and too rigid to deal with reality." Our Normative ethics can make us seem less trustworthy. They have a point. But their point makes more sense in a culture emphasizing Collectivism than in a culture emphasizing Individualism.

In *Figure 3,* we can see how China's reliance on Contextual ethics (+A) would be seen as not having ethics and lacking accountability by U.S. citizens (-B). "How can you even imply that you have 'ethics' if what is right or wrong is decided by the individual in any moment depending on their understanding of the circumstance? This will leave us adrift in moral ambiguity and no accountability." Their Contextual ethics can make them seem less trustworthy. We have a point. But our point makes more sense in a culture emphasizing Individualism than in a culture emphasizing Collectivism.

Think of how problematic it could be to attempt to impose Normative ethics as primary in China or Contextual ethics as primary in the U.S. In each case, you would lose the balancing benefit of the ethical system at play and end up in the downside of the cultural pole preference. China, with its lean toward Collectivism combined with an imposition of Normative ethics would be even more vulnerable to the downside of the Whole pole and Collectivism. It would be too oppressive. The U.S., with our lean toward Individualism combined with an imposition of Contextual ethics. would be even more vulnerable to the downside of the Part pole and Individualism. There would be an extreme lack of accountability.

The tension within the polarity of Normative ethics *And* Contextual ethics exists in the U.S. and in China. Because it is unavoidable and unsolvable, we will have an ongoing opportunity to leverage it well within each of our countries and between our countries. Attempting to address it with *Or*-thinking alone will not be very useful. Combining *Or*-thinking with *And*-thinking will not make it easy, but it will increase the likelihood of creating a mutually respectful relationship in which we keep our historical strengths and preferences, learn from each other, and thrive together.

In *Chapter 7*, we looked at john powell's focus on "targeted universalism" as a necessary dual strategy for <u>Racing to Justice</u>. His intuitive wisdom applies not just to creating a just and inclusive society. It also addresses the tension between normative ethics and contextual ethics because they both relate to the Part *And* Whole polarity. "Targeted" justice is like contextual ethics in responding to unique circumstances: it is just to treat those who are situated differently, differently. "Universalism" in justice is like normative ethics in responding to common circumstances: It is just to treat those who are situated similarly the same. This reinforces john powell's wisdom and the broader application of targeted universalism. It also reinforces the richness of the Part *And* Whole polarity as a resource.

Summary

A polarity lens can be helpful between nation states when each nation, as a culture, leans toward a different pole of a polarity; for example, the United States leaning toward the Part/Individualism pole *And* China leaning toward the Whole/Collectivism pole. Seeing the natural tension within the pole preference as a polarity dynamic allows us to leverage that tension in service of helping both countries and the relationship thrive.

When looking at the pole preference for Individualism or Collectivism within a country, we can appreciate how Individualism (USA) with its leaning toward the Part pole, would benefit from Normative ethics, which provides some of the upsides of the Whole pole. Similarly, Collectivism (China) with its leaning toward the Whole pole, would benefit from Contextual ethics, which provides some of the upsides from the Part pole.[R65]

Understanding the natural tension between the two cultures and the two ethical orientations and seeing them as polarities to be leveraged will be more useful than seeing either pole as a "solution" to a problem. It is possible to create a virtuous cycle from the tension to build rather than undermine the relationships between Collectivism in one culture and Individualism in another.

It is important, when looking at Hofstede's national dimensions of culture, to avoid looking at any dimension from only an *either/Or* perspective: *either* Individualism *Or* Collectivism defines your culture. To the degree that we are talking about a polarity, *both* will be present within every country. There will be an internal dynamic balancing going on, through ethics and other dimensions of the culture. And the lean, in preference within each national culture, will make it vulnerable to the downside of the pole toward which it leans. This reflection on national cultural polarities also holds true for the work of Charles Hampden-Turner and Alfonsus

Trompenaars.[35] Hampden-Turner has written several useful books on interdependent pairs, referred to as "Dilemmas."

John powell's "targeted universalism" not only provides a dual strategy for racial justice and inclusion, it provides a dual strategy for the natural tension between individualistic cultures that need universalism (normative ethics) *And* collectivist cultures that need the benefits of targeting (contextual ethics).

New Realities in Chapter 9

Reality 65 Normative ethics brings the upside of the Whole pole within cultures emphasizing Individualism (USA) that lean toward the Part pole. Contextual ethics brings the upside of the Part pole within cultures emphasizing Collectivism (China) that lean toward the Whole pole.

---

[35] Hampden-Turner, Charles; Trompenaars, Alfonsus. *Building Cross-Cultural Competence: How to Create Wealth from Conflicting Values.* 2000.

Chapter 10
The Part *And* Whole Energy Chain

A chain is as strong as its weakest link. Attending to the weakest Part is in service to the Whole.[R66]

I mentioned earlier that Polarity Thinking is scalable. What applies to the individual family applies to the "family of nations." I have also talked about a polarity as an energy system we can leverage. When we combine these two realities, we get the Part *And* Whole energy chain.

Figure 1 shows a simple ten-level chart, which begins at the bottom with Level 1, where the Part is the Individual *And* the Whole is the Family (or the Team). As you move up in system size, what was the Whole at one level of system becomes the Part at the next level. This goes all the way up to Level 10, in which the Part is all of Nature *And* the Whole is the larger dimension of Spirit. Within this book, I will not focus on all 10 levels, but I wanted you to see the multiple layers of Part *And* Whole that were possible. Many more could be included.

Figure 1

Part	*And*	Whole	Level
Nature	*And*	Spirit	10
Humanity	*And*	Nature	9
Country	*And*	Humanity	8
State/Province	*And*	Country	7
Community	*And*	State/Province	6
Neighborhood	*And*	Community	5
Organization	*And*	Neighborhood	4
Department	*And*	Organization	3
Family/Team	*And*	Department	2
Individual	*And*	Family/Team	1

The following *Figure 2* is a generic Part *And* Whole Polarity Map®. The content, dynamics, and realities for this map apply equally to all ten versions of the Part *And* Whole polarity in *Figure 1*. This is another way to picture the scalability of all polarities. Whether you are an Individual (Part) of a Team (Whole), as in Level 1, or you are a Country (Part) of Humanity (Whole), as in Level 8, there will be a desire, as a Part, for Freedom to express your Uniqueness and to take Initiative (+A). And, whether you are a Team Leader or a Leader in the United Nations, you will seek to develop some Equality, Connectedness, and Synergy among the Parts within the Whole (+C).

Figures 3 and 4 below, are two more versions of the ten-level chart in *Figure 1*. They capture another reality of the levels of system.

In *Figure 3,* we can see that the Individual is a Part of the Whole in each level of system. This represents each of us having access to and an ability to influence the many Wholes of which we are a Part. We are in a Part *And* Whole energy system as a member of our family or a team at work (1). We are also in a Part *And* Whole energy system as a citizen of our Country (7) or as a global citizen within our Humanity (8). We are a Part of Nature (9) and the Spiritual dimensions of life (10). At each level of system, we can leverage the polarity energy available. We can care for ourselves with that energy *And* we can care for the Whole of which we are a Part.

In *Figure 4,* we can see a similar arrangement when we focus on our organization. The organization that can access the energy available at all levels of system will be a better place to work and a more sustainable, thriving organization. In Levels 1–3, the organization is the Whole, needing to take care of its Parts (Departments, Teams, Individuals). In Levels 4–10, the

Figure 2

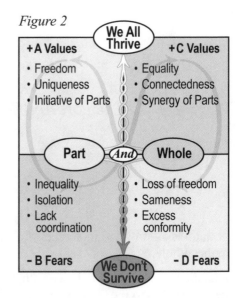

Figure 3

Part	*And*	Whole	Level
Individual	*And*	Spirit	10
Individual	*And*	Nature	9
Individual	*And*	Humanity	8
Individual	*And*	Country	7
Individual	*And*	State / Province	6
Individual	*And*	Community	5
Individual	*And*	Neighborhood	4
Individual	*And*	Organization	3
Individual	*And*	Department	2
Individual	*And*	Family / Team	1

Figure 4

Part	*And*	Whole	Level
Organization	*And*	Spirit	10
Organization	*And*	Nature	9
Organization	*And*	Humanity	8
Organization	*And*	Country	7
Organization	*And*	State / Province	6
Organization	*And*	Community	5
Organization	*And*	Neighborhood	4
Department	*And*	Organization	3
Family / Team	*And*	Department	2
Individual	*And*	Family / Team	1

organization is a Part, needing to take care of the Wholes of which it is a Part. Every level of system is a potential source of energy to be leveraged in service of the organization *And* in service of its internal Parts *And* its external Wholes.[R67]

It is always in the long-term interest of each pole to take care of both poles. In this case, we can see how that applies to all the Part *And* Whole polarities within *Figures 1–4*. In *Figure 3,* it is in my long-term interest to take care of myself *And* to take care of my: family/team, department, organization, neighborhood, community, state/province, country, humanity, nature, and spirit. *And*, it is in the interests of all these Wholes to take care of me. Even within the food chain, which can be seen as vicious in the attack of predator on its prey, there remains a need for a continuous supply of prey for the predator to live.

In *Figure 4,* it is always in the long-term interests of my organization to take care of its Parts *And* its Parts to take care of it. It is also in the long-term interests of my organization to take care of those Wholes of which it is a Part *And* for those Wholes to take care of my organization. This is another version of the wisdom within "enlightened self-interest."

In this book, the levels of system I am focusing on are primarily the Individual, Organization, Country, Humanity and some on Environment. You may choose to focus on other levels of system. For example, those of you working to strengthen your neighborhood might focus on that as the Whole and then look at the Parts within the neighborhood and the Wholes of which the neighborhood is a Part. What will be important from a Part *And* Whole polarity perspective is to leverage the natural tensions within the neighborhood and between the neighborhood and the larger Wholes of which it is a Part. Also, there will be many other polarities at play which you can leverage in service of a thriving neighborhood.

Nested Polarities

The Greater Purpose can be a pole of a larger polarity in which it is "nested."[R68]

The charts in *Figures 1, 3*, and *4* make it easy to see how the Whole at one level of system becomes the Part of the next level up. If we now pay attention to the energy system at play within each polarity at each level of system, we create a two-level Part *And* Whole energy chain shown in *Figure 5*.

If our work team does a good job of leveraging the polarity of Individual *And* Team, the Team will thrive. The Team Thriving becomes

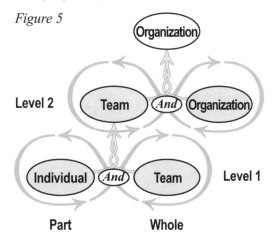

Figure 5

85

the Greater Purpose with the understanding that the Team Thriving is dependent upon the Individual Thriving as well. The popular quote, "There is no 'I' in 'TEAM'" is based on *Or*-thinking and is incomplete, from a polarity perspective. We need to empower both poles of each polarity in the chain. In Level 1, we need to empower the Individual *And* the Team.

The Greater Purpose of the original polarity (Level 1) becomes a pole of the larger polarity (Level 2). The Level 1 polarity (Individual *And* Team) is "nested" under the Team pole of the Level 2 polarity (Team *And* Organization). When the Individual *And* Team polarity is leveraged well (Level 1), the Team Thrives. At the same time, we cannot just use the energy from Level 1. We now must leverage the Level 2 polarity in which we need to empower the Organization pole as well. This is how the whole chain becomes an energy generating system.

Figure 6

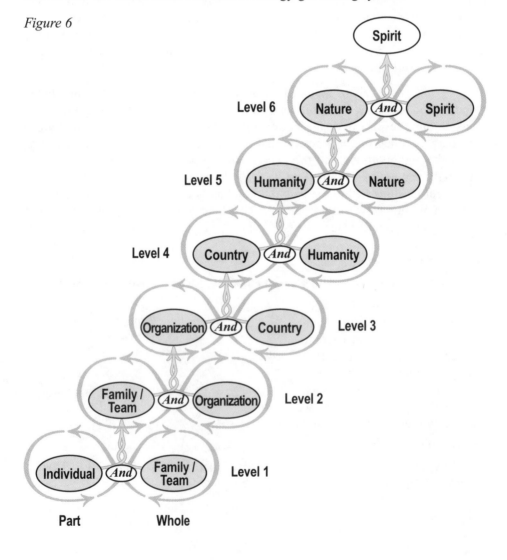

We could easily add a couple of links to the chain by having the Team nested within the Department, the Department nested within the Business Unit, and then the Business Unit nested within the Organization. You can add or subtract levels as desired. *Figure 6* is an expansion of *Figure 5* to include four more levels of the Part *And* Whole energy chain. This chain is the context for most chapters in this book.

No matter what level of system you want to focus your attention, it will be helpful to appreciate the larger context in which you are living and working.

When working with an individual, it is about them *And* it is about more than them. When I work with the United States Department of Defense, it is about serving and protecting our country *And* it is about more than serving and protecting our country. Just focusing on our country (the right pole in Level 3) will not serve and protect our country. For maximum service and protection of our country, we would pay attention to the whole energy chain.

This is my focus no matter which country I am working with, or which organization, or which team, or which individual. The wisdom is in them, the map is a wisdom organizer for them. Polarity energy is immediately available because it is living within them. When they can see the polarity and the polarity chain, they will be better equipped to fulfill their dreams and address their conflicts. *Or*-thinking, alone will not be up to the task. Supplementing *Or*-thinking with *And*-thinking is essential wherever *And*-thinking is required. It is required when dealing with the Part *And* Whole polarity at any level of system and it is required to address the Part *And* Whole energy chain.

Summary

The Part *And* Whole energy chain is a way to picture the scalability of Polarity Thinking. The Part *And* Whole polarity functions in predictable ways regardless of the size of the system. Sometimes the pole of one polarity is the Greater Purpose for a polarity that is "nested" within that pole. No matter which link you focus on, it will be helpful to see that link in the context of the whole chain. A chain (Whole) is as strong as its weakest link (Part). Attending to the weakest Part (link) is in service to the Whole (chain).

New Realities in Chapter 10

Reality 66   A chain (Whole) is as strong as its weakest link (Part). Attending to the weakest Part (link) is in service to the Whole (chain).

Reality 67   Every level of system is a potential source of energy to be leveraged in service of its internal Parts *And* its external Wholes.

Reality 68   Nested polarities – The Greater Purpose of one polarity can be a pole of a larger polarity in which it is "nested."

Chapter 11
The Part *And* Whole Polarity in Our Brain

We live inside polarities and they live in us. So far we have been looking at polarities in which we live. This chapter shows how they also live in the very structure and function of our brain. In terms of the Part *And* Whole polarity, we can look at our brain as an integrated Whole which has various Parts. We can also look at it as having several interdependent pairs of Parts (polarities). For example, the left *And* right hemispheres of our brain are a polarity.[R69]

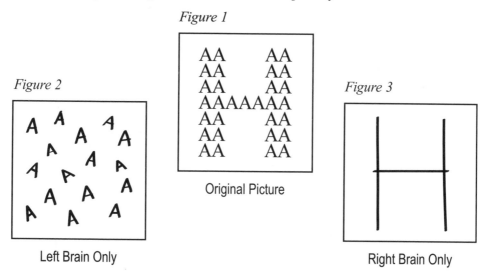

Figure 1

AA   AA
AA   AA
AA   AA
AAAAAAA
AA   AA
AA   AA
AA   AA

Original Picture

Figure 2

Left Brain Only

Figure 3

Right Brain Only

Figure 1 is a picture shown to people with damage to one of the two hemispheres of their brain. The picture is then taken away and they are asked to reproduce what they saw.[36]

Figure 2 is an example of what was drawn from memory by those with severe damage to their right hemisphere. This means they were reproducing the picture

---

[36] MacNielage, Peter F.; Rogers, Lesley J.; Vallortigara, Giorgio. *Origins of the Left and Right Brain*. Scientific American, July 2009.

using only their left brain as a memory source. What was remembered were the discrete Parts. There is some truth to the reproduction in that what they saw did contain many "A's." But it is not complete. What is missing is the pattern of the Whole: the shape of the "H."

Figure 3 is an example of what was drawn from memory by those with severe left hemisphere damage. They were reproducing the picture using only their right brain. What was remembered was the "H" pattern or Whole. There is also some truth to this reproduction in that what they saw did contain an "H." But it is not complete. What is missing are the "A's" or the Parts that made up the Whole.

It is the interdependency between the two hemispheres that allow those of us without brain damage to reproduce the full picture. It would be silly and inaccurate to tell those who produced *Figure 2* that they were wrong in showing a bunch of "A's," or to tell those who produced *Figure 3* that they were wrong in showing their "H." In each case you would generate unnecessary resistance. Each group can be confirmed that they reproduced a part of the picture *And* that there was more. Rather than contradict their memory of the picture, we can supplement it with what is missing. This is what we are doing with polarities all the time. Those who have one point of view within a polarity have half of the truth. They need the other half for a more complete picture of reality just as we need both hemispheres of our brain for a more complete picture.

Figure 4 is another version of the Part *And* Whole polarity reflecting the contribution of each hemisphere to each pole.

"You can't see the forest for the trees." (–B) "The devil is in the details." (–D). Each of these familiar quotes reflect our vulnerability of using one hemisphere to the relative neglect of the other.

It is important to be able to see and address the Details in our life. We need to "See the Trees." Our Left Brain helps us pay attention to the Parts (+A). At the same time, we need to see and address the patterns in our life. We need to "See the Forest." Our Right Brain helps us pay attention to the Whole (+C).

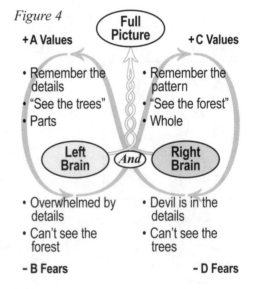

Figure 4

Full Picture

+A Values   +C Values

• Remember the details
• "See the trees"
• Parts

• Remember the pattern
• "See the forest"
• Whole

Left Brain   *And*   Right Brain

• Overwhelmed by details
• Can't see the forest

• Devil is in the details
• Can't see the trees

– B Fears   – D Fears

Polarity Thinking tends to focus on the pattern that is the infinity loop and how it functions over time within a Polarity Map® as an integrated Whole. *Or*-thinking tends to focus on the details and choices we need to make in the moment between the differentiated Parts. It is necessary to be clear about each part of the polarity map.

"The Whole is More Than the Sum of Its Parts."

This is a fundamental point in the origins of Gestalt Psychology which started off as a perceptual theory. Language is a great example. The word "tree" is more than the combination of 4 letters: e, t, r, e. They are arranged in a pattern that represents, in English, a big plant. Each letter (Part) is important *And* the pattern (Whole) is important. We are engaged in leveraging the Part *And* Whole polarity any time we read any language. This is true also of the sounds (Parts) that make a word (Whole) in spoken language. Words (Parts) become a collection of words that make up a complete sentence (Whole). This, of course, scales up to a paragraph, chapter, book, and library. This parallels the scaling up from Individual *And* Team to Nation *And* United Nations. This Part *And* Whole thing seems to be going on everywhere!

In his article, "Managing with the Brain in Mind,"[37] David Rock identifies a number of brain realities that are consistent with our understanding of polarities. For example, he indicates that we are more effective when our brain has a reward response than when it has a threat response. Within a polarity map, the reward response could be the GPS and the threat response could be the Deeper Fear. Effectively dealing with Status, Certainty, Autonomy, Relationships, and Fairness (SCARF) contributes to a reward response which supports our overall effectiveness. Each of these identified dimensions can be seen as contained within poles of a polarity rather than treating them as independent variables. Status and Autonomy parallels a focus on the Part while Relationships and Fairness both parallel a focus on the Whole. Certainty parallels Stability/Continuity while an improvement in Status parallels Chang*e*/Transformation. This will be explored in *Section Three*. For a more thorough look at the interface between polarity realities and brain research, see Ann Deaton's chapter in <u>*And*: Volume Two – Applications</u>.

Summary

It is no accident that we see Part *And* Whole polarities when we look at our families, teams, organizations, and nations. We are living inside them. It is also true that our brains are designed to help us see both. Thus, the polarities we see outside are also happening inside. Left *And* Right hemispheres, paralleling Part *And* Whole, are only one of the generic polarities dynamically operating within our brain. The Part *And* Whole polarity also corresponds to dimensions of life to which our brain has a reward response that contributes to effectiveness, or a threat response that contributes to ineffectiveness. Leveraging polarities is consistent with effective NeuroLeadership.

New Realities in Chapter 11

Reality 69   The Left *And* Right hemispheres of our brain are a polarity.

---

[37] Rock, David. *Managing with the Brain in Mind*. Strategy and Business issue 56, Autumn 2009.

SECTION THREE
Continuity *And* Transformation

We change most rapidly by first embracing who we are.

We call our process for leveraging polarities the "Polarity Approach to Continuity *And* Transformation" PACT. That is why I have chosen those pole names for this chapter. Remember, creating a Polarity Map®, including naming the poles, is always a values and language clarification process. Feel free to name the poles whatever will work for you and the stakeholders with whom you are working. Stability *And* Change is often used for this polarity. In <u>Built to Last,</u> Collins and Porras use "Preserve the Core Ideology *And* Stimulate Progress."[38] In <u>Managing Polarities in Congregations,</u> Roy Oswald and I use Tradition *And* Innovation.[39] No matter what you call it, we are living within it in our individual development and in every level of system explored in *Section Three*.

---

[38] Collins, John; Porras, Richard. *Built to Last*. Harper Collins, 1994.
[39] Oswald, Roy; Johnson, Barry. *Managing Polarities in Congregations*. Rowman and Littlefield, 2009.

Chapter 12
The Expansive Leader

The CEO of a large company has invited me to introduce Polarity Thinking to the executive team. The arrangement is for me to meet with each of the team members individually to get to know them a little and get their perceptions of the executive team and the organization. The plan was to use that information to identify some key polarities and address them with the executive team.

Because of scheduling problems, one of my interviews was with two members of the executive team. After we introduced ourselves, the two of them smiled at each other and one said, "Barry, if you are serious about being useful to the executive team and this organization, you'll just leave, now."

I smiled back and inquired, "Is there an option B?"

They continued, "Look, this has nothing to do with you or with Polarity Thinking, whatever that is. This is about our CEO's getting excited about one thing after another. Each time he brings in someone like you, we all get involved in the process and spend a lot of time and money making plans that never get implemented. We are tired of the lack of follow through and so are a lot of others in the organization. So, if you were to leave now, we would have one less thing to waste time and money on."

The second executive spoke up. "Can you get our CEO to stop this flavor of the month stuff and start following through on some plans so we can complete them? If you can do that, then your visit might be worthwhile."

I said, "Let's take a look at this issue through a polarity lens." I went to a flipchart in the room and started writing down what I was hearing.

The initial notes looked something like the following *Figure 1*.

First, I wrote what they seemed to be saying about the "problem" with the CEO's leadership: There was a lack of direction, projects weren't being completed, and the staff was overwhelmed and frustrated with a lack of accomplishment. Then I wrote what they wanted as a "solution": clear direction, completion of projects, and satisfaction for everyone with a sense of accomplishment.

They confirmed my notes. I then said that even if the CEO agreed with their description of the "problem" with leadership and with the "solution," the CEO would not do the proposed "solution."

They looked at each other with surprise on their faces. "How did you know that?" they asked. They told me they already had conversations with the CEO about these concerns. The CEO had agreed to the "solution" in *Figure 1,* but the behavior had changed only slightly if at all. They inquired, "How did you know that he wouldn't do what he agreed to?"

Figure 1

Solution:
• Clear direction
• Completion of projects
• Satisfaction and energy from sense of accomplishment

Problem:
• Lack of direction
• Projects not completed
• Staff overwhelmed with projects and frustrated with lack of accomplishment

I explained that the reason for the lack of compliance was that the CEO and the executive team saw these aspects of the CEO's leadership as a problem to solve when it would be more helpful to see it as a polarity to leverage. Their description of the problem and solution was accurate but incomplete.

Moving Through the SMALL Process

Without formally talking about the SMALL process (Seeing, Mapping, Assessing, Learning, and Leveraging), we moved through it together.

Seeing – I felt strongly that we were dealing with a leadership polarity in which the CEO was "stuck" in the downside of one pole. That downside was seen as a leadership "Problem" as shown in *Figure 1.* We know that it is easy when experiencing the downside of one pole to see the upside of the other pole as a solution. If it was a polarity, the question was, "What would be the names of the two poles that would work for them and, hopefully, for the CEO and others on the executive team?"

I raised this question with them and suggested that the name of the right pole might be for the CEO to be more "Focused." They were willing to try it as a temporary option. I then thought of the ability to "focus in on a few things" being balanced by the ability to be "expansive out on a lot of things." I suggested naming the other pole, "Expansive." I asked if that would fit for them and if it was a good description of their CEO. It made sense to them so we now had two, temporary poles. As you look at *Figure 2* on the following page, it is easy to see what is missing.

Mapping – Filling out the complete map had a solid start by the team members identifying concerns about the CEO's leadership (-B) and their suggestions for what might be done (+C). The poles became Expansive *And* Focused. We also agreed that they would like the CEO to become a more Effective Leader, which shows up as the Greater Purpose Statement. Ineffective Leader shows up as the Deeper Fear.

I suggested that the CEO probably had a strong value for being Expansive (+A) and an equally strong fear of losing that value (-D). If we could fill out those two quadrants, we would have a more complete picture of what was going on.

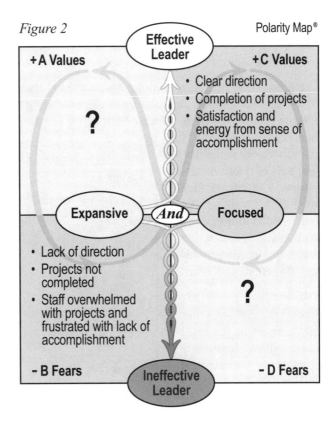

Figure 2   Polarity Map®

I asked them, "What are the positive results from the CEO's Expansiveness?" (+A)

If you would like to join in, jot down a few words or phrases on the blank lines that would be your answer to that question:

_____,

_____,

_____,

I then asked them, "What are the negative results the CEO would be afraid of if they over-focused on being Focused to the neglect of being Expansive?" (-D) This would be the opposite of what you have written above for (+A). What are a few words or phrases that would be your answer?

_____ , _____ , _____

If you decided to fill in some thoughts above, you probably came up with some words like what the two team members came up with in *Figure 3* on the following page.

They knew their CEO and they had a pretty good idea about what would be seen as positive results coming from a love of Expansiveness (+A): The CEO enjoyed being Flexible and responsive, liked Innovation and energy from new opportunities, and assumed others did as well.

Once (+A) was filled out, they had no trouble thinking of its opposite (-D): The CEO would not like to be Rigid and unresponsive, without innovation and creativity, and bored with a lack of new ideas or opportunities.

Assessing – Once we had filled out the map, a quick assessment could be summarized by the grey infinity loop in *Figure 3*. Notice how it loops low into the lower left quadrant (–B).

Learning – One message from the assessment is that there has been an over-focus on being Expansive to the relative neglect of being Focused. This has resulted in finding themselves in the downside of being Expansive. When in the downside of one pole, the upside of the other pole is the natural self-correction necessary. The reason they were not "walking the talk" had nothing to do with a lack of conviction and support for providing direction and completing projects (+C).

The resistance to what made sense in the head came from legitimate fears being experienced in the "gut." The CEO was "hooked" by a strong value for creativity (+A) and equally strong fear of its loss (–D), combined with *Or*-thinking. This combination creates a false choice between the two poles. This "choice" may be totally uncon-

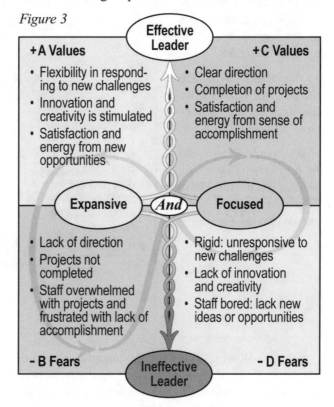

Figure 3

Effective Leader

+A Values
- Flexibility in responding to new challenges
- Innovation and creativity is stimulated
- Satisfaction and energy from new opportunities

+C Values
- Clear direction
- Completion of projects
- Satisfaction and energy from sense of accomplishment

Expansive –(*And*)– **Focused**

- Lack of direction
- Projects not completed
- Staff overwhelmed with projects and frustrated with lack of accomplishment

- Rigid: unresponsive to new challenges
- Lack of innovation and creativity
- Staff bored: lack new ideas or opportunities

– B Fears   **Ineffective Leader**   **– D Fears**

scious, but the result is that the CEO had difficulty going to the upside of the Focus pole (+C) and had gotten "stuck" in the downside of being Expansive (–B).

What was helpful was to look at the CEO's behavior in the context of a Polarity Map®, the dynamics of how polarities work, and the results of the assessment. This context is what made it fairly easy to predict the resistance to "walking the talk".

Leveraging – There was a shift in perception by the CEO and the executive team from seeing this as a problem to solve to seeing it as a polarity to leverage. The CEO was respected for and encouraged to continue Expansiveness (+A). Paradoxically, this freed them up to be more focused and more solid with project follow through. It also impacted their choice for the new Chief Operating Officer they were searching for at the time. They found a person who had a strong preference for the Focus pole.[R70] This was a solid Action Step to empower the Focus Pole. They explained the importance of this polarity to the new COO and how he/she/ they could help leverage it effectively over time. This was a more sustainable framework than the initial effort which saw being Focused (+C) as the solution.

Summary

When we look at individual development through a polarity lens, the person is much more likely to take on the desired areas of development (i.e., being more Focused) when they are seen as a self-correction within an ongoing polarity in which they are encouraged to hang on to their preferred pole (i.e., being Expansive). Paradoxically, we are most likely to "go after" the new pole when we have been encouraged to "hold on" to our historically preferred pole.

New Realities in Chapter 12

Reality 70   One way to empower a pole is by adding someone to the team or organization who has a strong preference for that pole and an ability to gain the upsides of that pole.

Chapter 13
Paradoxical Change and Getting Unstuck

The Paradoxical Theory of Change. ...change occurs when one becomes what he is, not when he tries to become what he is not.... By rejecting the role of change agent, we make meaningful and orderly change possible. ~ Arnold Beisser, M.D.[40]

As a young man in the 1960s wanting to make a difference, my goal was to become the best "change agent" possible. My hunch was that I needed to start with myself as the focus of change and expand out to larger and larger systems. Early in this personal journey, I was involved in a two-year training at the Gestalt Institute of Cleveland (1973–1975). It was in that training that I learned about what Beisser called "The Paradoxical Theory of Change."

I was shocked when I first read it. For eight years I had invested in learning to be an effective "change agent" and now I'm being told to "reject the role of change agent." There was a truth in there that I could not ignore. Beisser, from a polarity perspective, was identifying another pole of a polarity which needed attention. This was half right.

A simple example of the paradoxical theory of change: if I am angry with you for something I think you have done, trying to be "not angry" is a good way to get stuck in my anger. Paradoxically, in order to "change" from "being" angry to "becoming" not angry, I need to "be" angry. Being aware of my anger and expressing it—in ways that are not harmful to me or you—I move through and beyond the anger.

In the last chapter, the CEO was "Expansive" but wanted, along with the executive team and many in the organization, to become "Focused." Paradoxically, they were able to explore being more Focused when encouraged to "be" Expansive. In *Chapter 5*, the Fortune 100 company valued "Autonomous Business Units" but wanted to become a company of "Integrated Business Units." Paradoxically, they were able to take action steps toward Integration of their Business Units when first being supported with action steps to hold on to the Autonomy of their Business Units.

---

[40] Beisser, Arnold. *Gestalt Therapy Now.* Gestalt Journal Press, 1970.

"The premise is that one must stand in one place in order to have firm footing to move and that it is difficult or impossible to move without that footing." (Beisser)

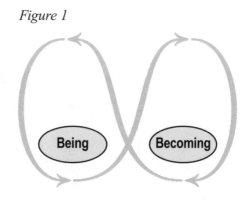

Figure 1

Figure 1 is a simple way to show paradoxical change from a polarity perspective.

The quickest and most sustainable way to "becoming" the individual, organization, or country you want to "become" is by "being" the individual, organization, or country you are at the moment.

Of course, if I am angry with you, I would like to get over it and move on with our relationship. I would like to "become" not angry. But I don't stop being angry by smiling at you and pretending that I am not angry or by trying to "be positive." I become not angry by "being" angry. I need to learn how to "be" angry in ways that build rather than destroy our relationship. This is only possible when I can let myself "be" angry in the first place.

In language that fits all polarities: if you want to embrace the other pole, first embrace the pole where you are.

Competing Values: "Holding On" *And* "Going After"

All transformation efforts, whether individual, organizational, or national, sit within the polarity energy system of Continuity *And* Transformation. This energy system, like all polarities, has two primary forces that are in tension with each other. This tension can be experienced within a person or between people.

On the one hand, there is a force attempting to Transform the situation shown in *Figure 2*. It is moving from "Missing" something valued, which is seen as a problem (-B), to "Going After" that which is "Missing," which is a vision for a preferred future (+C). This is energy to make things better.

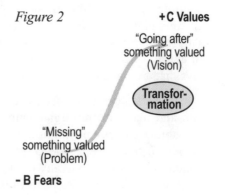

Figure 2

1. "We want our CEO to be more focused." (+C)
2. "We want our Business Units to be more integrated." (+C)
3. "Let's create a more equitable society." (+C)

On the other hand, there is a force for Continuity shown in *Figure 3*.

It is moving from avoiding the loss of something valued (-D) to "Holding On" to it with great Pride (+A).

1. "I like being expansive." (+A)
2. "We love our business unit Autonomy. It's one of our core values." (+A)
3. "I've worked hard for what I have and I don't want to lose it all to taxes. I'm Taxed Enough Already (TEA)!" (+A)

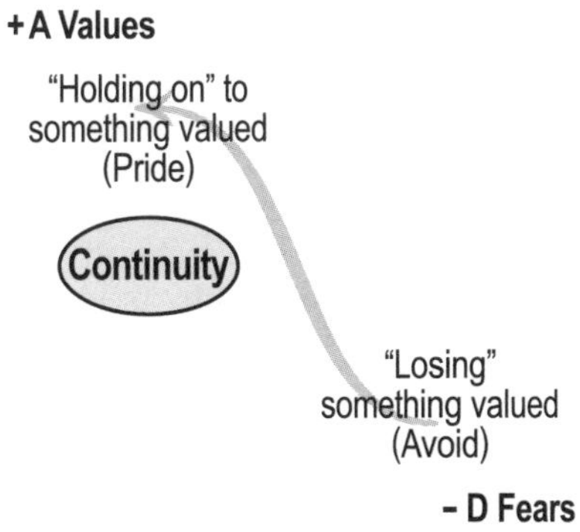

In *Figure 4*, these two forces, "Holding On" *And* "Going After," are the energy system in which we sit whenever we want to improve ourselves or get involved in an effort to make a positive difference. We live in it and it lives in us.

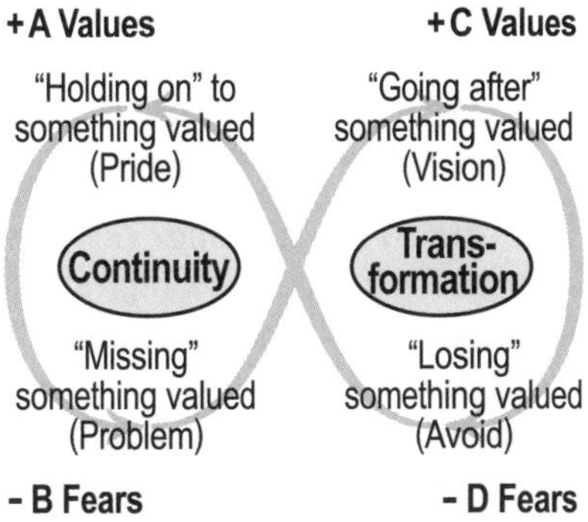

Since this polarity is present in any change effort, it is not surprising that parts of the map are found in various change strategies in the literature.

These change strategies fit in two groups: those focused mostly on the "Going After" energy (+C) and those focused also on the "Holding On" energy (+A).

Figure 3

+A Values

"Holding on" to something valued (Pride)

(Continuity)

"Losing" something valued (Avoid)

- D Fears

Figure 4

+A Values   **+C Values**

"Holding on" to something valued (Pride)   "Going after" something valued (Vision)

(Continuity)   (Transformation)

"Missing" something valued (Problem)   "Losing" something valued (Avoid)

- B Fears   **- D Fears**

Traditional change theories use some form of gap analysis, mentioned earlier, in which you:

1. Identify the present state in terms of its limits and what is "missing," (−B)
2. Create a vision for a preferred future worth "going after," (+C) and,
3. Create a strategy to bridge the gap.

Included in that group is Dick Beckhard's change model,[41] Kurt Lewin's force field analysis,[42] and Future Search,[43] which reminds us that our preferred future (+C) is more compelling and creates more possibilities than just focusing on solving today's problems (−B). All of these "Going After" orientations are essential ingredients in making effective change. A polarity approach builds on these essentials and includes a paradoxical dimension.

---

[41] Beckhard, Richard. *Organizational Development: Strategies and Models.* Addison Wesley, 1969.
[42] Lewin, Kurt. *Resolving Social Conflicts* and *Field Theory In Social Science.* American Psychological Association, 1997.
[43] Weisbord, Marvin; Janoff, Sandra. *Future Search.* Barnes & Noble, 2000.

When those "going after something valued" meet with resistance, the general orientation is to overcome or get around the resistance in some way in order to get what is valued. The transformation effort is seen as solving a problem and those involved should either "lead, follow, or get out of the way." We try to get everyone "aligned" to move in our chosen direction. This was my thinking as I was learning about being a "change agent." Yet, from a polarity perspective, the most effective way to undermine a transformation effort is to get everyone aligned to "Going After" the upside of one pole of a polarity. Such a strategy will reduce the likelihood of ever getting to the desired upside. If you do get there, it will have taken longer than necessary. And, the upside toward which you have been working will be inherently unsustainable and will be called a mistake later on. The Russian Revolution from Chapter 7 is an example.

Some more recent change theories are very intentional about including the "Holding On" force (+A/-D). Gestalt Therapy and Appreciative Inquiry[44] both appreciate that where we are (+A) is a good platform from which to go after our preferred future (+C). Immunity to Change[45] also recognizes that what we are going after (+C), and what we are going from (-B), is not enough to explain our immunity to change. We must also pay attention to competing demands (+A/-D).

This second set of change theories has a different orientation toward resistance to change. Rather than attempt to overwhelm or get around the resistance, it is seen as a resource that can be included in the process of making the transformation. The assumption is that there is wisdom in the resistance. Our Polarity Map® and principles incorporate the combined energy of "Going After" *And* "Holding On." The intent is to create a virtuous cycle rather than a vicious cycle with the natural tension between the two forces. This orientation will increase the likelihood of getting to the desired upside toward which you are working. It will increase the speed with which you get there. And, since the change is based on a polarity that is indestructible, the polarity will remain available as long as you or your organization exists. This orientation radically increases the sustainability of your change effort. The upside of the pole toward which you are headed will not be seen as a "mistake" later on because it was not identified as a "solution" in the first place. When you or the system experience the downside of the pole toward which you have been working, it is recognized as the natural flow between two poles of a polarity and that a self-correction is necessary. Not only is it not called a mistake, but you have anticipated the downside and built in Early Warnings to let you know, early on, as they are being experienced.

Getting Hooked and Stuck

Reality 51: A powerful value/fear diagonal when combined with *Or*-thinking gets us "hooked" by a false choice between the poles. We become blind to the other

[44] Cooperrider, David; Whitney, Diane. *Appreciative Inquiry, A Positive Revolution in Change.* Berrett-Koehler, 2005.
[45] Kegan, Robert; Lahey, Lisa Laskow. *Immunity to Change, How to Overcome It and Unlock the Potential in Yourself and Your Organization.* Harvard Business Press, 2009.

value/fear diagonal and over-tolerate the downside of our valued pole. We then get "stuck" there – unable to access the upside of the pole that is feared.

When we apply this reality to the Continuity *And* Transformation polarity, it looks like *Figure 5* – Getting Hooked and Stuck.

1. Hooked: The more powerfully we value something from our past (+A), the more powerfully we are afraid of losing it (-D). This strong value/fear combined with *Or*-thinking gets us hooked.

Figure 5: Getting Hooked and Stuck

2. Stuck: The hook (+A/-D) becomes a wall that blocks the natural flow of the force that knows something is missing (-B) and wants a transformation by going after it (+C). This leaves us stuck in the downside of Continuity.

Getting hooked and stuck is the primary reason that more than half of our change efforts do not achieve their desired outcomes. It is also why, if the "resistance" (+A/-D), is overcome by force or manipulation (Russian Revolution), you end up in the downside of the Transformation pole (-D) and it is called a mistake later on.

When, as a "change agent," I was going after my desired change (-B\+C) and I experienced this resistance (+A/-D), I would assume that I had a communication problem, which I did. My solution to this communication problem was to state, even more clearly and strongly, what is missing in the present and what is so terrific about my vision of what I was going after (-B\+C). The logic was clear. They would see the error of their ways (-B) and align with me toward the promised land! (+C)

I was seeing the situation as a problem (-B) with a solution (+C). The problem was with them and their resistance and the solution was, obviously, with me! When we treat the up side of one pole as a "solution" to a problem, the clearer the communication, the greater the resistance to that "solution".[R71]

As a "change agent," I was seen by those resisting as a "naïve complainer" – which I was. I was a "complainer" because I was pointing to the downside of the past and present (-B) which seemed to be complaining about what they valued, were proud of, and wanted to preserve (+A). And I was "naïve," in the minds of those resisting, because I was idealizing what the transformation would bring (+C) and talking as if there were no downside (-D). The more I emphasized my point of view as the only point of view (-B\+C), the clearer they were that I *either* did not see their point of view (+A/-D), *Or* I was rejecting it. In either case, the clearer my communication, the greater their resistance. As their resistance increased, I became more and more frustrated with their stubbornness! I needed to be more clever at getting around their resistance or organize enough power to overcome it. My lack of success in this venture, fortunately, could be blamed on those resisting.

Those resisting were also "naïve complainers." They were naïve to the downsides of Continuity and continuing as things are (-B). And they were complaining about the disaster that would happen (-D) if my proposed transformation (+C) would take place. Just as there is wisdom in the resistance by those "holding on," there is wisdom in efforts by those "going after."

We had two points of view in which each saw the other as the problem and ourselves as the solution. This led to a vicious cycle in which, no matter who won, the system lost and we could conveniently blame the other for the dysfunction.

Does this seem familiar?

Getting Unstuck

This is where the paradoxical theory of change is helpful. *Figure 6* shows our five-step process for getting unstuck.[R72] I will summarize the process here and demonstrate its application with an organizational case study in *Chapter 14*.

When promoting a personal or organizational transformation (+C), we can antici-pate that there will be resistance and that there will be wisdom in the resistance (+A/-D). With the resistance, we know that there is a value/fear diagonal that needs to be respected and learned from (+A/-D). We will:

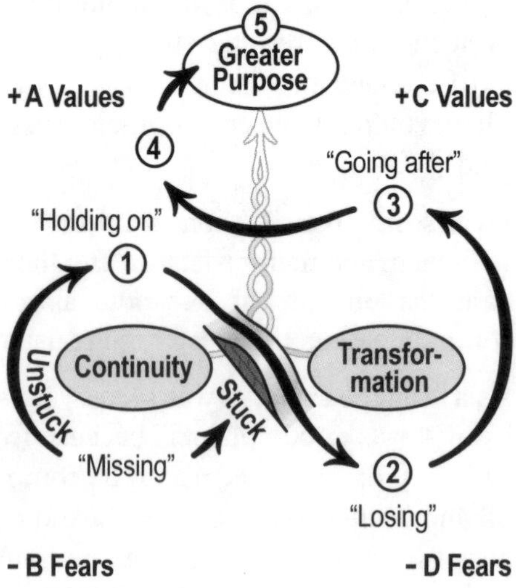

Step (1) – Seek out what Value is being held (+A). Listen to those who are resisting the move toward what we are "Going After" (+C). Affirm the value to which they are "Holding On" (+A).

Figure 6: Getting Unstuck

Step (2) – Once we know and affirm the value being held, what was a wall becomes a bridge to the fear of losing what is valued (-D). Listen to and respect the legitimate fear of losing what is valued.

Step (3) – After identifying and respect-ing the resistor's point of view (+A/-D), ask the question, "How might we (those holding on and those going after) gain what we are "going after"…

Step (4) – … without letting go of what the resistors value…

Step (5) – … in order to move toward a Greater Purpose that works for both groups?

The fear of those "Holding On" is that to join us in the transformation we are going after requires them to give up what they value. That is why, in any transformation effort, it is essential to first make sure we hear and respect their values (+A) and fears (-D) and to let them know that you are not asking them to let go of their point of view. That is why the first two steps in the process is focused on their point of view (+A/-D). Once they feel seen, heard, and respected and are assured that you are encouraging them to "Hold On" to their point of view, they are much more likely to supplement their point of view with your point of view. This is not a guarantee, but it does improve the odds.

Intrapersonal Transformation

It is important to remember that the Continuity *And* Transformation polarity is at play intrapersonally. Seeing my desired "transformed self" as the solution to the problem with me is a good way to find that, in spite of my best efforts, I have difficulty "walking my talk." This situation is seldom a lack of integrity or desire to walk my talk. It is a misunderstanding of the issue. Seeing it as a polarity helps us get in touch with our own resistance and the wisdom within it. Incorporating the values and fears within my resistance will increase the attainability, speed, and sustainability of my desired personal transformation. There is wisdom in the desired transformation as well as wisdom in your resistance.

In *Chapter 14*, I will share how this process worked with a large hospital system.

Summary

The Continuity *And* Transformation polarity is at play in any personal change or social change effort. It involves two forces: those "going after" the transformation and those "holding on" to a value or set of values they are afraid will be lost in the transformation process.

Many traditional change or transformation theories focus on the "going after" force and attempt to get around or overpower any resistance. Other change theories are paying attention to the "holding on" force and incorporating it within the transformation process. They have a paradoxical orientation toward change.

New Realities in Chapter 13

Reality 71　When we treat the up side of one pole as a "solution" to a problem, the clearer the communication, the greater the resistance to that "solution".

Reality 72　There is a 5-step process for getting unstuck.

1. Understand and respect the values of those "holding on."
2. Understand and respect the fears of those "holding on."
3. Ask, "How can we gain what we are "going after"…
4. … without letting go of the values of those "holding on"…
5. … in order to move toward a Greater Purpose that works for both groups?

And

Chapter 14
The Recalcitrant Oncologists

The CEO of a large hospital system wanted some help. They heard a presentation I made on Polarity Thinking and was wondering if it might be useful in their situation.

"Barry, I want us to be *the* leader in oncology for this metropolitan area. In order to do that, I need to make several million dollars in changes to upgrade our facilities and system. I can't make these changes, legally or politically, without the support of a group of 'recalcitrant oncologists' who have their own, independent group practice not far from our main facility. Some of the changes I want to make require an MD to sign off. This group is making a lot of money for themselves and for the hospital. I can't afford to alienate them, and they know it. Can you get them to support the changes I want? If you can, how would you do it?"

Figure 1

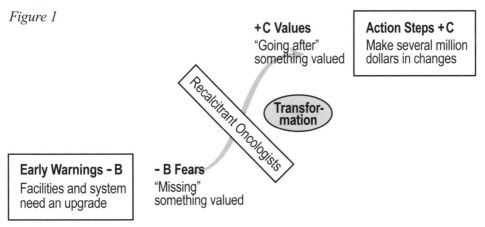

Figure 1 summarizes his view.

The CEO wants help in solving a couple of problems. The first is that the hospital facilities and system need to be upgraded (-B) and the solution is to make several million dollars in changes (+C). The CEO is personally invested in the "going after" energy to make some significant changes. The second problem is a group of 'recalcitrant oncologists' who have significant power in this situation. The CEO cannot afford to alienate them. They are very happy with the way things are and are "holding on" to the status quo. They are a roadblock to the vision.

I understand "going after" a vision (+C). And, from a Continuity *And* Transformation perspective, I assume there is wisdom in the resistance from the 'recalcitrant oncologists.' I have our SMALL process in mind which begins by engaging key stakeholders. I ask if it is possible to bring together some key players from the executive staff and some representatives from the independent oncology group. The response is, "That's not very easy to do because it is not a billable hour." I said, "We need to be figuring this out with them. What can you do to make that happen?" The reply, "I can get them to a 2-hour meeting if I feed them a meal." Notice the power in this relationship with the oncology group. The CEO has trouble even getting them to show up for a meeting, let alone being able to dictate to them the terms of the desired hospital transformation. I ask, "Can you arrange for two of these 2-hour meetings with meals?" The response, "I think I can do it if we have them at least a week apart." So, the following process happened within two, 2-hour meetings which included breakfast at each.

The SMALL Process (Seeing, Mapping, Assessing, Learning, Leveraging)

Seeing – I began with a brief introduction to Polarity Thinking including how polarities look and work. The message was clear that, with all polarities, it is essential to empower both poles. In this case, my intent was to make sure that *both* the oncologist group *And* the CEO's executive team had their interests included and respected. A brief discussion of desires and concerns led to an underlying polarity they named Traditional Care *And* Innovative Care. For them, these two pole names were both neutral and positive.

Notice how this parallels the names of the generic Continuity *And* Transformation polarity. This was language that worked for them. Once we agreed on the names of the two poles, we could create a map and include some of the information that had come up in the brief conversation about desires and concerns.

Mapping – As you will recall, the building of a Polarity Map® is always a values and language clarification process. We needed to make sure the content of the map worked for all those present. The first question was, "Where to start?" In one sense, it doesn't matter what the sequence is for filling out the map as long as all the parts get filled out. At the same time, there are some general guidelines worth considering.

If it seems relatively easy to identify a Greater Purpose Statement (GPS) that those present can agree to, having that GPS as a "True North" while filling out the rest of the map can be very useful. It becomes a constant reminder as to why we are investing in leveraging this polarity in the first place.[R73]

If it appears like it will be difficult to agree on a Greater Purpose Statement until those present have a chance to talk about their values and fears, you can start by filling in the four quadrants first. The agreed upon quadrants will then provide a richer context in which to create, together, a Greater Purpose Statement.[R74] In this case, there was agreement that they wanted to be a "Leader in Oncology" and that was the agenda the CEO had identified when inviting the executive team and the oncology group to the meeting. When you know your Greater Purpose, the Deeper Fear at the bottom of the map is the opposite. In this case, it was not being the Oncology care of choice.

We had an editable Polarity Map projected from a laptop to a big screen so it was easy for everyone to read. *Figure 2* is a cleaned-up outline of what we created together over breakfast at the first meeting. After agreeing on the two pole names, the Greater Purpose and the Deeper Fear, we focused on the four quadrants.

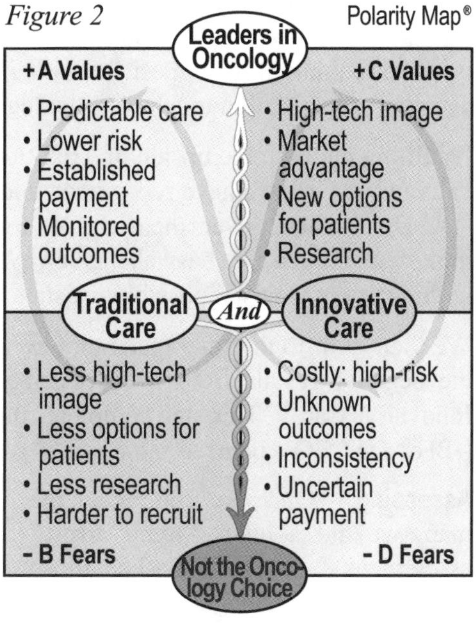

When filling out the four quadrants, as a general rule, it is useful to fill out the content of the two upsides first. That allows people supporting either pole to have their pole affirmed for what it brings.[R75]

When the upside of one pole represents a change that one or more people are "going after" (+C), it is often a good idea to first fill out the upside of the pole that others will be "holding on" to (+A). In this case, I first asked everyone to identify, "What would be the positive results if we did a good job of holding on to the benefits of Traditional Care?" (+A)

The message to everyone in filling out the upsides of Traditional Care

Figure 2   Polarity Map®

Leaders in Oncology

+A Values
- Predictable care
- Lower risk
- Established payment
- Monitored outcomes

+C Values
- High-tech image
- Market advantage
- New options for patients
- Research

Traditional Care *And* **Innovative Care**

- B Fears
- Less high-tech image
- Less options for patients
- Less research
- Harder to recruit

- D Fears
- Costly: high-risk
- Unknown outcomes
- Inconsistency
- Uncertain payment

Not the Oncology Choice

is that this upside exists and that it contains essential benefits for the hospital system. This is the pole that the "Recalcitrant Oncologists" valued and were holding on to. My message to them, after the completion of this quadrant, is that we will fill out the rest of the map and then come back to this quadrant and look at how we can make sure we hold on to this content when pursuing the Greater Purpose of becoming Leaders in Oncology.

I then asked, "What are the positive results from a good job of going after Innovative Care (+C)?" As we filled out the map, I made sure that both groups were contributing content to all four quadrants. This engages everyone in the process and it also asks everyone to identify, through their own words, that there is legitimate content in each quadrant.

Once you have both upside quadrants filled in, you can fill out both downsides. It is less important where you start with these than where you start with the two upside quadrants. At the same time, I suggest that you move next to the downside of the Innovative Care pole. The reason is to first acknowledge the legitimacy of the concerns of the Oncologists around the possible loss (–D) of what they value (+A) when going after Innovative Care (+C).

The question to ask when listing the content for the downside of Innovative Care is not, "What is the downside of innovative care?" The reason is that those favoring Innovative Care will have trouble identifying any downside to what they value. In this case, the CEO would have trouble identifying this content. He and others "going after" Innovative Care will be more likely to contribute content to this quadrant if asked something like: "We have already agreed upon a number of positive results if we do a good job at Innovative Care (+C). Now, what would happen if we over-focused on Innovative Care <u>to the neglect of</u> Traditional Care?" The answer is that we could lose the benefits of Traditional Care (+A). Everyone is asked to think of the opposite of (+A) in order to come up with content for (–D). This step puts us all in touch with the legitimate fears of the oncologists.

By filling out both the upside of Traditional Care (+A) and the downside of Innovative Care (–D), we have recognized and affirmed the oncologists' point of view (+A/–D). We have given them a place to stand which respects them and what is important to them. We have also given everyone the opportunity to see the wisdom within the oncologists' possible resistance to "going after" Innovative Care (+C).

We then went to the final quadrant (–B) and asked the question, "What would be the negative results from over-focusing on Traditional Care <u>to the neglect of</u> Innovative Care?" This step completes the affirmation of the values (+C) and fears (–B) of the CEO's point of view (–B\+C).

Assessing – Once we completed the map, we did a quick "trend arrow" assessment[R76] in which I asked those present, "If you imagine the polarity infinity loop moving as an energy system through the four quadrants, would you say, at this point in time, that it needs to move toward Innovative Care (+C) or toward Traditional Care (+A)?" (*Figure 3*) We have already established

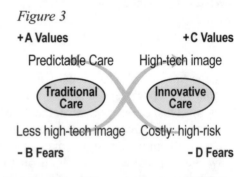

Figure 3

that over time, it will need to incorporate both upsides. There was a general agreement that while holding on to Traditional Care, there was a need to move toward Innovative Care at this point in time (–B to +C).

Learning – Given the trend toward Innovative Care and our paradoxical orientation toward change, I concluded the first two-hour breakfast letting them know that we would start the next breakfast by creating Action Steps to gain or maintain the upsides of Traditional Care.

Leveraging – When we gathered for breakfast a week later, we did a quick review of the process so far: Seeing, Mapping, Assessing and Learning. I then described the final step, Leveraging, which includes Action Steps and Early Warnings (*Figure 4*).

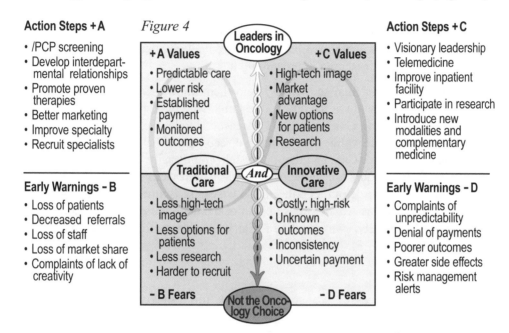

Action Steps +A

- /PCP screening
- Develop interdepart-mental relationships
- Promote proven therapies
- Better marketing
- Improve specialty
- Recruit specialists

Early Warnings – B

- Loss of patients
- Decreased referrals
- Loss of staff
- Loss of market share
- Complaints of lack of creativity

Figure 4

Leaders in Oncology

+A Values
- Predictable care
- Lower risk
- Established payment
- Monitored outcomes

+C Values
- High-tech image
- Market advantage
- New options for patients
- Research

Traditional Care *And* **Innovative Care**

- Less high-tech image
- Less options for patients
- Less research
- Harder to recruit

- Costly: high-risk
- Unknown outcomes
- Inconsistency
- Uncertain payment

– B Fears   **Not the Oncology Choice**   **– D Fears**

Action Steps +C

- Visionary leadership
- Telemedicine
- Improve inpatient facility
- Participate in research
- Introduce new modalities and complementary medicine

Early Warnings – D

- Complaints of unpredictability
- Denial of payments
- Poorer outcomes
- Greater side effects
- Risk management alerts

Action Steps – The question for creating Action Steps is something like: "What are we doing or could be doing to gain or maintain the upside of this pole?" We started with everyone thinking of Action Steps to gain or maintain the upsides of Traditional Care. I encouraged them to included things already being done and expand to new things. Like any project, it helps to have names of those accountable, dates for delivery and measurables for accomplishment.

This is a very transparent process. As everyone was contributing to the Action Steps to support Traditional Care, I would ask the people from the oncology group, "If the CEO and executive team agree to support these Action Steps (AS +A), are you convinced that we will do a good job of holding on to and improving the best of Traditional Care (+A)? They would say, "Not yet" and I would say, "What would it take?" I am clear with everyone that we will not move to looking at Action Steps in support of going after Innovative Care (AS +C) until everyone feels confident that we will do a good job of holding on to and improving Traditional Care (+A).

Once everyone felt confident about the Action Steps for Traditional Care (AS +A), we started creating Action Steps for Innovative Care (AS +C). To the surprise of the CEO and executive team, the recalcitrant oncologists came up with more ideas for Innovative Care than the executive team!!

The CEO got more than was hoped for in terms of Action Steps in support of Innovative Care. Several million dollars worth of Innovation was agreed to, in principle, and we had not yet finished our second 2-hour breakfast!

Why were the recalcitrant oncologists not so recalcitrant? I suggest that they saw this issue differently than seeing them as the "problem" getting in the way of the CEO's "solution." The reframe was to see this as a polarity that could be leveraged and their values were essential in leveraging it.

Early Warnings – This final step would help them know, early, when they were getting into one downside or the other. We started with the Early Warnings for the downside of Innovative Care (EW -D). The reason is to let the oncologists holding on to Traditional Care values know that we recognized that there is a potential downside to Innovative Care and that the system could easily find itself there. The question is, "How would we know early (what would we measure?) that we are getting into the downside of this pole (-D) so we can self-correct and pay attention to what we might do as Action Steps to gain or maintain the upside of Traditional Care (AS +A). Finally, we identified Early Warnings for the downside of Traditional Care (EW -B).

Summary

Clearly, not all processes are going to work this quickly but a lot can be accomplished in 4 hours or 1 day when the shift occurs from mis-diagnosing an issue as a problem to solve to recognizing it as a polarity to leverage. Once you know it is a polarity, all the polarity realities in this book are in play. And this powerful energy system in which you sit can be leveraged to serve you and the larger group of which you are a part. The wisdom within the map content and the Action Steps and Early Warnings was all within the participants and their two, equally valid points of view.

Think of what would have happened if I had joined the CEO in figuring out how to get around the resistance of the recalcitrant oncologists, or how to get enough power to overwhelm their resistance and move to implement the vision for Innovative Care.

Thirty years from now, this hospital system, if it exists, will be living within the Traditional Care *And* Innovative Care polarity. The only question will be how well they are leveraging it. There will be the natural tension between the two poles. If there is a change in leadership or, for some other reason, the reality of this being a polarity gets lost and the tension gets treated as a problem to solve, the tension is likely to become a vicious cycle which serves neither the receivers of care or the givers of care or the community in which the hospital system sits.

Constant hope: since polarities are indestructible, this polarity will always be immediately available as a gift with the opportunity to create, from the tension, a virtuous cycle which serves the receivers and givers of care and the community.

New Realities in Chapter 14

Reality 73   If it is seems relatively easy to identify a Greater Purpose Statement (GPS) that those present can agree to, having that GPS as a "True North" while filling out the rest of the map can be very useful. It becomes a constant reminder as to why we are investing in leveraging this polarity in the first place.

Reality 74   If it appears like it will be difficult to agree on a Greater Purpose Statement until those present have a chance to talk about their values and fears, you can start by filling in the four quadrants first. The agreed-upon quadrants will then provide a richer context in which to create, together, a Greater Purpose Statement.

Reality 75   When filling out the four quadrants, as a general rule, it is useful to fill out the content of the two upsides first. That allows people supporting either pole to have their pole affirmed for what it brings.

Realty 76   Once you have a Polarity Map, you can do a "Trend Arrow" assessment in which you are asking, "At this point in time, are we or should we be moving toward the upper left quadrant (+A) or toward the upper right quadrant (+C)?"

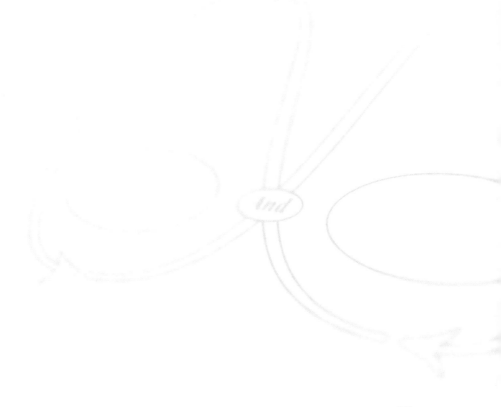

Chapter 15
"Pass One – Pass All" in South Africa

It is 1994. Apartheid is over. For the first time in its 125-year history, Potchefstroom University is integrated. A "transition team" has been created with black and white representatives from the administration, faculty, and students. Their job is to help address issues that might come up in this first year as an integrated school.

A few months into the first semester, a Black Student Union has formed on campus. At this particular meeting of the transition team, a few students from the Black Student Union have arrived with a list of demands. If they are not met, they threaten to shut down the administration building. One of those demands is "Pass one – Pass all." If you pass one student, you must pass all students.

Imagine yourself as a member of this transition team. What thoughts and feelings do you have when faced with a demand to pass all students? Fill in the blank: "If I were to comply with this demand, it could lead to..."

_____ , _____ , _____

One of the faculty members of the transition team, Leon Coetsee, is struck by his own anxiety about what would happen if they complied. He looks around at others on the transition team. He sees eyes rolling and expressions of confusion, frustration, and fear. It appears that others are reacting with feelings similar to his. The representatives of the Black Student Union are "going after" something and he feels his own, internal resistance to it. What to do!?

Leon is a professor of management at Potchefstroom. One year earlier, he had come to a management conference in the United States in which he participated in a workshop I was offering on "Polarity Management." He saw some potential in the concept and bought a copy of my book by the same title. He decided to include the book as required reading in one of his courses and started teaching about the power of *And*. His teaching contract included him spending 20% of his time consulting and training in both the private and public sector. He was introducing Polarity Management in those settings as well. By the time the Black Student Union presented its demands to the Transition Team, Leon had a year's worth of applying Polarity Thinking in both his teaching and his consulting.

No one else in the room knew anything about "Polarity Management" but it immediately seemed relevant to Leon. He knew that his own resistance to the demand "Pass one – Pass all" was very strong. He also thought he could see resistance in the faces of others. From a polarity perspective, he knew that there was wisdom in this resistance. If this was a polarity, there would be two points of view in which both were "right", and they needed each other.

What they needed to create and see, together, was the whole map. Leon suggested that it would be helpful to hear from those present including those who were supportive of the demand and those who had serious reservations. He suggested further that a Polarity Map® would be a good way to organize these two points of view. He didn't talk about polarities; he just used the map as a wisdom organizer, trusting there would be wisdom in both points of view.

Figure 1 represents the almost blank map he started with on a big flipchart. The Greater Purpose and Deeper Fear were not parts of the map in 1994. Leon put "Pass one – Pass all" as the possible right pole as a place from which to fill out the rest of the map. He knew that the demand had generated a lot of resistance in himself and others. That resistance contained some fear. There were two places in a Polarity Map in which to write down fears or concerns: the two downsides. The fears associated with the demand would go in the lower right quadrant, below "Pass one – Pass all."

Figure 1   Polarity Map®

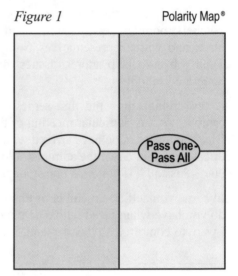

Leon knew that he and others were pre-occupied with concerns about the demands. He also knew that those fears needed to be acknowledged in order to free people up to look for content in other parts of the map. So, he started in the downside of over-focusing on "Pass one – Pass all". He asked the question, "If we were to take this demand seriously and implement it, what are some concerns people have about its impact on Potchefstroom?"

The list of concerns they generated is summarized in *Figure 2,* but I think you can imagine them: Students won't be accountable to show they have learned something. If anyone can graduate regardless of demonstrated competency, a degree from Potchefstroom will be meaningless. Where's the challenge and the pride in meeting that challenge? Those who do work hard are going to resent those who just occupy a chair in class, don't do any work, but somehow pass just for being present! This would be a disaster for the solid reputation Potchefstroom University has built over the past 125 years!

All good points. As you read and think about them, notice how important it is to get these fears out. Until they are expressed and heard, those holding these fears are not likely to hear another point of view.

In *Figure 2* we can see the first two steps in Leon's getting them to fill out the full map.

(1) Identify the fears of what could be lost (-D).

(2) Identify the values to which those resisting were "holding on." (+A)

The question for content in the upper left quadrant (+A) would be: What are the historical values that Potchefstroom University needs to hold on to which appear threatened by the "Pass one – Pass all" demand? Because the diagonal (+A/-D) are value/fear opposites, they just had to think of the opposite of their content in the lower right (-D).

Figure 2

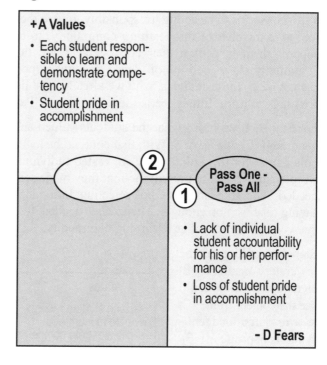

+A Values
- Each student responsible to learn and demonstrate competency
- Student pride in accomplishment

② ① Pass One - Pass All

- Lack of individual student accountability for his or her performance
- Loss of student pride in accomplishment

- D Fears

Again, the list is easy to come up with: We are proud of our high standards of academic excellence. Students are held accountable to demonstrate their learning through well-written papers and acceptable scores on exams. It has been a source of pride to be a graduate of Potchefstroom. We are recognized as a very good university, not only in South Africa but in the world.

Leon had provided an opportunity for all to appreciate the content and strength of the resistance to the demand to "Pass all." After getting clear on one point of view (+A/-D), it was time to get clear on the interdependent point of view (-B\+C). The initial source for this point of view was the students representing the Black Student Union. Leon suggested that "Pass one – Pass all" seemed like a means to an end. He asked for further clarification about what they were "going after" or attempting to accomplish with their demand.

The students were clear: "We are not asking you to lower the standards for entry or for graduation. We are talking about the University Community's responsibility to every student on campus. Each student has unique needs and circumstances which must be addressed to maximize their potential at Potchefstroom. Isn't it the job of every student, faculty, and administrator to pay attention to these needs and circumstances and respond to them effectively? We think so. If a student is struggling with a subject, isn't it the responsibility of others, including students, to be aware of this struggle and look at ways to support the student? We think so. If a student seems to be acting irresponsibly toward themselves or others, isn't it our job, as a member of this learning community, to confront them about this and support them in getting their act together? We think so. If we, as a learning community, do a good job of identifying and responding to the unique needs of each student, those students, who we already established are qualified to be here, are likely to learn. If they learn, they should pass. Pass one – Pass all."

For Step 3, Leon heard what the students valued and placed it in the upper right quadrant (+C) of *Figure 3*. With that content, he had a good idea of what might be pole names for this polarity. He suggested Individual Responsibility *And* School Responsibility. Those present thought they made sense and agreed that both were needed. The students were not rejecting Individual Responsibility. They were saying that is not enough. There *also* needed to be shared responsibility by everyone in the school as a learning community.

Step 4 was filling out the lower left quadrant (-B) Here again, they could use the content from (+C) as a resource for identifying its opposite in (-B). Leon asked the students from the Black Student Union what has been going on, for them, in the first few months of the semester that caused them to bring this demand to the transition team.

Again, the students were clear: "We are here because we can already predict that four years from now, there is going to be a disproportionate number of black South African students who will not graduate. When that

Figure 3

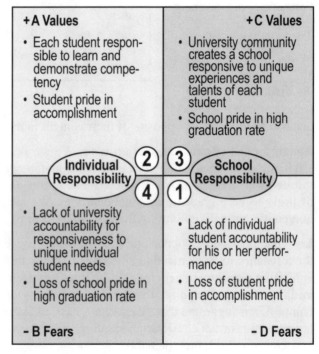

happens, you are going to explain this by telling us we are either lazy or stupid or both. You will be concluding that the individual student has failed in each case of non-graduation. We are saying that this culture is a setup against the way we have learned to learn. What we call 'collaboration,' you call 'cheating.'" Leon and the others present were hearing the wisdom in what they were resisting.

In this case, there was a natural tension between two cultural preferences. Potchefstroom University, like White South Africans generally, had a strong lean toward Individualism. This parallels a similar preference in the United States and Australia. The Black Student Union, like Black South Africans generally, had a strong lean toward Collectivism. The notion of "It takes a village" to educate a child comes from this more collectivist leaning.

This culture clash is around a polarity. Both points of view were not only right but they need each other over time. To the degree that the university could leverage both upsides of this polarity, they could not only keep the tension from becoming a vicious cycle between the black students and the administration, they could create a virtuous cycle between their two points of view, enhance the quality of education, and build on the proud tradition at Potchefstroom University.

Leon called me up the next day and was excited to share the richness of the conversation that had happened with the transition team. Leon continues to use Polarity Thinking in his consulting work in South Africa and several other countries in Africa.

Notice how the representatives from the Black Student Union were paying attention to the unique experiences and needs of the black students arriving on campus as an upside of School Responsibility. This fits well with john powell's focus on the "targeted" pole of "targeted universalism" (*Chapter 7*) and with contextual ethics (*Chapter 9*). The other pole, Individual Responsibility, to meet common performance demands fits well with john powell's focus on the "universal" pole of "targeted universalism" and with normative ethics.

Summary

In this case, there was the underlying polarity of Continuity *And* Transformation while the identified polarity ended up being Individual Responsibility *And* School Responsibility. The Transformation pole was what the Black Student Union was "going after": School Responsibility. It also paralleled the cultural pole of Collectivism. The Continuity pole was what Leon and many on the Transition Team were "holding on" to. It also paralleled the cultural pole of Individualism.

Those of us wanting to make a difference will often find ourselves, like the representatives from the Black Student Union, "going after" something that we believe will make a difference. To the degree that the difference we want to make is the upside of one pole of a polarity, it will be helpful to see and leverage the whole polarity. The Polarity Map® provides a place for people to stand who have points of view in tension with each other. It provides a place of legitimacy for their values and their fears. What appeared an *either/Or* choice, *either* accept *Or* reject this demand, became a rich discussion with conflicted energy becoming a virtuous cycle to benefit the students and the university. Leon made a difference by framing the tension within a Polarity Map which increased the opportunity for the Black Student Union representatives to make their difference.

A few other reflections on the process are worth mentioning.

- Leon was the only one in the room who knew much about Polarity Thinking, but the map and principles served them well.

- This was an emotionally-loaded issue with strongly-held values at stake, but was able to be handled by using the Polarity Map as a wisdom organizer and polarity principles guiding the process.

- Leon was able to use his own fears as a resource by imagining them in the downside of a pole of a polarity. This begged the question, "What is in the other quadrants?"

- Leon assumed there was wisdom in his (and others' resistance) *And* that there was wisdom in the students and the demand they were making even though it made him anxious.

- Sometimes the names of the poles either show up or are changed in the process of building a map. It is helpful to hold the content lightly, including the pole names, when building a map. As new stakeholders get involved, you may want to change them again.[R77]

- There is an inherent fairness in mapping a polarity which allows someone to facilitate the mapping even if they have a pole preference.[R78]

New Realities in Chapter 15

Reality 77   Sometimes the names of the poles either show up or are changed in the process of building a map. It is helpful to hold the content lightly, including the pole names, when building a map. As new stakeholders get involved, you may want to change them again.

Reality 78   There is an inherent fairness in mapping a polarity which allows someone to facilitate the mapping even if they have a pole preference.

Chapter 16
Mother Tongue *And* English in South Africa

I am in a large meeting room at Potchefstroom University in South Africa. I am doing a one-day workshop introducing Polarity Thinking to some faculty from the University, representatives from area businesses, and a few government agencies. They are working in table teams of five or six people.

The process includes each table team identifying an issue that is important to them. The issue could be based on excitement about moving toward a preferred future. It could also be based on a chronic tension between two or more groups within or between organizations. The reason they have been given these two areas of focus is that the two primary ways in which polarity tensions most frequently show up in organizations are:

1. The desire to make a change and experiencing resistance to the change.

2. A tension between groups with competing values or agendas. In this case, if the tension is based on a polarity, it will show up as a chronic conflict. It is chronic because the polarity is both unavoidable and unsolvable.

I then ask them to summarize their identified issue by completing this statement: With this issue, at this time, our organization is moving or should be moving from _____ to _____.

We then look at how the content of the "from _____ to _____" would be placed in a Polarity Map®, *Figure 1* is the most common arrangement. It represents the self-correction from the downside of one pole to the upside of the other (-B\+C). This is the gap analysis, problem solving arrangement moving **From:** <u>something not as good as you would like</u> **To:** <u>something better</u> that would make a positive difference. You have starting content for two quadrants (-B\+C), but still need to identify the pole names.

Figure 1

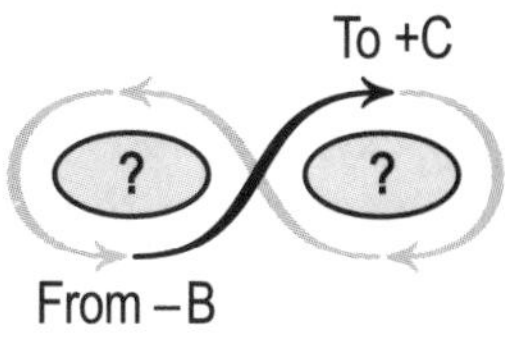

Figure 2 represents when both poles are either neutral or positive. In this case, you have the content for the two poles and need the rest of the map.

Figure 2

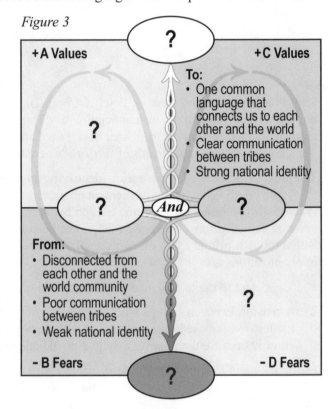

One of the table teams came from the Department of Education for South Africa. They were in the early stages of a project to have English become the common language throughout South Africa. English is one of eleven official languages in the Republic of South Africa.

Figure 3 shows the team's "From _____ to _____" statement. Their project goal was to move **From:** the various tribes being disconnected from each other and the world community, a community most probably unwilling to learn Zulu or any other of the 10 official tribal languages; poor communication between the tribes; and a weak national identity.

Figure 3

+A Values

To:
• One common language that connects us to each other and the world
• Clear communication between tribes
• Strong national identity

+C Values

And

From:
• Disconnected from each other and the world community
• Poor communication between tribes
• Weak national identity

– B Fears   – D Fears

They wanted to move **To:** having one common language that connected all parts of South Africa and South Africa to the world; clear communication between the tribes; and a strong national identity.

In their effort to make a difference, what they were going after was clear, but they had been experiencing a lot of resistance. They decided to use this polarity workshop as an opportunity to address the resistance. I explained to all the table teams present that whenever we attempt a change or transformation, if it is heard from an *either/Or* mindset, the message that will be heard is that you are asking them to reject something they value. You may not have told them that they have to reject it, but they will hear it anyway. The resistance to their desired change will come from a value or set of values they are "holding on" to; a fear of losing those values; and an assumption that *either* they can hold on to their values *Or* they can support your transformation effort. Given this choice created in their heads (consciously or unconsciously), they will choose to hold on to their values.

Each table team then proceeded to fill out the rest of their map. They were encouraged to keep key stakeholders in mind: "What words and language would work for everyone involved?" In most cases, their "from ____ to ____" statements fit in the lower left and upper right diagonal (-B\+C), like the education team.

The question then became, "What do we name the poles?" Naming the poles often provides a bridge between the downside and upside of a pole.[R79] Sometimes it is hard to identify the "upside" of something that is seen as very negative. For example, in the case of the education team's map in *Figure 4* below, it would be difficult to answer the question, "What are the upsides of (-B): being disconnected, having poor communications, and weak national identity?" It is the wrong question. Once they had "Mother Tongue" as the left pole name, the question became: "What are the upsides of focusing on and respecting Mother Tongue?" This is much easier to answer.

Similarly, without a right pole name, we ask the wrong question: "What are the downsides of (+C): being connected to each other, having good communication and a strong national identity?" With "English" as the right pole name, the question for (-D) becomes: "What happens if we over-focus on English to the neglect of Mother Tongue?" Since you already have content in (+A) you can identify its opposite for additional help in filling out (-D).

Filling out parts of the map can help us identify the poles and the reverse: filling out the poles can help us fill out parts of the map.

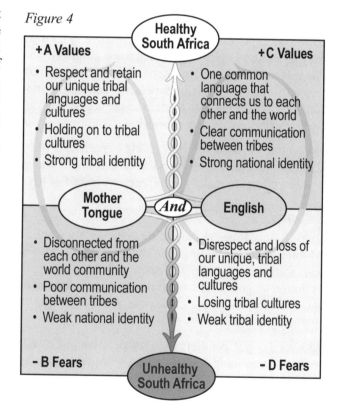

Figure 4

Also, the generic Part *And* Whole polarity is a good resource for imagining content in the Mother Tongue (Part) *And* English (Whole) polarity. It does not give you exact content but it does give you a general sense of themes you might look for when building the map. It also gives you potential insights into what the values and fears of the tribal chiefs might be even though they are not present. Seeing themselves as a unique Part of the Republic of South Africa as the Whole, you could appreciate what their values and fears might be.

In terms of the SMALL process, the teams had completed the Seeing and Mapping steps. The Assessing step was easy for the education team. It was clear that their "trend arrow" was wanting to go *from* being Disconnected, with Poor communication and Weak national identity (–B) *to* being Connected, with Clear communication and Strong national identity (+C). The Learning step includes appreciating where the resistance will come from and how to include the wisdom from that resistance in the final Leveraging step.

I explained our Getting Unstuck process and guided them through creating Action Steps and Early Warnings for their maps.

At a break in the middle of the workshop, the woman leading the national project for English as the common language came up to me with a big smile and excited look on her face. She said this polarity perspective helped her understand why the team was experiencing so much resistance to their project. She realized that when they promoted English as the "common language," tribal leaders were hearing that she was rejecting their "mother tongue." That was not her intent. However, without explicitly identifying it as a polarity and beginning with affirming their mother tongue and working with them to create action steps to preserve their mother tongue, their resistance was understandable.

It was one of those very rewarding experiences in which someone had combined their life experience with a polarity lens and it was going to be very useful to her and her efforts to make a difference on behalf of her country.

Summary

Two key polarities at play in this chapter are Continuity *And* Transformation and Mother Tongue *And* English. The education team was going after their version of transformation, which was their country getting the benefits of English as a common language. The natural resistance to this transformation was coming from those holding on to the other pole, Mother Tongue, which needed to be included explicitly in the process.

Mother Tongue parallels the Part pole while English parallels the Whole pole in the Part *And* Whole polarity. Thus, within this chapter we can integrate the insights from *Section Two* (Part *And* Whole) with the insights from *Section Three* (Continuity *And* Transformation).

New Realities in Chapter 16

Reality 79   Naming the poles often provides a bridge between the downside and upside of a pole.

Chapter 17
Countinuity *And* Transformation in Our Brain

"Practice Makes Perfect"

When I was in the 4th grade, I fell in love with basketball. I had dreams of playing in the NBA. These dreams persist, though at 78 my prospects do not look good! One of the things I needed to learn was how to dribble. This was a new skill which I practiced diligently in my basement. Brain research shows that when I was learning this new task, my brain activity was concentrated in one part of my brain that responds to the "new." As I got more comfortable with dribbling, I would practice blindfolded while dribbling between my legs and behind my back. As the task of dribbling became second nature, brain research indicates that the concentration of brain activity, when dribbling, shifted to another part of the brain which responds to the "familiar." In a sense, this freed up the part of my brain that concentrates on new things to take on something new, like going outside and shooting baskets. Dribbling outside on the basketball court, my brain activity was in the familiar part of my brain. When I attempt to combine a new shot with my dribbling, the brain activity shifted back to the part of my brain that concentrates on new things.

This process continues as I join others in playing on a team and take on more new things like passing and catching. As each new thing becomes familiar, I am able to take on more new dimensions of the game. It is not that linear a sequence of combining skills. It is more an oscillation between focusing on one skill, like dribbling, passing, shooting, and guarding that are each Part of the game *And* focusing on integrating them all into one Whole, playing the game. Focused practice on just dribbling or just shooting can create a familiarity with each that supports the other. Being able to dribble without looking at the ball frees me up to look for teammates getting open or gauge my distance from the basket for a shot.

This fits with all of life. As we take on new things, we stimulate one part of our brain. When the "new" becomes "second nature," the same activity stimulates a different part of the brain. Those things that have shifted to the "familiar" part of our brain have, in a sense, left room for more new things to be addressed in the "new" part of our brain. The familiar supports us doing new things *And* new things, over time, build our base of the familiar.

Too Much Newness, Too Fast, Reinforces the Familiar.

Let's look at a different, possible scenario with me and basketball in the 4th grade.

If I had no experience in dribbling or shooting or passing a basketball and my older brother, in his enthusiasm for basketball, takes me to a neighborhood court to join a game with experienced players, it could easily be overwhelming. I would be concentrating on trying to dribble and would have trouble looking up to see who I might pass to or where the basket was to try a shot. If I had a shot, I wouldn't know how to shoot the ball and I wouldn't have a clue about what it meant to "guard" somebody. This would be embarrassing, at best!

What would be going on in my brain is easy to track. When overwhelmed with too many new things, our brain shifts the location of where our activity is concentrated. The energy moves from the location for newness to the location for the familiar. This is a natural self-correction to protect ourselves from being overwhelmed. It is our brain's version of resistance to change. There is wisdom in this resistance. In this case, the natural self-correction might be to stop trying to play basketball and go back to riding my bike, which was something with which I was "familiar" and could do with confidence and ease. My older brother's transformation effort for me to become a basketball player would decrease rather than increase my interest in basketball. Instead of expanding my horizons with a new activity, I would be more deeply entrenched in one with which I am familiar. This reality within brain research fits exactly with our realities of how polarities work in teams, organizations, and countries.

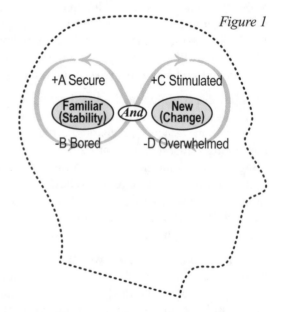

Figure 1

Figure 1 shows an overlay of a well-leveraged polarity on a head profile.

There is a natural tension between the Familiar *And* the New. There is also a natural oscillation between the two poles.

Each of us wants and needs a certain amount of Security which the Familiar brings to our lives (+A). It feels comfortable, like an old shoe. Yet there are limits to the focus on this pole. Over time, without some newness in our lives, it can become Boring (-B). When that happens, we are more and more drawn to something New that is challenging, fun, interesting, and Stimulating (+C). At the same time, too much of the New, without adequate support of the Familiar, can lead to being Overwhelmed (-D).

This dynamic between these two parts of the brain fits with our description of how polarities work and with what we are learning from brain research.

When we introduce a major change in an organization, within the brain of every stakeholder is the possibility of being overwhelmed. *Figure 2* shows what that looks like within a polarity. We know that when you over-focus on one pole to the relative neglect of the other, you get the downside of the pole on which you over-focus.

Figure 2

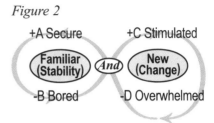

We also know that the natural self-correction from the downside of one pole is the upside of the other pole. With a major organizational change, the resistance we experience is not just from the "recalcitrant ones." It is going on, to some degree, inside the brain of everyone involved, including those advocating for the change.

From a polarity perspective, as summarized in *Figure 3*, we know that each individual brain involved in an organizational change can get "hooked" by the desire for Security and the fear of being Overwhelmed (+A/-D), which can get us "stuck" in the downside of the pole from which we want to move (-B).

Figure 3

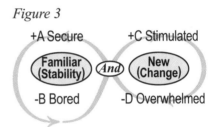

Figure 4 describes another reality. When we over-focus on one pole to the relative neglect of the other, first we get the downside of the pole on which we over-focus (*Figure 2*), then, if we persist in this over-focus, we get the downside of the other pole as well. We get what we are afraid of by our efforts to avoid it. In the case of a change or transformation effort, our effort to make the

Figure 4

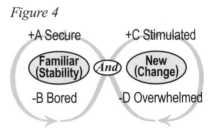

significant organizational change we want leads to over-focusing on the change pole without adequate attention to the stability pole. This leads first to being overwhelmed, then we find ourselves and the whole organization stuck in the very downside we wanted to avoid. We have unintentionally undermined the difference we are trying to make.

This has already been described in previous chapters. The point here is that this reality we experience with all polarities regardless of system size is not just happening in the team, organization, or nation; it is happening within the brain of all the stakeholders involved.[R80]

At this point, you will probably not be surprised that the recommendations for addressing the issue of our brain being overwhelmed with change correspond to our understanding of paradoxical change and our getting unstuck process. The suggestions made from the brain research fit as action steps to support the experience of Continuity as a support for the Transformation.

Summary

There is a solid correlation between what brain research has discovered about how our brain works in relation to Stability *And* Change and our realities of how polarities work in relation to Stability *And* Change. I am a novice at appreciating the richness and complexity of the brain and the extensive research in this area. What is exciting is that my initial understanding, from limited reading, is that brain research is a great potential resource for learning more about the phenomena of interdependent pairs. And, it is possible that what we have been learning about interdependent pairs could be useful in framing some of the insights of brain research. More on polarities and the brain is provided by Ann Deaton in *And*: Volume Two.

New Realities in Chapter 17

Reality 80   The realities we experience with all polarities regardless of system size is not just happening in the team, organization, or nation; it is happening within the brain of all the stakeholders involved.

SECTION FOUR
Justice *And* Mercy

All of us are accountable And all of us are loved – no exceptions!

~ Barry Johnson

Introduction

I was at the Parliament of World Religions as a resource and doing informal research for this book. I had the opportunity for a brief, warm conversation with a Tibetan Buddhist Monk. I introduced myself and said, "I was raised as a Christian within the Lutheran Church. In that tradition we talk about Law *And* Grace or Justice *And* Mercy in which God *both* loves us *And* holds us accountable for our actions. Is there a similar combination within Buddhism?" He smiled gently, put his palms together just below his chin and gave a slight bow. He then said, "Yes. On the one hand we have an all-loving God." He put his left hand out face up. "On the other hand, we have Karma." He put his right hand out face up.

I was struck by how effortless and obvious it was for him. This has been true in conversations I have had with people from other religions and in the limited reading I have done about our rich tapestry of religious traditions around the world. Each has a double message about the deity (deities) they worship: On the one hand, we are accountable for our actions (Justice). On the other hand, we are loved unconditionally (Mercy).

All our communities, sacred or secular, have agreements to live by. They may be written, spoken or "understood." These rules or laws are designed to protect the Individual (Part) *And* the Community (Whole). We need laws. We also need consequences for breaking the laws. Laws without consequences are meaningless. What our religious traditions bring to the focus on laws with consequences is its interdependent pair: mercy with forgiveness. This second focus is a huge gift to all of us.

Mercy with forgiveness is "built in" to our religious traditions. It sometimes occurs in secular communities, but it is not an integral part of secular society like it is in religious systems. Secular communities have consequences through which someone who has broken the law can "pay their debt to society." This might include a fine, time in prison, or, in some countries, the death penalty. Paying our debt to society for our shortcomings is different than mercy with forgiveness. Mercy is about being loved in spite of our shortcomings. It is the awareness that we are more than our shortcomings. It leads to restorative justice rather than abusive injustice in the name of justice.

In this section we will look at this ancient wisdom and how parallel forms of this generic polarity show up in our personal, organizational, national and international lives. For example, Justice *And* Mercy has parallel double messages we give at home and at work. At home, my parents gave me one message that they loved me (Mercy) *And* another message that I was not to hit my sister with a stick or speak to them in a way that showed disrespect (Justice). At work it is important that every person show up and do a good job for which they can earn "conditional respect" (Justice) *And*, every person deserves to be treated with "unconditional respect" regardless of performance (Mercy). Unconditional respect cannot be earned. There are no conditions we must meet to gain this type of respect. It is a birthright.

The awareness of being unconditionally loved is Part of a larger awareness of the universality of that love for all of creation – the Whole. Justice for all is sought not in order to be loved but as a natural response to the awareness of being one of the all who are loved. In order to avoid self-righteous cruelty, the pursuit of justice must be guided by the humbling reality of each of us falling short and being loved.

Mercy – "Only God decides what to anoint – which, thank God, is all of creation and all of humanity from the beginning. No exceptions."[46]

Justice – "The true contemplative, the truly spiritual person, then, must do justice, speak justice, insist on justice."[47]

---

[46] Rohr, Richard. *Richard Rohr's Daily Meditations: Christened Reality*. Center for Action and Contemplation, April 7, 2019.
[47] Chittister, Sister Joan. *Richard Rohr's Daily Meditations: The Path to Justice*. Center for Action and Contemplation, July 3, 2019.

Chapter 18
Justice *And* Mercy for the Individual

I am 13 years old and have just decided that I want to be a Lutheran Minister when I grow up. I have been attending Sunday School and Church at Bethany Lutheran Church two blocks from my home in Rice Lake, Wisconsin. It is a fairly conservative church, and I have come to believe that doing or thinking wrong things is a sin which leads to a very painful afterlife in hell. I have gotten the message that Jesus is, somehow, the way around this condemnation but I'm not sure how it works. I am thus very anxious about life after death and how to make sure I go to heaven rather than hell.

Amid this anxiety I read the following:

"And if your eye causes you to stumble, gouge it out and throw it away. It is better for you to enter life with one eye than to have two eyes and be thrown into the fire of hell." (Matthew 18:9 NIV)

The timing for reading this passage couldn't have been more powerful. I was experiencing a new-found attraction to girls. The attraction was strange and exciting. The stronger this attraction became, the more convinced I was that this was "lust" and was sinful thinking. Unless I could somehow stop this sinful thinking, I was headed straight to hell. When I read Matthew 18:9, the answer was clear; I would gouge out my eyes so I would not see girls and I would stop the "lust." I knew that gouging out one eye would not work because I could still see girls with the one good eye and the lust would continue.

I'm thinking, "If I use a large scissors, I can stab both eyes at the same time." Fortunately, I could not get myself to do it. Unfortunately, I now saw myself as both a sinner and a coward! Not the best for adolescent self-esteem!

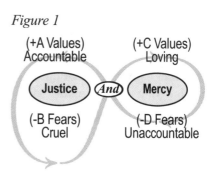

Figure 1

(+A Values) Accountable   (+C Values) Loving

Justice *And* Mercy

(-B Fears) Cruel   (-D Fears) Unaccountable

Figure 1 summarizes how my over-focus on being Accountable (+A) to the neglect of God being Loving (+C), led to my considering being cruel to myself (-B). It is important to recognize how powerful this polarity can be in the life of an individual. The sincere desire to do the right thing and to do it in order to positively affect our lives after death can lead to cruelty to ourselves or to others. In this case, it led to a thirteen-year-old thinking, seriously, about poking my eyes out with a scissors.

Justice without Mercy leads to cruelty. How do we prevent Accountability from becoming cruelty? We need to supplement Justice with Mercy – Consequences with Forgiveness.

Wisdom in Our Resistance

Before moving to Loving (+C) as the natural self-correction to Cruelty (-B), I suggest we look at our own resistance to such a move, *Figure 2*. Our resistance will come from our valuing Accountability (+A). When someone breaks the law, there should be consequences. Without laws and consequences (+A), we have a legitimate fear of lawlessness and no one being held accountable for bullying, stealing, rape, murder, you name

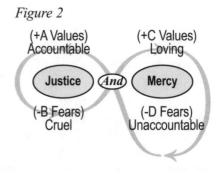

Figure 2

the crime (-D). There is wisdom in our resistance to Loving, alone, as a "solution" to cruelty in the world. Mercy without Justice is not sustainable. It over-tolerates cruelty without standing up against it. At the same time, there is also wisdom in our efforts to become more Loving. The question is, "How do we *both* hold ourselves and others Accountable *And* learn to be more Loving toward ourselves and others?"

A partial response is to use the SMALL process which begins by Seeing Justice *And* Mercy as a polarity. But the Seeing step is about much more than simply seeing the polarity.

In *Chapter 1*, I talked about Jack Gibb's quote, "Seeing is loving."

When we can see any person, organization or country completely, love is a natural result. Polarity Thinking helps us see ourselves and our world more completely, thus increasing our capacity to love. Love is not naïvely ignoring our times of being cruel with each other. It is the compassion that comes from seeing our moments of inhumanity in the context of a larger reality. It is the capacity to see ourselves, our organizations and our countries as more than our shortcomings. It is the Mercy pole of the polarity of Justice *And* Mercy. This polarity shows up, by different names, in all of our religious or spiritual traditions. It involves stopping the bullying *And* seeing the bully as more than a bully.

Allow me to expand. I am not saying that it is easy or that we are always able to see ourselves or others more completely. Sometimes we have trouble seeing beyond what someone is doing or has done. It might be an act of such cruelty to people I love, like my family or close friends, that I cannot see them beyond their cruel act. For example, if my family were killed in a suicide bombing, the Holocaust, Hiroshima, or any other example of our being cruel to each other, it would be very difficult for me to see the person or nation beyond what they have done to me and my loved ones. This is understandable. At the same time, my inability to see beyond whatever they have done or are doing does not mean that there is nothing more to see. It simply means that, at the moment, I cannot see beyond that which is so painful. The pain has me and is limiting my ability to see beyond it.

If we believe there is something more to see, we can choose to look. The very act of looking for more is a loving act that is self-fulfilling. The families of the nine African Americans (Cynthia Marie Graham Hurd, Susie Jackson, Ethel Lee Lance, Depayne Middleton-Doctor, Clementa C. Pinckney, Tywanza Sanders, Daniel Simmons, Sharonda Coleman-Singleton, Myra Thompson) who were killed in their Emanuel African Methodist Episcopal Church by a white man (Dylann Storm Roof) in Charleston, South Carolina, on June 17, 2015, were able to see Dylann Roof as more than the man that killed their family members. Some expressed forgiveness in the courtroom in which he was convicted. This is not a naïve ignoring of the cruelty of his act or the pain he caused. He needed to be held accountable for his actions. *And*, forgiveness was a gift to him and to those who forgave.

My hunch is that forgiveness is available to give to the extent to which one has experienced receiving it. In the case of the families of the nine killed in the Emanuel AME Church, they had a tradition in which they had experienced forgiveness personally and understood it universally.

One of the most dramatic examples of seeing a person as more than a "law breaker" or more than the cruelty they are delivering is Jesus on the cross. First, Jesus forgives the thief hanging on the next cross, seeing the thief as more than a thief. Then, while hanging from nails in hands and feet, Jesus is stabbed in the side, spit upon, and mocked. Amid this cruelty, Jesus sees those involved as more than people inflicting pain and says, "Father, forgive them for they know not what they are doing." (Luke 23:34 NIV)

The very request for forgiveness implies *both* wrongdoing *And* seeing beyond the wrongdoing. They were killing Jesus *And* they were people who did not know what they were doing. It is this tradition and their own experience of both needing forgiveness and receiving it that allowed some family members to see Dylann Roof as more than a murderer.

Hate is Naïve

Killing the nine African Americans in Emanuel AME Church was a hate crime. Their church was singled out because it was a proud symbol of African American religious tradition. They were killed because they were black. Those killed had welcomed and been kind to Dylann who, reportedly, told investigators he almost did not go through with his mission because members of the church study group had been so nice to him.[48]

Dylann Roof had been seeking out articles about black on white violence. He was contracting rather than expanding his ability to see any black person beyond their skin color and the evil he associated with it.

While "Seeing is Loving," Hating is not seeing. Hate is caught on a part of a person, organization, any identifiable group, or nation. It is naïve in that it is unaware of or blind to significant parts of a whole person or group. The love that I am talking about, in contrast, comes from seeing the whole person or group. This includes the good, the bad, and the ugly.

Three Levels of "Seeing"

1. The self that is *shown*
2. The self that is *hidden*
3. The *whole* self

Each of us tends to show parts of ourselves that we are proud of and hide parts of ourselves that we are not proud of. We tend to "put our best foot forward." We are especially likely to do this in situations with people we don't know very well. When we "love" people based on the parts of themselves they want us to see, that is naïve because we act as if there is nothing more to see. We haven't seen the parts of them that they are hiding, which we sometimes call their "dark side." To the extent that there are parts of them that we do not see, we are "naïve" (unaware) about those parts.

The reason we hide parts of ourselves is that we assume if someone saw the parts we are hiding there would be consequences we want to avoid. We all have experiences that support this assumption. When the "hidden" parts of ourselves get seen, those parts get identified as the "real me." Notice how this assumption is based on an *either/Or* mindset. *Either* the person is the one they showed, *Or* they are the one they were hiding. Polarity Thinking appreciates that they are what they are showing *And* what they are hiding *And* their whole history of life experience, which has brought them to where they are at this point in time. Paradoxically, the love we all desire is experienced only after our hidden self is seen and we find ourselves loved anyway.

Seeing others (or yourself) completely is the exact opposite of being naïve. It includes seeing all the parts, the whole person, the whole story, the context in which they grew up, the wrongs they have done and the wrongs done to them. It provides a basis for humility and connection. We share the reality of wrongdoing for which we are accountable (Justice) *And* the reality of being loved as the natural result of being seen completely (Grace). An all-seeing Deity is all loving.

---

[48] Borden, Jeremy; Horwitz, Sari; Markon, Jerry. *Officials: Suspect in church slayings unrepentant amid outcry over racial hatred.* The Washington Post, June 19, 2015.

The Power to Love

When we see Justice *And* Mercy as a polarity, we understand that we need to embrace both. One belief that will support us in this effort is the conviction that if we could see this person more completely, love would be the result. This puts a significant amount of power within ourselves. When we find someone we do not love, we can recognize that this is a reflection of our own inability, at the moment, to see them more completely. We can take initiative to see them more completely; to understand their context. The more our ability to love them is contingent upon them doing something different, the more we have shifted the power to them in controlling our capacity to love.[R81]

Polarity Map® as a Resource for Seeing More Completely

So far, this chapter has been about the first step of the SMALL process: **Seeing**. I would like to conclude with the second step: **Mapping**. This step is, essentially, an organized expansion of Seeing because it requires you to fill out the whole map. As each part is being filled out, more is being seen. If there is a part of the map that you have trouble filling out, you can look to key stakeholders, especially those resisting you, to help you see a more complete picture of the person, organization, or nation.

Use a Polarity Map to confront cruelty *And* to see more than the cruelty. Before describing this process, I want to be very clear that I believe in holding myself and others accountable for our actions. The effort to see a person, organization, or nation more completely is not intended to diminish accountability or to stand by and allow cruelty to continue unchallenged.

More Than a "Bully"

During the early years of the Vietnam War, I was a graduate student at Union Theological Seminary in New York City. In 1965, I was in a "secular internship program" in East Harlem. A small group of us were taking a year out of seminary to live in East Harlem, get a regular job, and participate in and learn about the issues facing the residents of East Harlem. The intent was to be more grounded in the realities of people living in an area of concentrated poverty and to have this experience influence our understanding of our own theology and ministry. We would meet two evenings a week to talk about our experiences and to discuss books on the issues of the time.

One reality that we faced was that all of us had a 4-D deferment with the Selective Service System. That meant we were not being drafted to fight in the Vietnam war. College students had a 2-S deferment meaning that they were, also, not being drafted. It was the young men in East Harlem who, without a solid education and unable to get into college, were being drafted. Those least benefiting from the privileges of our wonderful country were dying in disproportionately higher numbers than those who were benefiting most. This inequity became very personal as my friends I was playing flag football with in the school yard on 107th Street on Saturdays were being drafted and coming home in boxes.

In one of our evening meetings, we had a debate about the War in Vietnam. Sheldon Hughes was opposed to the war. Russ Fletcher saw it as necessary. The debate got me into studying the war. The more I read, the more convinced I was that the war could not be justified. I became the office manager of Clergy and Laity Concerned about Vietnam. Later, I decided I could not accept my deferment that was not available to the primarily black and Hispanic young men in East Harlem, so I turned in my draft card and refused the inequitably deferred status. We were called "draft dodgers," but the reality was that we were giving up the "dodge = deferment" that the Selective Service was giving us.

Russ followed his convictions and enlisted. He, like 56,000 other US soldiers, died in Vietnam. Though I was opposed to the war, it did not mean I would stop loving Russ or stop loving my country. Seeing my country as a bully in this situation meant I needed to do what I could to stop the bullying *And* to see my country as more than a bully. From a polarity perspective I can *both* recognize the cruelty within my country's history of slavery, mass relocation of Native Americans, Jim Crow laws, and contemporary mass incarceration *And* see that my country, like me and you, is much, much more than its shortcomings. Those who hate my country are caught in seeing our shortcomings as the "real" us when, in fact, each of us is more than our shortcomings. If they could see us completely, they would love us – and we them.

Russ saw North Vietnam as the bully. He also saw the spread of communism as an international bully. It would be disrespectful of Russ and all those who fought in Vietnam to not appreciate that they were standing up against bullying and putting themselves in harm's way to stop it – to serve and protect.

Mapping to See More Completely

When we see a person, organization, or nation overpower another and act cruelly toward them, we might call them a bully. The cruel acts could be so hurtful to us or those we love that we cannot see beyond the behavior. The person or nation is just a bully. That's all that needs to be said. "Let's stop the bullying."

Placing Bullying On a Map

In a Polarity Map, the lower quadrants (-B) and (-D) are places for things we consider negative and that need to be confronted. In *Figure 3* I have put the Bully with our Cruel acts in the lower left quadrant (-B).

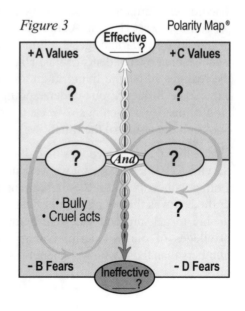

Figure 3   Polarity Map®

Effective ___?

+A Values   +C Values

?   ?

? And ?

• Bully
• Cruel acts   ?

- B Fears   - D Fears

Ineffective ___?

The question marks in the other seven spaces represent what is missing. Even if our description of our bullying acts of cruelty is accurate, we know, from a polarity perspective, that being accurate without being complete is a set-up.

"Anger Floats on a Sea of Fear" ~ Newt Fink

One of my mentors, Newt Fink, asserted that anger floats on a sea of fear. When you see an angry person or nation, you can appreciate that there is a fear below the anger. This awareness contributes to seeing the angry person or country as more than angry.[R82] They are also afraid. With this understanding, we can appreciate that the fear within each of the downside quadrants could show up as anger. When we experience the anger and the cruel acts coming out of the anger, it is easy to overlook the fear under the anger. The fear is important. Within a Polarity Map, the fear is connected to a value that is being threatened. The stronger the value, the stronger the fear. The fear can feed the anger that can lead to acts of cruelty we call bullying.

None of this is inevitable. Being fearful does not have to lead to being angry. Being angry does not have to lead to being cruel. What I am describing is a way to understand how we find ourselves being cruel to each other. Hopefully, the understanding will help reduce our own movement toward becoming a cruel bully and improve our effectiveness when addressing cruel, bullying behavior by others.

In *Figure 4* we can see a more complete map. Notice that the Greater Purpose Statement (GPS), at the top, and the Deeper Fear, at the bottom, are partially filled out. You can fill in the blank with whatever would work for you. For example, your GPS might be: Effective <u>Parent</u>, <u>Partner</u>, <u>Leader</u>, <u>Organization</u>, or <u>Nation</u>. The Deeper Fear would be the same word after "Ineffective."

Figure 4

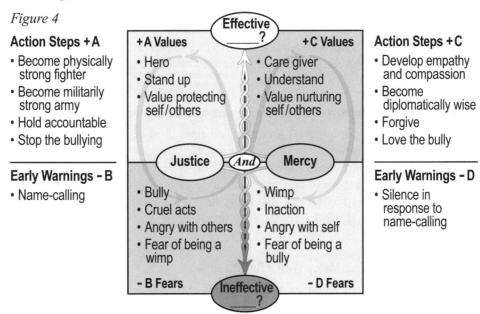

Action Steps +A	+A Values	+C Values	Action Steps +C
• Become physically strong fighter • Become militarily strong army • Hold accountable • Stop the bullying	• Hero • Stand up • Value protecting self/others	• Care giver • Understand • Value nurturing self/others	• Develop empathy and compassion • Become diplomatically wise • Forgive • Love the bully

Effective ___?

Justice *And* Mercy

Early Warnings – B			Early Warnings – D
• Name-calling	• Bully • Cruel acts • Angry with others • Fear of being a wimp	• Wimp • Inaction • Angry with self • Fear of being a bully	• Silence in response to name-calling

– B Fears   Ineffective ___?   – D Fears

In the lower left quadrant (-B) we see a Bully doing something cruel to another person. It might be an Early Warning like "Name-calling" (EW -B). They may appear angry, which we know is floating on a sea of fear. But what is the Bully afraid of? Being seen as a Wimp (-D). The Bully is "stuck" in the downside of Justice, doing cruel acts toward others because she/they/he has been "hooked" by a strong value of standing up for themselves (+A) and an equally strong fear of being seen as a wimp (-D). This value/fear diagonal combined with *either/Or*-thinking makes it very difficult for the bully to access the upside of the Mercy pole in which the bully would be a Care Giver and have some compassion and Understanding for others (+C).

Seeing more than the bullying behavior is like seeing additional layers:

- We see a person **behaving cruelly** – we label this person a Bully.

- Under their cruelty is anger – this person is **angry.**

- Under their anger is fear – this person is **frightened.**

- The fear is that something this person values is being threatened – in this case, the Bully values **standing up for him/her/their self** and is afraid of being **seen as a wimp.** As a way to confirm to themselves and to others that they are not wimps, they will identify someone else as a wimp and beat them up. *Or,* they can identify someone else as a bully and beat them up. This second option has a double advantage: not only are they demonstrating that they are not wimps, they are "heroes" protecting others from "bullies."

I will explore this more completely in *Chapter 21*. For now, it is just important to appreciate that a person or nation doing cruel things is more than the cruel things they are doing. There are powerful values and fears at play which need to be understood and addressed. The cruelty needs to be stopped (Justice) *And* the person or nation needs to be seen as more than the cruel things they are doing or have done (Mercy).

All Models and Accompanying Principles are Simplistic and Inadequate

Life is richer, more complicated and nuanced than the Polarity Map and set of polarity "realities" implies. Granting their limits, the question is whether they might be useful in dealing more effectively with our rich, complicated, and nuanced lives.[R83] I have found them to be useful and hope you will as well. I mention this at this time because I recognized that bullying by a person or a nation is more complicated than what can be contained within *Figure 4*. And, the polarity lens can be helpful.

Leveraging Justice *And* Mercy With a Bully

It is important to recognize that all four quadrants of the Justice *And* Mercy polarity in *Figure 4* are in us. Each of us has, within us, the capacity to Stand up to protect ourselves and others (+A); to Understand and be Nurturing to ourselves and others (+C); to be cruel to ourselves and others (–B); and to be silent and inactive when standing up is needed (–D).

Some of my proudest moments have been when I have stood up against cruelty as best I could (+A), or when I have brought understanding and compassion to those in need of it (+C). The moments I feel most badly about are when I have been cruel (–B), or when I have stood by silently as cruelty was happening to others (–D).

1. In other words, the first point in dealing effectively with bullying is to recognize the bully within ourselves.

2. The second point is to recognize that the person or nation doing the bullying is more than a bully – much more. If I could see them completely, love would be the result.

3. The third point is to stand up against the bullying which includes Action Steps to support the upside of the Justice pole (AS +A).

4. The fourth point is that accountability and standing up against bullying (+A) must be accompanied by love with forgiveness (+C). Bullying is not transformed by bullying the bully.

What Do You Do When You Think a Country is Acting Like a Bully?

Let's return to Russ, who died in Vietnam. From Russ's perspective, he enlisted because he saw the North of Vietnam as a bully and that the spread of communism was a bullying process with global implications. Russ saw himself in the upside of the Justice pole where he was Standing up and giving his life to serve and protect his country and those needing help in the South of Vietnam (+A). He was a true hero. And, he was more than a hero: He was a loving husband and proud son; a man who had shifted his dreams from becoming a minister to becoming a writer looking toward his Vietnam experience as a way to understand and empathize with those involved in the tragedy of war; a loyal friend that you could count on; a man who loved opera; a man with a dry sense of humor whose twinkling eyes gave him away.

I saw the war differently. I saw my country as a bully in violation of international law. I didn't want Russ or anyone else to die in that war. I did what I could to stop it. I also saw myself in the upside of the Justice pole attempting to stand up against what I thought was wrong and to protect against the cruelty that was happening to soldiers and their families on both sides and to Vietnamese civilians (+A).

This book is not about who was right. This book is about seeing the North of Vietnam as more than a bully *And* seeing my country as more than a bully. When we cannot see the more, we find ourselves becoming cruel in the name of standing up against it. For example, some people from the "Peace Movement" of which I was a part, engaged in name calling and disrespect for the men, women, and non-binary soldiers who fought in Vietnam when they returned home rather than thanking them for their service. What started off as standing up against the war (+A) became cruelty to those returning (-B). What is it like to risk your life and watch your buddies die to protect people back home and to return only to have them call you a "baby killer?" The impact of this cruelty to returning men and women can only be known by them. Some of us supposedly standing up against bullying had become the bully. They, the peace activists, like everyone else, need to be seen as more than these acts of cruelty.

Summary

Justice *And* Mercy is an ancient polarity that shows up in virtually all of our religious traditions. There are many names for the two poles, but what they all have in common is a sense of being accountable for our actions through rules with consequences *And* being loved in spite of our violation of the rules through grace with forgiveness.

Love is a result of seeing ourselves and others more completely: the parts we show, the parts we hide, and the whole of our life experience. A polarity lens can help us see more completely, increasing our capacity to love.

The bully we see is not just out there. The bully is in us. So is the caregiver, the one standing up and the one who is silent when speaking up is needed. None of us, no person, organization, and nation, is above accountability (Justice). And fortunately, none of us is below forgiveness (Mercy).

I want to conclude this summary with a poem by Thich Nhat Hanh. He is a Buddhist monk from Vietnam who has an ability to see himself in others and to see them more completely, enhancing his capacity to love.

Please Call Me by My True Names

Do not say that I'll depart tomorrow—
even today I am still arriving.

Look deeply: every second I am arriving
to be a bud on a Spring branch,
to be a tiny bird, with still-fragile wings,
learning to sing in my new nest,
to be a caterpillar in the heart of a flower,
to be a jewel hiding itself in a stone.

I still arrive, in order to laugh and to cry,
to fear and to hope,
the rhythm of my heart is the birth and death
of all that are alive.

I am the mayfly metamorphosing
on the surface of the river,
and I am the bird which, when Spring comes,
arrives in time to eat the mayfly.

I am the frog swimming happily
in the clear water of a pond,
and I am the grass-snake
that silently feeds itself on the frog.

I am the child in Uganda, all skin and bones,
my legs as thin as bamboo sticks.
And I am the arms merchant,
selling deadly weapons to Uganda.

I am the twelve-year-old girl,
refugee on a small boat,
who throws herself into the ocean
after being raped by a sea pirate.
And I am the pirate,
my heart not yet capable
of seeing and loving.

I am a member of the politburo,
with plenty of power in my hands.
And I am the man who has to pay his
"debt of blood" to my people
dying slowly in a forced labor camp.

My joy is like Spring, so warm
it makes flowers bloom all over the Earth.
My pain is like a river of tears,
so vast it fills the four oceans.

Please call me by my true names,
so I can hear all my cries and laughter at once,
so I can see that my joy and pain are one.

Please call me by my true names,
so I can wake up
and so the door of my heart can be left open,
the door of compassion.

~ Thich Nhat Hanh[49]

---

[49] Thich Nhat Han. *Call Me By My True Names: The Collected Poems.* Parallax Press, 1993.

New Realities in Chapter 18

Reality 81   The more our ability to love someone is contingent upon them doing something different, the more we have shifted the power to them in controlling our capacity to love.

Reality 82   Anger floats on a sea of fear. This means that an angry person is more than an angry person. They are also afraid. The fear is of losing something valued. Thus, an angry person or nation is afraid of losing something valued. This fear/value combination can be seen as a "point of view" made up of two diagonal quadrants in a Polarity Map®.

Reality 83   Life is richer, more complicated and nuanced than the Polarity Map and set of polarity "realities" implies. Granting their limits, the question is whether they might be useful in dealing more effectively with our rich, complicated, and nuanced lives.

Chapter 19
Justice *And* Mercy in Organizations

I have just completed a Leveraging Polarities presentation to 85 leaders at AMOCO in Chicago in the fall of 1992. A large, solid person comes forward to introduce himself as Dick Evans, Senior Vice President. Mr. Evans thanks me for the presentation and asks if there might be some polarities that would be especially relevant to union and management relations. He explains that this is important to him because his part of AMOCO has the highest percentage of union membership within the company.

I respond that two stand out immediately. The first is Employee Interests *And* Company Interests. I drew a simple map, like *Figure 1*, on a piece of paper.

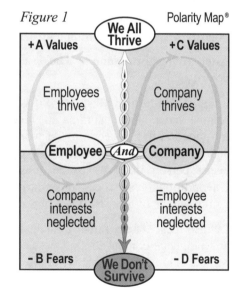

Figure 1 Polarity Map®

I point out that this polarity is present whether you have a union shop or not. There is always a natural tension between the interests of each employee (Part) *And* the interests of the company as a (Whole). Evan a not-for-profit, food co-op staffed with volunteer owners will be dealing with the tension between the interests of the volunteer owners *And* the interests of the co-op as a whole.

The early union movement can be seen as a self-correction in response to over-focusing on company interests to the relative neglect of Employee interests (-D). Unionization is neither just a "solution" in which Employees Thrive, as organized labor may see it (+A) or just a "problem" in which Company interests get neglected, as many owners and managers may see it (-B). With or without a union the question is the same: "How do we leverage the natural tension between Employee interests (+A) *And* Company interests (+C) in order that We All Thrive? (GPS)"

I shared an example of when this polarity was used in a Union contract negotiation. A manufacturing company in Detroit was a supplier to what was known at the time as "the big three": Ford, Chrysler, and General Motors. The employees were represented by the UAW. The owner told me it was time to renegotiate their contract and she was dreading it. Since the company had been created by her father shortly after World War II, they had never reached a new contract agreement before the old one expired. The hassles involved with not negotiating a new contract on time are significant. She asked if Polarity Thinking might help.

I had introduced Polarity Thinking to the owner and she asked me to present it to the leadership in her company. They, like Dick, saw it as potentially useful in working with the union. The manager decided to introduce Polarity Thinking to those involved, both management and union, in the new contract negotiations at the beginning of the process. They created an Employee Interests *And* Company Interests Polarity Map® <u>together</u> and kept it on the wall during the negotiations. Some elements of the contract showed up as Action Steps for gaining or maintaining the upside of Employee Interests. Others supported Company Interests. A few elements were high leverage Action Steps that showed up alongside both upsides. To the credit of all involved, the new contract agreement was completed well ahead of the end of the old contract and both sides felt good about the results. The manager was surprised and also grateful for taking less than an hour at the front end to create the Employee Interests *And* Company Interests Polarity Map with the Union representatives.

After giving this example, Dick said, "That's pretty clear. What is the second polarity?"

I said, "Conditional Respect *And* Unconditional Respect." These two kinds of respect have close parallels to Justice *And* Mercy. I mentioned this in the introduction to this section: "At work, it is important that every person show up and do a good job for which they can earn 'conditional respect' (Justice) *And*, every person deserves to be treated with 'unconditional respect' (Mercy). Unconditional respect cannot be earned. There are no conditions we must meet to gain this type of respect. It is a birthright."

I chose these names rather than Justice *And* Mercy because "respect" is a value and language common in business and industry. There is general agreement that respect is important. What is not often recognized is that respect can be broken out into two interdependent poles. When we talk about "respect" in an organization, we might be focusing on one form of respect and not the other. Not seeing respect as a polarity and leveraging the tension between its two poles can get us in trouble. Neither is sustainable, alone.

Figure 2 is a current version of the map I showed Dick from my first book.

The positive results from Conditional Respect (+A) are a sense of accomplishment and taking pride in what you have done; being able to recognize good work and to identify areas that need improvement and address them. All of the above requires measurement. The respect is conditional in that it is earned through measured results.

The positive results from Unconditional Respect (+C) are that each person experiences being treated with basic human dignity; they are listened to regardless of their status or performance. These forms of respect are independent of any measurement. For Unconditional Respect, measurement is irrelevant. There are no conditions attached to it.

For example, when I meet someone on the street or

Figure 2

We All Thrive

+A Values
- Pride in accomplishment: earned by doing
- Recognize good work
- Accountable to improve where needed
- Measurement essential

+C Values
- Experience our birthright of basic human dignity
- People listened to regardless of status
- Beyond performance
- Measurement irrelevant

Conditional Respect *And* **Unconditional Respect**

- Neglect human dignity
- People listened to based only on status
- Fear of mistakes
- People are "cogs": only a means to an end

- No pride in accomplishment
- Good work unnoticed
- No accountability for poor performance
- Measurement missing

- B Fears   **We Don't Survive**   **- D Fears**

am consulting with someone in an organization, I do not need to look at their performance review to know whether to treat them with basic respect. They cannot earn this respect and they do not need to. I believe each of us want and deserve this unconditional respect. The Beatles questioned what kind of respect they were getting from their throng of fans when they asked, "Will you still need me, will you still feed me, when I'm 64?" The question is, "Do you care about me only because I am in a band with hit songs or do you care about me in a way that will last when the hit songs are gone?" They were wondering, like the rest of us, whether they were getting any unconditional respect.

Just as it is tragic to see children attempting to earn the unconditional love they desire from their parents by performing well in school, it is tragic to see adults in organizations attempting to earn the unconditional respect they desire from others by performing well at work. In both cases, we are trying to gain something we strongly desire by performing well when it cannot be obtained through performance, no matter how great the performance.

In *Figure 2*, if we focus on Conditional Respect to the neglect of Unconditional Respect, we find ourselves neglecting the basic human dignity of others; we only listen to people based on status; we listen to our boss, but not those who work for us. We, and others, become afraid of making mistakes, and there is a sense that each of us is only a "cog" in a work machine, valued only for what we can contribute (-B).

This is one of two disasters that can happen with this polarity. The second disaster occurs when we over-focus on Unconditional Respect to the neglect of Conditional Respect. In this downside, we have no measures in place by which to take pride in our accomplishment; there is no way to recognize good work and we can't hold people accountable for poor work or to support them in improving by learning from mistakes (-D).

It is difficult to over-state how powerful this polarity is within the life of a person and an organization. The question remains the same as with all other polarities, "How do we maximize both upsides and minimize both downsides in order to create a virtuous cycle with the natural tension between the two poles?"

When negotiating a Union contract, it is easy to understand how owners and managers representing the company would assume that the contract was all about the conditions under which the employees will work, their pay, and their benefits (+A). This is half true. It is focused on the Conditional Respect pole, which is essential but not enough.

Equally powerful in the negotiating process is Unconditional Respect. This pole is focused on how the employee representatives feel they are being treated within the conversation about working conditions. Are they being treated with basic human dignity? Are they being listened to as if they had a head on their shoulders, a heart in their chest, and as much of a right to be at the table as those on the other side (+C)?

The same question could be asked about the treatment of management and ownership by the Union. Are they being treated with basic human dignity? Are they being treated as if they deserved basic respect independent of their status as a manager or owner?

Effective negotiators, whether company representatives or union representatives, are effective, in part, because they intuitively understand that both poles of this polarity are important. They show Unconditional Respect in the midst of talking about Conditional Respect items in the contract. If either side feels like they are not being given some Unconditional Respect, they will try to make up for the lack of Unconditional Respect by hard bargaining with the only pole left, Conditional Respect.

One of the most dramatic examples of workers demanding *both* Conditional *And* Unconditional Respect is the sign in *Figure 3*. "I AM A MAN."

Figure 3

Miami Herald / Tribune News Service via Getty Images

These men are sanitation workers in front of the Lorraine Motel in Memphis, Tennessee, where Dr. King was killed in 1968. Dr. King had gone to Memphis to support their strike.

Of course, the message is about working "conditions." *And*, it is about so much more. It is about Unconditional Respect which cannot be earned and need not be earned. It is a birthright. We all want it, we all deserve it.

Unconditional Respect, like Unconditional Love, is something available to give only after it has been received. Thus the paradox (polarity, dilemma): those unable to give unconditional respect need to experience it from us in order to give it to others.

Access to Russian Oil

A few weeks later, I was back at AMOCO presenting on polarities to another leadership group of 85 managers. This time, when I finished, Dick Evans came to the front of the room to tell the managers how he had been using Polarity Thinking since learning about it in the last session.

He told the following story, which I've paraphrased as best as I can remember:

"When Barry was here a few weeks ago, we talked about the polarity of Conditional Respect *And* Unconditional Respect and how it applied to Union/Management relations. It was clear to me that this polarity is very important. I arranged to have the map of this polarity enlarged and it is now hanging on my office wall as a reminder to pay attention to it."

"As some of you know, I was asked to lead the team that went to Russia to talk with them about access to their oil. Since the breakup of the Soviet Union, this was the first time that Russia had invited oil companies from around the world to come to Moscow. I wasn't sure how many oil companies they would give access to their oil, but I knew I wanted us to be one of them."

"I brought our team together in my office to plan our approach with the Russians. It occurred to me that the Conditional Respect *And* Unconditional Respect polarity would be at play in our negotiations. I pointed to this Polarity Map on my wall."

Dick then showed the Polarity Map on the big screen in front of the room.

"I asked the others on the team, 'Which pole do you think the other oil companies will focus on as they compete with us for access to Russia's oil?' We all agreed that the primary focus probably would be on Conditional respect, 'What are the *conditions* under which we can agree to have access to your oil?'"

"I suggested that we start with the other pole, Unconditional Respect. They asked, 'What would it look like to start the conversation on the Unconditional Respect pole?' I said, 'Let's look at the upside of Unconditional Respect. It seems to be about listening to people regardless of status and just respecting them as human beings with whom we share the planet.'"

"They said, 'OK, what do we listen about?'"

Dick smiled and some of the managers hearing his presentation laughed. He continued …

"I said, 'Look, the whole Soviet Union has just collapsed. Let's find out how the collapse has affected them and their families. Let's just try to understand what they have been going through since the breakup.'"

"They said, 'OK, how long do we listen?'"

Dick smiled again, and others in the room laughed as they imagined that they could have asked a similar question had they been in his office as a member of the team. Dick continued.

"We were asking ourselves when we would shift poles from Unconditional Respect to Conditional Respect. When we shifted poles, the primary emphasis would be on the conditions for access. It was quickly clear to all of us that we were the guests and that we did not shift to the Conditional Respect pole until our hosts invited us to shift."

"I am telling you this story because AMOCO is the only company that got access to Russian oil in this round of discussions. When we finished our meeting with them they said, 'We want to work with you. You are the only ones who have shown us respect.'"

"This is worth billions of dollars to AMOCO."

Dick raised up a copy of my book which they all had received and slammed it firmly on the podium in front of him while saying …

"This Polarity Thinking is good stuff. I encourage you to read it."

I was sitting in the back of the room listening to Dick tell this story and was thinking, "I wish I had that one on tape!"

It is worth pointing out that Dick Evans is the one who made the connection between how the Conditional Respect *And* Unconditional Respect polarity could be useful in negotiating for access to Russian oil. He combined his life experience with the Polarity Map and a brief application discussion with me to create a very significant agreement between AMOCO and the Russian government.

The same can be said for the manager I mentioned earlier in this chapter who negotiated the new contract with the UAW which was on time for the first time. He had attended a one-day workshop on Polarity Thinking and combined it with his life experience to make a positive difference in his relationship with the Union.

You can combine your life experience with a polarity lens and make a difference in areas that are important to you.

Summary

The polarity of Justice *And* Mercy has a parallel in organizational language which I call Conditional Respect *And* Unconditional Respect. Many companies talk about the importance of respect when listing their values. I agree. *And*, it is helpful to recognize that there are two kinds of respect, both of which are essential:

1. Conditional Respect, which you earn by doing good work for which you can be proud. Measurement is necessary.

2. Unconditional Respect, which is a birthright. It cannot be earned and need not be earned. Attempting to earn it is, at best, a waste of time. Measurement is irrelevant.[R84]

New Realities in Chapter 19

Reality 84   There are two kinds of "Respect," both of which are essential:

1. Conditional Respect, which you earn by doing good work for which you can be proud. Measurement is necessary.

2. Unconditional Respect, which is a birthright. It cannot be earned and need not be earned. Attempting to earn it is, at best, a waste of time. Measurement is irrelevant.

Chapter 20
Justice *And* Mercy Within a Nation

It's 1995, less than a year after Apartheid finally ended in South Africa. Nelson Mandela, who had served 27 years in prison for his struggle against Apartheid, is now president. This historic shift in power created an opportunity for black South Africans and their white allies to get some "Justice." But what would that mean? How would it be accomplished?

In his book, <u>No Future Without Forgiveness</u>[50], Archbishop Desmond Tutu describes the thinking and the process they went through in seeking "Restorative Justice." What they created became known as the "Truth *And* Reconciliation" process. It is a good example of a nation leveraging the polarity of Justice *And* Mercy. As in *Chapter 19*, the names of the poles are different but the underlying phenomenon is the same. On one hand, there is a need for accountability (Truth/Justice) *And*, on the other hand, there is a need for love and forgiveness (Reconciliation/Mercy).

It is no accident that Archbishop Tutu was invited to lead the process. During the brutality of the Apartheid years, he stood on his faith tradition, with a strong voice against Apartheid, demanding Justice for all. *And*, he brought something else from his faith tradition. He brought Mercy. This was the combination that Nelson Mandela and others intuitively knew would be important for the nation to move ahead.

It was not just the faith tradition of Justice *And* Mercy that informed the Truth *And* Reconciliation process. It was also their exploration of what Germany and Chile had done in response to similar situations of addressing a brutal past.

I would like to share a summary of that process laid out in a Polarity Map® with Action Steps in *Figure 1*. This is a good example of a group of people using their tacit wisdom about "*And*-thinking" to leverage a polarity without having heard explicitly about "polarities." Seeing the need for *both* Truth *And* Reconciliation was key. It was also valuable to recognize that *both* "Truth" *And* "Reconciliation" brought important upsides (+A, +C). Also, each had their own limit or downsides (-B, -D).

---

[50] Tutu, Desmond. *No Future Without Forgiveness*. Crown Publishing Group, 2000.

Figure 1

Action Steps

- Have people come forward and publicly own up to abuses they committed under apartheid
- Bring the victims and the victims family to the session in which the abuses to them or their family is admitted

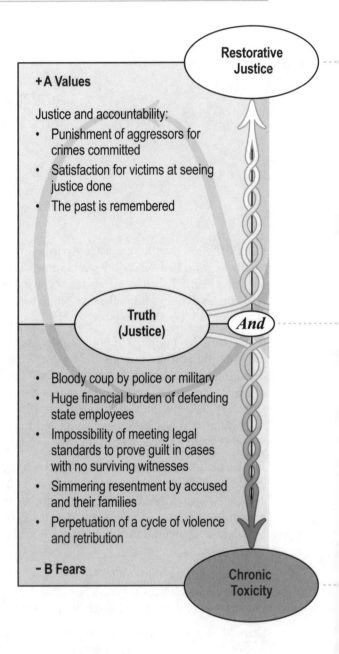

+A Values

Justice and accountability:
- Punishment of aggressors for crimes committed
- Satisfaction for victims at seeing justice done
- The past is remembered

Restorative Justice

Truth (Justice)

And

- Bloody coup by police or military
- Huge financial burden of defending state employees
- Impossibility of meeting legal standards to prove guilt in cases with no surviving witnesses
- Simmering resentment by accused and their families
- Perpetuation of a cycle of violence and retribution

– B Fears

Chronic Toxicity

Polarity Map®

Restorative Justice

+C Values

Peace and reconciliation:
- Focus on forgiveness, healing and the future
- Avoid provoking a military coup
- Save limited funds to build for the future
- Address the needs of the historically disadvantaged

And

Reconciliation (Mercy)

- National amnesia
- Simmering resentments by the victims of apartheid as their experiences were denied once again
- A past that continues to haunt because it has not been dealt with adequately

- D Fears

Chronic Toxicity

Action Steps

- Offer amnesty for abuses to which offenders have publicly admitted during the process
- Give victims and victims families an opportunity to forgive and lighten the load of resentment and rage
- Give the abusers an opportunity for admission and forgiveness

His summary of their thinking follows the normal flow of energy through the four quadrants of the map. He starts with the benefits of Justice (+A); followed by its limits (-B); then moving to the benefits of Mercy (+C); followed by its limits (-D). He then talks about the Action Steps they took. Some steps were intended to gain the benefits of the Truth pole (+A) *And* some were intended to gain the benefits of the Reconciliation pole (+C).

Learning From Germany and Chile

Truth (Justice) was the first focus (+A). They looked to Germany and the Nuremburg Trials. The benefits of those trials were that they responded to the demand for Justice and Accountability: punishment of aggressors for crimes committed; satisfaction for victims at seeing justice done; and support for remembering the past.

However, there were clear limits to focusing on the Nuremburg approach to Justice when applied to South Africa in 1995 (-B). There was a danger of a bloody coup by the police or military who were white and in control of all the weapons; there would be a huge financial burden on the government in defending state employees who were accused; the impossibility of meeting legal standards in the many cases in which there were no surviving witnesses; simmering resentment by the accused and their families; and the perpetuation of a cycle of violence and retribution.

Reconciliation (Mercy) became the second focus. With the limits of the Nuremburg Trials in mind (-B), the natural self-correction, from a polarity perspective, seemed to reside in Chile. They had given General Amnesty for those who committed human rights abuses during the 1973–1990 dictatorship of Gen. Augusto Pinochet. When thinking about its application to South Africa's situation, there were benefits worth considering (+C): it responded to the desire for peace and reconciliation; it provided healing of wounds and moving toward the future; it would avoid provoking a police or military coup; and it would allow limited funds to be used for the future and for addressing the needs of the historically disadvantaged.

Though these potential benefits were attractive, there was a downside to focusing on the Mercy pole alone (-D): there was a danger of "National Amnesia" – acting as if the crimes of Apartheid had never happened; simmering resentments by the victims of Apartheid as their painful experiences, denied for so long, would once again be denied; and concern for a past that would continue to haunt South Africa because it had not been faced and dealt with adequately.

Archbishop Tutu and the others working on the Truth *And* Reconciliation project knew that both the Nuremburg Trial approach and the General Amnesty approach had something important to offer but neither of them, alone, was desirable or sustainable. Though they may not have known about the writings on Polarity, Paradox, or Dilemma, they did know that the two options they studied were a false choice. Intrinsic polarities are always a "false choice."[R85]

There are such things as "chosen polarities," which are different than "intrinsic polarities."[R86] In this book, I am focusing on "intrinsic polarities." There are situations in which we can choose one pole or the other but have decided to choose both. Once we decide to include both, we can put the two poles on a Polarity Map and all the "realities" will apply except for it being unavoidable, unsolvable, indestructible, and unstoppable. For example, a country like Britain can choose to be a part of the European Union as long as present members of the EU agree. When that happens, a chosen version of the Part *And* Whole polarity is at play and all polarity realities apply. Yet it is not an intrinsic polarity because the country can decide to leave the EU, thus ending the formal interdependence created by joining. At the same time, as long as you are a country, you are a part of a larger whole (all of humanity) that cannot be avoided by leaving the EU. That Part *And* Whole is an intrinsic polarity which will be an ongoing tension whether in the EU or not.

Justice *And* Mercy is an intrinsic polarity which makes either pole a "false choice."

Given the reality of needing some form of both Truth (Justice) *And* Reconciliation (Mercy), the question for Archbishop Tutu was the same question posed by all polarities, "How do we maximize the benefits of each pole?"

Action Steps

Working with a Polarity Map, there will need to be some action steps to gain or maintain the upside of each of the poles. Here, again, it is easy to organize Archbishop Tutu's description of the Truth *And* Reconciliation process into two sets of actions that support one upside or the other of the Polarity Map in *Figure 1*.

Seeking Truth (Justice)

There were two actions designed to get the benefits of the Truth pole:

1. Invite people to come forward and publicly own up to the abuses they committed under Apartheid.
2. Bring the victim and victim's family to the session in which the abuses to them or their family are admitted.

Seeking Reconciliation (Mercy)

And there were three actions designed to get the benefits of the Reconciliation pole:

1. Offer amnesty for abuses to which offenders have publicly admitted during the process.
2. Give victims and victims' families an opportunity to forgive and lighten the load of resentment and rage.
3. Give the abusers an opportunity for admission and forgiveness.

This process allowed for some amazing transformations to happen. One example was the admission, to her parents, by two South African police officers who had murdered their daughter. She had come from the United States to work for the ending of Apartheid. They described what they had done and where their daughter was buried.

The parents knew their daughter would want them to engage in this Truth *And* Reconciliation process and to offer forgiveness, which they were able to do. The two officers, in response, created an organization in the daughter's name through which they dedicated their lives to addressing the residual issues from the brutal history of Apartheid.

They were murderers *And* they were more than murderers. The Truth *And* Reconciliation process allowed us to see the "more" and for them to be the "more."

Restorative Justice

The movement for Restorative Justice and the use of the Truth *And* Reconciliation process has spread all over the world. Like all polarities, Justice *And* Mercy is scalable. It can be used by each of us, individually, in our daily interactions and it can be used by an organization or a nation.

Summary

The polarity of Justice *And* Mercy was leveraged well by Archbishop Desmond Tutu and the Truth *And* Reconciliation Commission in South Africa after the end of Apartheid. It is a good example of leveraging this polarity at the national level of system. It is also a good example of leveraging it well at the individual level. Individual victims and individual family members of victims *And* individual perpetrators were able to be face-to-face with each other in a way that served them both. It also served the country of South Africa. The process started in South Africa now is serving victims and perpetrators in many parts of the world.

It is worth pointing out that the Truth *And* Reconciliation process grew out of both ancient wisdom from our religious traditions affirming *both* Justice *And* Mercy and learning from the application experiences of both Germany and Chile.

Archbishop Tutu is another example, like you, of a person who was successful, in part because of his intuitive ability to leverage a polarity. He did this even though he may never have heard of "polarities." I refer to this example as "like you" because I assume that there are times in your life when you have done something for which you are proud. It is an accomplishment or a contribution you have made, whether small or large. Because polarities are so present in our lives, I have a hunch that you were intuitively leveraging one or more polarities that contributed to your success. Maybe you were: "taking care of yourself *And* taking care of others" or, "pursuing a vision *And* staying grounded in reality" or, "holding your children accountable for their actions *And* loving them unconditionally" or, "getting the job done *And* building relationships."

My hope is that you give yourself credit for having experience, like Archbishop Tutu, in leveraging polarities fairly well before reading this book. I also hope the Polarity Map and realties make your implicit understanding of polarities explicit so you can be more intentional about leveraging them.

New Realities in Chapter 20

Reality 85   Intrinsic polarities are always a "false choice."

Reality 86   There are such things as "chosen polarities" which are different than "intrinsic polarities."

Chapter 21
Justice And Mercy on the Planet

A young person straps on a bomb, walks into a crowded marketplace and detonates it. Many are instantly killed and many more are wounded. Some of the wounded will be impaired for the rest of their lives. Families of the dead and wounded are in pain. What is going on? How do we become so cruel to each other and ourselves?

Understanding is Not Condoning

Our effort to understand how we become so cruel should not be confused with condoning it. On the contrary, it is part of our effort to reduce the violence to ourselves and others. Leveraging the polarity of Justice *And* Mercy can help. This polarity, like all others, has a natural tension between its two poles which can become a vicious cycle, leading toward suicide bombings, or it can become a virtuous cycle, leading toward Restorative Justice. This is true both in addressing the individual suicide bomber and the global issue of targeting the "evil other" for attack.

"Good" and "Evil" Through a Polarity Lens

I am proposing that "Good" comes in pairs that show up in a Polarity Map® as the two upsides. "Evil" also comes in pairs that show up in a Polarity Map as the two downsides. Paradoxically, the pursuit of one "Good" without also pursuing its interdependent partner, a second "Good," leads to an unanticipated "Evil."[R87]

Let's take a look at how this might work. All communities have laws guiding the conduct of its members. These laws may be written on tablets of stone or unwritten "understandings" that are passed down from one generation to the next. These laws are "good" and necessary. That's why we have them. They help us avoid the "evil" of lawlessness and chaos. At the same time, laws without consequences are meaningless. If there is no enforcement of the laws, they do not perform their function. Thus, laws with consequences are a "good" and necessary part of living in a community. They can help bring Justice.

If we look at "Good" and "Evil" from an *Or* mindset, the question becomes, "Do you choose Good *Or* Evil?" When put this way, it is clear that we want to move away from "Evil" and toward "Good." We thus find ourselves on a single line continuum with "Evil" at one end and a natural desire to move toward "Good" at the other end. In *Figure 1*, we see a continuum with Lawlessness and Chaos on the left which could be labeled "Evil." We have an arrow representing the desire to move from "Evil" toward "Good" which, in this case is Law Abiding Justice.

Figure 1

Figure 2 shows three assumptions about the move from "Evil" toward "Good" which are very logical within *Or*-thinking:

Figure 2

1. The more you move away from "Evil" the more you move toward "Good."

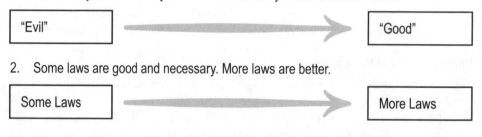

2. Some laws are good and necessary. More laws are better.

3. Consequences are necessary. More/harsher consequences are better.

It is easy to see how, in the pursuit of the "Good" associated with Justice, we can find ourselves with more and more laws with harsher and harsher consequences. But what if the "Good" we are pursuing were seen as one upside of a polarity?

If we put *Figure 1* within the Mercy *And* Justice polarity, it would look like *Figure 3*.

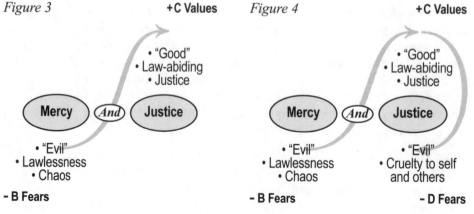

Figure 3   +C Values   *Figure 4*   +C Values

Seeing "Good," Law Abiding Justice (+C) as the upside of a pole within a polarity helps us anticipate, in *Figure 4*, the limits of Justice alone (-D). Though Justice is "Good" and necessary, Justice without Mercy leads to Cruelty to Ourselves and to Others, which is another form of "Evil" (-D). We do not have to be a "bad" person to become cruel to ourselves and others; we just have to pursue one form of "Good" (+C) as a solution to one form of "Evil" (-B).

This is how, as a 13-year-old, I seriously considered poking my eyes out to avoid being attracted to girls. This is how we find ourselves stoning a woman to death for being pregnant when not married. And we do it with self-righteous indignation! It is also how we find ourselves in a vicious cycle leading to suicide bombings.

Figure 5 shows the complete infinity loop with a Greater Purpose and Deeper Fear.

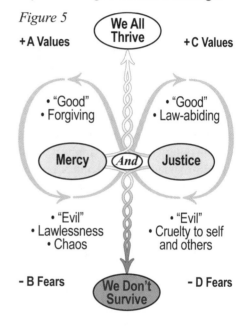

Figure 5

What is needed in this situation is the interdependent "Good." We do not stop our pursuit of being "Law Abiding" (+C). We supplement this necessary pursuit with being "Forgiving" (+A). An example of this, within the Christian tradition, is Jesus' response to stoning in the Bible: "Let the person among you who is without sin be the first to throw a stone at her." John 8:7 International Standard Version.

In the case of a suicide bombing, *Or*-thinking without *And*-thinking leads to a vicious cycle from the tension between Mercy *And* Justice. We experience both Chaotic Lawlessness (-B) and Cruelty to Self and Others (-D). This leads to the Deeper Fear in which We (both the suicide bomber and the other victims of the blast) Don't Survive.

Mercy Without Justice is Equally Problematic

Just as Mercy is a necessary partner with Justice, Justice is a necessary partner with Mercy. If we pursue the "Good" of being Forgiving (+A) to the neglect of the "Good" of being Law Abiding (+C), we find ourselves tolerating lawlessness and not holding ourselves and others accountable for our actions (-B). The question becomes, "How do we leverage the natural tension between Mercy *And* Justice?" Put another way, "How do we create a virtuous cycle in which We All Thrive rather than get ourselves caught in a vicious cycle in which We Don't Survive?" Seeing the underlying polarity is an important first step.

Dr. Martin Luther King, Jr. spoke about the need for *both* Love (Mercy) *And* Power (Justice): "Power without love is reckless and abusive, and love without power is sentimental and anemic. Power at its best is love implementing the demands of justice, and justice at its best is power correcting everything that stands against love."

Notice how readily this quote fits within a polarity infinity loop in *Figure 6 (read sequentially 1–4)*. Dr. King is aware of the limits of either pole "without" the other (1) and (2). He is also aware of how each upside is the necessary self-correction for the limits of the other pole (3) and (4).

This is another example of the Polarity Map as a wisdom organizer. The wisdom is in the experience, knowledge, and intuition of Dr. King. The Polarity Map helps us appreciate that this is another interdependent pair in which all of our polarity realities apply. I would like to expand on Dr. King's point in *Figure 6* that "Power without love is reckless and abusive."

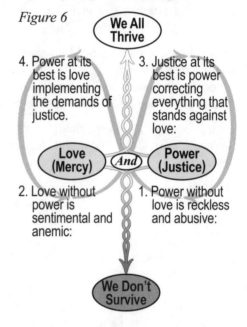

Figure 6

We All Thrive

4. Power at its best is love implementing the demands of justice.

3. Justice at its best is power correcting everything that stands against love:

Love (Mercy)   *And*   Power (Justice)

2. Love without power is sentimental and anemic:

1. Power without love is reckless and abusive:

We Don't Survive

Our Fear of Owning Our Own "Shortcomings" – Justice Without Mercy Leads to Deflection and Projection

As I mentioned earlier, virtually all Religious Communities have, within their traditions, some version of Mercy *And* Justice. When, within the Religious Community, there is an over-focus on Justice to the neglect of Mercy, there is an increase in laws and an increase in the harshness of the consequences for breaking those laws. When this happens, a culture is created in which it is increasingly difficult to take responsibility for our "own" shortcomings.[R88]

We end up with so many laws that we find ourselves in violation of them from moment to moment. It is not just acting correctly that is required, it is thinking correctly. The consequences of admitting to falling short have become so harsh (eternal life in hell or getting my hand cut off for stealing an apple) that I can't admit my shortcomings to anyone. Eventually, I can't admit some of them to myself. So what do I do with parts of myself I can't "own" or "admit" are a part of me? I deflect what I can't own away from me and project it on to someone else or another group. The "evil" I cannot own becomes the "evil other."

This is a natural process we all learn growing up. For example, as a child, my mother might find some money missing from her purse and would ask me if I had taken it. I could simply say, "No, I didn't." This is a form of deflection in which I take the pressure off me by claiming innocence. It takes the pressure off, a little.

But my mother would not be sure I was telling the truth, so I wouldn't be completely off the hook. If, however, my older sister Beverly later explained that she had taken the money to buy some groceries, I would be totally free and clear. My mother would even apologize for doubting me! My claim that "It was not me" (deflection) would really get its power when combined with identifying someone else: "It was Beverly" (projection).

This insight gets reinforced through books and movies of mysteries in which we know that someone claiming innocence (deflection) may be guilty until we discover that it was someone else who committed the crime. Once the real culprit is identified, everyone else who was a suspect is back in good standing. All these experiences teach us that just denying one's guilt is not nearly as effective as denying one's guilt (deflection) combined with identifying a "guilty other" (projection).

Thus, we all learn what to do with the things about ourselves that we are unable to own: deflect away from ourselves and project onto another person or group. Once we have projected our shortcomings on to the "other," we need to seal the deal by standing on a platform of self-righteous indignation. "They" become a target of our rage. We can't let them get away with this shortcoming. In the name of all that is good and just, we find ourselves handing out the stones and throwing them, we hand out the guns and start shooting, we hand out the suicide vests and go to market, we build planes and start bombing, we hand out rockets and start launching. God is on our side as we fight the "good fight" against the "evil other."

Below is a summary of the sequence of deflecting, then projecting, and then getting self-righteous about it. The "other" could be as small as another person or as large as another country.

The "other" as a person: When I can't own my own shortcomings (thoughts and actions related to my own sexuality), I am more likely to identify an unmarried, pregnant woman and demonstrate to myself and others that:

1. Deflection – "I am not a person guilty of anything in relation to my own sexuality."
2. Projection –"She is the guilty one. Let's stone her." We literally project stones at her. (The projection could also be name-calling, spitting, hitting, or kicking, etc.)
3. Self-righteous –"I am so upset by her behavior; I am filled with self-righteous indignation. You can see, by my indignation, how far removed I am from doing anything like what she has done."

The "other" as a country: When we, as a country, can't own our country's shortcomings, we are more likely to identify another country as an "evil empire."

1. Deflection –"We are not guilty of anything as a county."
2. Projection – "They are the guilty ones. Let's bomb them."
3. Self-righteous –"We are filled with self-righteous indignation with the other country's behavior. You can see, by our indignation, how far removed we are from doing anything like what they have done."

We Need Justice With Mercy

I find myself doing some version of this every day. When I see myself as someone trying to "make a difference," or to "make a better world," I easily get very judgmental about those I think are making things worse. The other person or group or country becomes the "problem." As I pursue Justice, I stand against injustice. My pursuit of Justice, like yours and that of your group and your country, is essential. *And*, we need Mercy to keep our pursuit of Justice from becoming a new form of injustice.

Remember the young person mentioned at the beginning of the chapter who strapped on a bomb and went to market to kill themselves and others? They were, from their perspective, doing "good" in the face of "evil." The same could be said for other acts of violence we impose on each other daily all over the world. We self-righteously shoot abortion clinic doctors, fly planes into a World Trade Center, invade other countries, conduct the holocaust, and implement mass incarceration of African American men. This is what "Justice" looks like without "Mercy" and what "Mercy" looks like without "Justice." This is why it is so important to see Justice *And* Mercy as an interdependent pair. We need *both*.

Who Makes the Best Projection Screen?

Whether I am an individual unable to own my own shortcomings, or a group, or a nation, what is not within our capacity to own as a part of ourselves will be deflected away from ourselves and projected on to a targeted "other." To project on the "other," just like a movie projector needs a good screen for a clear picture, we need a good projection screen to most effectively deflect from ourselves and on to an "other."

Two qualities for a good projection screen are: (1) the person or group on which I want to project must be readily available, and (2) the person or group must be obviously "not me." They have to be obviously "not me" to ensure that others will not confuse me with the person or group on which I want to project.

The less able I am to own my own shortcomings, the more I need to have a screen to project them on and the more I need the screen to be clear. It has to be absolutely clear who "we are" and who "they are."

For example, as a white male in the United States, the two most available and obviously "not me" groups are people of color and women. This is a significant basis for my own racism and sexism and for racism and sexism on the planet. We will explore this more thoroughly in *Section Eight*.

The Star of David

During the rise of the Third Reich in Germany, the Jews became a projection screen for whatever the Nazi government and its followers did not want to own. As a projection screen, the Jews were available but it was not always obvious who was Jewish. This lack of clarity undermined the effectiveness of using Jews as a projection screen. It needed to be more obvious who were the "not us." This need was filled by requiring all Jews to wear a Star of David on their outer garment. The star made it clear whom to self-righteously hate, demean, and put in the ovens.

The "Evil Enemy" as a Projection Screen

One simple way to identify the "not me" on whom to project is to identify an "enemy" from whom we must protect ourselves, our loved ones, our way of life. Notice how easy it was in the paragraph above to identify the Nazi Party as needing to project on Jews. It is important for me and you to also recognize our possible need to make a projection screen of the WWII Nazi Party or present-day Neo-Nazis for parts of ourselves that we have trouble owning.

This brings us back to the beginning of the chapter with a focus on suicide bombings and how to stop them. It brings us to our "enemies." It brings us back to ourselves. It also brings us back to the polarity of Justice *And* Mercy.

Our "Not Me" is Me

In the effort to understand and reduce suicide bombings, it is important to appreciate that self-righteous indignation and doing "evil" in the pursuit of "good" is something that all of us have done, in our own way. The suicide bomber is giving up her/his/their life to fight the "evil other." There is a self-righteousness within this act that is not unlike my own country's invasion of Iraq. In both cases, many innocent civilians, let alone "fighters for justice," have become the casualties.

Mercy Supports Ownership

In order to own the suicide bomber in ourselves, we need to know that we are loved as we are. We need this message of Mercy to go along with the Justice we demand of ourselves and others. When I am loved in spite of my shortcomings, it is easier to own my shortcomings. This reduces my need to find an "other" on whom to project them.

To ask the question, "How do we stop the suicide bombings?" is to ask the questions, "How do we stop our invasion of one country by another?" "How do we stop our cruelty to each other?" I am suggesting that one underestimated and powerful element in responding to these questions is the polarity of Justice *And* Mercy. It is some version of stopping the bullying while acknowledging the bully in ourselves *And* loving ourselves and the bully. Loving the bully is about seeing the bully and ourselves more completely. In that effort to see another and ourselves more completely, a polarity lens will be helpful.

Standing With and Standing Against Without Standing Over

In *Figure 7* on the next page, we can see where taking a stand might fit within the polarity of Mercy *And* Justice. (1) Justice requires us to *stand with* those who are experiencing the abuse of power and to *stand against* those who are abusing power. (2) Mercy allows us to own our own abuse of power and to love ourselves and others as more than power abusers. (3) *Not standing with* those abused by power and *not standing against* those abusing power perpetuates the injustice because of an overfocus on Mercy to the neglect of Justice. (4) Self-righteously *standing over* those abusing power becomes our own abuse of power as we project on the "evil other." This is a result of over-focusing on Justice to the neglect of Mercy. In our own use of power, we need to *stand with* and *stand against* without *standing over*.

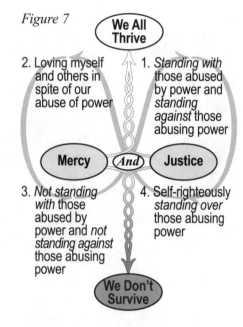

Figure 7

We All Thrive

2. Loving myself and others in spite of our abuse of power

1. *Standing with* those abused by power and *standing against* those abusing power

Mercy *And* **Justice**

3. *Not standing with* those abused by power and *not standing against* those abusing power

4. Self-righteously *standing over* those abusing power

We Don't Survive

In summary, none of us has a platform of self-righteous indignation on which to stand. Such a platform is based on two assumptions: That "we" are above accountability and that "they" are below forgiveness. All our religious traditions teach us a different truth about this polarity: We are all accountable *And* We are all loved as we are.

Leaders as Heroes and Villains

So far, I have talked about deflecting and projecting negative things (shortcomings) about ourselves that we have trouble owning. This part of our self, in dramatic terms, could be called the "villain" in us. We also have trouble owning our own goodness, our beauty, our preciousness, our greatness. When we have trouble owning those parts of ourselves, we will do the same thing we do with our shortcomings. We deflect and project the very best of ourselves onto an "other" who becomes our "hero."

Leaders make good projection screens. The leader stands out as a "not me" for the followers. He/she/they become an easy target for us to project the best of ourselves and become a hero or the worst of ourselves and become a villain. President Donald Trump, for example, has become a villain onto whom some of us project the worst of ourselves. At the same time, he has become a hero onto whom others of us project the best of ourselves. The question is, "Is he a Hero or a Villain?" The answer is, "Yes." Just as each of us is a hero and a villain. Think of the polarization that happens between us when my "Hero" is your "Villain" and the reverse.

When a leader does something quite unacceptable by both those for whom the leader has been a hero and those for whom the leader has been a villain, that leader is in trouble. The leader has reinforced the projection screen for those who already saw a villain. When we frame them as the villain, they can't do anything right.

If we acknowledge that they have done something right, it would mess with our projection screen and make it less easy for us to project the worst of ourselves onto them. In order to preserve our projection screen, we need to self-righteously pounce on our villain.

At the same time, the unacceptable behavior has created a problem for those of us seeing the leader as our hero. When we frame them as a hero, they can't do anything wrong. If we acknowledge that they have done something wrong, it would mess with our projection screen and make it less easy for us to project the best of ourselves onto them. In order to preserve our projection screen, we need to protect our hero. We assert that the non-hero behavior is not true of our hero. It must be lies or fake news.

The Flip

At the point where we can no longer deny the truth of the non-hero behavior by our hero, we can easily resent them for messing with our needed projection screen. They are no longer, for me, clearly a hero on whom I can project the best of me. The leader remains a "not me" projection screen but is no longer available as a "Hero" screen. If I can no longer project the hero in me onto a leader, that leader is very vulnerable to becoming the one on whom I project the villain in me. This is how leaders can flip from Hero to Villain. They are resented not only for doing something I consider wrong, but for destroying my much needed "Hero" projection screen. This helps us understand our cruelty toward people who were simplistic heroes that became simplistic villains.

People in Uniform as Heroes and Villains

People in uniform are also great projection screens, becoming our heroes or our villains. Uniforms identify who we are and give us a community to belong to. They give us a chance to not only belong but to be a part of the hero group with our hero leader at the top. The soldiers and leaders that are on "our side" become heroes. The soldiers and leaders that are on the "other side" become villains. This may help us out, psychologically, with our need to project parts of ourselves that we can't own but it is a source of a lot of the suffering we impose on each other.

The uniformed police officers in any community in the world are also easy targets for our projections. Seeing them as only heroes or only villains is as much a comment about us as it is about them.

The more we can own our own goodness and greatness *And* own our own shortcomings, the less we have a need for our Heroes to be pure goodness and greatness or our Villains to be pure evil. We can acknowledge that we are our heroes and we are our villains. This will not end our having heroes and villains. It just allows us to hold both our heroes and our villains accountable *And* to forgive both our heroes and our villains. Seeing ourselves, our heroes, and our villains completely results in love for all three. Therefore, a polarity lens – in this case the lens of Justice *And* Mercy – is so important for each of us and all of us.

Is the young suicide bomber a villain or a hero? Yes. Stopping them *And* loving them is part of the same interdependent pair: Justice *And* Mercy.

With the Polarity of Justice *And* Mercy, Religious Communities are a Part of the Problem and a Part of the Solution

Our Religions are a great resource for leveraging Justice *And* Mercy. It is our various religious communities (religions) that bring us the message of unconditional love (Mercy). Experiencing this unconditional love can be a great source for sharing this love with others. Unfortunately, in our religious communities, we often find ourselves over-focusing on Justice to the neglect of Mercy. This has led to extreme cruelty in the name of our religions. In addressing our cruelty to each other, it is easy to underestimate the influence of religious communities in the lives of individual suicide bombers and invading nations.

The Power Advantage Religious Communities Have Relative to State Communities

When dealing with suicide bombers, there is no "holding them accountable" beyond what they have already done to themselves. This leads us to focus on prevention rather than retribution. This prevention must be focused not just on individual suicide bombers but on the interface between our Religious Communities and our State Communities.

What I mean by Religious Communities are the different Religions or belief systems that have a community of "believers." What I mean by a State Community is a Nation State like India, Germany, or Brazil.

There are at least four areas in which Religious Communities have relatively more power or influence than State Communities. This power imbalance is an important consideration if we are a State Community attempting to effectively deal with a segment of a Religious Community whose behavior we want to address. Religious-based terrorism and suicide bombings are one example.

1.   While both Religious Communities and State Communities have laws for their members to live by, Religious Communities have leverage not available to State Communities (unless they are one and the same). Religious Communities have a claim on one's status not only during this life, but also after this life. This is huge for the believer within the Religious Community. In an effort to promote compliance with the rules (Justice), a State Community can threaten to lock their citizens up for as long as they want and in some countries, kill them for breaking the laws. But life in prison or the death penalty is the most powerful leverage State Communities have for controlling their citizens.

     Most Religious Communities, on the other hand, suggest to their members that what we do in this life has an impact on what happens to us after this life. The threats of "Eternal suffering in hell" or, by contrast, the "Eternal bliss of Heaven" become a powerful influence over the believers within a Religious Community. This influence cannot be matched by the State Community. For example, there was nothing in my being a 13-year-old citizen of the U.S. that would cause me to consider poking both my eyes out with a scissors in order to be a "good citizen." That form of self-imposed cruelty came from wanting to be a "good Lutheran!"

This type of cruelty to ourselves *and/or* others is more possible within the context of any Religious Community's influence over its members. It shows up when the polarity of Justice *And* Mercy gets over-focused on Justice to the relative neglect of Mercy. Though people will die and kill for their country, the power to influence such dramatic behavior is much stronger within our Religious Communities than within our State Communities.

2. A second difference is that State Communities attempt to control the behavior of its citizens through laws. Religious Communities, by contrast, attempt to control their members' behavior and their beliefs; their thinking. As a matter of fact, correct belief is a condition of membership. Thus the intended and real reach of control of those within the Religious Community is greater than that of State Communities.

3. A third difference is that Religious Communities believe in a "Higher Power" that is given priority over allegiance to the State Community when the two are in apparent conflict. This belief, which is a condition of membership in most religious communities, has demonstrated an amazing resilience against state community persecution throughout history. Here, again, the Power of a Religious Community over its members is relatively stronger than that of a State Community.

4. A fourth difference is that State Communities, by definition, have national borders while Religious Communities have no such limitation. Religious Communities can operate in any country in the world. This is true even if they are explicitly banned by the State Community. The Religious Community will just go underground within the "banning" State Community and get support from their members in other countries. This global reach and ability to operate from within many countries is another significant influence advantage for Religious Communities.

Given these four influence advantages that Religious Communities have over State Communities, fighting against a radical element within a Religious Community is a greater challenge than a State Community might appreciate. Fighting a Religious Community, or a radical element of a Religious Community, by attacking another State Community is, at best, a waste of time. At its worse, it is a recipe for extreme suffering in a military fight that cannot be won. Occupying and totally dominating a country will not prevent a Religious Community from surviving underground within the occupied country. And, it will serve to build the Religious Community in many other countries. It is like playing "whack a mole," a game in which a "mole" pops up in one hole and you hit it with a hammer. It disappears from that hole and immediately pops up in another. This might be temporary entertainment for a child but is not a good military strategy for a State Community dealing with a segment of a global Religious Community.

State Communities Respectfully Collaborating With Religious Communities

The United States, for example, fighting a radical element within Islam, will not succeed by invading and occupying any country or combination of countries. Radical elements within any Religious Community can only be addressed effectively by respectful collaboration with that Religious Community. One basis for the collaboration is the appreciation of the Mercy *And* Justice polarity as a fundamental and powerful force within the tradition of that Religious Community. The "radical element" within the Religious Community is caught in the downside of Justice. Attempting to kill them only increases their being stuck in their self-righteous pursuit of "Justice." We, of course, have now gotten caught in our own self-righteous pursuit of "Justice." This vicious cycle will not be effectively addressed by an *Or* mindset alone. It will also not be effectively addressed by a State Community solution alone.

So, what do we do as concerned national citizens, as concerned global citizens, and as concerned Religious Community members? I am not suggesting there are simple answers. At the same time, I believe there are ways of looking at this complexity that will undermine us and ways that will support us going forward.

If Our Greater Purpose is that "We All Thrive":

1. **It will undermine us** to pursue Justice as a "solution" to terrorism, whether State Community sponsored or Religious Community sponsored.

    It will support us to see and intentionally leverage the polarity of Justice *And* Mercy. *Either* Justice *Or* Mercy without the other will contribute to a vicious cycle leading to unnecessary suffering.

2. **It will undermine us** to create more laws and harsher consequences as the way to control our citizens and our Religious Community members. It will lead to cruelty to ourselves and others in the name of Justice. It will lead to evil in the pursuit of good.

    It will support us to supplement Justice with Mercy in order to create settings in which as individuals, nations, and cultures, we can own our own shortcomings. When we can own our own shortcomings, we reduce the need to deflect them from ourselves and project them onto an "evil other." We must hold ourselves and others accountable (Justice) *And* be able to forgive ourselves and others for our shortcomings (Mercy).

3. **It will undermine us** to fight elements of a Religious Community who have over-focused on Justice to the neglect of Mercy by attacking nation states in which those elements exist. We cannot fight elements within a Religious Community on a state-by-state basis; it is unwinnable.

It will support us to recognize that all Religious Communities have, within their traditions, the polarity of Justice *And* Mercy and that any Religious Community will have elements that over-focus on Justice to the neglect of Mercy. We must appreciate the tradition of Justice *And* Mercy within each Religious Community and support those leaders from each Religious Tradition who are seeking to leverage both poles of the Justice *And* Mercy polarity. Through this collaboration, their Religious Community can thrive and the relationships between Religious Communities and State Communities can thrive.

4. **It will undermine us** to see small elements within a Religious Community as representing the whole Religious Community. To project on all Christians, Muslims, Hindus, or Jews the acts of a segment of that community is simplistic, false, and contributes to a vicious cycle in which a whole Religious Community becomes a projection screen on which the other Religious Communities will project the parts of themselves that they can't own.

    It will support us to be welcoming and respectful of other Religious Traditions and recognize that our own Religious Tradition is not above accountability or below forgiveness.

5. **It will undermine us** to stand by and do nothing in the face of injustice or to seek Justice without Mercy.

    It will support us with our families, our organizations, our nations, and our planet to enhance our capacity to seek Justice *And* Mercy.

Summary

The primary point of this chapter is that we misdiagnose the situation when we see "Good" as a solution to "Evil." Pursuing one "Good" without also pursuing its interdependent partner will lead to an unanticipated "Evil." This does not make the initial pursuit of one "Good" somehow wrong. Just like "Activity" is "Good" for our bodies and minds, the goodness of Activity is undermined when its interdependent "Good = Rest" is neglected. "Good" and "Evil" is just powerful language to describe one point of view containing the downside of one pole (Evil) and the self-correcting upside of the pole partner (Good). What is missing is the other point of view which contains the downside (Evil) of the pole being pursued for its upside (Good) and the upside (Good) of the pole being avoided for its downside (Evil). See earlier *Figures 4* and *5*.

Pursuing Justice as a "Good" to the neglect of its "Good" partner, Mercy, leads to an excess of laws and an excess of punishment for breaking those laws. This excess leads to individuals, organizations, and nations who are less and less able to own their own shortcomings. As this happens, there is an increase in the need to deflect away from ourselves those things we have trouble owning and projecting them onto some "other."

The "other" needs to be as good a "projection screen" as we can find. Two aspects of a good projection screen are that the "other" be both handy and clearly "not me."

Just as we sometimes have trouble owning our shortcomings and project them onto others as "villains," we sometimes have trouble owning the best of ourselves and project those things onto others as "heroes." When my hero is your villain and the reverse, we can become very cruel with each other. When I can own my shortcomings and my greatness, I can hold my heroes accountable and forgive my villains.

Religious Communities have significant, often underestimated, influence over their members and are not bound by national boundaries, which gives them significant power relative to State Communities. When State Communities do not understand the polarity of Justice *And* Mercy and underestimate the power and influence of Religious Communities, significant unnecessary suffering will follow for both communities.

When State Communities can appreciate the Justice *And* Mercy Polarity within various Religious Communities and collaborate with leaders from those Religious Communities, they will be much more effective in addressing concerns about violent subgroups within any religious community.

New Realities in Chapter 21

Reality 87   "Good" comes in pairs that show up in a Polarity Map® as the two upsides. "Evil" also comes in pairs that show up in a Polarity Map as the two downsides. Paradoxically, the pursuit of one "Good" without also pursuing its interdependent partner, a second "Good," leads to an unanticipated "Evil."

Reality 88   The greater the pursuit of Justice to the neglect of Mercy, the greater the number of laws and the harsher the consequences. This decreases our ability to own our shortcomings and increases the need to project them onto an "other" who is convenient and obviously "not me."

SECTION FIVE
Part *And* Part
From Polarization to Optimization

The issues that cross my desk are hard and complicated, and oftentimes involve the clash not of right or wrong, but of two rights. And you are having to balance and reconcile against competing values that are equally legitimate. ~ President Barack Obama[51]

Introduction

President Obama may not have heard of Polarity Thinking yet notice how he, like many others, has combined his life experience and intuition to identify the importance of interdependent pairs. He describes them as "competing values" and as "two rights."

Figure 1, the polarity of Us *And* Them, serves as an organizer of President Obama's wisdom. The two competing values are located in the two upper quadrants (+A: Freedom and +C: Equality).

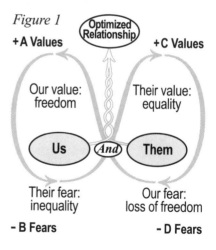

Figure 1

The group of Us holds the value of Freedom that We think is right. The group of Them holds on to the value of Equality that They think is right. The map is a good example of Obama's point about "two rights," Freedom *And* Equality. They are also competing values. The map offers more. The two values are attached to fears in the diagonal downsides (-B: Inequality and -D: Loss of Freedom).

From an *Or*-thinking perspective, *either* we are right, *Or* they are right. This assumption triggers Us with a fear that we could lose our Freedom (-D). The same

---

[51] Wenner, Jann S. *President Barack Obama.* Rolling Stone, October 14, 2010.

171

Or-thinking triggers Them with a fear that they would find themselves in a situation of gross Inequality (-B). The stronger the value, the stronger the fear. *Or*-thinking about competing values leads to polarization between Us and Them. This creates a vicious cycle where both sides experience a loss of values. *And*-thinking can create a virtuous cycle elevating the system toward its Greater Purpose. In this case, a Greater Purpose Statement could be an Optimized Relationship between two Parts: Us *And* Them.

Figure 1 summarizes the subject of *Section Five*, the relationship between two Parts of a system; i.e., Part *And* Part. One Part could be you and the other Part could be any other person (Self *And* Other). One Part could be your group and the other Part could be any other group (Us *And* Them). Within a family, the Part *And* Part could be any two members of the family. In an organization, the Part *And* Part could be two individuals, two teams, or two departments. In the United States, the Part *And* Part could be Republicans *And* Democrats. In the United Nations, the Parts could be two countries or two groups of countries. Regardless of the system size, *And*-thinking allows us to leverage the natural tension between two Parts to build a relationship that moves from polarization to optimization.

Four Chapters

As discussed previously, there is a need to empower both poles of any polarity. With that in mind, *Chapter 22*, Claiming Power *And* Sharing Power, addresses each Part's right to claim its power *And* the need to share power. *Chapter 23*, Organizational, is about the tension within the U.S. Department of Defense concerning its need to provide both security *And* access to data. *Chapter 24*, National, deals with the polarization in the United States between President Trump Support *And* President Trump Opposition. *Chapter 25*, International, is about the global nuclear arms tension between Us *And* Them.

Chapter 22
*Claiming Power **And** Sharing Power*

Power With Others Builds Powerful Relationships 1+1=3

Each of us has a right to claim our power. Claiming individual power within a relationship is a positive act *And* there is the possibility of much more – the power of the relationship itself. Believing that we can *both* claim power *And* share power creates the possibility for relationship power. This is a power that maximizes individual potential *And* the potential of the relationship. Relationship power is only available by supplementing *Or*-thinking with *And*-thinking.

Reflect on a relationship where you feel empowered. It could be with a close friend, a colleague at work, a boss, or someone who works for you. Regardless of your relative hierarchical status with this person, you feel energized by being with them. Most of the time, you feel good about your time together and the creativity that comes out of it. When you disagree, both of you feel like you are heard and respected and can influence the outcome. In this relationship, you feel like you can claim your own power to make a difference *And* it feels like the other person is also free to claim their power to make a difference. The relationship itself is power-ful. It brings something beyond just what each of you bring to it alone. As a two-person team, you each become stronger. There is a synergy between you that is more powerful than the sum of the two of you. This is power with others.

The following *Figure 1* shows "Power With Others" on a Polarity Map®. When Claiming Power *And* Sharing Power, the natural tension can become a virtuous cycle that benefits you, the other person, and the relationship itself. What could be polarized becomes optimized: 1+1=3.

Figure 2 shows "Power Over Others" in a Polarity Map. In this scenario, power in your relationship is seen as a zero-sum game – the more power the other has, the less power you have. If there were a limited power of 10 units between you and another person and the other person's power increased from 5 units to 7, your power would be reduced from 5 units to 3. With *Or*-thinking, the natural tension between each of you claiming power becomes a vicious cycle that undermines the relationship. When we engage in an *either/Or* power struggle, initially one of us "wins" and the other is disempowered. Then, both of us are disempowered and the relationship is undermined. *Or*-thinking without *And*-thinking polarizes the relationship and undermines the potential synergy between the two Parts: 1+1 = less than 2.

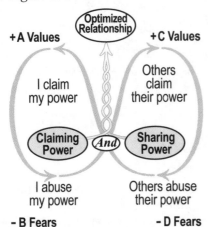

Figure 1: Power With Others

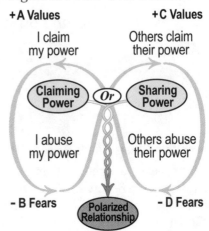

Figure 2: Power Over Others

Claiming Power Without Sharing Power Causes an Abuse of Power[R89] (*Figure 3*)

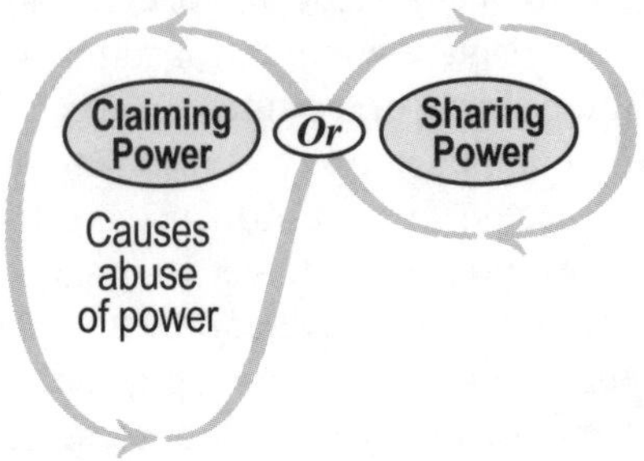

I used to become irritated when I would return home late at night from a trip and find our door locked. "Why is this door locked?" I would grumble to myself. I believed our neighborhood was safe. My irritation was clueless. It changed radically through a phone call from my 23-year-old daughter, Shalom. In tears, with a sadness I cannot begin to imagine, she tells me she has been raped. After the call, she comes to our home. I hold her gently for a long time as we cry

Figure 3

together. Shalom has given me permission to share this story because she knows this abuse of power is far too common and wants it to be acknowledged and addressed.

Shalom was raped by a man because he had the power to do it. We men have the power to do that. Why does it take the rape of my daughter for me to wake up to the power difference between men and women and the regular abuse of that power? I do not know. It may be because those of us with power over others lack sensitivity to our impact. I am no longer irritated that our door is locked when I come home from a road trip late at night. Dana has just been self-protective in my absence.

The day after holding Shalom in the wake of her attack, I was walking down the halls of a large hospital. For the first time in my life, I was aware that some of the women coming toward me, going the opposite direction down the hall, could be afraid of me or even angry with me. After the rape, I understood. It was not about their vulnerability in the busy hallway of the hospital. It was about the power imbalance between men and women and the regular abuse of that power. I was afraid and angry with us (men) out of concern for my wife, my daughters, grand-daughters, women friends, and women everywhere.

Explicit Power

There are many kinds of power. Explicit power over others is raw, physical power – the power to override another person's "no." This is the power to dictate the conditions for others' lives, to put indigenous people on reservations, to define some as white and enslave those defined as black,[52] to put people in concentration camps, to invade another country, to pay some less than others for the same work, to write and enforce the laws, and to escape punishment for breaking those laws.

Figure 4 could relate to any country in the world. In more specific terms, consider U.S. history where those Claiming Power were wealthy white men. Claiming power for Us (wealthy white men) without sharing power with Them (anyone not wealthy, white, and male) has caused sexism, racism, and poverty. It dehumanizes Us and Them. Over time, it polarizes and disempowers Us, Them, and the relationship.

Figure 4

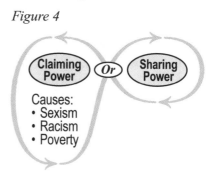

Claiming power without sharing power is a reality everywhere. It is the source of revolution and war within and between countries throughout history. Rwanda, for example, has a long history of the minority Tutsi claiming power and not sharing power with the majority Hutu. This history was part of a vicious cycle resulting in the genocide of Tutsis.[53] Genocide anywhere is a powerful example of abuse of power by an Us over Them. These situations are always more complicated than the tensions within a few polarities. At the same time, the underlying Us *Or* Them tensions and power dynamics are at play.

At the global level, the basic physical power imbalance men have over women combined with *Or*-thinking about power is a primary cause and perpetuator of sexism. It has contributed to the underrepresentation of women in positions of power in business, politics, and religion. This underrepresentation has led to a host of other inequities for women.

---

[52] Battalora, Jacqueline. *Birth of a White Nation: The Invention of White People and Its Relevance Today.* Strategic Book Publishing and Rights Co, 2013.

[53] Chen, Anson; Viswanathan, Balu. *The Rwandan Genocide.* Modern History Project 2012, www.ModernHistoryProject2012.wordpress.com/history-of-hutu-tutsi-relations/.

Within the United States, it is smart for those of us in dominant groups (i.e., wealthy white, cis men) to claim power *And* to share power with marginalized groups (i.e., women, LGBTQI+, Black, Indigenous, and People of Color (BIPOC), and poor people) as they claim their right to power. As mentioned earlier, seeing this power relationship as *either* We have power *Or* They have power leads to an abuse of power. Seeing and intentionally leveraging this power polarity will help us address these chronic issues while affirming the humanity of Us *And* Them.

Religion as a Basis for Power Over Them Leads to Abuse

For ages, we have used religion as a basis for power over Them. This is a tragic denial of the central message of our religious traditions that all are loved and there are no barriers to ultimate unity. Despite this ancient wisdom, we have had power struggles between two parts of a religion such as between Catholics and Protestants within Christianity and between Sunni and Shia within Islam. Power struggles also have occurred between religions. In each case, both sides claim that "God is on our side." For example, in 1455, Pope Nicholas V declared an African trade monopoly for the Portuguese.

> *We ... granted among other things free and ample faculty to the aforesaid King Alfonso – to invade, search out, capture, vanquish, and subdue all Saracens and pagans whatsoever, and other enemies of Christ wheresoever placed, ..., and all movable and immovable goods whatsoever held and possessed by them and to reduce their persons to perpetual slavery, and to apply and appropriate to himself and his successors the kingdoms, dukedoms, counties, principalities, dominions, possessions, and goods, and to convert them to his and their use and profit....*[54]

The Pope's proclamation, known as the Doctrine of Discovery, reflects an assertion of power by a white, male Christian leader over black, indigenous people of color, and people of other religions.

What happens when we "win" a power struggle between Us and Them? We are in trouble, They are in trouble, the relationship is in trouble, and our humanity is in trouble.

"To The Victors Go The Spoils" and "Might Makes Right"

These two quotes reflect the common results for the "winner" of a power struggle. For example, in the early history of European settlers in North America, We (wealthy white men), used guns to gain power over Them (indigenous people). Through slavery, We exercised power over Them (black people) who arrived in chains. We needed land for cotton and removed indigenous people from the land. We needed cheap labor, bought slaves, and kept them in slavery. In the wake of "victory," We made assertions that We were superior and They were inferior.

---

[54] Pontifex, Romanus; Davenport, Frances Gardiner, editor. Published in *European Treaties bearing on the History of the United States and its Dependencies to 1648*. Carnegie Institution of Washington, 1917, pp. 20-26, English translation of Latin text.

As victors, We claim that We won because We are smarter, stronger, more industrious, courageous, committed, creative, persistent, loving of our families and country, and more virtuous. We can claim that we won because God is on our side. We can quote the Pope! We deserve what We got and Those who lost deserve whatever We decide they deserve. Our superiority becomes a given that has been blessed by Christian leadership.

Power We Have Gained Over Others Must Be Maintained

The *Or*-thinking that drives Us to gain power over Them drives us to maintain that power. We claimed our power while systematically undermining or outlawing efforts that would allow Them to claim Their power. We became slave owners, and They became criminals for attempting to escape. We became the smart ones, and They were punished for learning to read. Teaching slaves to read was prohibited because We would not allow Them an empowering skill. From an *Or* perspective, sharing the power of reading would have undermined Our power advantage. If They gained power, We would lose it. In Our power over Them, We became the civilized ones, and indigenous people became the savages. We became the elected leaders, and They were not allowed to vote. There are numerous examples from U.S. history:

President Andrew Jackson – Slavery and Removal

President Andrew Jackson is an example of how claiming power without sharing power was an abuse of power. Before becoming president, Andrew Jackson was a slave owner, an inherently cruel role imbued with Power Over Others. Gaining power over slaves by purchasing them led to additional cruelty to maintain power over them. This is reflected in the advertisements placed by slave owners.

"Stop the Runaway," Andrew Jackson urged in an ad placed in the Tennessee Gazette in October 1804. The future president gave a detailed description: A "Mulatto Man Slave," about thirty years old, six feet and an inch high, stout made and active, talks sensible, stoops in his walk, and has a remarkably large foot, broad across the root of the toes – will pass for a free man...."

Jackson, who would become the country's seventh commander in chief in 1829, promised anyone who captured this "Mulatto Man Slave" a reward of $50, plus "reasonable" expenses paid.

Jackson added a line that some historians find particularly cruel. It offered "ten dollars extra, for every hundred lashes any person will give him, to the amount of three hundred." The ad was signed, "ANDREW JACKSON, Near Nashville, State of Tennessee."[55]

---

[55] Brown, DeNeen L. *Hunting down runaway slaves: The cruel ads of Andrew Jackson and 'the master class'.* Washington Post, May 1, 2017.

Power Over Indigenous People in North America – Removal

In 1830, President Andrew Jackson signed the Indian Removal Act, which forcibly relocated most indigenous people in the South. The power of wealthy white men to "remove" indigenous people from the land worked hand in hand with the power to own slaves. As noted above, We removed Them (indigenous people) from the land and bought Them (slaves) to work it.

At the beginning of the 1830s, nearly 125,000 Native Americans lived on millions of acres of land in Georgia, Tennessee, Alabama, North Carolina and Florida – land their ancestors had occupied and cultivated for generations. By the end of the decade, very few natives remained anywhere in the southeastern United States. Working on behalf of white settlers who wanted to grow cotton on the Indians' land, the federal government forced them to leave their homelands and walk thousands of miles to a specially designated "Indian territory" across the Mississippi River. This difficult and sometimes deadly journey is known as the Trail of Tears.

Scott and his troops forced the Cherokee into stockades at bayonet point while whites looted their homes and belongings. Then, they marched the Indians more than 1,200 miles to Indian territory. Whooping cough, typhus, dysentery, cholera, and starvation were epidemic along the way, and historians estimate that more than 5,000 Cherokee died as a result of the journey.

By 1840, tens of thousands of Native Americans had been driven off of their land in the southeastern states and forced to move across the Mississippi to Indian territory. The federal government promised that their new land would remain unmolested forever, but as the line of white settlement pushed westward, "Indian country" shrank and shrank. In 1907, Oklahoma became a state and Indian territory was gone for good.[56]

The Cherokee Nation, to legally claim their power, appealed the plan to remove them from their land to the U.S. Supreme Court and won.

John Marshall's opinion for the Court majority in *Cherokee Nation v. Georgia* was essentially that Georgia had no jurisdiction over the Cherokees and no claim to their lands. But Georgia officials simply ignored the decision, and President Jackson refused to enforce it. Jackson was furious and personally affronted by the ruling, stating, "Mr. Marshall has made his decision. Now let him enforce it!"[57]

This flouting of the Supreme Court was a tragic example of claiming power while denying the Cherokee Nation their legal claim to power. This abuse of power over Them undermined the U.S. constitutional system of government itself.

[56] History.com editors. *Trail of Tears*. A&E Television Networks, November 9, 2009, www.History.com/topics/native-american-history/trail-of-tears.

[57] *The Trail of Tears – The Indian Removals*. U.S. History Online Textbook, March 11, 2020, www.USHistory.org/us/24f.asp.

Power Over Also Leads to Poverty

Those with power over, when focused on self-interest and the short term, are likely to abuse that power to gain and maintain wealth while tolerating poverty and blaming it on the poor. This results in an increasing concentration of wealth among a decreasing percent of the population.

The Stanford Center on Inequality and Poverty ranks the most well-off countries in terms of labor markets, poverty, safety net, wealth inequality, and economic mobility. The U.S. comes in last of the top 10 most well-off countries and 18th among the top 21.[58]

Since 1980, the top 0.1% have captured as much income growth as the entire bottom half of world's adult population. For the group of people in between the bottom 50% and top 1% – mostly the lower- and middle-income groups in North America and Europe – income growth has been either sluggish or flat.[59]

Sharing Power Without Claiming Power Allows Abuse of Power[R89]

Often, the intimidation of those with power leads to accommodation by those with less power. This accommodation looks like *Figure 5*. Sharing Power without Claiming Power allows the abuse of power.

Figure 5   *Figure 6*

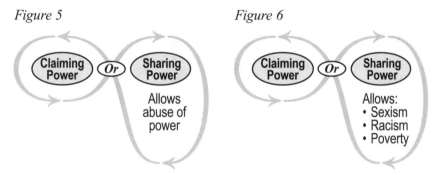

Three examples of allowing abuse of power are sexism, racism, and poverty shown in *Figure 6*. The abused person in an abusive relationship often is afraid of claiming power because of the potential violent reaction. A woman accepting unequal pay for the same work can be afraid of claiming power out of fear of losing a job. Slaves may not claim power by running away or revolting out of fear of the consequences for themselves and their family. A tribe of indigenous people may not claim power and right to land but agree to move beyond the Mississippi River to prevent a slaughter of their people. The poor and disenfranchised may not revolt for fear of its consequences. Potential allies of women and other marginalized groups may not stand with them out of fear of the consequences. The result of

---

[58] Alston, Philip. *Statement on Visit to the USA*. United Nations Special Rapporteur on Extreme Poverty and Human Rights, December 15, 2017.

[59] Nelson, Eshe. *Thomas Piketty says the US is setting a bad example on inequality for the world*. World Inequality Report, December 14, 2017.

these understandable fears is that those abusing power can continue the abuse. What might start off as a willingness to share power becomes a fearful abdication of power despite a desire to claim it. Just as an over-focus on claiming power to the neglect of sharing power leads to dysfunctions including sexism, racism, and poverty, so does an over-focus on sharing power to the neglect of claiming power.

Hope for Equity Within and Between Governments

Democracy is at its best when it successfully optimizes the polarity of Claiming Power *And* Sharing Power. *Figure 7* summarizes this tension. In the upside of Claiming Power (+A), the claimer gains power. The claimer could be any one of us or any group with which we identify: our tribe, our country, our religion, our race, our gender. Claiming power is a right worth affirming. *And,* what is needed to go along with claiming power is sharing power with Them (+C). Claiming Power *And* Sharing Power can Optimize the relationship (the Greater Purpose Statement at the top). An optimized relationship benefits Us, Them, and the relationship. It also will reduce sexism, racism, and poverty.

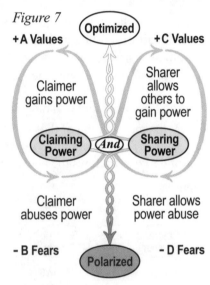

Figure 7

If we look at the rise and fall of apartheid in South Africa through the lens of this map, it will help us appreciate what Nelson Mandela did when he became President. White South Africans claimed power and with it created apartheid. This State-sanctioned discrimination based on color was a systematic way to deny power for indigenous, black South Africans. This moved the country into the lower left quadrant (–B) in which white South Africans abused their power. When Mandela became President, he and black South Africans claimed power as full citizens (+A). Rather than abuse his new-found power (–B), President Mandela shared power with white South Africans by allowing them to continue to claim their power as full citizens. There was another level of benefit for white South Africans. They were freed from power abuse anxiety. When We have power over Them, with the inherent abuse in gaining and maintaining it, We harbor a fear that if They claim their power, We will experience their retribution (–D). This power abuse anxiety comes from imagining what We would do if We had been treated like We have treated Them. By avoiding retribution and creating the Truth *And* Reconciliation process instead, President Mandela freed white South Africans from power abuse anxiety and black South Africans from the burden of perpetual resentment. Thus, President Mandela's Claiming Power *And* Sharing Power (+A *And* +C) was a gift to both white and black South Africans. It was a gift to his country and to all of us who can see and appreciate the potential of *And* in relation to power.

What we can learn from President Mandela is that We (our group) have a right to claim power *And* They have a right to claim power even if they have abused their power in the past. Anything less gets us into the downside of Claiming Power without Sharing Power (-B) where the abused become the abusers. There are many examples of this with revolutionary shifts in power throughout history, such as the genocide of the Tutsis by the Hutu in Rwanda mentioned earlier in this chapter. Looking beyond wealthy white men in the U.S. and beyond Tutsis in Rwanda, each of us, individually and as part of a group, have claimed power without sharing power, resulting in abuse of power. Fortunately, we can understand how this happens and we can be intentional about leveraging this polarity better in the future.

Power Within *And* Power Beyond

There are other important dimensions of power: power within ourselves *And* power beyond ourselves.

We each have the Power Within to make meaning for ourselves.[R90] This power was a significant support for those during and after their incarceration in concentration camps during World War II. Those with Power Over Others have limits. Nelson Mandela was imprisoned for 27 years by those who had power over his legal status. While they had power over him, he had power within. He created meaning for himself and other prisoners by preparing to lead the country after the end of apartheid. This power within is a source of hope as we address power inequities.

Another source of hope is Power Beyond. This power is inherent within all religious traditions. It is the belief that there is a power beyond us individually and beyond us collectively. This power is not dependent upon us to figure it out or do it right. This power is the gift of universal, unconditional love.[R91]

Knowing we are loved, and those abusing Power Over Us are loved, is a power richer than any Power Over Others. It is a gift we already possess, a power to receive with gratitude rather than to obtain through any effort.

Summary

Power with others – Claiming Power for Us *And* Sharing Power with Them is possible. When this happens, it creates a virtuous cycle which elevates Us, Them, and the relationship.

Power over others leads to abuse – *Or*-thinking about power leads to abuse of power with Us striving to gain power over Them.

The assumption of superiority – Superiority in battle feeds the assertion of superiority in any dimension the victors desire. Victors can assign all sorts of positive attributes for themselves and negative attributes to those they now have power over. The negative attributes assigned to those who lost were used as reasons for gaining power over them in the first place and for maintaining it into the future.

Sexism – Power over women by men has led to abuse including inequity in virtually every dimension of life. **Racism** – In the United States, "power over" by wealthy white men manifested itself with slavery of African Americans and removal of indigenous people from their land. **Poverty** – As long as those with Power Over Others consciously or unconsciously believe that we must choose between self-interest and the interests of the many, the income gap will continue to build until the system cannot contain the imbalance.

Power Within *And* Power Beyond – Power Within provides hope in creating meaning for ourselves regardless of the Power Over Us that others may have. Power Beyond is living in the gift of universal, unconditional love for Us *And* Them.

New Realities in Chapter 22

Reality 89   Claiming Power without Sharing Power causes an abuse of power, while Sharing Power without Claiming Power allows an abuse of power. This is a fundamental source and perpetuator of sexism, racism, and poverty.

Reality 90   Power Within – There is a power within each of us to make meaning for ourselves in whatever situation we find ourselves.

Reality 91   Power Beyond – This is the power within all religious traditions. It is the awareness that there is a power beyond us individually and beyond us collectively. This power is not dependent upon us to figure it out or do it right. This power is the gift of universal, unconditional love.

Chapter 23
Information Sharing *And* Information Security

Meeting David Wennergren

I am sitting at a large, round table at a restaurant in Monterey, California, with senior officers from the information professional community of the U.S. Department of the Navy. The officers are in the middle of a two-week executive leadership course. I will be spending the next day with them with a focus on leveraging polarities. Also at the table is David (Dave) Wennergren, Chief Information Officer (CIO) for the Navy.

Jeanne and Barry Frew had created the course which they led at the Naval Postgraduate School (NPS) in Monterey. Their firm, Frew & Associates, created an executive program to merge four communities within the Navy. They are both great at what they do, and I felt privileged to be part of it. Barry Frew is a retired Naval Officer and an emeritus faculty member at NPS, who has many years of experience in leadership development. I had arrived early so that I could meet Dave, who was attending as a guest resource. I sat in the back of the room listening to the discussion between Dave and the senior officers. I was struck by his warmth as well as the way he listened intently and responded directly to questions and suggestions.

As we sat around the dinner table, one of the officers asked what this "polarity stuff" was all about. My response generated more questions and a series of hypothetical situations, such as "What would you do if … ?" It was a lively conversation. Dave did not say anything, he just watched and listened.

At the end of the meal, Dave took me aside and said, "I think the notion of leveraging polarities is very interesting. I'm disappointed that I won't be able to be at your session tomorrow. Can I call you later?" I said I would welcome a call.

Seeing

Three months later, I received a call from the Pentagon. It was Dave. Since we met, he was promoted to Deputy CIO for the Department of Defense (DOD). In his new position, he has spent a lot of time listening, as he shifts from focusing on the Navy to focusing on the DOD.

He shared an issue that he found repeatedly: "Barry, there is a real fight going on between two groups. On the one hand, we have people who insist that we have good information sharing. Without that, the right hand doesn't know what the left hand is doing and it can lead to disasters like 9/11. We cannot serve and protect the American people without good information sharing. At the same time, there is another group who insist on strong information security. Without that, the enemy will know what we are doing and can create disinformation and confusion within our system. We cannot serve and protect without information security. Barry, these two groups are each trying to protect the country from the other group! Is this one of those polarity things?"

I laughed and said, "I think so, sir." He then asked me if Barry Frew and I would meet with the executive team to discuss how to leverage this polarity. Dave was very clear, "The fight between these two groups is not serving and protecting our country, and we need to do something about it."

With the benefit of a few conversations on Polarity Thinking with Barry Frew and the dinner conversation I mentioned above, Dave was able to **See** the polarity of Information Sharing *And* Information Security. This is the first step in the 5-step SMALL process. Barry Frew and I spent six hours at the Pentagon completing the remaining four steps with Dave Wennergren and the executive team. He has given me permission to share the process and the results.

Mapping

Barry Frew served as a bridge between the executive team and me. I was anxious about doing a good job, and I wanted a polarity lens to be useful. I was aware of the polarity of Humility *And* Self-assurance. On the humility side, I had no military service experience. Respect for all who serve in the military is a far cry from being someone who has served. There was plenty of reason to approach this effort with Humility. On the Self-Assurance side, I had experience joining people worldwide in leveraging polarities. I also knew that building a Polarity Map® was a values and language clarification process, and that the Polarity Map we would build together was a wisdom organizer. The wisdom was within Dave and the executive team. My self-assurance came from respect for their experience and wisdom and my own, combined with respect for the power and predictable func-tioning of all polarities.

We worked together to fill in a Polarity Map projected on a large screen. We started with a brief explanation of polarities and how they look and work, and then we started mapping Information Sharing *And* Information Security. Version 1.0 is shown in *Figure 1* on pages 186 and 187.

First, we filled out the two upper quadrants. We asked, "If we did a good job with this pole, what would the positive results be?" Then, we filled out the lower quadrants, asking, "What would the negative results be if we over-focused on this pole to the neglect of the other pole?" We used the content of the two upper quadrants as a source for putting its opposite in the diagonal downside quadrant.

Notice that the first positive result identified for Information Sharing is "Innovation." The first negative result of over-focusing on Information Security, to the neglect of Sharing, is "Stifles Creativity."

One of the results of mapping is that both points of view (upper lef*t*/lower right) and (upper righ*t*/lower left) are identified and respected. The map provides a "place to stand" for those valuing each pole[R92] The Polarity Map also clarifies that fighting over the two poles does not serve and protect the country. Once we had filled out the four quadrants, we discussed and agreed on a Greater Purpose Statement (Information Advantage) and Deeper Fear (Irrelevance and Insecurity).

Assessing

Once we had filled out the Polarity Map, we did a quick assessment. I shared a couple of visual possibilities with them. *Figure 2* is a simple picture of what would happen if, within the DOD, the power was concentrated with those wanting good Information Sharing and they treated the tension as an *Or* issue.

Figure 3 pictures what would happen if the power was concentrated with those wanting solid Information Security.

Figure 2   *Figure 3*   *Figure 4*

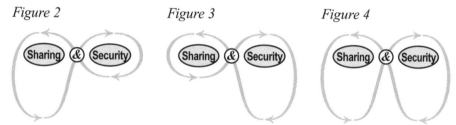

When I asked if one of those represented the present situation, they said, "No, we are in the downsides of both!" They agreed the picture should look more like *Figure 4*.

To serve and protect the country most effectively, the DOD needs to intentionally leverage the natural tension between Information Sharing *And* Information Security. If it does this well, the assessment results would look like *Figure 5*.

Figure 5

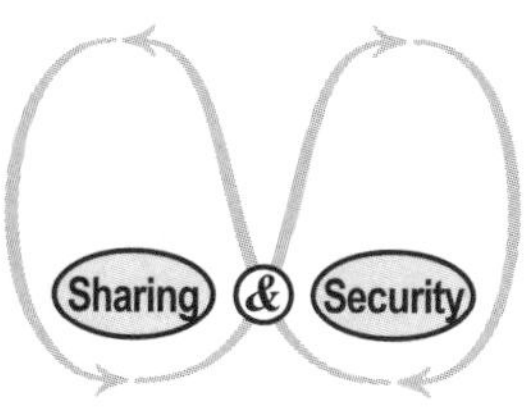

Learning

Learning occurs when we interpret the assessment results.
In this case, the assessment made it clear that the DOD was experiencing the downsides of both poles described in *Figure 1*. The map also shows that creating Action Steps for only one upside will not be sustainable. We must create Action Steps for both upsides and identify Early Warnings for both downsides.

Figure 1

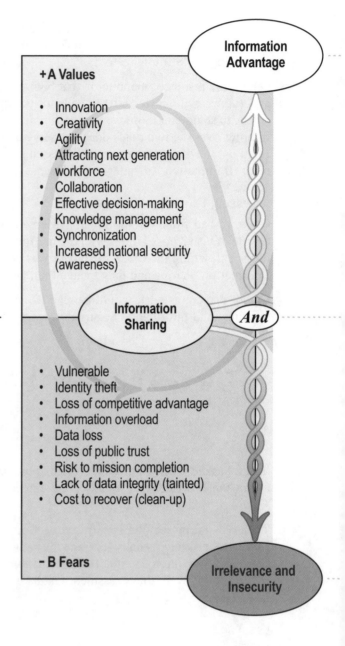

Action Steps

- Marketing (understand imperative to share)
- Training (how/why to share)
- Integrate security solutions into sharing activities
- Implement Intel Community Information Security Marking (ICISM) standards
- Implement good governance and oversight (HL)
- Implement the DoD Net-Centric Data and Services Strategy by mission area and community
- Implement ABAC (HL)

Early Warnings

- Loss of Personally Identifiable Information (PII) up
- Successful Intrusions/Data exfiltrations up

+A Values

- Innovation
- Creativity
- Agility
- Attracting next generation workforce
- Collaboration
- Effective decision-making
- Knowledge management
- Synchronization
- Increased national security (awareness)

Information Advantage

Information Sharing

And

- Vulnerable
- Identity theft
- Loss of competitive advantage
- Information overload
- Data loss
- Loss of public trust
- Risk to mission completion
- Lack of data integrity (tainted)
- Cost to recover (clean-up)

– B Fears

Irrelevance and Insecurity

Polarity Map®

Information Advantage

+C Values

- Protected
- Reduce loss
- More costly for attacker
- Increased national security (protection)
- Identity protection
- Data integrity
- Continuity of operations
- Integrated security and risk management

And

Information Security

- Stifles creativity
- Inflexibility
- Negative workforce attraction
- Creating stovepipes
- Lack of Information
- Lack of choice/access
- Increased time to collaborate
- Increased costs (inefficiencies)
- Technology restrictions

- D Fears

Irrelevance and Insecurity

Action Steps

- Marketing (understanding the value of security)
- Training (practicing good security hygiene)
- Providing good security tools
- Implement good governance and oversight (HL)
- Develop better metrics to measure security vulnerabilities
- Implement ABAC (HL)

Early Warnings

- Information in newly-fielded systems not visible/accessible outside of the enclave
- Time to get required information up
- Access to information denied

Leveraging: includes Action Steps and Early Warnings

Action Steps (*Figure 1*)

We started by defining Action Steps for gaining and maintaining positive results from Information Sharing (broad Action Steps shown in *Figure 1*). Each Action Step can be seen as a small or large project. Notice how the map develops parallel thinking. For example, Action Step 1 on both upsides relates to marketing:

Marketing	*And*	Marketing
(understand imperative to share)		(understand the value of security)

When the same action step leverages both upsides simultaneously, we label it HL for "High Leverage". For example, "Implement good governance and oversight (HL)" and "Implement ABAC (HL)" show up as action steps for both upsides. ABAC = Attribute Based Access Control.

Early Warnings (*Figure 1*)

Early Warnings need to be as early as possible and measurable. To help the executive team think of measurable indicators, we asked them to consider what might be increasing or decreasing that would indicate early that they are getting into the downside of that pole.[R93] For example, the first early warning of the downside of Information Sharing is that "Loss of Personally Identified Information" increases. Because this could be measured and is likely to be an early indicator, it could serve as a key early warning.

Evolution of the Information Sharing / Information Security Polarity Map®

Frew & Associates used the version 1.0 map in subsequent executive workshops for the DOD and the Navy. Each learning session involved more stakeholders and the map matured. In addition, Polarity Thinking enabled Dave to discuss the tension between Information Sharing *And* Information Security in speeches and talks with stakeholders in a powerful, culture-changing way. He began to talk about the need for "secure information sharing;" a phrase incorporating the values of both Information Sharing and Information Security. The change in language reshaped the thinking, beliefs, and behaviors regarding the natural tension for the DOD. Advocacy for a single pole of the interdependent pair was dramatically reduced. The same process can be used to address other polarities encountered while serving and protecting the country.

Summary

It does not take a great deal of formal learning experience to begin to see and leverage polarities. David Wennergren quickly identified a polarity between Information Sharing *And* Information Security. Seeing was step one of the five-step process. Dave's executive team could **See** a polarity, create a **Map**, **Assess** it, **Learn** from it, and **Leverage** it (**SMALL**). The essence of this process can be accomplished in less than a day. While the ongoing leveraging of the polarity will require sustained attention and effort, those involved gained the fundamental knowledge that the DOD can increase its effectiveness and make a difference by leveraging polarities.

New Realities in Chapter 23

Reality 92   One of the results of mapping is that both points of view (+A/-D) and (-B\+C) are identified and respected, providing a "place to stand" for those valuing each pole.

Reality 93   To help think of measurable indicators, consider what might be increasing or decreasing that would indicate early that they are getting into the downside of that pole.

Chapter 24

President Trump Supporters *And* President Trump Opposition

This chapter examines polarization in the United States between those who support President Trump *And* those who oppose him. As the polarization increases, it becomes more difficult for either side to see beyond what is most upsetting for them about the other side. This is exactly the type of situation in which a Polarity Map® can be useful. It can help Trump Opposition understand how anyone could support him. It can help Trump Support understand how anyone could oppose him. Without a polarity lens, those who Support Trump and those who Oppose Trump tend to view the other as "naïve," "stupid," "evil," or all three.

If a particular tension between Trump Support *And* Trump Opposition is over a polarity, each side focuses on a single point of view within the polarity. Each side feels that the other viewpoint threatens its values. The greater the threat, the greater the polarization. A Polarity Map is useful because it respects the values and fears within both points of view.

Diplomacy *And* Candor – One Key to Trump's Victory in 2016

Among the forces contributing to President Trump's election was the Candor *And* Diplomacy polarity seen in *Figure 1*. Politicians must Consider voters' opinions and respond to them with Compassion (+A). When politicians over-focus on voters' opinions to the neglect of their own beliefs (+C), they say what they think voters want to hear and are labeled as "Politically correct" and "Dishonest" (–B).

In the summer of 2016, the congressional approval rating dropped to 12.2%.[60]

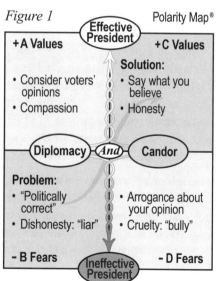

Figure 1   Polarity Map®

Effective President

+A Values   +C Values

Solution:
- Consider voters' opinions
- Compassion
- Say what you believe
- Honesty

Diplomacy —*And*— Candor

Problem:
- "Politically correct"
- Dishonesty: "liar"
- Arrogance about your opinion
- Cruelty: "bully"

– B Fears   – D Fears

Ineffective President

---

[60] *Congressional Job Approval: Poll Average*. Real Clear Politics, August 20, 2016.

Voters saw politicians as "Politically correct" and "Dishonest" (-B) and this contributed to the low rating.

The arrow in *Figure 1* going from (-B) to (+C) indicates the change in voter opinion at the time. "Politically correct" mainstream politicians were labeled dishonest and seen as the "problem" (-B). The "solution" was to support candidates who would be Honest and Say what they believe (+C).

Both Donald Trump and Bernie Sanders rode the flow of this energy system from (-B) to (+C) by being willing to be politically incorrect. Though their policies were at odds, they were praised for their honesty. People said, "I may not agree with everything they say, but at least they're being honest about what they believe."

During the presidential campaign between Donald Trump and Hillary Clinton, Trump Support praised Trump as standing in the upside of Candor (+C) and characterized Clinton as standing in the downside of Diplomacy (-B). At the same time, Trump Opposition criticized Trump as standing in the downside of Candor. Candor without Diplomacy results in Arrogance and Cruel name calling (-D). Candidate Trump made statements without regard for the impact on others. For example, he referred to Mexican immigrants as rapists and drug dealers and called Clinton a "liar." Trump supporters viewed the statements as "Honest" (+C) and praised him for not succumbing to "Political correctness" (-B). In this way, candidate Trump made statements that, at another point in time, would have set back a candidate. Instead, his poll numbers often increased after one of these statements. The more he made politically incorrect statements, the more Trump Support believed he was honest. They increasingly saw him in the upside of the Candor pole (+C). At the same time, Trump Opposition saw him in the downside of the Candor pole (-D). Trump Support saw him as honest and trustworthy. Trump Opposition saw him as an untrustworthy, arrogant bully.

Within this polarity, Trump Support has an important point of view (-B\+C). Honestly saying what you believe is a benefit of Candor (+C) and dishonestly saying what one thinks people want to hear is a limit of Diplomacy (-B). Trump Opposition also has an important point of view (+A/-D). Compassionately considering voters' opinions is a benefit of Diplomacy (+A) and cruel name calling and arrogance about one's own opinion are limits to Candor (-D). Both points of view are valid, and they need each other over time.

Though many may have wanted to move from the downside of Diplomacy (-B) to the upside of Candor (+C) during the 2016 election, that pole preference alone was not sustainable because it can lead to the downside of Candor without Diplomacy (-D). When that happens, the movement toward the upside of Candor is likely to be seen as a mistake. It was not a mistake to support Candor, but it also was not a "solution."

The Greater Purpose in *Figure 1*, an Effective President, is someone who can maximize the upsides of Candor *And* Diplomacy. Focusing on Candor (+C) can generate votes if that is the preference of the general population at the time of an election. However, it can decrease the likelihood of re-election if the candidate focuses only on Candor to the exclusion of Diplomacy. Over time, the downside of Candor (-D) increases and the upside of Diplomacy (+A) will become more attractive. President Trump will reduce his effectiveness as president and reduce his chances of re-election if he does not embrace Diplomacy (+A) as a supplement to Candor (+C).

"America First" – National Focus

Trump Support's focus on Nationalism, reflected in President Trump's "America first" rhetoric, is one pole of the Nationalism/Globalism polarity; an example of a Part/Whole polarity as detailed in *Section Two*. As mapped in *Figure 2*, Trump Support (TS) sees "America First" as the upside of Nationalism (+A). They value the United States' freedom to claim uniqueness and to act unilaterally. They have a point. There are benefits to this pole.

Trump Opposition (TO) worries that over-focus on "America first" (+A) could lead to "America alone" (-B) with inequality between countries, isolation of America, and chaotic relationships between the U.S. and other countries. They also have a point. There are limits to Nationalism. Trump Opposition advocates the upside of Globalism (+C), valuing an "America with others," where equality, connectedness, and synergy can be achieved in a global community. Trump Support fears that over-focusing on "America with others" would result in "America last" (-D). They are afraid that the nation would lose the freedom to take independent initiative to pursue unique, national interests. They have

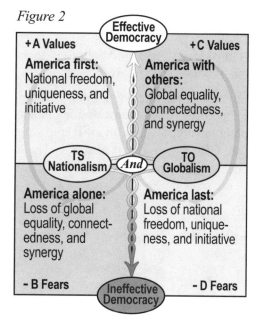

Figure 2

+A Values	Effective Democracy	+C Values
America first: National freedom, uniqueness, and initiative		**America with others:** Global equality, connectedness, and synergy
TS Nationalism	*And*	**TO** Globalism
America alone: Loss of global equality, connectedness, and synergy		**America last:** Loss of national freedom, uniqueness, and initiative
- B Fears	Ineffective Democracy	- D Fears

a point. There are downsides to Globalism. The more Trump Support fears the downside of Globalism (-D), the more they support Nationalism (+A).

When this polarity is seen as *either* "America first" *Or* "America with others," the natural tension between these two poles becomes a vicious cycle. If there is a power struggle between the two poles and "America first" wins, the nation will find itself in the downside of the Nationalism pole: "America alone" (-B). Eventually, the nation will also find itself in the downside of the Globalism pole: "America last" (-D).

The Polarity Map® and Principles are Inherently Fair

Diplomacy *And* Candor along with Nationalism *And* Globalism are two polarities in which there is a natural tension between Trump Support *And* Trump Opposition. The Polarity Map identifies opposing values and fears and recognizes them as essential. There is an inherent fairness within a Polarity Map and the process of leveraging polarities.

In *Figure 3*, any pole Trump Support prefers will have its benefits (+A) and limits (-B). Trump Opposition fears (-B) because they value the upside of their preferred pole (+C).

Figure 3

The Opposition's preferred pole also will have downside limits (-D). Trump Support's value and fear viewpoint (+A/-D), is matched by Trump Opposition's equally valid viewpoint (-B\+C). Both viewpoints are essential for optimizing polarities that are the source of conflict.

Both sides are right, and both need each other to be successful over time.

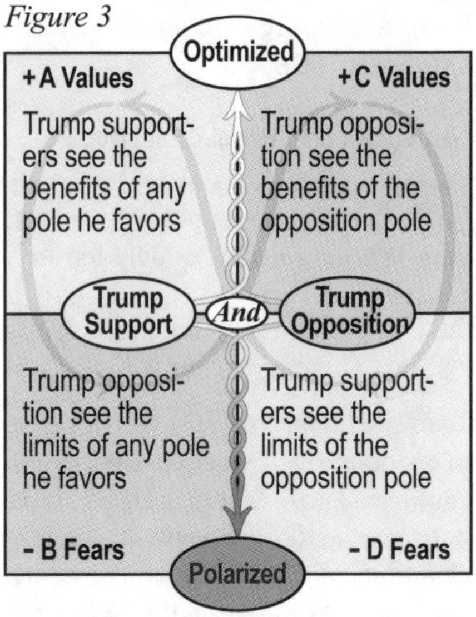

From an *Or* perspective, the more Trump Support advocates for the upside of their preferred pole (+A), the more Trump Opposition will fear the downside of the same pole (-B). The reverse is also true. The more Trump Opposition advocates for the upside of their preferred pole (+C), the more Trump Support will fear the downside of the same pole (-D). *Figures 4* and *5* separate the two points of view.

Figure 4

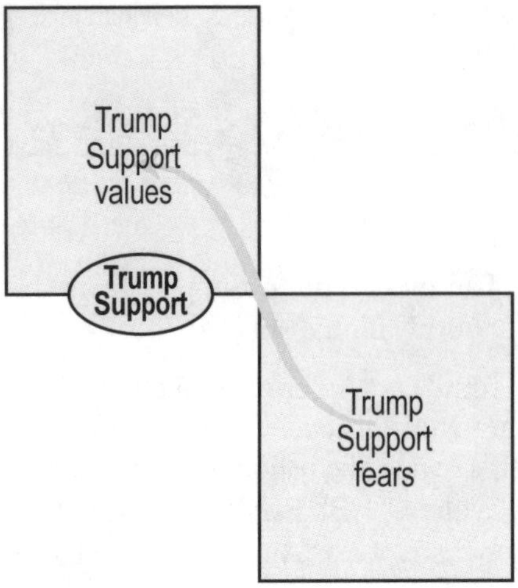

Figure 5

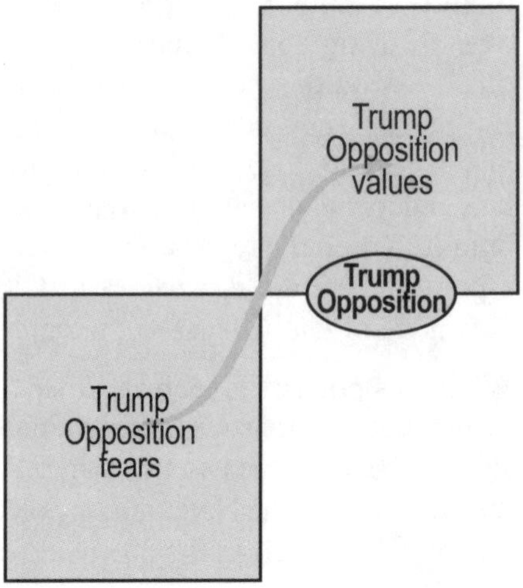

In *Figure 4*, the Trump Support point of view shows the natural movement away from what they fear and toward what they value. In *Figure 5*, the Trump Opposition point of view shows the same natural movement away from what they fear and toward what they value. When each group believes that they must choose to follow *either* "our values" *Or* "their values," they will choose their own values claiming, "We are right; They are wrong" and polarization increases. The tension between the two points of view becomes a vicious cycle in which everyone loses.

Switching Poles

Figure 6 is a simple version of the Open Communication *And* Strategic Communication polarity. This polarity pair shows how the view of Trump Support has altered regarding talks with North Korea.

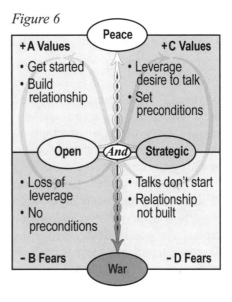

Figure 6

When then-candidate Barack Obama was asked whether he would talk with North Korea without pre-conditions, he said he would. His rationale was that it would start a conversation that could Build a relationship (+A). In contrast, historically, the U.S. had been leveraging the North Korean desire for talks as a basis to set pre-conditions (+C). Fox News and Obama opposition were upset with the thought of talking with North Korea without pre-conditions (-B).

Later, President Trump agreed to talk with North Korea without pre-conditions. Fox News and Trump Support praised him for taking the initiative to Build a relationship (+A), while Trump Opposition pointed out that Trump had lost leverage by Not requiring pre-conditions (-B).

What happened in this change of perspective? When a politician chooses a pole, it will always be true that the pole chosen will have an upside and a downside. Supporters will look for the upside, find it, and praise its benefits. Opposition will look for the downside, find it, and warn of its limits. If the politician switches poles, supporters again look for the upside, while opposition looks for the downside. No matter which pole a politician chooses, supporters will find its upside and opposition will find its downside. Both sides will see a value threatened and their fear will increase. Both sides will have a legitimate viewpoint.

Converting an Accusation Into a Question

The question that Trump Opposition often asks – "How can you support this guy?" and the question that Trump Support often asks – "How can you oppose this guy?" – are often accusations rather than an inquiry in search of an answer. When the question is heard as an accusation, it increases polarization. A Polarity Map can help an accusation become a question.

For example, when Trump announced his candidacy for president, he promised to secure our borders from illegal immigrants entering from Mexico. He was both tapping into an existing fear and increasing it. He announced: "They're bringing drugs. They're bringing crime. They're rapists. And some, I assume, are good people."[61] If you believe candidate Trump, you are likely to support him because you value security and protection for your family. You are not likely to pay attention to information questioning the validity of his claim, such as studies concluding that immigrants are less likely to commit crimes than people born in the U.S.[62] Trump Support likely considers this "fake news."

In *Figure 7*, Trump Support's fear of drugs, crime, and rape is located in the downside of Welcoming (-B). Whether these fears are based on anxiety for family safety or racist assumptions or both, they generate support for Trump and his promise to build a wall. Wanting to protect one's family (+C) is not a crazy idea. It is very understandable. Welcoming others without Protecting one's own group is a potential vulnerability (-B). Trump Support has fears for which his responses increase support. Concern for family security is one example.

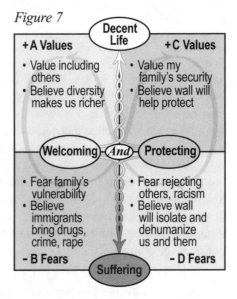

Figure 7

From a polarity perspective, there is a pattern here. When people fear the downside of a pole, they view the downside as a "problem" (-B) and they support the candidate who proposes a "solution;" a candidate who emphasizes the upside of the other pole (+C). If the fear is sufficiently powerful, they will even overlook other statements and actions by their candidate that they do not support.

Trump Opposition's viewpoint within this polarity (+A/-D) is different than Trump Support's viewpoint (-B\+C). They are moved by the poem on the Statue of Liberty, "Give me your tired, your poor, your huddled masses yearning to breathe free."[63] They value including others and the richness it can bring to their family and

---

[61] Washington Post Staff. *Donald Trump Announces a Presidential Bid.* Washington Post, June 16, 2015.

[62] Pérez-Peña, Richard. *Contrary to Trump's Claims, Immigrants Are Less Likely to Commit Crimes.* New York Times, January 26, 2017. "... several studies, over many years, have concluded that immigrants are less likely to commit crimes than people born in the United States. And experts say the available evidence does not support the idea that undocumented immigrants commit a disproportionate share of crime."

[63] Lazarus, Emma. *New Colossus.* From an engraved on a plaque inside the Statue of Liberty pedestal.

country (+A). They fear that Protecting without Welcoming will lead to rejecting others based on race, and that a wall will lead to isolation and dehumanization of both those promoting it and those barred from entering (-D). There is a potential vulnerability to Protecting one's own group without Welcoming others. The desire to include and benefit from diversity is not crazy. It is very understandable.

Finding a Greater Purpose Can Be Useful

Both Trump Support *And* Trump Opposition would like a "Decent Life" for themselves and their families so it is shown as the Greater Purpose at the top of *Figure 7*. A Decent Life would include quality relationships (+A) *And* would provide adequate protection so those relationships could be enjoyed (+C).

"Suffering" is shown as the Deeper Fear. Suffering occurs when approaching any polarity with *Or*-thinking. As with all Polarity Maps, if this Greater Purpose and Deeper Fear does not work for you, create your own. The map created will need to work for you and for those preferring the other pole.

Fearing Something Strongly Does Not Make It True

The fears in each downside of a Polarity Map can be very powerful and significantly influence our actions regardless of how grounded they are in reality.[R94] Understanding another's fears is not the same as agreeing with the basis for the fears. We might also understand the actions coming from those fears, but that is not the same as condoning those actions. For example, being afraid of immigrants from Mexico can be understandable given the history of racism in the culture. But understanding how some may have that fear does not mean I agree that there is a need to be fearful of immigrants from Mexico. Also, understanding how this fear could lead to wanting a boarder wall does not mean I support building the wall.

The Polarity Map can help us understand another's values, fears, and behavior without agreeing with it or condoning it. Understanding can give us answers to the questions, "How can you support this guy?" or, "How can you oppose this guy?" without considering the other group naïve, stupid, evil – or all three. Understanding can provide a more helpful starting point for building a relationship even if we prefer different poles.

All Polarities Can be Optimized

For numerous polarities, Trump Support prefers the upside of one pole *And* Trump Opposition prefers the upside of the other. Each is fearful of the downside of the disfavored pole. From a polarity perspective, the two points of view are necessary to complete the four quadrants of the Polarity Map. The goal is to maximize the upsides while minimizing the downsides. Seeing the polarity as a problem to solve will increase polarization. Seeing it as an interdependent pair of values and intentionally empowering both poles can move the issue from polarization to optimization.

We have already looked at four polarities:

Diplomacy	*And*	Candor
Nationalism	*And*	Globalism
Open Communication	*And*	Strategic Communication
Welcoming	*And*	Protecting

The following additional polarities are commonly seen in the tension between Trump Support *And* Trump Opposition:

Self-Assurance	*And*	Humility
Style	*And*	Substance
Direction	*And*	Participation
Spontaneous (tweets)	*And*	Planning
Protecting Us	*And*	Protecting Them
Freedom	*And*	Equality

Trump Support tends to favor the values in the left column, *And* Trump Opposition tends to favor those in the right column. If Trump Opposition were to gain power and focus on the right column to the neglect of the left, the country will find itself in the downsides of those values and eventually in the downsides of both poles. The polarization will continue and none of the polarities will be optimized. It is important to see these interdependent pairs (also called polarities, paradoxes, or dilemmas) and intentionally leverage them, regardless of who is supporting which pole at any point in time.

We Are All Accountable *And* We Are All Loved

When we look at President Trump, Trump Support *And* Trump Opposition through the lens of the Justice *And* Mercy polarity, we can see our common humanity. The upside of the Justice Pole is universal accountability for our actions and inactions. The upside of the Mercy Pole is universal, unconditional love. The polarity question is, "How do we pursue Justice by holding ourselves and others accountable *And* take in the Merciful awareness that all of us are loved as we are, as we have been, and as we will be?"

We Are All Accountable

Whether we are not preventing suffering by our inactions, causing suffering by our actions, or allowing suffering to continue by our inactions, we are accountable for the suffering.[R95] Pursuit of one pole of a polarity to the neglect of its interdependent pole always leads to some degree of suffering and dysfunction. For example, if Candor without Diplomacy leads to bullying, we are accountable for that bullying. If Diplomacy without Candor leads to allowing the bullying, we also are accountable. In either case, when we find ourselves or others in the downside of a pole, it needs to be identified and addressed. Ideally, we have understood the polarity and intentionally leveraged it to minimize the downside in the first place.

The question is not, "Which pole is chosen by Trump Support and which pole is chosen by Trump Opposition?" The question is, "Will the group choosing a pole be able to embrace the interdependent pole sufficiently to keep from getting stuck in the downside of their preferred pole?"

When Trump Support says "America first" to advocate for Nationalism, they have a point. At the same time, if they over-focus on Nationalism to the neglect of Globalism, we can find ourselves primarily in the downside of Nationalism as summarized in *Figure 8*. This is the fear of Trump Opposition. When we experience this downside, it is important to call attention to it and to do our best to address it.

Figure 8

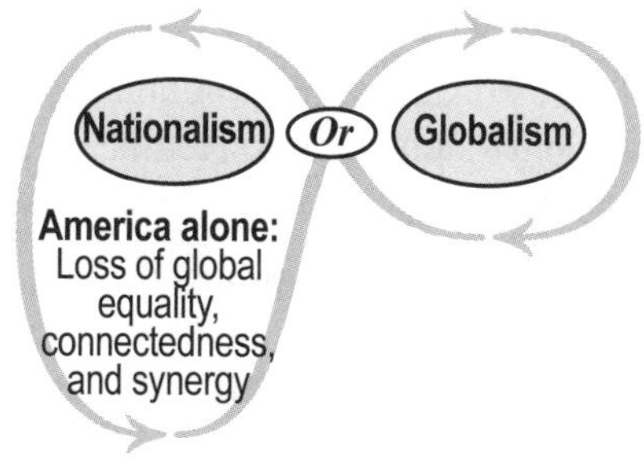

Nationalism *Or* **Globalism**

America alone:
Loss of global equality, connectedness, and synergy

How we address it is important. If we identify the downside of Nationalism as a "problem" with Globalism as a "solution," we will find ourselves in the downside of Globalism, as summarized in *Figure 9*. This is the fear of Trump Support. It will not benefit the country for both groups to engage in an *either/Or* power struggle over their legitimate fears of the downside of the other's preferred pole. The result will be to find ourselves in the downside of the winner's preferred pole first:

Figure 9

Nationalism *Or* **Globalism**

America last:
Loss of national freedom, uniqueness, and initiative

Figure 8 or *Figure 9*. Then, if we persist in pursuit of one pole to the neglect of the other, we will find ourselves in the downside of both poles.

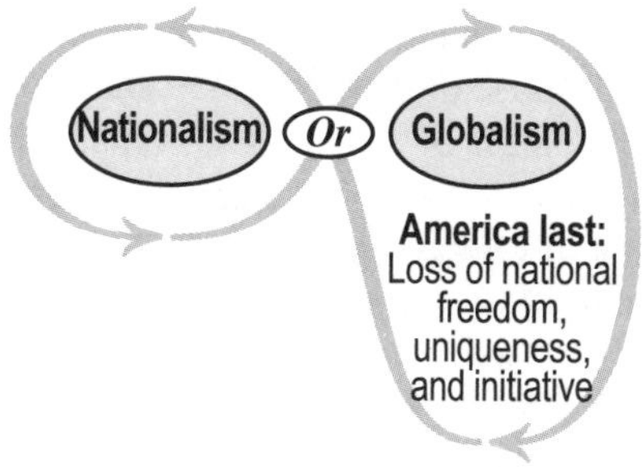

Figure 10 summarizes an alternative that respects the values and fears of both Trump Support *And* Trump Opposition. Not only is it possible to have national freedom, uniqueness, and initiative *And* global equality, connectedness, and synergy between countries, it is essential in order for the United States *And* the global community to thrive. A polarity perspective can maximize these two upsides and minimize getting caught in a downside of either pole.

Figure 10

America first:
National freedom, uniqueness, and initiative

America with others:
Global equality, connectedness, and synergy

Nationalism *And* **Globalism**

In our community of nations, the tension between Nationalism *And* Globalism exists within each country and between countries. Treating the tension as if it were a problem to solve has led to cruelty and terrible suffering as we kill each other in our struggles and create refugee camps from the struggles. A polarity lens can help us understand how we can become so cruel to each other at times. This understanding is not condoning. It just provides a more solid ground from which to reduce the cruelty and increase our compassion.[R96]

A Polarity Perspective on "Moral Equivalency"

When President Trump equates "White Supremacy" demonstrators with counter demonstrators, he implies that both groups have equal moral legitimacy.[64] From a polarity perspective, they are not morally equivalent positions.

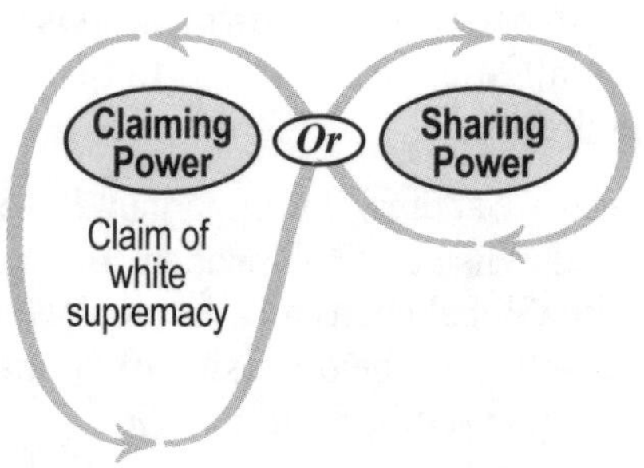

In *Figure 11*, the claim of "White Supremacy" can be seen as the abuse of power by people who claim power without sharing it, as discussed in *Chapter 22*. This downside is a source of suffering and dehumanization for black, indigenous, and people of color. It is also dehumanizing for white supremacists and those of us who fail to stand up against the claim of "White Supremacy". We are accountable to stand against abuses of power not just out of caring for the humanity of the abused; it is about caring for our own humanity and the humanity of all of us.

Figure 11

Claiming Power   *Or*   Sharing Power

Claim of white supremacy

We Are All Loved

As we discussed in *Section Four*, Justice without Mercy becomes cruelty. The universal unconditional love of the Mercy pole includes President Trump, Trump Support *And* Trump Opposition. The Mercy pole reminds us of another important message from *Chapter 1*, "seeing is loving." As we find ourselves disagreeing with Trump Opposition or Trump Support, we may have difficulty seeing beyond the words and actions we find offensive or cruel. It is easy to deny that such words and actions could be ours had our personal history been more like theirs.

It helps to remember that each of us is more than our worst moments. We do not have to deny our own cruelty or the cruelty of others to see that we and they are more than our cruel acts. If we can see ourselves and those we oppose completely, including the cruelty, love is the natural result. This gift of Mercy is easiest to give when it has been received. A polarity lens can help us see Trump Support, Trump Opposition, and ourselves more completely. In other words, it can increase our capacity to love. The "enemy" does not have to change to be loved. They just need to be fully seen.

---

[64] Shear, Michael D.; Haberman, Maggie. *Trump Defends Initial Remarks on Charlottesville; Again Blames "Both Sides"*. New York Times, August 15, 2017.

Summary

Diplomacy *And* Candor was an important polarity in the 2016 United States election. At the time, the country was frustrated with the downside of Diplomacy and attracted to the upside of Candor. Trump and Sanders appealed to voters because they favored Candor and were seen as honest.

When Trump Support *And* Trump Opposition disagree over a polarity, each side has an essential point of view. Each point of view includes a value and a fear of losing that value. *And*-thinking is needed to maximize the values of both poles. When President Trump prefers a pole within a polarity, Trump Support will look for the upside of that pole and find it. Trump Opposition will look for the downside of the same pole and find it. What is missing in focusing on the upside and downside of one pole is the upside and downside of its interdependent pole. Seeing the more complete map with two upsides and two downsides and intentionally going after both upsides can help the natural tension between the poles become a virtuous cycle rather than a vicious cycle.

Fearing something strongly does not make it true, although it can significantly influence our actions. Fearing for our family's safety can cause us to support a border wall even if crime statistics show we are less vulnerable to crime by immigrants than to crime by people born here.

We are Accountable *And* Loved. We are accountable for our part in getting into the downside of a pole and the negative impact it has on others. We are also accountable for doing what we can to keep us from getting into a downside and for helping us get out of one. There is no "moral equivalency" between those causing and perpetuating the downside of a pole and those standing against those downside actions.

Seeing is loving. If we can see President Trump, Trump Support, and Trump Opposition completely, love is a natural result. A polarity lens can help us see ourselves and others, including our opposition, more completely. This supports us in holding ourselves and others accountable (Justice) *And* loving ourselves and others (Mercy).

New Realities in Chapter 24

Reality 94   Fearing something does not make it true. It is important to recognize that our fears located in each downside of a Polarity Map® can be very powerful and significantly influence our actions regardless of how grounded they are in reality.

Reality 95   We are all accountable. Whether we are not preventing suffering by our inactions, causing suffering by our actions, or allowing suffering to continue by our inactions, we are accountable for the suffering.

Reality 96   A polarity lens can help us understand how we can become so cruel to each other at times. This understanding is not condoning. It just provides a more solid ground from which to reduce the cruelty and increase our compassion.

And

Chapter 25

The Global Nuclear Arms Race
Between Us And Them

On March 5, 1970, the nuclear Non-proliferation Treaty went into effect. In 1995, it was extended indefinitely. There are three primary parts to the treaty that are dependent upon a verification process:

1. **Non-proliferation** of nuclear weapons in non-nuclear weapon states.
2. **Disarmament** of nuclear weapons states that already have nuclear weapons.
3. **Peaceful** use of nuclear power.

This chapter focuses on the first two elements of the treaty: Non-proliferation and Disarmament. There is a natural (part/part) tension between nuclear weapons states[65] *And* non-nuclear weapons states. The nuclear weapon states have armed themselves for protection. Their threat of a nuclear response is intended to keep others from attacking. The more a country feels threatened, the more willing it may be to invest in nuclear weapons. In the name of self-protection and power balance with states that have nuclear weapons, several non-nuclear weapons states might want nuclear weapons. The more states that have nuclear weapons, the more likely it is that a conflict between states would result in nuclear war. The fear of this proliferation led to an effort, especially by nuclear weapons states, to stop other states from acquiring them.

This interest is represented in (+A) in *Figure 1* on the following page. Though it is in everyone's interest to keep nuclear weapons from proliferating, it is especially in the interest of those who already have nuclear weapons because it gives them a power advantage over those without nuclear weapons. We talked about claiming power *And* sharing power in *Chapter 22*. In this situation, those claiming nuclear weapons power without sharing it could easily abuse their power.

Smaller, poorer counties cannot compete in a nuclear arms race, so how are their security interests protected? They are protected by the nuclear weapons states

---

[65] Kristensen, Hans M.; Korda, Matt. *Status of World Nuclear Forces.* Federation of American Scientists, 2016, www.fas.org/issues/nuclear-weapons/status-world-nuclear-forces/. "Warheads (Deployed / Total): Russia – 1,950 / 6,800, United States – 1,800 / 6,600, France – 280 / 300, China – ? / 270, UK – 120 / 215, Pakistan – 0 / 120-130, India – 0 / 110-120, Israel – n.a. / est. 60-400, North Korea – 0 / 15)"

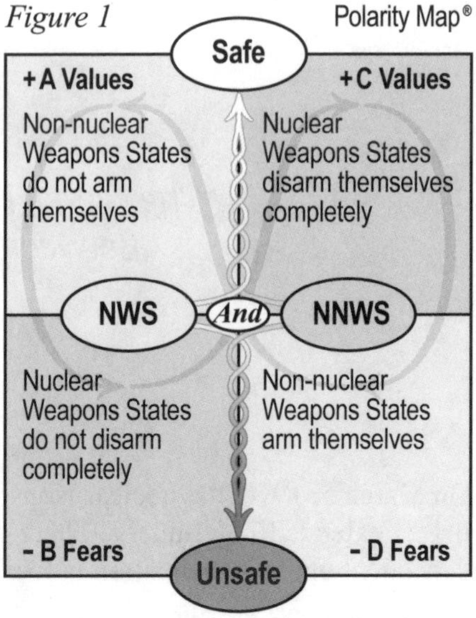

agreeing to disarm completely (+C). This is the second part of the Non-Proliferation Treaty. Non-proliferation (+A) *And* complete nuclear disarmament (+C) are both necessary for all to be safe from a nuclear attack. Non-proliferation without complete disarmament maintains the vulnerability of non-nuclear weapons states (-B). Nuclear power states disarming without stopping proliferation creates vulnerability of those who gave up nuclear power to those who have gained it (-D). If the goal is to protect the citizens of your country from experiencing a nuclear attack, we need to commit to, and effectively monitor, *both* non-proliferation *And* complete nuclear disarmament in every country.

Figure 2 summarizes the nuclear weapons negotiations between the United States *And* Iran as a part/part polarity. It would protect the U.S. if Iran complied with non-proliferation and complete nuclear disarmament (+A). It would protect Iran if the U.S. complied with non-proliferation and complete nuclear disarmament (+C). If the U.S. complies and Iran does not, the U.S. is vulnerable to nuclear attack by Iran (-D). If Iran complies but the U.S. does not, Iran is vulnerable to nuclear attack by the U.S. (-B).

Monitoring compliance is the key issue. Both countries need to trust the compliance of the other. The monitoring cannot include only the United States and Iran.

Figure 1   Polarity Map®

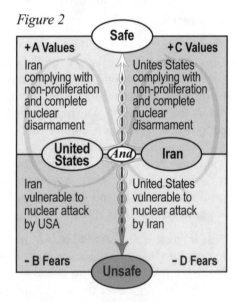

Figure 2

Neither country would agree to non-proliferation and complete disarmament without the same commitment from other countries as well. This takes us back to the Non-Proliferation Treaty.

When a county with a large stockpile of nuclear weapons, like the U.S., is negotiating with a county with no nuclear weapons like Iran, the country with nuclear weapons focuses on the non-proliferation part of the treaty and demands compliance. The country with nuclear weapons has more than nuclear weapons power inequality over the country without nuclear weapons, it has financial power inequality over non-nuclear weapons countries. It can use financial power inequality to impose sanctions and a variety of pressure tactics to make sure others do not get nuclear weapons. This effort to stop proliferation is necessary to reduce the chance of nuclear attack for all countries.

But what about the other pole of this polarity? The second part of the treaty requires complete disarmament of nuclear weapons by all countries. Iran, along with all other non-nuclear weapons states, has a right to expect the U.S. and other nuclear weapon countries to completely disarm. From a polarity perspective, we need to empower both poles. How do we empower the nuclear disarmament pole? Those with nuclear weapons have the financial power to impose meaningful sanctions. They would have to impose sanctions on themselves with the same intensity toward disarmament as imposed toward non-proliferation. This is where claiming power needs to be balanced with sharing power. Nuclear weapons states (richer states) need to share power with non-nuclear weapons states (poorer states) to prevent nuclear attack. This is the essence of the nuclear Non-Proliferation Treaty.

A new nuclear non-proliferation treaty is not needed. The existing treaty is sufficient so long as there is adequate monitoring and compliance is enforced. Paradoxically, the way for nuclear weapons states such as the United States to protect its citizens from nuclear attack is to invest in collective monitoring and disarm itself of nuclear weapons. While nuclear weapons have been reduced, clear commitment with trustworthy monitoring are required to reach full disarmament.

Adequate monitoring requires access. The global community could continue to look to the International Atomic Energy Agency (IAEA) for monitoring with additional support and access to countries. A starting point for agreeing on adequate access could be what was demanded of Iraq by the United Nations prior to the invasion to get their "weapons of mass destruction." With Iraq, the demand was for access to any site desired without warning. We could agree to an equally or even more open access to monitor whether countries are complying with their agreement to not create nuclear weapons and/or to completely disarm of all nuclear weapons.

The process for monitoring disarmament should include countries with and without nuclear weapons as well as those suspected of having or building nuclear weapons. Claiming power *And* sharing power might include:

1. Strengthening the IAEA's capacity to monitor by adding more personnel and providing a more thorough "foolproof" access.

2. Establishing a baseline through the monitoring of the countries that have or are suspected of having nuclear weapons. This would include determining which countries have nuclear weapons, how many, and what kind.

3. Diminishing the number of weapons proportionately or join the disarmament when others have lowered to your level. The intent would be to reach full disarmament together.

- o   All countries with nuclear weapons would reduce their stockpile by 25% within a mutually agreed timeframe. For example, the U.S. with 6,600 nuclear weapons would reduce to 4,950; North Korea, with 15 nuclear weapons would reduce to 11 by the same date.

- o   Alternatively, China with 270 nuclear weapons would start reducing its stockpile when Russia, the U.S., and France got their count to 270. Then they would reduce together, picking up lower number countries along the way as their number was reached.

4.   Monitoring nuclear weapons states who are disarming with the same high degree of access established for those attempting to build nuclear weapons or suspected of doing so.

5.   Establishing consequences for non-compliance with the Treaty.

The circumstances around the nuclear Non-Proliferation Treaty are complicated and there is more to consider than what is addressed in these few pages. At the same time, a polarity perspective can aid in understanding the perspective of those advocating for either pole. In each of the two polarities in this chapter, *Figure 1*: Nuclear Weapon States *And* Non-nuclear Weapon States, and *Figure 2*: United States *And* Iran, there are legitimate interests for both poles. In each case, there is more power in the left pole because it is easy for those with the power to make demands of those with less power and to avoid putting reciprocal demands on themselves. Nuclear weapon states, including the United States, can resist disarmament while using economic power to sanction and pressure non-nuclear weapon states, including Iran, for building or buying nuclear weapons. These arrangements are not making anyone safer from a nuclear attack. They are allowing those claiming power to abuse that power by imposing on others what they are not willing to impose on themselves.

In this situation, claiming power is not creating a stockpile of nuclear weapons *And* sharing power is not allowing others to create a stockpile of nuclear weapons. The Non-Proliferation Treaty supports each county's right to claim power to protect themselves from nuclear attack. Countries also are encouraged to share power with others to decide, collectively, how to monitor and enforce nuclear non-proliferation and disarmament. Those with nuclear power and the strongest econo-mies can claim power to support the nuclear Non-Proliferation Treaty by holding themselves accountable. They also can share power by engaging with those with-out nuclear power to effectively fulfill the commitment of the treaty. Whether a country has nuclear weapons or not, it is in the national interest of each country to comply with and enforce the Nuclear Non-Proliferation Treaty. Think of the difference this would make in national *And* international security.

Summary

In the world community, there is a natural tension between two key elements of the nuclear Non-Proliferation Treaty: **1) non-proliferation** of nuclear weapons to those *who do not have nuclear weapons,* and **2) complete disarmament** of those *who have nuclear weapons.* It also shows up between two countries like between the United States *And* Iran. The United States will not agree to total nuclear disarmament with Iran unless other nuclear weapons countries also agree to completely disarm. The tension in the world community cannot be resolved by any two countries. In this case, claiming power *And* sharing power is about claiming national influence and collaborating with others to claim their national influence to prevent proliferation *And* to completely disarm.

SECTION SIX
The Genius of *Or And* the Genius of *And*

The rejection of Or-thinking is an example of Or-thinking.[R97]
~ Barry Johnson

Introduction

In this section, we will look at the source of our strong, automatic inclination to "solve" any difficulty we experience. We will put *Or* with *And* on a Polarity Map® to see their interdependence more completely. We will identify 6 ways polarities show up in our lives. We will also look at how to distinguish problems to solve from polarities to leverage.

Chapter 26
The Genius of Or And the Genius of And

At this point, it is probably clear to you that polarities are everywhere. It is also probably clear that *Or*-thinking and basic problem solving are not up to the task of dealing effectively with polarities. Your enthusiasm for *And*-thinking could lead to recommending to others that they shift <u>from</u> *Or*-thinking <u>to</u> *And*-thinking. This is understandable, but not helpful. It demonstrates that we automatically see every difficulty as a "problem" for which we must find a "solution." In this case, we choose *And* as a solution. Notice how our advocacy for *And* fits within an *Or*-thinking framework. "Should we choose *Or*-thinking, *Or* should we choose *And*-thinking?" The solution, we think, is to choose *And*.

This tendency brings us back to the first two polarity realities:

1. *Or*-thinking is essential for learning and for solving problems.
2. *And*-thinking is a supplement to *Or*-thinking, not a replacement.

Or-thinking and solving problems is one pole of a polarity. The other pole is *And*-thinking and leveraging polarities. They are an interdependent pair.[R98]

Solving Problems *And* Leveraging Polarities

As a young child, we are taught language by naming things and activities. "This is your hand. This is your foot. The dog is running. The girl is laughing." We are asked questions to see if we are learning. My older sister might say, "What is this?" as she puts her finger gently on my nose. The naming of things and activities is an introduction to problem solving. Soon, we are the ones asking the questions, "What is this? What is going on here?"

That is just the beginning. In addition to learning how to communicate, we learn to explore, "What is 4 plus 4?" "Who was the first president, or Emperor, or King of my country?" "Why do apples fall down from trees rather than up?" "What is love?" "Why am I here?" In the process of learning language, mathematics, history, science, philosophy, spirituality, and other dimensions of life, we are given problems to solve to demonstrate that we are learning. In this way, one generation passes its culture on to the next, and we learn to solve the difficulties we encounter in life. Solving problems is necessary for survival. "How do I get food to eat?" "How do I keep warm when it's cold and cool when it's hot?"

We learn from a very early age that solving problems is important. In school, every question on every test is a problem to solve. In this process, we learn about the world and we are rewarded for getting correct answers. High test scores help us move to the next grade, get into college, and get a better job. We also learn:

1. If you have a difficulty, solving it is a good thing and the quicker the better.
2. If your solution is right, those who disagree with you are wrong.

We come by these two understandings naturally. When we experience a difficulty in our lives, there is a natural, automatic tendency to see it as a "problem" and to do our best to "solve" it. This is the responsible and helpful thing to do. Solving it will contribute to society, and we will feel a sense of accomplishment at overcoming the challenge the problem represents.

The second understanding, "If I am right and we disagree, then you are wrong," is also natural and automatic. For example, as a grade school student in the United States, I could have a history test with the multiple-choice question:

Who was the first president of the United States? (Put an "X" by the right answer)

☐ Franklin   ☐ Jefferson   ☐ Lincoln   ☐ Washington

I put an "X" by Washington. While walking home from school that day with my classmate, Greg, we start comparing our answers on the test. Greg says, "I checked Jefferson." I ask myself, "Do I feel confident it is Washington?" The more convinced I am that I am right, the more convinced I am that Greg is wrong.

We experience this thousands of times as we encounter problems to solve. We learn that when we are in a disagreement, we need to find out who is right and this identifies who is wrong. *Either* I am right *Or* the person with whom I disagree is right. *Or*, we could both be wrong. This process of solving problems with right answers is reinforced moment to moment in our lives. Thus, anytime we are in a difficulty, we automatically look for a solution. We presume that the difficulty is a problem to solve with a right answer and that those who disagree are wrong.

To summarize, *Or*-thinking and problem solving is powerful, instinctive, and automatic. It is necessary for survival and for passing culture from one generation to the next. Through the process of education and acculturation, we all develop an unconscious bias for *Or*-thinking. This unconscious bias does not serve us well when addressing a Polarity/Paradox/Dilemma because a polarity is different than a problem to solve.[R99] The reality of a polarity is that what I believe to be true can be true *And* the belief of the person who is disagreeing with me can also be true. More than that, the two truths need each other to be sustainable over time.

Figure 1

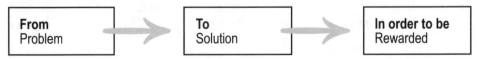

Figure 1 represents the process we go through when confronted with a difficulty. We want to move from the difficulty, which we have defined as a problem, to a solution in order to be rewarded. The reward can be any goal such as: a sense of accomplishment in making a difference, satisfaction in overcoming a challenge, a good grade on a test, recognition from others, a promotion, or a better world. Once we have solved the problem, we are ready to move on to the next one.

Figure 2

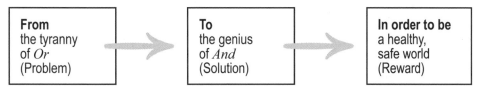

Figure 2 shows how those aware of the limits of *Or*-thinking could see it as a problem and call it the "tyranny of *Or*." They could view the advantages of *And*-thinking as a solution and call it the "genius of *And*."[66] "Let's get everyone to shift from *Or*-thinking to *And*-thinking to have a healthy, safe world."

Figure 3 shows the ideas from *Figure 2* in a Polarity Map®. When experiencing the tyranny of *Or*, the natural correction is to go to the genius of *And*. Those advocating such a move are half right.

Figure 3   Polarity Map®

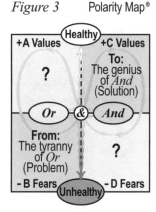

And-thinking is a correction to the limits of *Or*-thinking, but it is not a sustainable solution. *And*-thinking has its own limits (the downside of *And* without *Or*). *Or*-thinking is the necessary correction (the upside of *Or*).

Figure 4 provides a complete picture. Just as not every difficulty is a problem to solve, not every difficulty is a polarity to leverage. Choosing *And*-thinking to the neglect of *Or*-thinking will lead to the tyranny of *And*.

Figure 4

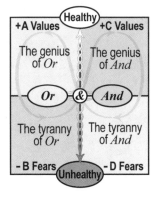

In *Figure 5*, the double-page spread on pages 212 and 213, we can see an even more complete picture of this polarity. It shows the values and fears associated with *Or*-thinking and with *And*-thinking and how they contribute to leveraging this polarity more effectively.

---

66 Collins, James C.; Porras, Jerry. *Built to Last*. Harper Business, 1994.

Figure 5

Action Steps

- Teach reading, writing, and subject matter to everyone
- Teach the values of right, wrong and consequences
- Teach problem solving

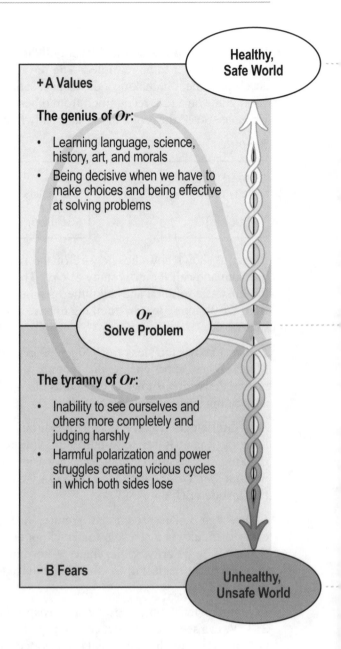

+A Values

The genius of *Or*:

- Learning language, science, history, art, and morals
- Being decisive when we have to make choices and being effective at solving problems

Or
Solve Problem

Healthy, Safe World

Early Warnings

- Increased power struggles
- Increased identification of the opposition as "evil"
- Increased comments like, "You are either with me or against me."

The tyranny of *Or*:

- Inability to see ourselves and others more completely and judging harshly
- Harmful polarization and power struggles creating vicious cycles in which both sides lose

– B Fears

Unhealthy, Unsafe World

Polarity Map®

Healthy, Safe World

+C Values

The genius of *And*:

- Learning to see ourselves and others more completely and to love
- Creating a virtuous cycle with the natural tension between poles leading to the GPS (i.e. leveraging well)

***And*
Leverage Polarity**

The tyranny of *And*:

- Inability to learn language, science, history, art, and morals
- Being indecisive, vulnerable to inaction and unable to solve problems

Unhealthy, Unsafe World

- D Fears

Action Steps

- Teach everyone to identify and leverage polarities
- Supplement "either/or" thinking with "both/and" thinking when useful
- Listen to others' stories with the desire to see them more completely

Early Warnings

- Increased complaints like, "We are acting like everything is a polarity!"
- Decreased agreement on what is right or wrong
- Increased complaints about indecisiveness

The upside of *Or* (+A) shows the important values of *Or*-thinking. It is fundamental to learning language and culture, and it helps us solve problems. Without it, the downside of *And* (-D) is the result and these essential values are lost. This is the tyranny of *And* without *Or*. This point of view needs its interdependent point of view. The upside of *And* (+C) shows the important values of *And*-thinking. We see ourselves and others more completely with love as a result.

We can learn to leverage the natural tensions between poles of polarities to create a virtuous cycle leading to our greater purpose. Without it, we find ourselves in the downside of *Or* (-B) in which we limit our ability to see ourselves and others more completely, which reduces our ability to love ourselves and others. The "other" becomes the enemy. The result is harmful polarization; a vicious cycle where both sides lose.

To combine the best of *Or* with the best of *And*, follow the **SMALL** process: **See** it as a polarity; **Map** it with language that works for our stakeholders; **Assess** how well we have been leveraging it recently; **Learn** from that assessment what self-corrections might be useful; and **Leverage** the polarity by creating Action Steps for each upside and Early Warnings for each downside.

Action Steps

It is no accident that the very first polarity reality affirms *Or*-thinking. The second reality identifies *And*-thinking as a supplement *to* rather than a replacement *for* *Or*-thinking. This is consistent with the paradoxical change model. To supplement *Or*-thinking with *And*-thinking, it is important to first acknowledge the value of *Or*-thinking.

One way to do that is to start with Action Steps to support *Or*-thinking. They might include: teaching everyone reading and writing and a wide range of subjects; teaching the values of right and wrong with consequences for each; and teaching children to solve problems, both simple and complex.

We can then supplement with Action Steps to support *And*-thinking. They might include: teaching everyone to see and leverage polarities; supplementing *Or*-thinking with *And*-thinking when useful; and listening to others' stories with the desire to see them more completely.

Early Warnings

Just as it is helpful to start with Action Steps in support of *Or*-thinking, it is helpful to identify the Early Warnings for *And*-thinking before *Or*-thinking. The reason is the same for each. We want those with the point of view we are trying to supplement to understand that we are not trying to replace their viewpoint with ours.

By looking at Early Warnings for the downside of *And*-thinking before looking at Early Warnings for the downside of *Or*-thinking, we make it clear that we know *And*-thinking has a downside and that we are willing to join in identifying Early Warnings to help minimize those downsides. In this case, Early Warnings for the downside of *And*-thinking to the neglect of *Or*-thinking might include: increased complaints like, "We are acting like everything is a polarity"; decreased agreement about what is right and wrong; and increased complaints about indecisiveness.

Next, we can join those who favor *Or*-thinking to create Early Warnings that we have over-focused on *Or*-thinking to the neglect of *And*-thinking. They might include: increased power struggles and polarization; increasingly identifying others as "evil"; and increased comments like, "You are either with me or against me."

Use *And* Rather Than "Versus" to Connect the 2 Poles of a Polarity.

There is a natural tension between the two poles of a polarity. When we view this tension from an *Or* mindset, it is natural to use the word "versus" to connect the two poles: Centralization versus Decentralization, Short Term versus Long Term. "Versus" is another word for *Or*. The message can be heard as, "There is a conflict between these two in which one pole must win or be chosen." Using the word "versus" reinforces our tendency to solve problems and to assume that if one answer is right, the alternative is wrong. If you have an interdependent pair, connecting the two poles with "versus" can be as misleading as connecting them with *Or*.[R100]

And-thinking Includes and Transcends *Or*-thinking While *Or*-thinking Cannot Include *And*-thinking.[67],[R101]

There is no place within the mental frame of *Or*-thinking for *And*-thinking. In order to incorporate *And*-thinking, we must go beyond (transcend) *Or*-thinking. *And*-thinking, on the other hand, can include *Or*-thinking. This chapter has demonstrated how *And*-thinking can include *Or*-thinking: put each as a pole of a polarity.

Summary

We tend to see all difficulties as problems to solve as a result of the process of learning to survive, to succeed in school, and to get rewarded for getting solutions fast. Again and again, when our solution is the right answer, those who disagree with us are wrong. When we disagree, we believe that *either* I am right *Or* you are right. This is true in so many situations that it is natural to use the word *Or* to address the tension between the two poles of a polarity.

This mindset is so strong that it becomes the context in which we become enthusiastic about *And*-thinking. We find ourselves recommending to others that they move from *Or*-thinking to *And*-thinking. This, of course, is an example of *Or*-thinking.

The more useful move is from *Or*-thinking alone to *Or*-thinking as a pole of a polarity with *And*-thinking as the other pole. They are an interdependent pair. Paradoxically, if you want to have others embrace *And*-thinking, it is important to first embrace *Or*-thinking.

---

[67] I learned of this reality from Charles Hampden-Turner.

New Realities in Chapter 26

Reality 97   The rejection of *Or*-thinking is an example of *Or*-thinking.

Reality 98   *Or*-thinking and solving problems is one pole of a polarity. The other pole is *And*-thinking and leveraging polarities. They are an interdependent pair.

Reality 99   Through the process of education and acculturation, we all develop an unconscious bias for *Or*-thinking. This unconscious bias does not serve us well when addressing a Polarity/Paradox/Dilemma because a polarity is different than a problem to solve.

Reality 100   If you have an interdependent pair, connecting the two poles with "versus" can be as misleading as connecting them with *Or*.

Reality 101   *And*-thinking includes and transcends *Or*-thinking, while *Or*-thinking cannot include *And*-thinking. I learned of this reality from Charles Hampden-Turner.

Chapter 27
Six Ways Polarities Show Up

In the midst of a complex, messy situation, polarities seldom show up as the names of the two poles of a Polarity Map®. Instead, they often appear as a part of a Polarity Map such as a value, a fear, an Action Step, or an Early Warning. You might think of the Polarity Map as a 12-piece puzzle with the infinity loop constantly flowing through all four quadrants (see *Figure 1*).

The numbers are included to identify the 12 parts of the puzzle, not the order in which any part might appear. Any piece or combination of pieces could appear first.

There are 6 primary ways that polarities surface.[R102]

Figure 1

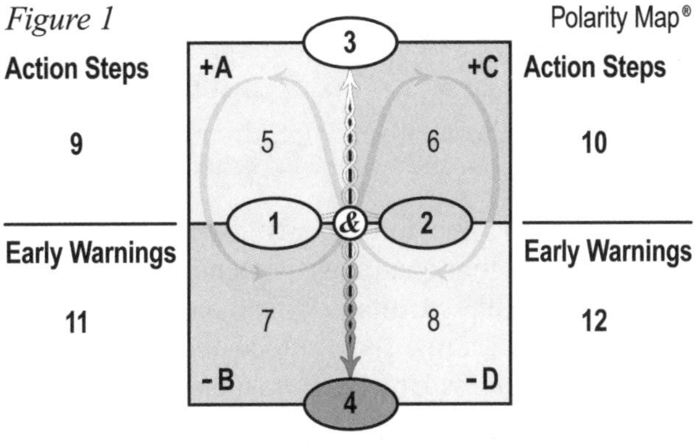

Action Steps	+A			+C	Action Steps
9		5	6		10

Polarity Map®

Early Warnings					Early Warnings
11		7	8		12

1. Polarities Emerge as a Value or Set of Values.

In *Chapter 5*, the polarity appeared in a company's value list as Autonomous Business Units. As a value, it could be the name of a pole (1) or (2), it could be one of the upsides (5) or (6), or it could be the Greater Purpose Statement (3). In that situation, I decided to put it as the left pole name (1) because it was easy to see an Autonomous Business Unit as a Part of all the business units in an Integrated Whole. Seeing Autonomous Business Units as a pole within the Part *And* Whole polarity generated ideas about other pieces of the puzzle. The upsides and downsides of the generic Part *And* Whole map in *Chapter 5* could be used to identify content here.

Figure 2 shows the Autonomous Business Unit as the left pole. It is the first piece of the puzzle. Since all Polarity Maps have two poles connected by the word "*And*," we know to look for a right pole. The infinity loop segment from the upside to the downside of the left pole is a clue. It reminds us that Autonomous Business Units brought some Benefits and these benefits over time lead to some Limits. What are these Benefits and Limits?

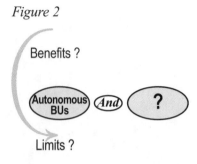

Figure 2

Figure 3 answers these questions. The right pole could be Integrated Business Units. A benefit of Autonomous Business Units is Entrepreneurial Initiative. A limit of only focusing on Autonomous Business Units is that they become Silos. *Figure 3* also includes two more infinity loop segments, from Silos to the Benefits of Integrated Business Units and from the Limits of Integrated Business Units to Entrepreneurial Initiative. We can identify what is missing because the two ends of the diagonal arrows are always opposites. The Benefits of Integrated Business Units will be the opposite of Silos, and the Limits of Integrated Business units will be the opposite of Entrepreneurial Initiative.

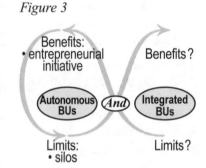

Figure 3

Figure 4 shows the full infinity loop and content for the four quadrants. A Benefit of Integrated Business Units is Effective Collaboration. A Limit of only focusing on Integrated Business Units is Bureaucracy.

Figure 4

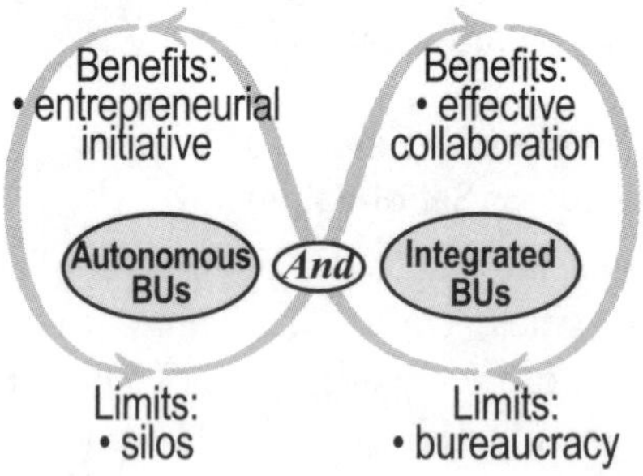

For a full Polarity Map, additional pieces are needed, including the Greater Purpose Statement and Deeper Fear, the two sets of Action Steps, and the two sets of Early Warnings. A Polarity Map is useful even when it is incomplete. Just knowing that you have a polarity enables you to stop making things worse by treating it as a problem to solve and to instead start making a difference by treating it as a polarity to leverage.

2. Polarities Show Up as Resistance Based on a Fear of Something that Could Happen.

In *Chapter 15*, the Black Student Union's demand to "Pass one – Pass all" made Leon and the transition team afraid. Leon first put the demand as a right pole but soon he realized that the demand created fear and the real starting point for creating a Polarity Map was that fear. There are two places in a Polarity Map for locating fear and the desire to avoid something: the downsides.

Figure 5 shows that identified fear, "Lack of individual student accountability", in the downside of the students' demand. Once the lower right quadrant had content, it was easy to determine its opposite and complete the diagonal upper left. The content of the upper left quadrant would be the benefits of the other pole, that is, something they were proud of and were afraid of losing if they complied with the students' demand.

Figure 5

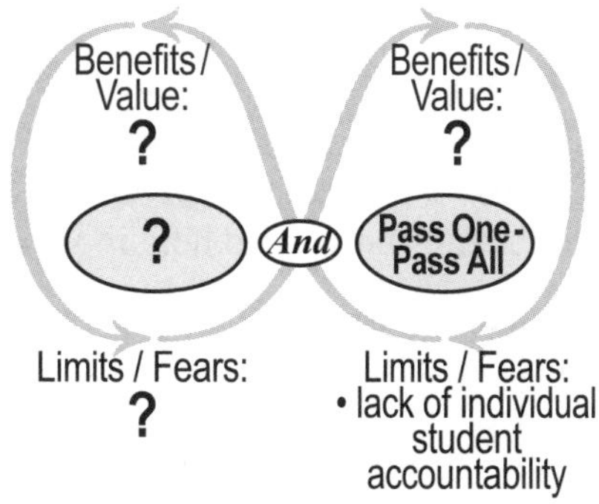

Benefits/
Value:
?

Benefits/
Value:
?

? *And* **Pass One-
Pass All**

Limits / Fears:
?

Limits / Fears:
• lack of individual
student
accountability

Figure 6 is an even more complete picture. The opposite of the lower right quadrant, "Lack of individual student accountability," became the upper left quadrant, "Each student responsible to demonstrate competency." This led Leon and the team to name the left pole Individual Responsibility. With that name in place and input from the students, they renamed the right pole School Responsibility.

Figure 6

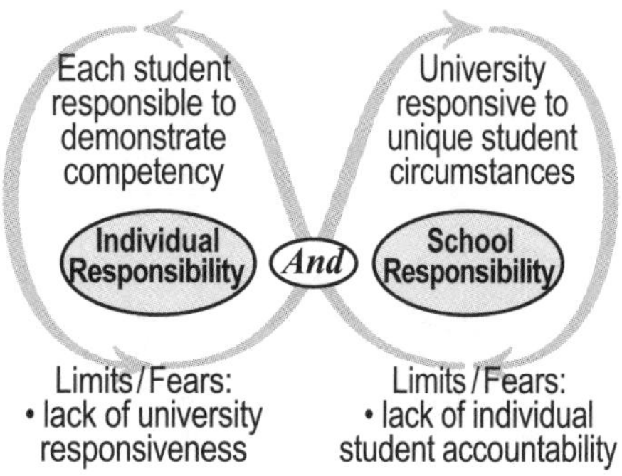

Each student
responsible to
demonstrate
competency

University
responsive to
unique student
circumstances

**Individual
Responsibility** *And* **School
Responsibility**

Limits/Fears:
• lack of university
responsiveness

Limits/Fears:
• lack of individual
student accountability

3. Polarities Show Up as One or More Action Steps.

When we decide to "take action," there is a reason behind it; some goal that we want to accomplish. The action we want to take could be an Action Step that would appear on the Polarity Map beside one or both upper quadrants. If it supports both upsides, we would put it beside both upsides with an (HL) after it indicating that it is High Leverage.

As the Polarity Map shown in *Figures 5* and *6* was developed, it became clear that the Pass One – Pass All demand was an Action Step that the Black Student Union wanted the university to take.

In *Figure 7*, the Pass One – Pass All demand appears as an Action Step in support of the right pole. Leon asked the

Figure 7

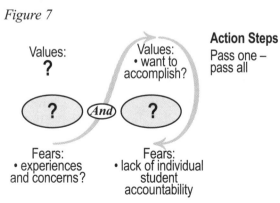

Values:
?

Values:
• want to
accomplish?

Action Steps
Pass one –
pass all

? *And* **?**

Fears:
• experiences
and concerns?

Fears:
• lack of individual
student
accountability

Black Student Union representatives what they wanted to accomplish through their demand in order to understand the content for the upper right quadrant. He also asked about their experiences and concerns that led to the demand. This provided content for the lower left quadrant.

4. Polarities Show Up as a Complaint or a Complaint Combined with a Solution.

This is very common because we tend to see difficulties as problems to solve. In *Chapter 12*, members of an executive team had a complaint about company leadership and wanted help in solving the "problem with the CEO."

Figure 8 illustrates the polarity as a complaint (lack of direction) with a logical solution (clear direction). The remaining pieces of the puzzle are missing. The arrows from the infinity loop show that there is an upside to the pole with a downside complaint and there is a downside to its solution. Also, the two poles need labels that are neutral or positive.

Figure 8   *Figure 9*

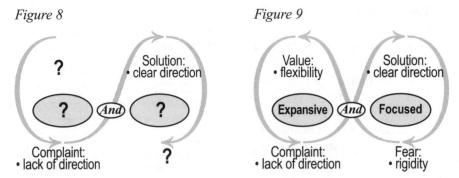

To name the upside of the left pole, we asked: "What is a parallel value to Clear Direction?" As shown in *Figure 9*, we decided on Flexibility. We then asked, "What is a neutral or positive name for a pole with Flexibility as an upside and Lack of Direction as a downside?" We arrived at Expansive.

We asked, "What is the opposite of Flexibility?" This is the downside of the right pole. We chose Rigidity. For the name of the right pole, we asked two more questions: "What is a parallel to Expansive that is neutral or positive?" and "What is a pole with an upside of Clear Direction and a downside of Rigidity." In answering these questions, we named the right pole "Focused." With these additional pieces in place, we have a good start to completing the puzzle.

5. Polarities Show Up as a Vision or Dream for a Preferred Future.

Chapter 16 discussed the South African government's proposal that English become a "common language" for the country. This vision for their future was placed in the upper right quadrant, as shown in *Figure 10*.

The infinity loop from the lower left to the upper right reminds us to look for the complaint that led to the vision. The infinity loop from the upper right to the lower right reminds us to look for a possible fear of the limits of this pole. This fear in

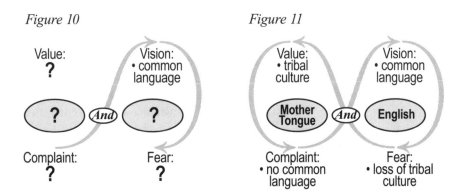

Figure 10

Value: ?

Vision:
• common language

? *And* ?

Complaint: ?

Fear: ?

Figure 11

Value:
• tribal culture

Vision:
• common language

Mother Tongue *And* English

Complaint:
• no common language

Fear:
• loss of tribal culture

the lower right, combined with its opposite that is of "Value" in the upper left will identify a source of resistance to the "Vision." In this case, the content of the upsides and downsides clarified the names of the poles.

The more complete map looked like *Figure 11*. The complaint that led to the vision was No Common Language. The value of Tribal Culture led to the fear that the vision for a Common Language could lead to a Loss of Tribal Culture. In this case, the content of the four quadrants led to identifying the two pole names – Mother Tongue *And* English.

The remaining pieces of the puzzle could be filled in from there.

6. Polarities Show Up as a Conflict.

If a conflict is based on a polarity, there will be two points of view that need each other over time. In *Chapter 7,* we looked at the conflict between the Tea Party *And* the Occupy Wall Street movement in the United States. When examining a conflict, listen to each side with a focus on values and fears. These will be connected. In a polarity, when one group affirms its value, it triggers the fear of the other group of losing what it values.

In *Figure 12*, when the Tea Party (TP) talks about Freedom, it triggers a fear in Occupy Wall Street (OWS) of Big Business. When OWS advocates talk about Equality, it triggers a fear in the Tea Party of Big Government.

Figure 12

TP values freedom

OWS values equality

TP *And* OWS

OWS fears big business

TP fears big government

Each side will hold on to its value when it fears the value is threatened. Each side will pursue the value when it has been neglected. When one side holds onto a value from an *either/Or* perspective, it will resist the other value. If OWS's pursuit of Equality overpowers the Tea Party's hold on their Freedom value, the result is Big Government and the roles shift. Now, OWS becomes the group holding on to Equality and the Tea Party becomes the group pursuing Freedom.

Summary

The Polarity Map® is a 12-piece puzzle. The six primary ways polarities surface involve pieces of the puzzle. Once the initial pieces are in place, the rest of the puzzle can be completed easily with a basic understanding of how polarities function. Completing the puzzle with key stakeholders is a good way for you, with them, to make a difference. The difference will be sustainable because it is tied to a polarity that is indestructible. Filling out the puzzle is a problem to solve in the service of leveraging the polarity.

New Realities in Chapter 27

Reality 102   There are six primary ways polarities show up:

1. As a value or set of values.
2. As resistance based on a fear of something that could happen.
3. As one or more Action Steps.
4. As a complaint or a complaint combined with a solution.
5. As a vision or dream for a preferred future.
6. As a conflict.

Chapter 28
Is It a Problem *Or* a Polarity?

The first 25 chapters described how polarities look (Polarity Map®) and how they work (Polarity Realities). Knowing how they look and work distinguishes them from problems to solve. *Chapter 26* explained that solving problems *And* leveraging polarities is itself an interdependent pair. *Chapter 27* looked at six ways polarities commonly appear. This chapter demonstrates how to distinguish between a problem we can solve *And* a polarity we can leverage.

Figure 1

Problems to Solve	Polarities to Leverage
They are not ongoing. There is an endpoint. They are solvable – there is a correct answer or solution.	They are ongoing. There is no endpoint. They are not solvable – neither pole offers a solution.
Have *in*dependent alternatives.	Have *inter*dependent alternatives.
A solution can stand alone. There is no need to include an alternative for the solution to work.	Neither pole can stand alone. The alternatives need each other to optimize the situation over time.
Often contain mutually exclusive choices: 1. Should we relocate? 2. What should we include in our employee survey? 3. Should we buy the 200-ton press? 4. Is climate change happening? 5. Should we remove one level of management?	Always contain mutually inclusive choices: 1. Stability *And* Change 2. Company interests *And* Employee interests 3. Cost *And* Quality 4. Care for our country *And* Care for the environment 5. Centralize *And* Decentralize
Can have one right answer in which case, "If I am right, my opposition is wrong."	Have two right answers that are interdependent.
Can have two or more right answers that are independent. "There is more than one way to skin a cat."	"I and my opposition are not only both right, we are each dependent on the other's truth over time."

Figure 1 contrasts basic attributes of Problems and Polarities. The key differentiator is whether the variables are *in*dependent or *inter*dependent. Sometimes we experience tension or ambivalence over tough choices. Since there is tension and ambivalence within interdependent pairs, we might assume that tension or ambivalence always indicates a polarity, paradox, or dilemma. However, it is possible to have tension or ambivalence without an interdependent pair. This has led to some confusion in the literature about what is meant by polarity, paradox, or dilemma. This two-book set discusses the phenomena of the interdependent pair which we call a polarity. If the difficulty does not involve an interdependent pair, it does not meet the definition of "polarity" as the term is used here. Words that could indicate either an interdependent pair or independent alternatives include tension, polarity, dilemma, paradox.

Tension – A polarity involves tension between poles. However, tension over the solution could indicate that there is a problem to solve. For example, there can be tension over who to vote for in an election. Just because there is tension does not make the difficulty a polarity. Voters can make their choice on the ballot and the election will solve the problem by declaring a winner.

In *Figure 2*, there can be tension over the question: "Should we focus on National interests or Environmental interests?" Since this is a polarity, the question is a false choice. We need to do both, so the connecting word is *"And."*

Figure 2

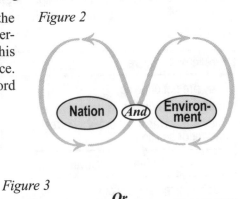

At other times, as in *Figure 3*, we may experience tension over two independent options: "Should I leave my job *Or* stay." You can choose to stay *Or* to leave without having to include the alternative any time in the future. The alternatives are independent. In that case, the tension is over a problem to solve.

Polarity – In Gestalt Psychology, client internal tension over a choice is often called a "polarity" without distinguishing between whether the choice tension is over an interdependent pair (*Figure 2*) or an independent, *either/Or* choice (*Figure 3*). The question is not what it is called but whether there is an interdependence between the alternatives about which the client feels tension. This is a distinction worth making in supporting the work of the client.

Dilemma or Paradox – Like tension and polarity, some situations called a "dilemma" or "paradox" are an interdependent pair. Others are just a difficult choice. We talk about being on the "horns of a dilemma" in which either choice seems to have negative consequences. In this case, it is possible that the two negative consequences are the two downsides of an interdependent pair.

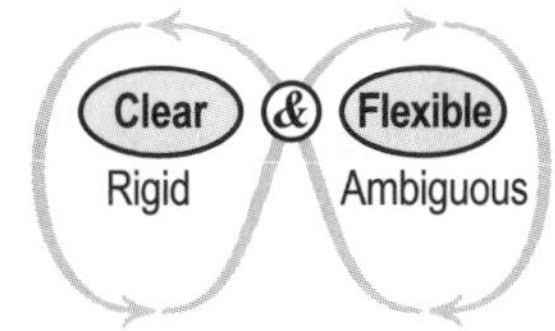

For example, in *Figure 4*, the dilemma or paradox could be that I don't want to be seen as rigid, but I also don't want to be seen as ambiguous. This is a polarity, an interdependent pair, where the poles could be Clear *And* Flexible.

Figure 4

In other situations, called "dilemma" or "paradox," the negative consequences are just bad results from two independent options. For example, in *Figure 3*, my tension over leaving *Or* staying on my job might be seen as a dilemma or paradox. If I leave my job in protest of my company's actions which are against my values, I may not find another job and my family could suffer from lack of income. At the same time, if I keep my job when my company's actions are against my values, I will compromise my integrity and collude in perpetuating actions I oppose. Do I leave my job *Or* keep it? There are underlying, interdependent pairs worth considering in making this choice. One could be Realism *And* Idealism.

Yet, the decision to keep my job does not require me, sometime in the future, to leave it. Also, the decision to leave my job does not require me, sometime in the future, to take it back. The alternatives are independent. One does not require the other over time. If it were an interdependent pair, one would be required to include both alternatives over time. Though the situation might contain tension or may be called a polarity, paradox, or dilemma, it is not an interdependent pair. It is essentially a problem to solve.

Four Questions

There are four questions that help in deciding whether an issue is a polarity or a problem.[R103] If the answers are "Yes," the issue is probably an interdependent pair; a polarity.

1. **Is the issue ongoing, like breathing?** Thinking ahead, is some form of this issue likely to exist? As long as we are alive, we will be inhaling *And* exhaling, active *And* resting. Any organization with two or more people will continue to centralize for coordination *And* decentralize for responsiveness.

2. **Is there an interdependence between two alternatives such that if we choose one alternative for the moment, we will be required to include the other at some point in the future?** We can inhale for the moment and we know that life is unsustainable without including exhaling sometime in the future. We can pursue our national interests *And* we will have to make sure we have an environment that continues to support human life.

Once we have created a Polarity Map including a Greater Purpose and a Deeper Fear, the second two questions can be asked.

3. **Is it necessary over time to have both identified upsides?** In *Figure 5*, "Is it necessary over time to be *both* stimulated *And* rejuvenated?" If so, it is probably a polarity. In *Figure 6*, "Is it necessary over time to take care of both Evan's needs and his friends' needs?" The answer is "Yes."

4. **Will focusing on one upside to the neglect of the other eventually undermine your efforts to move toward your Greater Purpose?** In *Figure 5*, will focusing on either stimulation or rejuvenation to the neglect of the other undermine a healthy life? In *Figure 6*, if Evan focuses on his needs to the neglect of his friends' *Or* focuses on his friends' needs to the neglect of his own, will that eventually undermine his desire for Good Relationships. The answer is "Yes."

Quiz: Problem or Polarity?

Based on the distinctions between problems and polarities set forth in *Figure 1*, combined with the four questions above, take the quiz on *Figure 7* and decide for each **Issue** whether you think it is a problem or a polarity. The four questions **(Q#)** provide lenses through which to look at the situation. If your answer is "Yes" to all four of the questions, it is quite likely that you have an interdependent pair/polarity. If you think the issue is essentially a polarity, what might be the **Name of Poles**?

Figure 5 — Polarity Map®

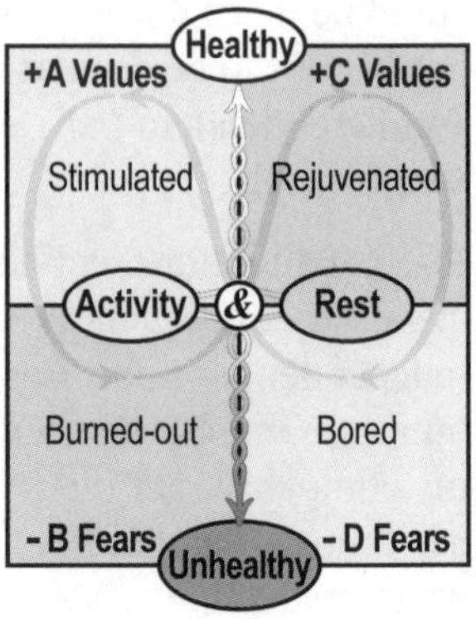

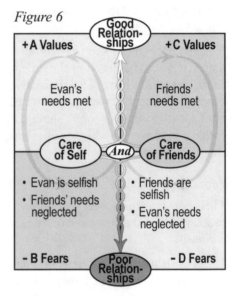

Figure 6

The first two questions are most important for this quiz. Questions three and four are useful to the extent that you create a map for a polarity you identify within the issue. If you create a map on paper or in your head, see if questions three and four are answered "Yes" to further confirm you have identified a polarity.

1. Is the issue ongoing, like breathing?
2. Is there an interdependence between two alternatives such that if we choose one alternative for the moment, we will be required to include the other alternative in the future?
3. Is it necessary over time to have both identified upsides?
4. Will focusing on one upside to the neglect of the other eventually undermine efforts to move toward your Greater Purpose?

Please take the quiz before looking ahead.

Figure 7

Issue	Q #	Yes	No	Name of Poles?
1. Where do we go for lunch? Sam likes Wanda's Wonder Bar and Linda likes The Nostalgic Noodle.	1 2 3 4	Y Y Y Y	N N N N	
2. We have to get rid of our silo mentality. Let's break down the barriers and become an integrated team.	1 2 3 4	Y Y Y Y	N N N N	
3. How do we get to the top of this mountain?	1 2 3 4	Y Y Y Y	N N N N	
4. We are becoming an international company. How do we get our people to think globally?	1 2 3 4	Y Y Y Y	N N N N	
5. Should we merge with Mega-Corporation? It would help our capitalization.	1 2 3 4	Y Y Y Y	N N N N	
6. How do we get union support for our major, company-wide change effort?	1 2 3 4	Y Y Y Y	N N N N	
7. Our Swedish partners have to talk to everyone before deciding. How can we get them to decide faster?	1 2 3 4	Y Y Y Y	N N N N	

Quiz Reflections

1. **Where do we go for lunch? Sam likes Wanda's Wonder Bar and Linda likes The Nostalgic Noodle.** This is a problem to solve. Once we have chosen to go to either place for lunch, there is nothing that says we must eat at the other place in the future. The choice is not ongoing. We can choose one restaurant, and the problem is solved. If Sam and Linda are in an ongoing relationship, there is an underlying polarity between Sam's interests *And* Linda's interests. If there are a series of choices between the two of them and one of them always gets their way, it could undermine the relationship. You might have identified this potential ongoing relationship issue as a polarity. However, this particular lunch decision is a problem to solve. Tension in the relationship or calling the choice a "dilemma" does not make "where do we go for lunch?" an interdependent pair.

2. **We have to get rid of our silo mentality. Let's break down the barriers and become an integrated team.** This complaint about "silos" is a common concern about the downside of the Part pole in the Part *And* Whole polarity. The silos could be teams, departments, or larger parts of an organization. As long as the organization has two or more people in it, there will be an ongoing tension between decentralizing to allow responsiveness by the parts *And* centralizing to work as an integrated whole. This is a polarity to leverage.

3. **How do we get to the top of this mountain?** There could be many right answers to this question. We could hike following a trail *Or* climb up a steep face. We could go by car *Or* helicopter. Though we might feel tension about the choices, this is essentially a problem to solve. Once we have decided to take a helicopter, we do not have to include the other alternatives because the problem is solved. We are not required to use any of the other alternatives in the future. They are independent alternatives.

4. **We are becoming an international company. How do we get our people to think globally?** This is another example of the generic Part *And* Whole polarity. Focusing on the Part could be Thinking Locally *And* focusing on the Whole could be Thinking Globally. One might say that once you have all the employees thinking globally, you have solved the problem. But there will be an ongoing tension between Thinking Locally *And* Thinking Globally that is important to appreciate. Focusing on thinking globally as a solution to a problem will generate resistance from those who appreciate the equally important focus on thinking locally.

5. **Should we merge with "Mega-Corporation?" It would help our capitalization.** This is a problem to solve. If we decide to merge, there is nothing inherent in the merger that will require us to unmerge later. Also, if we decide not to merge, there is nothing inherent in not merging that will require us to merge sometime in the future. We could make one decision now and make another decision later. The two decisions are not interdependent and do not require us to focus on both over time. There are polarities we could focus on to help us to decide and to implement the choice. If the company decides to merge, there will be polarities to manage such as Maintaining the Best of Organization X Culture *And* Maintaining the Best of Organization Y Culture.

6. **How do we get union support for our major, company-wide change effort?** In this case, it depends on what you are asking about. If it is union support for one change effort, it is a problem to solve. If you are examining the ongoing relationship with the union, the polarities to leverage would include Employee Interests *And* Company Interests as well as Stability *And* Change.

7. **Our Swedish partners have to talk to everyone before deciding. How can we get them to decide faster?** This question is based on a real situation where a U.S. company had merged with a Swedish company and three years later, they agreed to unmerge. Leaders from both companies wanted to unwind the merger because of communication problems. The merged company had not recognized

and leveraged an underlying polarity between Directive *And* Participative decision-making. The Swedish partners saw the U.S. partners as "cowboys." "They get a few leaders in a room and make major decisions without input from the rest of the organization. They then try to get 'buy-in' from those who have been left out of the process. That's a terrible way to make decisions. You are quick to decide but slow to implement." The U.S. partners viewed the Swedish partners are "decidaphobic." "They want to include everyone on everything. If you want to change the shape of the water cooler, you have to call a team meeting to discuss it. Even if no one cares about the shape of the water cooler, you have to have a meeting to include people in decisions. This wastes time and money." Both were complaining about the downside of the other's preferred pole. The polarity of Directive *And* Participative decision-making will not disappear just because they unmerged. The separated companies will still be challenged with a need to leverage both poles of this polarity.

Polarities Always Contain Problems to Solve.[R104]

Polarities include a host of problems to solve. The problems must be solved in order to leverage the polarity effectively. We looked at the 12 pieces of the polarity puzzle as a problem to solve in *Chapter 27*. A few basic problems that accompany any polarity include:

1. What do we name the poles?
2. What content do we put in the four quadrants, the Greater Purpose, and Deeper Fear?
3. What Action Steps should we take to maximize each upside?
4. What Early Warnings will help us minimize each downside?
5. How will we assess our ongoing progress with leveraging this polarity?
6. How do we engage key stakeholders in answering the above questions?

Just because an issue is a polarity does not mean that there is no need for problem solving. It just means that problem solving needs to take place within a polarity context.

Problems to Solve Can be a Part of a Polarity and Can Have Polarities Within Them.[R105]

Question 5 of the quiz asked whether or not to merge. Deciding whether to merge is a problem to solve. Even so, consideration of polarities is important to making a merger decision. For example, a merger of two centralized companies or two decentralized companies may look like a good fit. But the merged organizations could be in trouble if they lack ability to embrace the alternate pole to the one they both prefer. Centralization *And* Decentralization is a polarity. While the merger of a highly centralized company with a highly decentralized company may seem like a bad fit, such a merger might provide a synergy that allows the merged organization to maximize the benefits of *both* Centralization *And* Decentralization. Such a synergy is only possible if both organizations see it as an interdependent pair worth leveraging.

Summary

The key to distinguishing a problem from a polarity is the interdependence of the variables being considered. Though an interdependent pair will be accompanied by tension, the tension does not make it an interdependent pair. An interdependent pair may be called a polarity, dilemma, or paradox, but these words are also used to describe pairs that are not interdependent.

There are four questions that help us decide whether an issue is a polarity or a problem:

1. Is the issue ongoing, like breathing?
2. Is there an interdependence between two alternatives such that if we choose one alternative for the moment, we will be required to include the other alternative at some point in the future?
3. Is it necessary over time to have both identified upsides?
4. Will focusing on one upside to the neglect of the other eventually undermine efforts to move toward your Greater Purpose?

Polarities always contain problems to solve. Problems to solve can be part of a polarity, and they can have polarities within them.

New Realities in Chapter 28

Reality 103   There are four questions that help us decide whether an issue is a polarity or a problem:

1. Is the issue ongoing, like breathing?
2. Is there an interdependence between two alternatives such that if we choose one alternative for the moment, we will be required to include the other alternative at some point in the future?
3. Is it necessary over time to have both identified upsides?
4. Will focusing on one upside to the neglect of the other eventually undermine efforts to move toward your Greater Purpose?

Reality 104   Polarities always contain problems to solve.

Reality 105   Problems to solve can be a part of a polarity, and they can have polarities within them.

SECTION SEVEN
Stacking Polarities

Introduction

When we over-focus on one pole of a polarity to the neglect of its interdependent pole, the result is the downside of the favored pole. The reason we over-focus on one pole to the neglect of the other is because we connect the two poles with the word *Or* when *And* is required. When we over-focus on one pole in multiple polarities, the difficulties are compounded. The vicious cycle caused by poorly leveraging one polarity becomes a hyper vicious cycle when combined with other poorly leveraged polarities.[R106]

Figure 1 shows a "stack" of four polarities representing four sections we have already covered. Notice that the poles of each polarity are connected by *Or*. *Chapter 29* explains how the hyper-vicious cycle from this stack of poorly-leveraged polarities is a root cause and perpetuator of poverty, racism, and sexism.

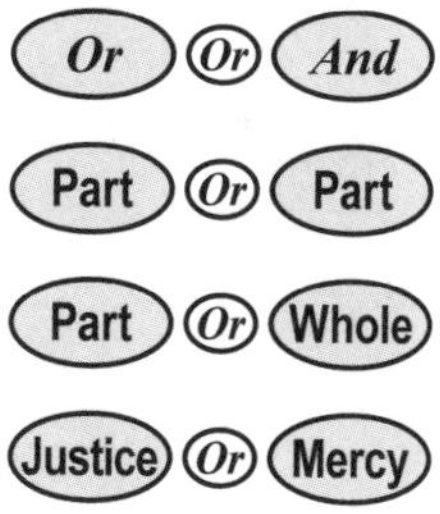

It also provides hope in addressing these chronic issues.

Figure 1

Supplementing *Or* with *And* creates a virtuous cycle in each of the polarities in a stack. This results in a hyper-virtuous cycle in which the benefits are multiplied, providing equity in quality of life for all.[R107] *Chapter 30* explains how another stack of polarities is a primary contributor to the climate crisis and how *And* is a helpful response. Addressing these chronic issues without explicitly supplementing *Or* with *And* will unintentionally undermine our efforts.

Chapter 31 Identifies why having women and other marginalized groups in shared leadership is both right and smart. Cis male dominated cultures tend to focus more on *Or*-thinking and the other left poles of the stacks in *Chapters 29* and *30*. Women and other marginalized groups tend to focus more on *And*-thinking. Both are essential. Women and other marginalized groups sharing leadership is one important step for more effectively addressing the issues identified in *Chapters 29* and *30*.

Chapter 29

Or With *And* Helps Us Address Poverty, Racism and Sexism

Root Causes *And* Symptoms

China is an 8-year-old who lives in the Avondale neighborhood of Cincinnati, Ohio. Avondale is the location of Cincinnati Children's Hospital Medical Center. China is one of hundreds of children Dr. Victor Garcia has treated at the hospital trauma center. China was shot multiple times while walking on the sidewalk with an adult friend who was the intended target. Dr. Garcia and the trauma unit team were able to save China. But, in the process, the 8-year-old lost one eye and is paralyzed from the waist down.

Dr. Garcia knew that creating and running the trauma center was absolutely necessary, *And* he knew that China and the many other wounded children he kept seeing on the operating table were symptoms. He wanted to run the best trauma center possible *And* to address the root causes for the flow of wounded children. Dr. Garcia asked for help in a presentation about his situation at a Systems Thinking conference we both attended. After hearing each other's presentations, we decided to see if a polarity lens might be useful.

Figure 1 framed our concerns. Dr. Garcia wanted to continue running the trauma center to help the children arriving with various gun and knife wounds (+C). Yet that was not enough because it was focused only on the Symptoms. This focus, without also focusing on Root Causes, would lead to more wounded children (-D). He needed to also address the Root Causes to reduce the number of wounded children (+A) without neglecting the wounded children (-B).

Before ever hearing of Polarity Thinking, Dr. Garcia understood the need for addressing *both* Root Causes *And* Symptoms. This intuitive wisdom led him to create an organization called CoreChange that was

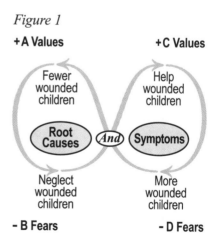

Figure 1

+A Values   +C Values

Fewer wounded children   Help wounded children

Root Causes *And* Symptoms

Neglect wounded children   More wounded children

- B Fears   - D Fears

focused on addressing Root Causes. *Figure 1* became a wisdom organizer for his intuitive wisdom.

As we explored the polarity of Root Causes *And* Symptoms, often we found that a root cause behind one symptom was also a symptom with a root cause. *Figure 2* is a simple example of a Root Cause viewed as a Symptom.

(1) The fact that China was shot can be viewed as a Symptom with (2) Poverty and Racism as Root Causes. Also, (3) Poverty and Racism can be seen as a Symptom with (4) Systemic Institutional Prac-

Figure 2

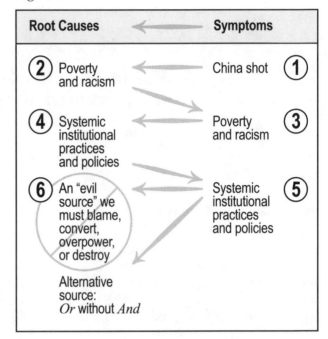

tices and Policies as Root Causes which themselves (5) become Symptoms. As we move deeper toward more basic Root Causes, we find ourselves in search of (6) an "evil intent" or "evil source" which we must blame, convert, overpower, or destroy. But what if there is no evil source? An alternative to an "evil intent" or "evil source" as a root cause for China's situation can be found in a stack of polarities in which *Or*-thinking is used when *And*-thinking is required.[R108]

Chapter 21 showed that focusing on one "good" to the neglect of its interdependent "good" leads to an unintended "evil." This reality is compounded within a stack of polarities. For example, below is a list of "good" things that most of us would value.

We would like to:

1. Be effective problem solvers,
2. Protect "Us" (our family, our organization, our country),

Figure 3

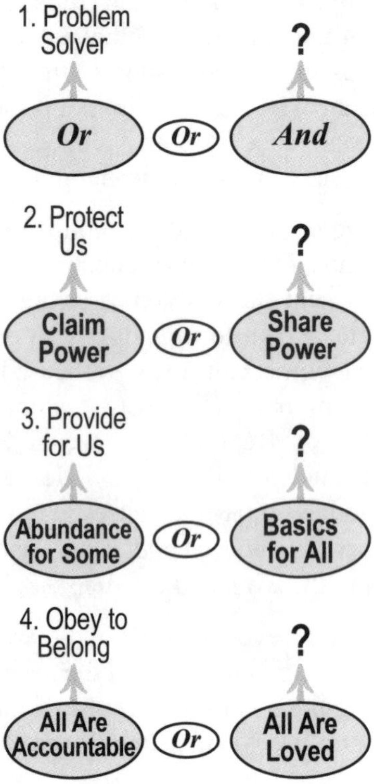

1. Problem Solver

?

Or   *Or*   *And*

2. Protect Us

?

Claim Power   *Or*   Share Power

3. Provide for Us

?

Abundance for Some   *Or*   Basics for All

4. Obey to Belong

?

All Are Accountable   *Or*   All Are Loved

3. Provide for "Us" (ourselves and our family),
4. Belong within our group – be one of "Us."

These natural desires can be seen as the upside of the left poles in *Figure 3*. There is nothing wrong with any of them. They only become a source of dysfunction when they are pursued to the neglect of their interdependent upsides whose absences are indicated by question marks in *Figure 3*. Interdependent upsides are invisible to us when we unconsciously approach this stack of polarities with an *Or* mindset.

1. Be an Effective Problem Solver

Figure 4 shows a Polarity Map® of the top polarity in *Figure 3*. When the two poles are connected by *Or,* we assume that we must choose between being a Clear, Decisive Problem Solver (+A) *Or* an Ambiguous, Hesitant person who is unable to Solve Problems (-D). This false choice leads to an over-focus on being Clear without being Flexible and becoming Rigid; being Decisive without Thoughtfulness and becoming Reactive; and Solving Problems without Leveraging Polarities. This leads to Vicious Cycles because we frame this and other polarities as if they were problems to solve.

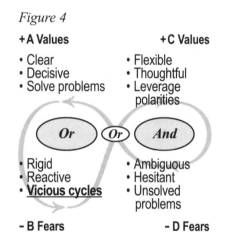

Figure 4

+A Values	+C Values
• Clear	• Flexible
• Decisive	• Thoughtful
• Solve problems	• Leverage polarities

Or   Or   And

• Rigid	• Ambiguous
• Reactive	• Hesitant
• **Vicious cycles**	• Unsolved problems

- B Fears   - D Fears

Figure 5 summarizes *Figure 4,* allowing us to stack it on top of the Claim Power/ Share Power polarity. Vicious Cycles represents also being Rigid and Reactive. We bring these downsides with us as we address the question of whether we should Claim Power *Or* Share Power.

Figure 5

Or   Or   And

Vicious Cycles

Claim Power   Or   Share Power

Notice that there is also a dotted arrow from the *Or* pole to the ellipse between Claim Power *Or* Share Power. This indicates how the unconscious bias for *Or*-thinking in the first polarity is also used for all the polarities below it in the stack. As we look at the polarity below, our view of this second polarity is radically influenced because the polarity below is already in the downside of *Or*-thinking.

2. Protect "Us" (Our Family, Our Organization, Our Country)

Figure 6 shows claiming power to protect Us (whoever Us is anywhere in the world) (+A) while not sharing power to protect Them is an abuse of power (-B).

Where does the drive to claim power over Them come from? It comes naturally through wanting to protect ourselves and our families. It expands as we want to protect our company, our tribe, and our country. If we assume that *either* We claim power to protect Us (+A) *Or* We allow abuse of power over Us (-D), we will not consider sharing power to protect Them (+C). We will make sure that We claim power while preventing Them from claiming power. We must have power over Them to protect Us from Them. The result is We abuse power over Them (-B).

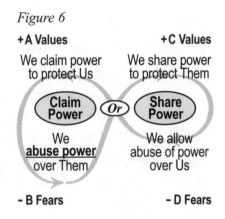

Figure 6

When I work with the U.S. military, I join them in their mission to "Serve and Protect." Many men, women, and members of the LGBTQI+ community have given their lives to protect their families and their country. This same desire to protect family and country is a fundamental motivation for those of other countries, our allies and enemies. In the United States, this desire to protect has resulted in us spending more on national defense than China, Saudi Arabia, Russia, United Kingdom, India, France, and Japan combined.[68]

Our desire to protect those we love and the country we love is natural and powerful. This deep, essential desire becomes dysfunctional when it is combined with *Or*-thinking about power. From an *Or* perspective, my country must have more power than any other country. Alternatively, my country must join with others so that the Us becomes a group of allies with enough collective power over other countries to protect Us from Them. One example of Us is NATO (the North Atlantic Treaty Organization), with Them being non-NATO countries.

Figure 7 summarizes the increasingly dysfunctional effects of combining the vicious cycles from *Or* without *And* with the Abuse of Power from Claiming Power without Sharing Power. We bring these combined downsides with us as

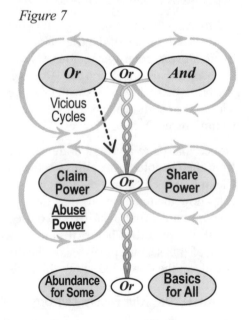

Figure 7

---

[68] Alston, Philip. *Statement on Visit to the USA.* United Nations Special Rapporteur on Extreme Poverty and Human Rights, December 15, 2017.

we address the question of whether we should provide Abundance for Some *Or* Basics for All.

3. Provide for "Us" (Ourselves and Our Family)

Protecting Us is not enough. *Figure 8* summarizes our desire for the freedom to provide abundance for Us. We want Us to have the basics: food, water, shelter, clothing, education, work with a living wage, healthcare, and if possible, the joy of living in abundance (+A). If we frame this issue as Abundance for Some *Or* Basics for All, we will seek power over Them in order to provide abundance for Us. This results in gross inequality with a loss of the basics for more and more (-B).

Efforts to bring equality in providing basics for all (+C) will be resisted either consciously or unconsciously because of the fear that we will lose the freedom to provide abundance for Us resulting in our loss of abundance (-D). To the degree that we have an unconscious bias for *Or*-thinking, we will have an unconscious bias against providing basic healthcare, food, and shelter for everyone. This will be true even among those dedicating time and money to providing these basics for all.

Recall the story in *Chapter 5* of a multinational organization that had alignment of everyone to go from the downside of Autonomous Business Units (-B), which was costing them millions of dollars, to the upside of Integrated Business Units (+C). Even with unanimous agreement that they needed to move toward Integrated Business Units and that the cost of not going was high, they were not able to gain the benefits of Integrated Business Units (+C).

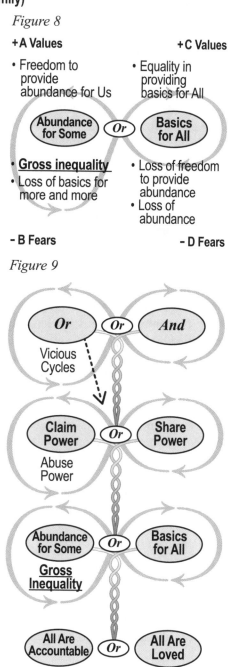

Figure 8

+A Values

• Freedom to provide abundance for Us

+C Values

• Equality in providing basics for All

- B Fears

• Gross inequality
• Loss of basics for more and more

- D Fears

• Loss of freedom to provide abundance
• Loss of abundance

Figure 9

The reason is the same as for those in *Figure 8* who find themselves not gaining basics for all (+C). In both cases, the issue is framed as a problem to solve with (–B) as the problem and (+C) as the solution. In both cases, there is a powerful value not being recognized (+A) and an equally powerful, often unconscious fear (–D) that keeps them from gaining the desired outcome they want (+C). Until we see Abundance for some *And* Basics for all as a polarity in which *both* are possible, the present framing of Abundance for some *Or* Basics for all will continue to be a primary cause and perpetuator of poverty worldwide.

Figure 9 on the previous page summarizes an increase in dysfunction as polarities are stacked. Vicious Cycles and Abuse of Power are combined with Gross Inequality. This disastrous combination is what we bring with us as we address the question of whether All are Accountable *Or* All are Loved.

4. Belong Within Our Group: Be One of "Us"

We all have a need to belong. Because this need is not as conscious or as obvious as our want to protect and provide, it is easy to underestimate its influence on how we think and act. Our need to belong is satisfied, in part, by creating an Us, i.e., our group. *Figure 10* shows that a way to stay a member of Us is to obey our laws which creates our form of Justice (+A).

Figure 10

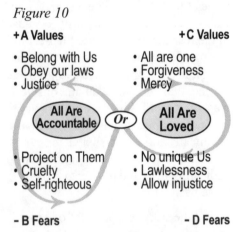

There is another sphere of belonging in which we realize we all are already one (+C). This unity consciousness has been identified by mystics from various religions over the ages. Martin Buber describes it as the "I and Thou" relationship.[69] We all belong from before our life, throughout our life, and after our life. This unconditional belonging is not based on our obedience or lack of obedience to the laws we create or to our enforcement of them in the name of justice. It is a belonging based on unconditional love, forgiveness, and mercy. This universal belonging includes belonging to our many subgroups of Us and our need to obey our laws and to seek justice. It contains the double message that All are Accountable *And* All are Loved.

This understanding is not available in the world of *Or* without *And*. In a world where *either* we support the Us to which we belong and obey its laws and seek its justice (+A) *Or* we lose our unique form of Us and allow lawlessness and injustice (–D). That way of framing belonging leads to Us projecting on Them the things we cannot admit to about Us, and to cruel and self-righteous treatment toward Them (–B).

---

[69] Buber, Martin. *I and Thou*. Charles Scribner's Sons, 1937, reprint Continuum International Publishing Group, 2004.

One beautiful, positive example of creating an Us *And* Them internationally is the opening ceremony of the Olympics. Each team arrives with their own national flag and clothing that proudly identify Our team and Our country where We belong. This sense of belonging as a part of Us is a great feeling. There is an Us and there are other teams representing their countries who become Them. When the team from my country (Us) is competing with a team from another country (Them), I cheer for my team and celebrate if they win. In this context, the identification of Us *And* Them becomes a source of enjoyment and life enhancement for all.

Drawing a line as a circle around Us and a circle around Them (differentiating Us from Them) is perfectly natural. Where we draw the line is not as important as how we treat those on either side of the line. In our effort to belong, we draw a circle around Our country, Our race or ethnic group, Our gender, Our sexual identity, Our religious group, or Our economic group, and call those inside the circle: "Us." Two questions arise from creating our membership within the circle: "How do we treat those inside the circle (Us)? *And*, how do we treat those outside the circle (Them)?"

When we ask these questions from an Us *Or* Them perspective, combined with the need to belong, we are likely to choose Us over Them. We are likely to claim positive things about Us: to contrast Us from Them in ways that favor Us; to agree to protect Us from Them; to be clear to the world that we are not one of Them; and we pledge allegiance to Us.

For example, citizens of the United States affirm belonging through our pledge of allegiance:

> *I pledge allegiance to the Flag of the United States of America, and to the Republic for which it stands, one nation, under God, indivisible, with liberty and justice for all.*

When you read this pledge, think about the questions raised earlier: How do we treat those inside the circle (our fellow citizens)? How do we treat those outside the circle (citizens of other countries)?

From a polarity perspective, we recognize the false choice between those on either side of the line no matter where we draw the line. We recognize that to see Us completely is to love Us *And*, to see Them completely is to love Them. We recognize that it is in Our interest to claim Our power *And* to share power with Them. It is also in their interest to claim their power *And* to share power with Us.

In summary, the unconscious need to belong leads to our claiming membership in different subgroups we call Us, which creates other subgroups we call Them. We tend to see the relationship as Us *Or* Them rather than Us *And* Them. This is because of our tendency to see things from an *Or* perspective in the first place. Also, seeing the relationship as Us *Or* Them helps secure my belonging with Us. For example, a statement like, "I am not a Muslim, I am a Christian," reinforces my belonging to My group (Christian) by clearly differentiating Myself from Them in another group (Muslim). I can further solidify my belonging with Us by demonstrating my commitment to protect Us and provide for Us. This combination increases my tendency to embrace Us while decreasing my tendency to embrace Them.

Chapter 21 discussed our need to identify a Them who look different than Us (an obvious "not us") on whom to project those things we cannot admit are true of Us. For me, as a white male, the two most obvious "not us" groups are people of color and women. The stronger the need to project on Them, the stronger the unconscious need for power over Them.[R109] If we have power over them, we can define Our "reality" about Us and Them. For example, we can define Us as smart, caring, and industrious and deny the fact that at times we are stupid, ruthless, or lazy. The unconscious need to project can be as strong as the need to protect, provide, and belong.

If we can identify Them as evil, savages, gangs, terrorists, infidels, animals, or criminals, we can rationalize our right, even our obligation, to claim power over them. The degree of inhumanness we employ to gain and maintain power over Them will be matched by the degree of inhumanness We need to project on Them. They become less than human so We can live with being less than human to Them.[R110]

With our power over them, we create a justice system which protects Us from Them, gives Us financial advantage, establishes that we belong and they do not, and allows Us to project on Them any negative thing we do not want to recognize as true of Us. For wealthy, white, cis men in the United States, the most obvious "not me" are poor people, people of color, and women. This becomes an unconscious source of poverty, racism, and sexism.

A Hyper Vicious Cycle Causing and Perpetuating Poverty, Racism, and Sexism

The four polarities identified above are not a complete picture. There are more polarities involved. At the same time, combining the four downsides from choosing the left pole to the neglect of the right pole demonstrates how we can significantly contribute to poverty, racism, and sexism without identifying an "evil intent" or an "evil source."

In *Figure 11*, The four upsides of the left poles without their interdependent partner (the four upsides of the right poles) leads to the downsides of the left poles combining in a downward spiral, a hyper vicious cycle that is a primary cause and perpetuator of poverty, racism, and sexism.

Figure 11 provides a summary. The desire to be a problem solver without leveraging polarities leads to being rigid and reactive, contributing to vicious cycles. The desire to protect Us without protecting Them leads to claiming power without sharing power, which becomes an abuse of power. The desire to provide for Us without providing for Them leads to gross inequality. The need to belong to Us by obeying our laws and supporting our justice system without experiencing universal belonging, forgiveness, and mercy leads to projecting what We cannot own on Them with self-righteousness cruelty.

When we persist in focusing on the four left poles, first we get the downsides of the left poles, then we get the downsides of the right poles as well. Those of us wanting to make a difference by reducing poverty, racism, and sexism would benefit greatly from understanding and leveraging these four polarities.

The Temptation to Find an "Evil Source"

Before moving on, I would like to clarify what I mean by, "There is no evil source." It is tempting to identify a person or group or country as an "evil source" to explain the reality of "evil" in our world. From my perspective, there are evil acts that we have done and continue to do toward each other. This includes any form of abuse of ourselves or others. The suicide bombing described in *Chapter 21* is an example. There are evil results from those evil acts. This includes the death of the suicide bomber, others killed in the bombing, and all those impacted by the deaths. It is important to recognized evil acts and evil results and to hold ourselves accountable for them. At the same time, there is a difference between identifying a suicide bombing as an evil act with evil results and identifying a suicide bomber as an inherently "evil source."

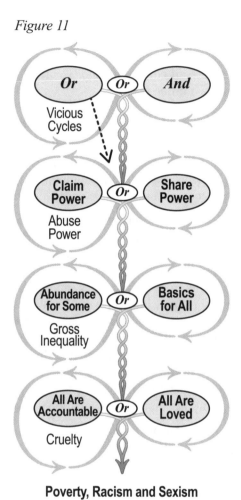

Figure 11

Poverty, Racism and Sexism

The bomber is not inherently evil. No person, group, or country is inherently evil. The actions and results of the slave owner, the dictator, the child molester, the invading country, or the leader and followers of acts of genocide might all be identified as evil. Yet, to identify the perpetrators as "evil" denies the reality that they are more than the acts we identify as evil. A person or group or country is always more than our worst selves. It is dehumanizing to them and to us to see them as simply "evil." To see them as simply evil is to see them as less than human and beyond forgiveness. It is to disconnect them from us as if we could. The very act of de-connecting is de-humanizing. By doing so, we are claiming to be categorically not them. They are evil and we are not. This shift in our relative status with them gives us the right and even the responsibility to destroy them. If we can only destroy the "evil source," we will bring good to the world. Notice how we have arrived at the very argument for the genocide of some group as an "evil source!"

We can identify evil actions and evil results without the need to identify ourselves or anyone else as inherently evil. Whatever our contribution toward evil in the world, fortunately, it cannot disconnect us from the rest of humanity and nature. We are all connected, and we are all loved unconditionally as we do our best to make a difference.

Replacing *Or* with *And* Within this Stack of Polarities Provides Hope in Addressing Poverty, Racism, and Sexism

You can leverage the natural tension between the poles of a polarity so it becomes a positive, self-re-enforcing loop or virtuous cycle lifting you and your organization to goals unattainable with *Or*-thinking alone.

Figure 12 connects the poles of the four stacked polarities with *And* building from the bottom up. By leveraging these polarities well, the positive synergy of benefits from the polarities can move us toward Equity in Quality of Life. We can Solve Problems *And* Leverage Polarities; Protect Us *And* Protect Them; Provide for Us *And* Provide for all; Belong with Us while pursuing Justice *And* Experience the reality that All are one in the Mercy of unconditional love.

This power of universal, unconditional love protects us, our loved ones and our enemies from hate, retribution, and lifelong efforts to obtain that which cannot be obtained because it is already ours; provides food for the soul from an unlimited source, which expands in the giving and receiving; affirms that all of us Belong and there is nothing we need to do or think or not do or not think in order to belong; removes the need to Project parts of ourselves we cannot acknowledge on to Them because we can acknowledge all of it with accountability (Justice) And know we are loved (Mercy).

Figure 12

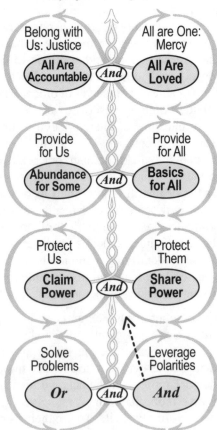

Equity in Quality of Life

And-thinking is not a solution to poverty, racism, or sexism, but it is a required mental framework. Without supplementing *Or*-thinking with *And*-thinking, our most sincere efforts will be radically undermined, and no amount of money, commitment, or alignment will compensate.[R111]

New Realities in Chapter 29

Reality 106 The vicious cycle caused by poorly leveraging one polarity becomes a hyper-vicious cycle when combined with a number of other poorly leveraged polarities.

Reality 107 Supplementing *Or* with *And* creates a virtuous cycle in each of the polarities in a stack. This results in a hyper-virtuous cycle in which the benefits are multiplied providing equity in quality of life for all.

Reality 108 An alternative to an "evil intent" or "evil source" as a root cause for chronic issues like poverty, racism, and sexism can be found in a stack of polarities in which *Or*-thinking is used when *And*-thinking is required.

Reality 109 The stronger the need to project on Them, the stronger the unconscious need for power over Them.

Reality 110 The degree of inhumanness we employ to gain and maintain power over Them will be matched by the degree of inhumanness We need to project on Them. They become less than human so We can live with being less than human to Them.

Reality 111 *And*-thinking is not a solution to poverty, racism, or sexism, but it is a process requirement. Without supplementing *Or*-thinking with *And*-thinking, our most sincere efforts will be radically undermined, and no amount of money, commitment, or alignment will compensate.

Chapter 30

Or With *And* Helps Us Address
the Climate Crisis

This chapter focuses on a second stack of polarities with a focus on climate change. *Figure 1* provides the same starting point as *Chapter 29* with "*Or*" *Or* "*And*" as the first of four polarities we will combine in a stack. As described in prior chapters, we have an unconscious bias for *Or*-thinking. The desire to be a clear, decisive problem solver (+A) with its corresponding fear of being an ambiguous, hesitant person who cannot solve problems (-D) leads us to over focus on *Or* to the neglect of *And*. The result is that we lose the upside of *And*, being flexible, thoughtful, and able to leverage polarities (+C). Instead, we find ourselves mired in the downside of *Or*, becoming rigid, reactive, and caught in vicious cycles (-B).

Figure 2 shows the Family/Environment polarity. "Family" in this context means close relatives: parents, siblings, children, grandchildren, and others to whom we feel closely bonded. "Environment," as used here, means all families and all of nature. *Figure 2* also shows us bringing the downsides from our *Or* choice in *Figure 1* to our question about whether we should choose our Family *Or* the Environment. The dotted arrow reminds us that the *Or* bias continues through all the remaining polarities in the stack.

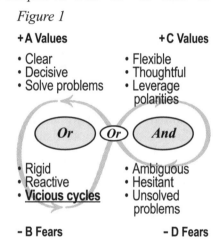

Figure 1

+A Values	+C Values
• Clear	• Flexible
• Decisive	• Thoughtful
• Solve problems	• Leverage polarities

Or | *Or* | *And*

• Rigid	• Ambiguous
• Reactive	• Hesitant
• **Vicious cycles**	• Unsolved problems

– B Fears   – D Fears

Figure 2

Or   *Or*   *And*

Vicious Cycles

Family   *Or*   Environment

Figure 3 summarizes the results of choosing between Family *Or* Environment. Given that choice, almost everyone will choose Family. It becomes a more obvious choice from the (+A/-D) point of view. The question is, "Do I want to Protect my family (+A) *Or* Neglect my family (-D)?" The arrow between (-D) and (+A) reflects the choice and indicates the movement of energy on the infinity loop toward Protect Family (+A). Love of family combined with the unconscious, false choice between Family *Or* Environment leads to an over-

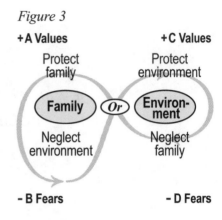

Figure 3

focus on protecting the Family to the neglect of protecting the Environment. The result is to neglect the Environment (-B).

Two important dimensions that impact the decision to choose Family over Environment are connection and urgency.

1. Connection to my Part of the Whole – The Family is a small Part of the Environment which is the Whole. For many it is easier to feel connected to and protective of our immediate Family (Part) than the larger and more abstract notion of the Environment (Whole). This closer connection to Family increases the likelihood that we will choose Family over Environment.

2. Urgency for protecting my part – The connection with Family brings with it an urgency to make sure the Family is protected. The Environment is large and complex, and it feels less urgent and more like a long-term issue. As a result, we are likely to choose Family and get to the Environment later.

Figure 4 shows these two dimensions with "Part – Now" above the left pole and "Whole – Long-Term" above the right pole. This combination of connection and urgency explains why we favor Family when making the false choice between Family *Or* Environment.

From an *Or* perspective, those focusing on the Environment (Tree Huggers) appear to have chosen the Environment over Family. From that perspective, it is easy to see why some people would resist seriously looking at the climate crisis. This understandable choice leads to an over focus on protecting

Figure 4

Part - Now	**Whole - Long Term**
+A Values	+C Values
Protect family	Protect environment
Family *Or* Environment	
Neglect environment	Neglect family
- B Fears	- D Fears

Family Now (+A). The result is to Neglect the Environment and the Long-term survival of the family. (-B).

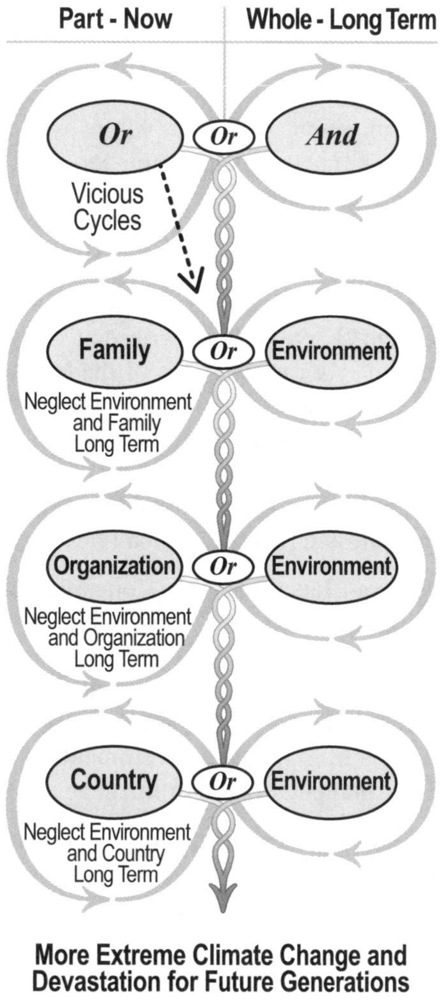

Figure 5 contains the stack of four polarities with *Or* connecting the poles. Moving down the stack, the left poles are expanded from Family to Organization to Country. Though the left pole Part gets bigger, the right pole Whole remains the Environment. As with the Family in *Figure 4*, we tend to have more direct and immediate concerns for protecting our Organization or Country than for protecting the Environment.

When given the false choice between protecting my Organization and providing work for our employees now *Or* protecting the Environment sometime in the future, I am likely to choose to protect my organization now. This *Or* choice leads us to Neglect the Environment and the long-term interests of my company. An Environment that does not support human life will also not support my company.

The same is true when given the false choice between protecting my Country now *Or* protecting the Environment sometime in the future. I am likely to choose to protect my Country and its immediate needs to be strong and healthy. This choice leads us to neglect the Environment and the long-term interests of the Country. An Environment that does not support human life also will not support the Country.

Figure 5

More Extreme Climate Change and Devastation for Future Generations

As mentioned earlier, *Or*-thinking undermines the ability to consider the science behind climate change let alone invest time and energy in addressing it. *Or*-thinking leads to the following assumption: "If climate change is real, I cannot protect my family, my organization, or my country." With that assumption, I will grasp for any indicator that climate change is not real. I will welcome the possibility that there is still confusion over the issue. Confusion is a form of resistance. It protects us from harsh realities. It can be comforting to think, "Maybe it isn't true." I group climate change confusion as a type of climate change denial because they both have the same impact of not giving the climate crisis the attention it deserves. The climate crisis is real, *now.* Denial only makes things worse.

Or-thinking was an important reason that the U.S. Senate voted 95–0 against signing the Kyoto Protocol. *Or*-thinking also served as the basis for President Trump's withdrawal from the Paris Climate Accord 20 years later.

Though it is understandable that any of us would choose to protect our Family, Organization, and Country now over choosing the Environment in the future, these are false choices that combine to result in more extreme climate change and devastation for future generations. This is indicated at the bottom of the stack in Figure 5.

Addressing the Climate Crisis Now

Focusing on the Part we feel most connected to (Family, Organization, and Country) gives us an unconscious sense of urgency to take care of those parts. We assume we can take care of the Whole (Environment) in the long-term. Those of us appealing for attention to the climate crisis now have an increasing sense of urgency. It comes from the conviction that climate change already has a negative impact, and in the long-term it will have a disastrous impact on our Family, Organization, and Country. Also, we are concerned about the impact on the other animals and plants that share our planet.

My son, Luke, has been concerned about the climate crisis for many years. His sense of urgency increases with every report on climate change and its impact now and in the future. I have joined him in my own sense of urgency about the climate crisis. This chapter is not intended to convince readers that climate change is real and its impact will be devastating. I encourage you, instead, to look at current reports from the Intergovernmental Panel on Climate Change (IPCC) and the U.S. Environmental Protection Agency (EPA).

I believe the scientists studying climate change are right; we have urgent work to do. The question is not whether we protect our Family/Organization/Country *Or* the Environment. This is a false choice. We can and must do both. The question is, "How do we protect them *And* the environment Now *And* Long-Term?"

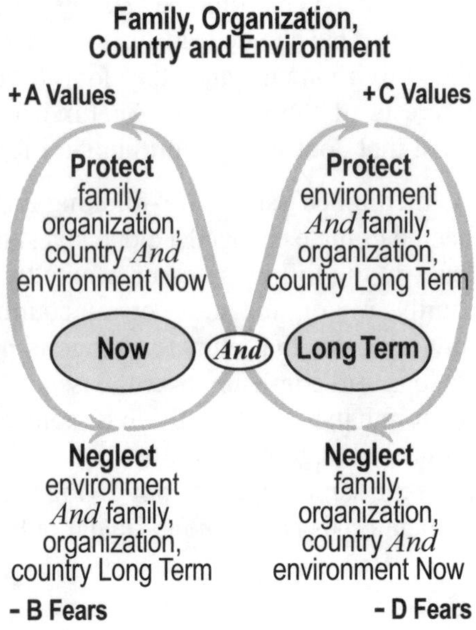

Figure 6 reframes the question. This map is a modification of *Figure 3*. The pole names have been changed to Now *And* Long-Term. Each quadrant begins **in bold** with the content from *Figure 3* and then includes what is missing to reflect the new poles.

In this map, the greater purpose statement includes Family, Organization, Country *And* Environment. This reflects

Figure 6

Family, Organization, Country and Environment

+A Values   +C Values

Protect family, organization, country *And* environment Now

Protect environment *And* family, organization, country Long Term

Now   *And*   Long Term

Neglect environment *And* family, organization, country Long Term

Neglect family, organization, country *And* environment Now

− B Fears   − D Fears

the reality that all of us want to protect our Family, Organization, Country *And* all of us want to protect the Environment. It is a false assumption that those of us wanting to protect Family do not care about the Environment. It is also a false assumption that those of who want to protect the Environment do not care about Family.

When we put *And* between the poles, Family *And* Environment combined with Now *And* Long-Term, notice what happens in each upside of *Figure 6*. We affirm that we can and must protect our Family, Organization, Country *And* Environment now (+A). The natural, sometimes unconscious urgency we feel about protecting our Family, Organization, Country is supplemented with the conscious urgency that we protect them by protecting the Environment. We can and must protect both now.

Leveraging this polarity also affirms that we can protect our Family, Organization, Country *And* the Environment long term (+C). We can maintain an Environment in which our great, great, grandchildren can flourish. For that to happen, we need to ensure that plant and animal life are allowed to flourish.

And Brings Possibilities to the Climate Crisis Discussion

Figure 7 provides the possibilities that come from supplementing *Or* with *And*. In this new stack, we build from the bottom up using the natural tension between the two poles to lift the system toward a Greater Purpose: Sustainability for Family, Organization, Country *And* Environment.

Starting at the bottom, we can solve problems (upside of *Or*) *And* leverage polarities (upside of *And*). The dotted arrow from *And* in the right pole indicates that we bring *And*-thinking to the other polarities going up the stack. We can protect Family *And* Environment now (upside of Family) *And* long-term (upside of Environment); protect Organization *And* Environment now (upside of Organization) *And* long-term (upside of Environment); protect country and Environment now (upside of Country) *And* long-term (upside of Environment). Leveraging one polarity well helps in leveraging the next one well.

Figure 7

Sustainability for Family, Organization, Country and Environment

249

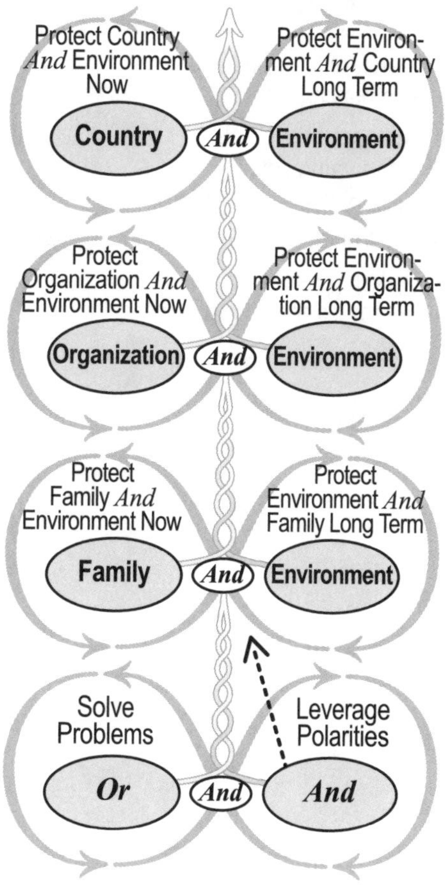

Figure 8

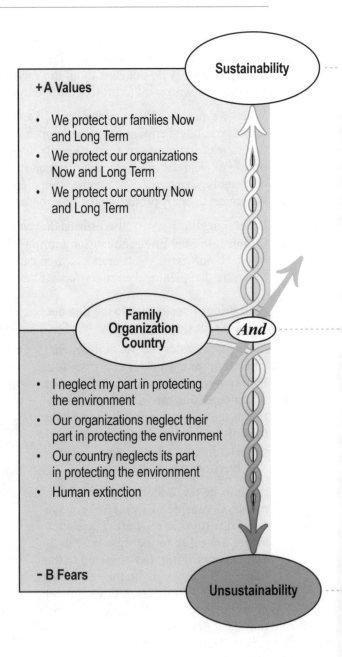

Action Steps

- Provide the basics, including job training for families losing work in transition to renewable energy
- Create renewable energy businesses (HL)
- Retain/gain country strength with renewable energy (HL)
- Explicitly use *And* (HL)

Early Warnings

- Denial/confusion about climate change
- Increase in average temperature, etc.
- USA Senate votes 95-0 not to sign Kyoto Protocol
- Trump pulls U.S. out of Paris Climate Accord 2017

+ A Values

- We protect our families Now and Long Term
- We protect our organizations Now and Long Term
- We protect our country Now and Long Term

Sustainability

Family Organization Country

And

- I neglect my part in protecting the environment
- Our organizations neglect their part in protecting the environment
- Our country neglects its part in protecting the environment
- Human extinction

- B Fears

Unsustainability

Polarity Map®

Sustainability

+C Values

- We do our part to protect the environment Now and Long Term
- Our organizations do their part to protect the environment Now and Long Term
- Our countries do their part to protect the environment Now and Long Term

And — Environment

- I neglect protecting my family: no food or shelter
- We neglect protecting our organizations and their employees: go under
- We neglect protecting our country: become weak and vulnerable

– D Fears

Unsustainability

Action Steps

- Retain/gain legislation protecting our environment from pollution and excessive climate change
- Create renewable energy businesses (HL)
- Retain/gain country strength with renewable energy (HL)
- Explicitly use *And* (HL)
- U.S. recommits to Paris Climate Accord and future accords

Early Warnings

- Increase in families losing fossil fuel related jobs without alternative means to care for families
- Increase in fossil fuel and related businesses closing
- Identifying others as "evil" deniers and polluters: feel self-righteous indignation

Taking Action to Address the Climate Crisis – the SMALL Process

Seeing: The first step in seeing is to remember that seeing is loving. If we could see, completely, those denying or confused about the climate crisis and those organizing to address the climate crisis, love would be the result. The second step in seeing is to see relevant polarities. In this chapter, I have focused on a version of the Part *And* Whole polarity: protecting Family, Organization, Country *And* protecting the Environment. Family, Organization, and Country are three polarities stacked with the *Or/And* polarity. The other polarity that emerged as important was Now *And* Long-Term.

Mapping: The reason to map a polarity is to see beyond the two poles connected by *And*. The full map allows us to Assess, Learn, and Leverage the polarity through Action Steps and Early Warnings.

Figure 8, on previous pages 250 and 251, is a full Polarity Map® with Action Steps and Early Warnings.

Family, Organization, and Country is the left pole *And* the Environment is the right pole. Within each quadrant, the focus is on Now *And* Long-Term. The Greater Purpose Statement is Sustainability and the Deeper Fear is Unsustainability: an environment that will not sustain life.

The map does not include all possible content within each quadrant or all possible Action Steps and Early Warnings. Instead, it frames the conversation, valuing and respecting the upsides of both poles.

Assessing: The map uses a "trend arrow". The trend arrow question is, "At this time, is the energy trending (or needing to trend) toward the upside of Family, Organization, Country (–D toward +A) or toward the upside of Environment (–B toward +C)? In my assessment for the United States in 2020, the energy needs to trend toward the upside of Environment (+C) because we have over-focused on protecting our Family, Organizations, and Country to the neglect of the Environment.

Early Warnings (EW –B) causing me to make this assessment included:

- Denial/confusion about the climate crisis. This denial/confusion comes from wanting to protect Family, Organization, Country combined with the false assumption that we must choose between those things *Or* the Environment.

- Increase in average temperature and growing indicators of problems resulting from climate change.

- In 1997, the U.S. Senate voted 95–0 against ratification of the Kyoto Protocol. This unanimous vote was not an indication that the senators did not care about the environment. It indicated the unconscious bias for *Or*-thinking.

- In 2017, President Trump withdrew from the Paris Climate Accord. Support for this decision came from citizens and legislators who saw it from an *either/Or* perspective and chose Family, Organization, and Country.

These Early Warnings contributed to my assessment that the trend arrow needs to point from (-B) toward (+C). If you see it the other way, switch the arrow so it points from (-D) toward (+A). You also could see it differently for a different country or at a different time. Regardless of where the trend arrow points, Action Steps are needed for each upside.

Learning: If we determine that we need to go to the upside of the Environment (+C), it means, paradoxically, that first we should focus on Action Steps to protect the Family, Organization, and Country (AS +A). Then, we should focus on Action Steps to protect the Environment (AS +C). Before planning to protect the Environment, we need to be very explicit about plans to protect our Family, Organization, and Country. This paradoxical change process was described as "getting unstuck" in *Chapter 13*.

Leveraging: This final step in the SMALL process includes Action Steps to maximize the upsides and Early Warnings to minimize the downsides. Because we are wanting to move to (+C), we begin, below, with identifying Action Steps for (+A).

Action Steps (AS +A) to gain (or maintain) the upsides of Family, Organization, Country (+A) include:

- Provide the basics, including job training for families losing work in the transition to renewable energy. Advocates for the Environment first must be clear that we are committed to protecting families impacted by the switch from fossil fuel to renewable energy. The *And* message is that we can protect Families *And* the Environment. This commitment fits with the polarity of Abundance for Some *And* Basics for All in *Chapter 29*. Coal miners, oil and gas industry employees, and others affected by the shift to renewable energy deserve the basics: food, water, shelter, clothing, education, work with a living wage and healthcare. We can and must protect them *And* the Environment, now and long-term. Legislation to protect the Environment should also protect the Family. We cannot allow legislation to perpetuate the false choice between Family *Or* Environment by addressing only one side of the polarity.

- Create renewable energy businesses. Just as we can and must protect the Family *And* Environment, we must do our best to protect our Organizations *And* the Environment. For example, how might we protect businesses reliant on fossil fuel by supporting them in shifting to renewable energy? How do we address the impact on owners and employees when businesses do not survive the shift? We can and must protect Organizations *And* the Environment. This action step is High Leverage (HL) because it contributes to retaining/gaining the upsides of both poles.

- Retai*n*/gain country strength through renewable energy (HL). Many wars have been fought over access to fossil fuels located within national boundaries. Sun and wind are more widely available. Energy independence through renewable energy is a good way to protect our Country *And* protect the Environment. We can enhance national security while caring for the Environment.

- Explicitly use *And* (HL). Our communications and actions must be clear that we are leveraging key polarities in order to protect our Families, Organizations, and Countries *And* the Environment Now *And* Long-term. Efforts to address the climate crisis without explicitly leveraging these key polarities undermine those efforts radically.

Early Warnings (EW −D) of over-focusing on the Environment to the neglect of Family, Organization, Country (−D) include:

- Increase in families losing fossil fuel related jobs without alternative means to care for those families.

- Increase in Fossil fuel and related businesses closing. These concerns need to be acknowledged, respected, and addressed by the Action Steps in support of the upside of Family, Organization, and Country (+A).

- Identifying others as "evil" deniers and polluters – feel self-righteous indignation. This is a version of the Justice *And* Mercy polarity. When we have trouble admitting our own contribution to the climate crisis, it is easier to project our shortcomings onto "them."

Action Steps (AS +C) to gain or maintain the upside of Environment (+C) include:

- Retain/gain legislation protecting our environment from pollution and climate change. What I list here is simply placeholder examples to represent an ongoing need for legislation and enforcement to slow down and reverse the impact of the climate crisis.

- Create renewable energy businesses (HL).

- Retain/gain country strength with renewable energy (HL).

- Explicitly use *And* when addressing the tension within polarities that are part of the climate crisis struggle (HL).

- Re-affirm Paris Climate Accord and future accords.

Planning *And* Implementing

The SMALL process is done with key stakeholders first as a planning discussion in which possible Action Steps and Early Warnings are identified. When moving to implementation, high leverage Action Steps are a helpful place to start because they simultaneously support both upsides. It is also important to make sure that enough Action Steps are implemented to support the upside of the pole you are moving from to avoid the downside of the pole you are moving toward. When that is done, it will be easier to implement the Action Steps to gain or maintain the upside of the pole you want to move toward at this point in time.

Summary

The issue of the climate crisis is more complicated than this chapter can begin to reflect. At the same time, a polarity lens can be useful in addressing complicated issues by identifying underlying tension patterns and leveraging them.

When asked whether we want to protect our Family, Organizations, and Country *Or* protect the Environment, we will likely choose Family, Organization and Country. Connection and urgency drive this choice. For example, we are likely to feel more connected to Family than the Environment and to feel more urgent about protecting Family now than the environment, which we feel we can address long-term.

When we stack Family, Organization, and Country on the left side with Environment on the right side and connect the two sides with *Or*, the Environment pole is neglected. Connecting the two sides with *And* changes how we communicate about, and influences the actions we take, to slow down and reverse climate change.

Both advocates for the Environment and those denying the climate crisis care about protecting Family, Organization, and Country. Also, both care about the Environment. Both also feel a sense of urgency. Those denying climate change unconsciously feel that it is urgent to protect their Family now. Those organizing to reverse the climate crisis consciously feel that it is urgent to protect the Environment Now in order to protect our Families Now *And* Long-term.

The SMALL process is useful. Viewing the issue through a polarity lens encourages respect for the values and fears of *both* those denying the climate crisis *And* the Environmental advocates. When planning, if the present trend needs to move from the downside of Family, Organization, and Country to the upside of Environment, it is important to identify Action Steps to protect Family, Organization, and Country first and then identify Action Steps to protect the Environment. When implementing, it is often helpful to do high leverage Action Steps first because they support the upside of both poles. It is also helpful to make sure enough Action Steps supporting the present pole are being carried out to hold on to the benefits of that pole while going after the upsides of the interdependent pole. In many cases, the Action Steps for both upsides can then be carried out simultaneously.

And-thinking is a framework for making a difference with climate change. Without supplementing *Or*-thinking with *And*-thinking, efforts to reverse the climate crisis in time to protect future generations are undermined radically. The survival of future generations is dependent, in part, upon supplementing *Or*-thinking with *And*-thinking.[R112]

New Realities in Chapter 30

Reality 112   *And*-thinking is a framework for addressing climate change. Without supplementing *Or*-thinking with *And*-thinking, efforts to reverse the climate crisis in time to protect future generations are undermined radically. The survival of future generations is dependent, in part, upon supplementing *Or*-thinking with *And*-thinking.

Chapter 31

Women and Other Marginalized Groups
in Shared Leadership is Right And Smart

A targeted universal strategy is inclusive of the needs of both dominant and marginalized groups but pays particular attention to the situation of the marginalized group. ~ Dr. powell, pg. 14

In *Chapter 7*, I referenced john a. powell's book, <u>Racing to Justice</u>,[70] in which he talks about the Dominant Group *And* Marginalized Groups:

In virtually every area of dominance and marginalization, I am a member of the dominant group that is responsible for creating the marginalization and for perpetuating it. A few areas include being rich, white, cisgender and male. It is my responsibility as a member of the dominant group to speak out against our marginalization of others and to do what I can to change the practices and policies that perpetuate it. Sharing our Polarity Map® and principles is one way I am trying to do just that.

There is a second responsibility as a member of the dominant group. It is to listen to members of the marginalized groups for their perspective and insights and to share power with them in creating a better world for all of us. To that end, Polarity Mastery graduates who are members of marginalized groups – women, LBGTQI+ community, Black, Indigenous, and People of Color (BIPOC) – are the authors of four chapters in the first section of *And*: Volume Two–Applications. They provide us with their perspective on applying Polarity Thinking to the issues of marginalization, power and privilege.

In this chapter, the primary focus will be on the marginalization of women with the understanding that those who are marginalized, regardless of the basis, have a more solid, experiential understanding of the tension within polarities than those in the dominant group. This is true because those of us in the dominant group have the power to override the tension within any polarity by just choosing one pole as the "solution." We have the decision-making power to make a false choice between the poles of any polarity and to impose that false choice on the people and systems over which we dominate.

---

[70] powell, john a. *Racing to Justice: Transforming Our Conceptions of Self and Other to Build an Inclusive Society.* Indiana University Press, 2012.

This does not make dominant group members "bad," but it does make us, the systems we control, and members of marginalized groups all vulnerable to the dysfunctions that occur when we treat key polarities as if they were problems to solve. Since women and other marginalized groups experience the tension within polarities more profoundly, they are a natural resource to help us identify and leverage polarities well. It is right that women and other marginalized groups share in leadership because they are a part of our community. It is also smart, from a polarity perspective, because they increase our ability to leverage polarities well. Below are some experiences that expand on this point.

"I Live With These Tensions Every Day!"

When I give a polarity presentation to an audience of men and women,[71] most men will respond by saying something like, "This is very interesting." They have a point. Polarities are very interesting. From the same presentation, many women say something like: "This is so powerful! I live with these tensions every day." These responses are a generalization. Some men talk about living with these tensions and some women do not. Yet, there is a pattern. Women are much more likely to talk about how strongly they experience polarity tensions in their daily lives.

To understand why this is true, consider that when a disagreement over a polarity occurs between two people, the boss (who is more often male) has the final say. *Figure 1* is an example. Michael is the department head where Jennifer works and he points out the need to Centralize. Jennifer suggests the need to Decentralize. They both have a valuable point of view. Given Jennifer's suggestion, Michael quickly reflects on whether he has good reasons to Centralize. He thinks of upsides including being more

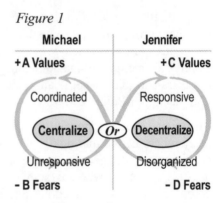

Figure 1

Coordinated (+A). The more important it is for him to be Coordinated, the more he will want to avoid being Disorganized (-D). If his question is framed as "Should we be Coordinated *Or* Disorganized?" he will do what leaders are expected to do, he decides. He thanks Jennifer for her input and informs her that the department will Centralize.

When Michael goes home that evening, he is not likely to experience much tension over the conversation with Jennifer. Any tension he might have experienced between the two poles was removed by deciding to Centralize. When Jennifer goes home,

---

[71] Some of those in the audience may appear to me as men or women but may self-identify as non-binary and / or as a part of the LGBTQI+ community. In virtually all of the settings in which these examples take place there was not an open and clear identification of how those present self-identify. I will talk about men and women based on my perception recognizing that male or female gender attribution could be inaccurate and overlook those for whom those categories do not fit.

she continues to hold the tension within the polarity because she knows that there are good reasons to Decentralize including being Responsive (+C). She also knows that there are vulnerabilities when you Centralize including being Unresponsive (−B). She is living with his decision to Centralize while holding on to her own preference to Decentralize. She is living with the tension. He is not. He is living with the *Or*. She is living with the *And*.

The time lag between when Michael decided to Centralize and when the department experiences the downsides of the decision might be long enough that many other variables intervene and are seen as the cause for those downsides. These variables hide the fact that the false choice between "Centralize *Or* Decentralize" contributed to the problems. Michael also might have moved on to another job before experiencing the downsides of his choice. If he is still head of the department when the downsides of Centralize occur, he might not remember the points that Jennifer mentioned a few years earlier. Jennifer will remember them. Thus, the tension within the polarity is reinforced for Jennifer but still not experienced by Michael.

Since polarities are everywhere, there will be multiple occasions when Michael and Jennifer identify with different poles of a polarity. In those situations, Michael, with decision-making power, can remove tension for himself by using *Or*-thinking, choosing his favored pole and moving on. Jennifer will experience the tension of *And*-thinking as she lives with Michael's pole preference and with her own. This is why, when I introduce Polarity Thinking to their organization, Michael is likely to say, "That's interesting," and Jennifer is likely to say, "I live with these tensions every day!"

Women and other marginalized groups experience polarities more powerfully, in part, because the world is cis male-dominated. A group that has decision-making power over others is more insulated from experiencing a polarity's tension because they have the power to choose one pole *Or* the other. We can override those supporting the alternate pole. Those with less decision-making power have richer direct experience with the power differential and with the tension between one pole *And* the other. This gives them an advantage in seeing polarities, valuing their potential, and learning to leverage them.[R113]

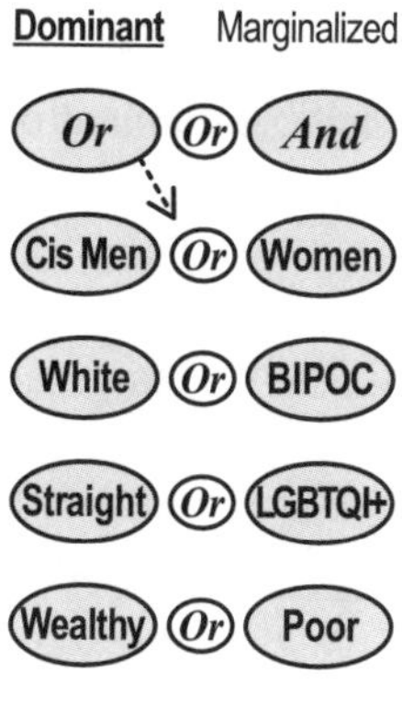

Multiple Marginalization: Intersectionality of Marginalization

Figures 2 and *3* show the same stack of polarities with the left poles associated with the dominant cultures in the U.S., while the right poles associate with marginalized cultures. This is an overview, graphic pair.

In *Figure 2, Or*-thinking is associated with the four dominant groups below the *Or* pole in the stack: Cis Men, White, Straight, Wealthy. *And*-thinking is associated with the four elements of marginality below the *And* pole of the stack: Women, Blacks, Indigenous, People of Color, LGBTQI+,

Figure 2

Dominant   Marginalized

Or   (Or) And

(Cis Men) (Or) (Women)

(White) (Or) (BIPOC)

(Straight) (Or) (LGBTQI+)

(Wealthy) (Or) (Poor)

Poor. Notice that "Dominant" is bold and underlined. This represents the dominant group using its dominance to focus on *Or*-thinking and its preference for the left poles. With all four of the dominant groups, *Or*-thinking reinforces our need for dominance and our dominance reinforces *Or*-thinking. To the degree that the dominant group brings only *Or*-thinking to this stack of polarities, a vicious cycle is created that undermines the system and everyone in it.

In *Figure 3*, notice that both "Dominant" and "Marginalized" are bold and underlined. This represents the marginalized group using *And*-thinking to claim and share power with the dominant group. For all four of the marginalized groups, *And*-thinking supports them in surviving and thriving in spite of their marginalization and their marginalization supports them in developing *And*-thinking. To the degree that the dominant group can supplement *Or*-thinking with *And*-thinking, both groups can create a virtuous cycle which supports the system and everyone in it.

Figure 3

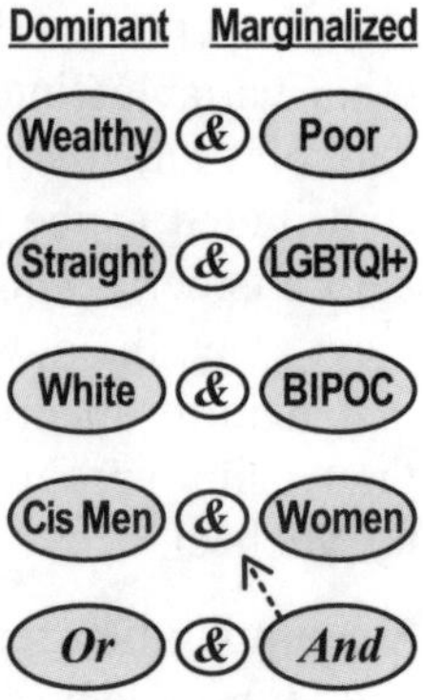

Dominant   **Marginalized**

(Wealthy) *&* (Poor)

(Straight) *&* (LGBTQI+)

(White) *&* (BIPOC)

(Cis Men) *&* (Women)

(*Or*) *&* (*And*)

People who have an intersection of more than one form of marginalization understand each facet of their marginalization and the depths of the combined effect. For example, in the United States, the marginalization of woman leads to them making 80% of what non-Hispanic white men make for the same work. The marginalization of black people, when combined with the marginalization of being a woman leads to black women making 61%.[72] Each layer of marginalization takes its toll as an accumulated weight of micro-aggressions and macro-aggressions. At the same time, each layer of marginalization provides a possibility for empathy and connection with others who are marginalized. Each layer of marginalization provides an opportunity to forgive those who dominate in that layer of domination as we have been forgiven for our own times of domination and insensitivity to it. Each layer of marginalization also provides another level of awareness of the power difference between the dominant groups and the marginalized groups and the tension within the polarities being overlooked by the dominant groups. Paradoxically, the greater the intersectionality of marginalization, the greater the potential resource to the larger community to help us own our shortcomings and reclaim our humanity; to be forgiven that we might forgive; to celebrate our interdependence; and to see and leverage the many polarities in which we live.

Multiple Domination: Intersectionality of Dominance

For the dominant group in each layer of dominance and marginalization, we have a collection of blind spots about our impact on the marginalized. Each layer of domination reduces the possibility for empathy and connection with those whom we have marginalized and with those in our dominant group which leads to insensitivity and isolation. Each layer of domination creates a need for forgiveness which dehumanizes when it goes unrecognized. It undermines our opportunity to

---

[72] American Association of University Women. *Black Women and the Pay Gap.* August 21, 2018.

experience forgiveness and our ability to forgive. Each layer of domination creates another level of insolation and denial of the power difference between dominant groups and marginalized groups. Each layer of dominance insolates us from experiencing the tension within polarities and our ability to see and leverage them. Paradoxically, the greater the intersectionality of domination, the more we need the humility, wisdom, and humanity and forgiveness from those we have marginalized to recover from our own dehumanization of ourselves and of those we have marginalized.

Right *And* Smart

It is right to respect human rights. It is a human right to Claim *And* Share decision-making power over how we live together and how we impact the rest of the planet.[73] This human right is reinforced by the democratic claim of one person – one vote. Women, who are virtually half of the adult population, combined with men from other marginalized groups and members of the LGBTQI+ community, make up a significant majority of our population. It is right that this marginalized majority Claim *And* Share decision-making power with the dominant minority.

It is also smart. In the beginning of this book, I stated that individuals and organizations that leverage polarities well outperform those that do not. In 45 years of learning with others about applying Polarity Thinking around the world, I have found that women, on average, more readily see and leverage polarities than men. While many men are very good at seeing and leveraging polarities and some women are not, in my experience, women generally have an enhanced capacity to see and leverage polarities. It is not as dramatically obvious, but this generalization about women also applies to other marginalized groups. It is smart to take advantage of this.

If we were to assess the ability to leverage polarities as an essential leadership capacity, we would have more effective leaders of all genders. In addition, the percent of women and other marginalized group leaders would increase. It would be both right and smart to have polarity-leveraging people in decision-making in all areas of life, including business, industry, government, religion, education, and the military.

Decision-Making Power Reinforces *Or*-thinking While *Or*-thinking Reinforces the Desire to Claim Decision-Making Power Without Sharing It

In *Chapter 26,* we looked at how education and acculturation contribute to us unconsciously favoring *Or*-thinking and problem solving. *Or* works well when addressing the problems we face daily. It does not work well in addressing the polarities we face daily. As we have seen in *Chapters 22* and *29*, when we bring an unconscious *Or*-thinking bias to concerns about protecting loved ones, we assume that *either* we claim power to protect those we love *Or* those we love go

---

[73] *Universal Declaration of Human Rights.* UN General Assembly resolution 217 III A, December 10, 1948, www.un.org/en/universal-declaration-human-rights/.

unprotected. Within this *either/Or* choice, it is understandable that we will claim power for ourselves and those we love. In this way, *Or*-thinking reinforces claiming power.

If we succeed in claiming power, such power insulates us from experiencing the tension within polarities. The power we claim allows us to choose one pole *Or* the other of a polarity with few, obvious, short-term consequences. As a matter of fact, we are rewarded for solving problems. We are affirmed for bringing the upside of *Or*-thinking to the organizations and countries where we have decision-making power. This reinforces seeing all difficulties as *either/Or* problems to solve and distances us from the ability to see and leverage polarities. With our power, we decide that leadership itself is defined as the upside of *Or*-thinking including being clear and decisive. Thus, claiming decision-making power reinforces *Or*-thinking.

Worldwide, there are more men in positions of power. There are likely many complex reasons for this. One reason is that cisgender men are, on average, physically bigger and stronger than women. Historically, physical dominance gave men an advantage when claiming power to protect loved ones and when seeking decision-making dominance.

Regardless of historical origins, the reality is that men hold more decision-making power in the major institutions that control our governments, workplaces, and religious institutions. Since we all live with polarities, we all have some tacit wisdom about them. At the same time, the longer men have primarily held decision-making power, the more likely that position has reinforced an unconscious bias for *Or*-thinking and undermined *And*-thinking. The longer women and other marginalized groups have been kept out of decision-making power, the more likely they have experienced the tension within polarities and have learned to see and leverage them in order to survive and even thrive in spite of being marginalized.

For example, at the time of the founding of the United States, most states allowed only white male property owners to vote. This group was 6% of the population. The 15th Amendment of the U.S. Constitution in 1870 gave black men the right to vote and the 19th Amendment in 1920, gave white women the right to vote. The intersectionality of race and gender kept black women without a vote. Both the 15th and 19th Amendments were based on *And*-thinking by the marginalized groups seeking the right to vote. The message was, "You keep your claim on your right to vote *And* share that right with us. We are claiming our right to vote *And* are happy to share that right with you." It was about claiming *And* sharing power. Notice how different this is from, "*Either* you have the vote *Or* we have the vote and we are going to take it from you because you have kept it from us." Such a proposition would be neither right nor smart for the country. The message from the marginalized groups was about sharing power, which comes from an *And* assumption about power. The resistance from the dominant group comes from an *Or* assumption of power in which to share it is to lose it.

A False Choice: *Or*-thinking *Or And*-thinking

Progress has been made in terms of women and men sharing decision-making power *And* there is more work to be done. The fundamental polarity at the core of this work is *Or*-thinking *And And*-thinking. All polarities become mired in their downsides when we approach them from an *Or*-thinking mindset. That is why, in *Chapters 29* and *30*, the first polarity in each stack is *Or And And*.

Or-thinking and having decision-making power are not inherently bad and they are not a basis for disparaging white, cis men in the United States. At the same time, *And*-thinking is the only way to successfully leverage polarities. As mentioned above, women and other marginalized groups, with a stronger connection to *And*-thinking, are a valuable, underutilized resource when leveraging polarities.

All Genders Are Potential Resources for Leveraging the Tension Between *Or And And*

Figure 4 is a map of the *Or And And* polarity. When a cis man has decision-making power, it is easier to be Clear and Decisive (+A). Having power makes him less vulnerable to accusations of being wrong or misguided. When a woman works for a cis man with decision-making power, she is smart to be Flexible and Thoughtful (+C). With less decision-making power, she is more vulnerable to accusations of being wrong or misguided. In this context, it is smart of her to bring Flexibility to any situation and be more Thoughtful about her decisions. It is smart for the organization because she brings what is needed to keep Clarity and Decisiveness (+A) from becoming Rigid and Reactive (-B). Shared leadership could embrace both upsides by being Clear and Decisive while being Flexible and Thoughtful. *Or*-thinking without *And*-thinking undermines this opportunity.

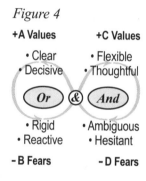

Figure 4

Resistance to Women and Other Marginalized Groups Bringing *And*-thinking To Decision-Making

Figure 5 reminds us that all polarities contain two points of view. Within the *Or*-thinking mental framework, *either* I am Clear and Decisive (+A) *Or* I am Ambiguous and Hesitant (-D); there is no room for *And*-thinking. This reality is represented with the *Or* between the two poles and the absence of (+C) or (-B). The stronger the dominant group values the upside of *Or*, including being Clear and Decisive, the more that becomes our turf (+A). It takes on the quality of "my turf" because, from an *Or*-thinking perspective, we cannot share it. *Either* it is mine, *Or*

Figure 5: "Or" Point of View

+A Values	+C Values
My turf - I am:	
• Clear	• ?
• Decisive	• ?
Or Or And	
	She is:
• ?	• Ambiguous
• ?	• Hesitant
- B Fears	**- D Fears**

it is yours. We also have an equally strong aversion for being Ambiguous or Hesitant. *Either* I am Clear and Decisive *Or* I am Ambiguous and Hesitant. The often-unconscious orientation for many men and dominant group members is, "I am Clear and Decisive and declare it as the right way to lead. I certainly am not Ambiguous or Hesitant. Those who hesitate are lost." The decision between being Clear and Decisive *Or* being Ambiguous and Hesitant is, itself, Clear and Decisive. We are half right when claiming this point of view. What is necessary is to supplement it with the upside of *And*.

Women and Other Marginalized Groups Who Bring the Upside of *And* Get Accused of Its Downside

Figure 6 shows what happens when women and other marginalized groups bring *And*-thinking as a supplement to *Or*-thinking. They contribute the upside of *And*: Flexible and Thoughtful (+C). These words are printed in grey to demonstrate that their contribution is "hidden" or out of view for many men. This is because of the preoccupation, for many men, with an *Or* point of view (+A/-D). Though it is not easy for many men to see, it is the exact perspective needed to keep our Clarity and Decisiveness (+A) from becoming Rigid and Reactive (-B). They are also in grey because they are hidden from the *Or* point of view.

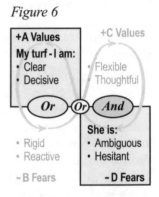

Figure 6

I cannot be both Clear/Decisive and Ambiguous/Hesitant. So, which is it? This makes it difficult for me to acknowledge the reality that I am, in fact, sometimes Ambiguous and Hesitant. What I cannot own as true of me, I will tend to project on an obvious "not me" which, in this context, would be women and other marginalized groups. I need them to occupy the downside of *And* in my place so I do not have to own it. "I am not Ambiguous and Hesitant. They are." I use my power to claim my turf and to put them in "their place." We say something like, "Women are just too soft spoken and Hesitant. In order to become leaders, they need to be Clearer and more Decisive."

If I start from an assumption that *either* men have Clarity and Decisiveness *Or* women have it, I cannot allow a woman to claim it. If I lose my identity as a Clear and Decisive man, I become an Ambiguous and Hesitant man and that is just not acceptable. This is often an unconscious bias. The impact is the same whether it is conscious or not. This is how a woman, being Flexible and Thoughtful (+C), gets accused of being Ambiguous and Hesitant (-D). She may bring the upside of *And*, but she is seen as in its downside. She who is thoughtful is called "hesitant." And, as we all know, "She who hesitates is lost."

Those seeing her that way have a point. The downside of *And* is real just like the downside *Or* is real. It is true that if you over-focus on being Flexible and Thoughtful (+C) without also being Clear and Decisive (+A), you become Ambiguous and Hesitant (-D). This awareness is accurate but incomplete. The problem occurs when some men, being afraid of the downside of *And*, have trouble being Flexible and Thoughtful. This is not good for men or the organizations and countries they lead. Both are vulnerable to becoming Rigid and Reactive (-B).

Women and Other Marginalized Groups Bringing the Upside of *Or* Get Accused of Its Downside

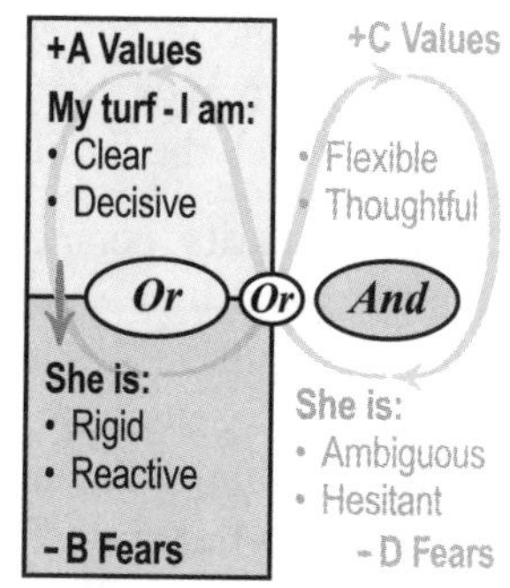

In Figure 7, when a woman who is accused of being Ambiguous and Hesitant (-D) supplements her Flexibility and Thoughtfulness (+C) with being powerfully Clear and Decisive (+A), many men have trouble sharing the upside of *Or* (+A). From an *Or* perspective, the unconscious question is, "Does this turf (being Clear and Decisive) belong to me *Or* to her?" The answer? "This is my turf. I am the Clear and Decisive one."

Figure 7

If being Clear and Decisive belongs to me, where do I put her? I have traditionally simply stereotyped her as Ambiguous and Hesitant (-D). But that space, in grey text, is unavailable because it is obvious that she is not being Ambiguous or Hesitant. She is being powerfully Clear and Decisive (+A). She is not being Flexible and Thoughtful (+C), also in grey text, because it is not an available place to put her at the moment. She has already been Flexible and Thoughtful and has received little or no credit. She shifted poles, which she can do more easily because *And*-thinking includes both poles in the first place. Her *And*-thinking orientation allows her to more easily access the upside of both poles while my *Or*-thinking orientation results in me choosing one upside and denying me access to the other upside because, from an *Or* perspective, I cannot have both.

If I am unwilling or unable to share the upside of *Or* (+A), the only place within the *Or* half of the map to put her is the downside of *Or* (-D). That is how women, by doing the same things that men do to be defined as Clear and Decisive leaders (+A), get accused of being Rigid and Reactive (-B).[74]

Those with decision-making power can claim the upsides of their preferred pole for themselves and assign the downsides of both poles to those over whom they have power. This is why those with less decision-making power dislike being differentiated by and from those with more power. The differentiation itself is

---

[74] This same experience is reported by Black, Indigenous, People of Color and LGBTQI+ people when they claim their power and become very Clear and Decisive (+A). Some white people and some cisgender straight people will accuse them of being Rigid and Reactive (-B). When women and other marginalized groups claim the upside of *Or*-thinking, they are sometimes called names such as "bitchy," "uppity," "pushy," "nasty," or "loud". The list is long. There is also the reality of internalized marginalization in which those marginalized, like those in the dominant group, take in the messages within the culture about their status and have an unconscious bias against themselves and against others in their marginalized group. They sometimes join the ranks of the dominant group in putting down those in their marginalized group.

disempowering. The power differential is painfully re-asserted as they often become identified with the downsides of both poles of any polarity that is the focus of attention.[R114]

A cis male-dominated system is more likely to have trouble accessing the upsides of *And* than a system where leadership is shared by people of all genders. The absence of marginalized groups in leadership increases the likelihood of getting caught in the downside of *Or* and becoming Rigid and Reactive (-B). It also increases the likelihood that the system will apply *Or*-thinking to polarities. This leads to vicious cycles and unnecessary polarization. It is not good for the dominant group or the marginalized groups. It is not good at any level of system – the individual, the family, the organization, the nation, our humanity, or the planet.

From a polarity perspective, it is smart to supplement *Or*-thinking with *And*-thinking, and it is smart to supplement dominant culture leadership with marginalized culture leadership. When marginalized people are in positions of leadership, we increase the likelihood that *And*-thinking will be used and valued. With *And*-thinking, we continue to value and include *Or*-thinking. *And*-thinking includes *Or*-thinking. From a polarity competency perspective, the question is not whether a person identifies as a man, a woman, or as a non-binary person. The question is, "Can the person solve problems *And* leverage polarities?"

Summary

"A targeted universal strategy is inclusive of the needs of both dominant and marginalized groups, but pays particular attention to the situation of the marginalized group." – john a. powell

In the United States, elements of decision-making dominance include being rich, white, cisgender, and male. Marginalized groups include women, the LGBTQI+ community, Black, Indigenous, and People of Color (BIPOC). Having decision-making power insolates those of us from the tensions within polarities because we can remove the tension for ourselves by making a false choice and choosing one pole as the "solution." We get rewarded for being problem solvers, which is useful when addressing problems but is dysfunctional when addressing polarities.

Women and other marginalized groups live with the tension in polarities because they do not have the decision-making power to impose one pole of a polarity on the dominant group. Experiencing more clearly the tension within polarities results in women and other marginalized groups becoming valuable resources in helping our organizations and countries see and leverage polarities. It is right that women and other marginalized groups share in leadership because they are a part of our organizations and citizens of our countries. It is smart because they bring a more direct access to *And*-thinking which is needed to supplement the *Or*-thinking upon which the dominant culture has over-focused.

New Realities in Chapter 31

Reality 113 A group that has decision-making power over others is more insulated from experiencing a polarity's tension because decision makers
have the power to choose one pole *Or* the other. They can override
those supporting the alternate pole. Those with less decision-making
power have richer, more direct experiences with the power differential and with the tension between one pole *And* the other. This gives
them an experiential advantage in seeing polarities, valuing their potential and in learning to leverage them.

Reality 114 Those with decision-making power can claim the upsides of their
preferred pole for themselves and assign the downsides of both poles
to those over whom they have power. This is why those with less
decision-making power dislike being differentiated by and from
those with more power. The differentiation itself is disempowering.
The power differential is painfully reasserted, as they often become
identified with the downsides of both poles of any polarity which is
the focus of attention.

Chapter 32
Yang *And* Yin

Whenever we stack polarities, it is helpful to think of an organizing principle or common theme for the left poles and the right poles.[R115] One of our most universal, inclusive, and ancient polarities is Yin *And* Yang energy. These two energies are an interdependent pair available to all of us.[R116] I have chosen these two energies as the organizing theme for the stacks of polarities in the three previous chapters in this section.

In the stacks of polarities, I identify all the left poles with traditional Yang energy and I identify the right poles with traditional Yin energy. Historically, we tend to think of "Yin *And* Yang" but I am switching them in these stacks to "Yang *And* Yin." Within a Polarity Map®, the names of the two poles are completely interchangeable, so either name can go first to identify the left pole. When the pole names are switched, their upsides and downsides move with them.[R117] I changed the order for two reasons:

1. To remind us that the normal balance implied in Yin *And* Yang has been disrupted by an over-focus on Yang energy.

2. Most languages read left to right so when we describe the change process, we talk about what we are moving "from" first and then what we are moving "to." For that reason, in our generic, getting unstuck process, we have put the pole we are moving from on the left. In the case of Yang *And* Yin energy, our over-focus on Yang energy makes the Yang poles the ones we need to move from, so I have put them on the left. Paradoxically, in our effort to supplement the Yang focus with the Yin focus, we need to start, in each case, by affirming the pole we are moving from (Yang) as essential and then affirm the pole we are moving toward (Yin) as an equally essential supplement.

People of All Genders Live in a Rich Combination of Yang *And* Yin Energy

Historically, Yang energy has often been identified with the Masculine in each of us and Yin energy with the Feminine in each of us. These associations, combined with *Or*-thinking, has led to stereotyping men and women. From an *Or*-thinking perspective, we create a false choice that men and women are *either* Yang *Or* Yin.

We then assign Yang to men and Yin to women. These stereotypes are not only inaccurate, they are harmful to men, women, our LGBTQI+ community, and our organizations.

When we supplement *Or*-thinking with *And*-thinking, our focus on Yang *And* Yin energy is more inclusive. People of all genders live with a rich combination of *both* Yin *And* Yang energy. What is important, as with all polarities, is to be able to access both energies as needed. Yang energy provides the necessary differentiation between the two poles, while Yin energy makes both poles accessible as an inter-dependent whole.

Figure 1 provides a picture of three rows of icons: non-binary, female, and male, each on a Yang *And* Yin continuum. The light grey on the left represents Yang energy. The dark grey on the right represents Yin energy. Each icon has both Yang and Yin shading. This represents each of us using a combination of Yang *And* Yin energy all the time. Each icon has a different ratio of dark and light grey indicating the strength of their lean toward the Yang or Yin energies.

Figure 1

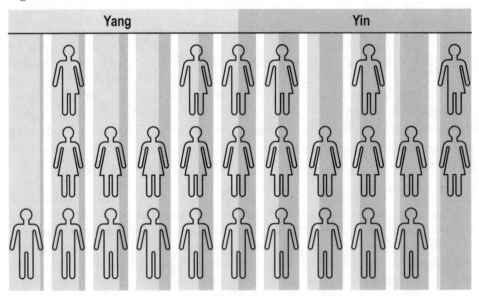

The more the shading is light grey, the stronger the lean toward Yang energy. The icons farthest to the left have the strongest lean toward Yang energy. The more the shading is dark grey, the stronger the lean toward Yin energy. The icons farthest to the right have the strongest lean toward Yin energy. The three icons stacked in the exact middle represent those who feel like they are straddling the two energies without a lean one way of the other.

On an individual basis, you are the best judge of where you would put yourself on the continuum from a slight to a strong attraction to Yang energy, or a slight to strong attraction to Yin energy, at any given time. Or, in the middle: being undecided or clear that your leanings are equal. Wherever we place ourselves, we can contribute to leveraging polarities if we can embrace our own pole preference *And* the alternate pole. This includes the ability to welcome those people who lean toward the alternate pole from our own and those in the middle.

Within *Figure 1,* the three non-binary, five women, and four men who lean toward Yin energy are more likely to welcome those in the middle and those who lean toward Yang energy than the reverse. This is because the mental framework of *And*-thinking (Yin) can include *Or*-thinking (Yang), but the mental framework for *Or*-thinking (Yang) does not have a place for *And*-thinking. At the same time, even those non-binary people, women, and men on the far left of their continuum that have the strongest leaning toward Yang energy, have access to Yin energy. It is within them and is part of their intuitive wisdom and life experience. A polarity lens can support them in continuing to claim their own Yang energy *And* in sharing power with those who lean toward Yin energy.

For years I have conducted an exercise in which I asked people to put themselves on a continuum line, as in *Figure 1*, in which they would stand somewhere from a strong Yang preference to a strong Yin preference. Until recently, I have not considered those who might identify as non-binary. Because of this lack of awareness on my part, I can only guess what their distribution might be on the Yang *And* Yin continuum. In the exercises I have done, the results were not an even 50/50 distribution for those who appeared to be men or women. Instead, it usually looks something like the middle and bottom rows in *Figure 1* in which, among the women, more than half will identify a lean toward Yin energy and, among men, more than half will identify a lean toward Yang energy.

Figure 1 is not intended to imply that 2/6 of non-binary, 4/10 of women and 5/10 of men lean toward Yang energy. It is only a generalization. *Figure 1* depicts the concept that in a group of 6 non-binary, 10 men, and 10 women, a majority of non-binary and women identify with Yin energy and a majority of men identify with Yang energy. The strength of their lean toward either would vary by individual. For example, some non-binary and women will have a much stronger lean toward Yang energy than most men. This is depicted by their icons on the far left of the Yang energy section having a larger amount of lighter shading (Yang) than the male icons below and to the right. The opposite also is depicted. The male icon on the far right of the Yin energy section has a larger amount of darker shading (Yin) than the non-binary and female icons above and to the left.

It is easy to see, from this generalization in *Figure 1*, how men get identified with Yang energy and women with Yin. Non-binary are less easy to stereotype because their non-binary identification does not fit into male and female stereotypes. It is also easy to see how inaccurate the stereotype is that all women should be identified with only Yin energy and all men should be identified with only Yang energy. Many men and non-binary lean toward Yin energy and many women and non-binary lean toward Yang energy.

The dominant culture elements in the United States, described in *Chapter 31*, lean toward Yang energy and expect men to do so. This could result in non-binary people and men who lean toward Yin energy shutting down their personal leaning in order to conform to stereotypes and avoid harassment.

When we look at the stacked polarities, we can see that organizations led by all men are more vulnerable to the downsides of the Yang energy poles, and organizations led by all women and non-binary are more vulnerable to the downsides of the Yin energy poles. Though each group is vulnerable to the downsides of their preferred pole, the degree of vulnerability is greater for organizations led by all men. This is because *Or*-thinking does not include *And*-thinking. *And*-thinking can include *Or*-thinking, so organizations led by all women and non-binary are more able to embrace the upsides of *both* Yang *And* Yin energy. This makes them less vulnerable to the downsides of Yin energy.

As mentioned in *Chapter 31*, in the United States, because white, cis male dominance in decision-making is pervasive, the understanding of the tension within polarities is richer for women and other marginalized groups, even those who lean toward Yang (*Or*) energy. This is one reason why, in the U.S., white, cis men sharing decision-making power with women and other marginalized groups is smart. Accessing Yin energy will make an organization more productive and a better place to work for everyone, including the men.

Organizing the Polarity Stacks Around Yang *And* Yin Energy

In *Chapter 29*, we looked at poverty, racism, and sexism through the lens of *Figure 2*. In *Chapter 30*, we looked at the climate crisis through the lens of *Figure 3*. In *Chapter 31*, we looked at dominant and marginalized cultures through the lens of *Figure 4*. In all three stacks, we have historically over-focused on the left poles (Yang energy) to the relative neglect of their partners on the right (Yin energy).

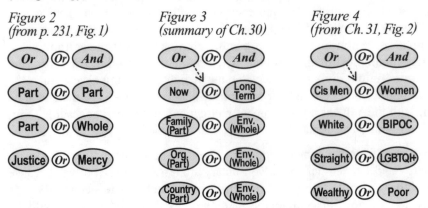

Or And And are the first polarity on top of each stack. We talked about the resistance women and other marginalized groups experience when bringing *And*-thinking as a supplement to *Or*-thinking to their organizations. This reflects a pattern of resistance which occurs when women and other marginalized groups bring any of the right poles as a supplement to the left poles in *Figures 2, 3,* and *4.*

The pattern includes:

1. Women and other marginalized groups bringing the upside of the Yin poles are associated with the downsides of those poles without getting credit for their upsides.

2. Women and other marginalized groups, behaving similarly to white, cis men in claiming the upside of the Yang poles, are associated with the downsides of those poles without getting credit for their upsides.

3. The people from dominant and marginalized groups and their organizations all lose by having limited access to the upside of the Yin poles and by getting stuck in the downsides of the Yang poles. If the imbalance persists, all involved and their organization will also become vulnerable to the downside of the Yin poles.

Often, men who lean toward Yin energy are accused by some Yang-leaning men and women of not being "real men." They, like many women, are associated with the downsides of Yin without getting credit for bringing its upside. This further limits men's access to the upsides of Yin energy while undermining men, women, the LGBTQI+ community, and the organization.

People of all genders who lean toward Yang energy need to claim decision-making power for themselves *And* share power with people who lean toward Yin energy. Also, people of all genders who lean toward Yin energy need to share decision-making power with those who lean toward Yang energy *And* to claim power for themselves.

Each group needs to hold onto their favored pole *And* embrace the other pole. The alternative point of view is always a resource to seeing and experiencing the whole picture of the Polarity Map®.[R118] From a power perspective, the powerful need to listen to the less powerful because they bring the alternate pole that is needed to leverage the polarity well. The greater the power differential, the greater the need for those with more power to listen to those with less power[R119] This is different than the common assumption within a democracy in which, if you have the needed majority of votes, you feel little or no need to listen to the minority view.

Defining Yang *And* Yin Energy

Besides the polarities in *Figures 2, 3,* and *4*, here are some additional polarities that help clarify my associations with Yang *And* Yin energy.

- **Doing *And* Being**: The Nike® slogan, "Just do it! ®" is a great example of Yang energy. When we are busy doing, we are in Yang energy. The Beatles' song, "Let It Be" is a great example of Yin energy. When we are just relaxing and letting ourselves be, without a need to accomplish something, we are in Yin energy.

- **Competition *And* Collaboration:** "The thrill of victory. The agony of defeat. Either is better than neither." This is a Yang energy, competition statement. Planning the Olympics is a Yin energy, collaborative process.

- **Projecting Out – Talking *And* Taking In – Listening:** When writing and talking, I am in Yang energy. When reading and listening I am in Yin energy.

- **Action *And* Contemplation:** Richard Rohr's Center for Action and Contemplation by name and function embraces Yang *And* Yin energy. Its focus on Action embraces Yang energy while its focus on Contemplation embraces Yin energy.

- **Focus on Self – Intent, Candor *And* Focus on Other – Impact, Diplomacy:** When I am clear about my beliefs and intentions, I am in Yang energy. When I focus on others and impact on them or us, collectively, I am in Yin energy.

- **Self-Assured *And* Humble:** Confidence is an example of Yang energy. Humble acknowledgment of one's limitations and mistakes is an example of Yin energy.

- **Task *And* Relationship:** When asked, "How are we doing?" a Yang energy response would focus on how close we are to completing the task. A Yin energy response would focus on how our relationships are doing. "How strong is our team spirit?"

- **Cost *And* Quality:** A value proposition is often a combination of a Yang energy focus on Cost *And* a Yin energy focus on Quality. Paying attention to the "bottom line" is a Yang energy focus. Paying attention to multiple "bottom lines" is a Yin energy focus.

This list of polarities within the umbrella of Yin *And* Yang energy could be much longer. All the poles within Yang energy *And* all the poles within Yin energy are essential. Look at the stacks of polarities in *Figures 2–4*. Imagine the loss that occurs if we over-focus on the left, Yang energy poles, to the neglect of the right, Yin energy poles. This is the vulnerability of all white, cis male leadership. Most men are likely to lean toward Yang energy. We do this because of the wonderful and essential upsides of the Yang energy poles. The problem is not with embracing the Yang energy poles. The problem is with making an unconscious, false choice between those upsides *Or* the wonderful and essential upsides of the Yin energy poles. We bring *Or*-thinking (Yang) to these interdependent pairs when *And*-thinking (Yin) is required.

Supplementing Yang With Yin is Good for Men

Male dominance in leadership has led to dehumanizing half-truths like, "Big boys don't cry." This slogan reflects an effort to avoid the downsides of Yin energy and to instead "stand up and be a man" in the upside of Yang energy. The cost to men raised to embrace Yang energy and to avoid Yin energy is the loss of the ability to know our own feelings and to empathize with others (the upside of Yin). This undermines our relationships and our ability to lead with head *And* heart. It also undermines our ability to hear the message that we are loved just as we are. Supplementing Yang energy with Yin energy is a smart and caring move for men, women, non-binary people, and our organizations.

Assessing for Leadership Effectiveness

We have developed polarity assessments for leaders and for organizations to determine how effectively they are leveraging polarities.[75] The leadership assessment provides helpful criteria for identifying effective future leaders. From a polarity perspective, the primary question is not whether the applicant identifies as a man, a women, or non-binary. The primary question is, "How effective are they at solving problems *And* leveraging polarities?" Because women and other marginalized groups generally see and leverage polarities more readily, a polarity leadership assessment would result in more women and other marginalized groups in leadership.

A similar point has been made by Tomas Chamorrow-Premuzic in his book, <u>Why Do So Many Incompetent Men Become Leaders? (And How To Fix It)</u>.[76] He identifies Emotional Intelligence (EQ) as an important leadership capacity. He points to research indicating that women and men score the same on IQ while women, on average, score higher on EQ. I identify IQ with Yang energy and EQ with Yin energy. Using high EQ as a hiring criterion for leaders will have the same effect as using polarity competency. It will lead to more effective leadership and an increase in women and other marginalized groups as leaders.

Results

Leveraging polarities is helpful in addressing polarization and in increasing profitability. If women, in general, gravitate toward collaboration and are a natural resource for leveraging polarities, shouldn't that be reflected in government and corporate profitability? Glad you asked.

Women more frequently collaborate to sponsor legislation in the U.S. Senate. In 2015, it was reported that women were 54% more likely to co-sponsor a bill with other woman than men with other men and 32% more likely to co-sponsor a bill with a member of the opposite party.[77] This is evidence of collaboration (Yin).

Women in corporate leadership also make businesses more profitable. In 2016, a study surveyed nearly 22,000 firms and found that going from having no women in corporate leadership (the CEO, the board, and other C-suite positions) to a 30%

---

[75] See Appendix A for information on Polarity Assessments.

[76] Chamorrow-Premuzic, Tomas. *Why Do So Many Incompetent Men Become Leaders? (and how to fix it).* Harvard Business Review Press, 2019.

[77] Stolberg, Sheryl Gay. *Proof That Women Are the Better Deal Makers in the Senate.* First Draft, February 19, 2015.

female share is associated with a one-percentage-point increase in net margin. This translates to a 15% increase in profitability (Yang) for a typical firm.[78]

Summary

Yang *And* Yin energy is one of the most universal and inclusive polarities. It has been used as the basis for the list of poles in the polarity stacks in *Chapter 29*, focusing on poverty, racism, and sexism; in *Chapter 30*, focusing on the climate crisis; and in *Chapter 31*, focusing on dominant and marginalized cultures. People of all genders who lean toward Yang energy need to claim decision-making power for themselves *And* share power with people who lean toward Yin energy. Also, people of all genders who lean toward Yin energy need to share decision-making power with those who lean toward Yang energy *And* to claim power for themselves.

New Realities in Chapter 32

Reality 115 Whenever we stack polarities, it is helpful to think of an organizing principle or common theme for all the left poles and all the right poles.

Reality 116 One of our most universal, inclusive, and ancient polarities is Yang *And* Yin energy. These two energies are an interdependent pair that are available to all of us *And* in all of us.

Reality 117 Within a Polarity Map®, the names of the two poles are completely interchangeable so either name can go first to identify the left pole. When the pole names are switched, their upsides and downsides move with them.

Reality 118 From a polarity perspective, the alternative point of view is always a resource to seeing and experiencing the whole picture of the Polarity Map.

Reality 119 From a power perspective, the powerful need to listen to the less powerful because, in a polarity disagreement, they bring the alternate pole that is needed to leverage the polarity well. The greater the power differential, the greater the need for those with more power to listen to those with less power.

---

[78] Noland, Marcus; Moran, Tyler. *Study: Firms with Women in the C-Suite are More Profitable.* Harvard Business Review, February 8, 2016.

SECTION EIGHT
Doing *And* Being

Introduction

This final section is an opportunity to take a break from concentrating on making a difference by leveraging polarity, paradox or dilemma. It is a time to pay attention to two polarities that are not about making a difference, but are essential for making a difference. The first of two chapters is about enjoying life and letting ourselves be. Being is the absolutely essential sister to doing.

The second chapter is an appreciation of the limits of this whole book, with its words and graphs and fun ideas that might be useful to some. Relax and enjoy.

Chapter 33
Making a Difference *And* Enjoying Life

It is 9:00 am on a summer morning in 1994. I am feeling great. My wife, Dana, has just called to let me know she is bringing lunch to the office. She has invited two of my closest friends to join us, my partner David Perkins and John Otterbacher.

I'm thinking, "This is just like Dana." The day before, we had finished a six-month project with Amoco and it was time to celebrate with my wife and friends.

Dana arrives with a picnic basket. I am helping her set the small table in my office for lunch when David arrives. He is his usual warm self but does not mention yesterday's completion of the Amoco project or seem all that excited about this celebration. John is close behind and he too seems a bit tempered for a festive gathering.

After we settled in and started enjoying our sandwiches, Dana tells me why she has planned this lunch. It related to the Amoco project, but not in the way I was thinking. She tells me that all three of them love me very much and they are angry with me. They are angry because my preoccupation with bringing Polarity Thinking to the world is undermining my health and my relationships with family and friends. It has resulted in my doing things that threaten my own safety and the safety of others.

One of many examples they cited was when I had worked all night preparing for a workshop. Early the next morning, without any sleep, I drove five hours to arrive at the workshop. When it was over, I drove home, arriving at 11:00 pm. They pointed out that had I fallen asleep at the wheel, I could have killed myself and others. They also cited examples of many missed opportunities to spend time with Dana, our five children, and our friends. The examples were undeniable and powerful when listed by these frightened, angry people who loved me.

I was embarrassed and saddened by what they said. I was also moved by the love and concern in their voices. Here I was, two years after my first book on how to leverage polarities was published, and loved ones were pointing out what a terrible job I was doing at leveraging the polarity of Work *And* Home. So much for my anticipated celebration lunch! The difference between the celebration I was

279

expecting and the intervention I experienced was a clear demonstration of how out of touch I was with this issue.

It has been twenty-six years since that lunch. On average, with the help of Dana, I am doing a better job of leveraging this polarity. I have changed the names of the poles to Making a Difference *And* Enjoying Life. Making a difference, for me, is any effort driven by the desire to contribute to the quality of life on the planet. Writing this book is one example. Enjoying life, for me, includes everything else: spending time with friends and family, sitting outside with my face toward the sun, eyes closed, listening to the sounds around me; quiet meditation; and kayaking down the Pine River in rural Michigan. While I enjoy my efforts to make a difference as well, the "Enjoying Life" pole for me is enjoying life beyond efforts to make a difference. If you build your own map on this tension, I encourage you to name the poles whatever works for you.

The day of the lunch intervention, Dana and I created a map for Work *And* Home with action steps and early warnings. *Figure 1* is a summary version, which has been useful to us and others. It might give you ideas for creating one that will work for you.

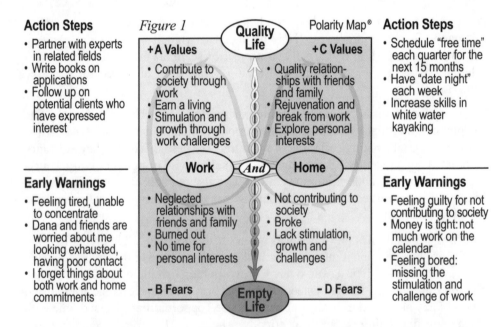

Action Steps
- Partner with experts in related fields
- Write books on applications
- Follow up on potential clients who have expressed interest

Figure 1   Polarity Map®

Quality Life

+A Values
- Contribute to society through work
- Earn a living
- Stimulation and growth through work challenges

+C Values
- Quality relationships with friends and family
- Rejuvenation and break from work
- Explore personal interests

Action Steps
- Schedule "free time" each quarter for the next 15 months
- Have "date night" each week
- Increase skills in white water kayaking

Work *And* **Home**

Early Warnings
- Feeling tired, unable to concentrate
- Dana and friends are worried about me looking exhausted, having poor contact
- I forget things about both work and home commitments

- B Fears
- Neglected relationships with friends and family
- Burned out
- No time for personal interests

- D Fears
- Not contributing to society
- Broke
- Lack stimulation, growth and challenges

Early Warnings
- Feeling guilty for not contributing to society
- Money is tight: not much work on the calendar
- Feeling bored: missing the stimulation and challenge of work

Empty Life

As you read through the map, the only part that might not be self-explanatory is the first action step for the upsides of Home: Schedule free time each quarter for the next 15 months. "Free time" is a concept from Dan Sullivan's Strategic Coach program. This is time on my calendar which is clearly separated from work and work-related activity. I build in 6 to 8 weeks per year of free time, scheduling it 15 months in advance. In January through March each year, I plan with Dana what we will do for free time in April through June of the following year. This provides planning time and also helps both of us connect with how we are feeling in the January–March timeframe that would influence what we would want to do in April–June the following year. This action step and the others have been very useful.

Over the past twenty-six years, I have continued to feel the tension between work *And* home. I continue to be vulnerable to over-focusing on work to the neglect of home, but I am doing a much better job of getting the upsides of each pole and avoiding getting caught in the downsides of the work pole. Our quality of life is better, and we are experiencing more of the upsides of *both* work *And* home.

Individual Responsibility *And* Organizational Responsibility

I had a big advantage in attempting to leverage the Work *And* Home polarity because the company was small and I was an owner. I have worked with some large organizations who wanted my help to support their employees in leveraging the Work *And* Home polarity. When the conversation begins, those inviting me are often thinking about what the employees can do to address the tensions in their commitment to work and to home. The focus on individual responsibility is important because there is a lot that the individual can do and it is very empowering to identify the things you can do that are within your control.

After acknowledging the importance of individual responsibility, I point out that there is another important polarity at play. It is the polarity of Individual Responsibility for Work *And* Home **And** Organizational Responsibility for Work *And* Home. If the organizational culture is one that expects 100-hour work weeks in order to demonstrate commitment, the individual attempting to leverage Work *And* Home will not have a chance. There is often collusion between the employee and the organization. The employee is willing to work long hours to support the company, and the company rewards the long hours with promotions and bonuses. This is an understandable agreement, but over time it can undermine the employee and the company. It undermines the employee who neglects their home life and becomes burned out. It undermines the company because burned out employees make more mistakes and eventually leave to take care of themselves and their family. When they leave, they take their hard-earned expertise with them. It also undermines the community because there is no energy or time available to get involved in the important aspects of making the community a community.

Figure 1 focused on Individual Responsibility for Work *And* Home. *Figure 2* on pages 282 and 283 is a generic map focusing on Organizational Responsibility for Work *And* Home. It offers some generic possibilities to support you in thinking about how your organization can support employees' efforts to leverage the polarity of Work *And* Home.

Figure 2

Action Steps

- Create clear projects with measurable outcomes
- Tie compensation to performance
- Align talents with responsibilities
- Create learning opportunities on the job
- Listen and respond to client needs

Early Warnings

- Increase in sick time
- More expressions of frustration with work
- Increase in complaints about being overwhelmed
- Increase in concerns of absence or neglect by partner/family

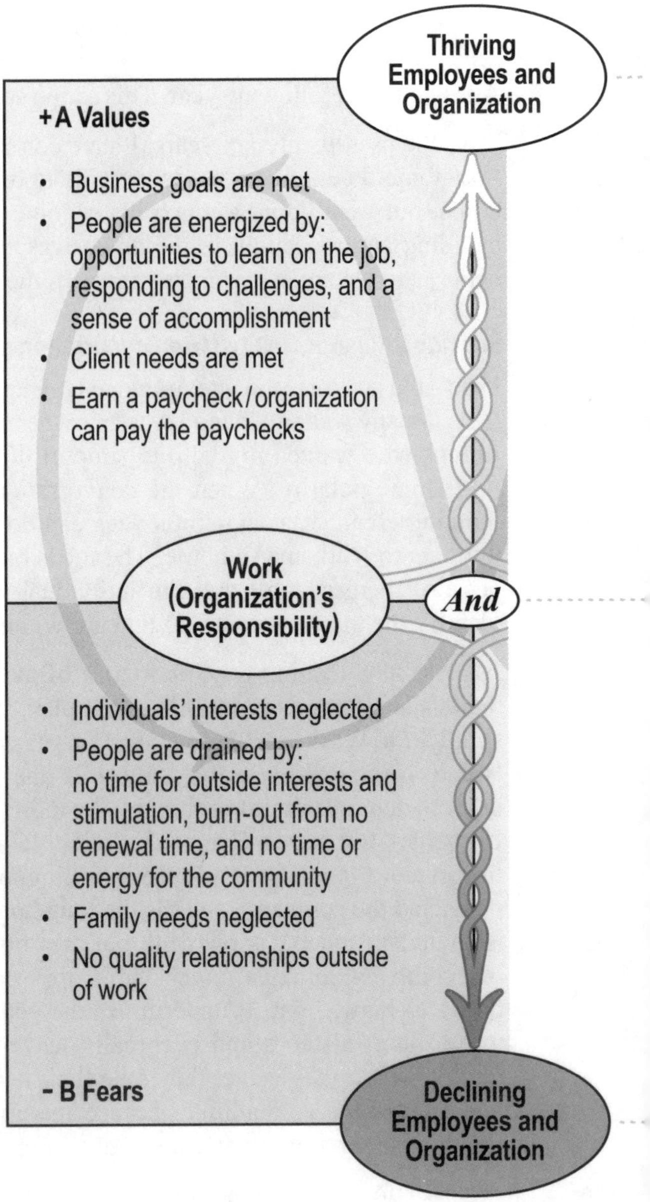

Thriving Employees and Organization

+A Values

- Business goals are met
- People are energized by: opportunities to learn on the job, responding to challenges, and a sense of accomplishment
- Client needs are met
- Earn a paycheck/organization can pay the paychecks

Work (Organization's Responsibility)

And

- Individuals' interests neglected
- People are drained by: no time for outside interests and stimulation, burn-out from no renewal time, and no time or energy for the community
- Family needs neglected
- No quality relationships outside of work

– B Fears

Declining Employees and Organization

Thriving Employees and Organization

+C Values

- Individuals' interests are met
- People are energized by: pursuing outside interests, time for mental and physical renewal and contributing to community
- Family needs are met
- Have quality relationships outside of work

And

Home (Organization's Responsibility)

- Business goals not met
- People are drained by: lack of professional learning opportunities, lack of work challenges and no sense of work accomplishments
- Client needs are neglected
- No paycheck and no money for others' paychecks

- D Fears

Declining Employees and Organization

Action Steps

- Allow for planned vacations
- Allow time to pursue outside interests
- Provide recovery time after intense project completion
- Respect individual family needs and traditions
- Recognize work done in the community

Early Warnings

- Reduction in profit margin
- Clients complaining about neglect or poor service
- Increase in complaints about lack of accomplishment and boredom
- Paycheck reductions

You Can Do Both – Make a Difference *And* Enjoy Life

One of the common aspirations I hear is our shared desire to make a difference. It is my hope that this book will make a difference and be useful to you in some way. I hope you are reminded that you are loved as you are, you are unique, *And* you are connected to the rest of us and all of life. I hope that you feel encouraged to enjoy life while making your difference. The motivation for making a difference is not in order to be loved, it is that we are loved.

How do you go about enjoying life in the midst of making a difference in the lives of others? The possibilities probably will be an ongoing discovery that changes over time. There are unlimited ways to make a difference, and there are unlimited ways to enjoy life. From a polarity perspective, it is important that you recognize that you can do both and you can be intentional about doing both.

The more powerfully you are driven to make a difference and to live your mission, the more vulnerable you are to over-focus on making a difference to the neglect of enjoying life. As with all polarities, when you over-focus on one pole, you first get the downside of that pole and then you get the downside of the other pole as well. When we over-focus on making a difference, first we lose our enjoyment of life and the richness of joyful relationships and then we move toward burnout. When we get burned out, we reduce our ability to make a difference. Focusing on enjoying life (celebrating life *And* just being) supports us in sustaining our efforts at making a difference.

Summary

If we want to make a difference in a sustained way, over time, we also need to pay attention to enjoying life (celebrating life *And* just being in the beauty of life). I began this chapter acknowledging what a poor job I was doing at leveraging this polarity twenty-six years ago. I am still living with this tension and, at times, find myself over-focused on making a difference. With Dana's help, I am doing a better job at regularly gaining the upsides of both poles. It supports me (*And* us) in such a way that I believe I will never retire from this polarity even if I retire from an income-producing job. Making a difference is too important to me *And* enjoying life is too much fun to let go of either. Good luck in your own version of leveraging this polarity.

Chapter 34

I – It *And* I – You:
The Limits of Polarity Thinking

One cannot live in the pure present: it would consume us if care were not taken that it is overcome quickly and thoroughly. But in pure past one can live; in fact, only there can a life be arranged. One only has to fill every moment with experiencing and using, and it ceases to burn. And in all the seriousness of truth, listen: without it a human being cannot live. But whoever lives only with that is not human.[79] ~ Martin Buber

Here, Jewish mystic Martin Buber makes a powerful statement. He points to a polarity I – It *And* I – You. This whole book is contained within one pole of this polarity, I – It. As important as this book is, it is equally important to acknowledge its interdependent pole.

Figure 1

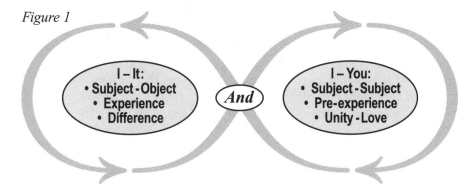

Figure 1 summarizes this polarity. In the dimension of I – It on the left, we are the subject and the world we experience is the object of our experience. In this dimension, we are aware of all the wonderful, beautiful, and sometimes painful aspects of our life in the world. This book is about making a difference. It is about experienceing a need, a person who is hungry or a system that is not functioning well, and responding to that need. We distinguish between problems to solve and

[79] Buber, Martin. *I And Thou*. Scribners, 1923.

polarities to leverage. We create maps and take action. These things take place in the world of experience, within the dimension of I–It.

I–You is a dimension of non-differentiated unity and love. Buber calls it "the pure present." The message: "We are all one. We are all loved. Now." I–You is pre-experience because when we become aware that we have been in that dimension, we have returned to the dimension of I–It in which we "experience it." We can write about it and celebrate it. Writing about and celebrating the I–You dimension of unity and love happens within the dimension of I–It. Visiting the dimension of I–You radically influences our relationship with ourselves, others, and all of nature as we work in the dimension of I–It. The experience of unity and love impacts our efforts to make a difference.

We make a difference in order to affirm our universal unity and to live the reality that we are all unconditionally loved. This is very different than making a difference in order to create a unity with others or in order to make ourselves or our "enemy" more loveable. It brings peace to our struggle with war. It brings joy to our struggle with suffering. It brings love to our struggle with our cruelty to ourselves and others. It brings hope to our struggle with despair.

Our efforts to make a difference are one pole of a polarity that is interdependent with, and supported by, the pole of universal unity and unconditional love. The richness, the energy, and the wonder of life and death is in the oscillation between these poles.[R120]

The mystics from various traditions are the ones who both affirm and go beyond their traditions as they emerge from recurring visits to the pole of I–You.

Martin Buber

The unlimited sway of causality in the It-world, which is of fundamental importance for the scientific ordering of nature, is not felt to be oppressive by the man[80] who is not confined to the It-world, but free to step out of it again and again into the world of relation. Here I and You confront each other freely in a reciprocity that is not involved in or tainted by any causality; here man finds guaranteed the freedom of his being and of being.[81]

The man to whom freedom is guaranteed does not feel oppressed by causality. He knows that his mortal life is by its very nature an oscillation between You and It, and he senses the meaning of this.[82]

Sri Aurobindo

It would only affirm the truth of the differentiating movement along with the truth of the stable unity, regarding them as the upper and lower poles

---

[80] I encourage you to consider substituting "person" for "man" to address the unconscious bias reflected in the writing at the time.

[81] Buber, Martin. *I And Thou*. Scribners, 1923. p. 101

[82] Ibid. p. 102.

of the same truth, the foundation and culmination of the same divine play; and it would insist on the joy of the differentiation as necessary to the fullness of the joy of the unity.[83]

Matthew Fox

Deep down, each one of us is a mystic. ... Getting in touch with the mystic inside is the beginning of our deep service.[84]

Pat Hawk

The true contemplative does not strive for unity of Divine and human only at specific times of prayer, but in all circumstances and conditions of daily life: washing dishes, caring for children, family, work, sleeping.[85]

Judy Cannato

Emergent theories seem to confirm what mystics have been telling us all along—that we are one, not just all human beings, but all creation, the entire universe. As much as we may imagine and act to the contrary, human beings are not the center of the universe – even though we are a vital part of it. Nor are we completely separate from others, but live only in and through a complex set of relationships we hardly notice. Interdependent and mutual connections are integral to all life.[86]

Richard Rohr

Humans are wired to scapegoat and project our shadow elsewhere. Being able to recognize our own negativity takes foundational conversion and transformation of the egoic self. Unitive consciousness – the awareness that we are all one in Love – lays a solid foundation for social critique and acts of justice. I hope we will let God show us how to think and live in new ways; ways that meet the very real needs of our time on this suffering planet.[87]

The Center for Action *And* Contemplation

All of the above quotes, except those of Martin Buber and Sri Aurobindo, came to my attention through my reading of Richard Rohr's Daily Meditations. They are available from the Center for Action and Contemplation.[88] I have been humbled and inspired by Richard Rohr's writing and the rich collection of writings by people of all faiths made available through these meditations. It is no accident that

---

[83] Aurobindo, Sri. *The Life Divine*. Sri Aurobindo Ashram Press, 1939.

[84] Fox, Matthew. *Christian Mystics: 365 Readings and Mediations*. New World Library, 2011, p. 3.

[85] Hawk, Pat. *Pathless Path Newsletter, Vol. 1, no. 4*. 2002, p. 3.

[86] Cannato, Judy. *Quantum Grace: Lenten Reflections on Creation and Connectedness*. Ave Maria Press, 2003, pp 13-14.

[87] Rohr, Richard. *Richard Rohr's Daily Meditation, Unity And Diversity, One in Love*. Center for Action and Contemplation, June 2, 2019.

[88] The Center for Action and Contemplation. Meditations@cac.org.

this organization, by title and practice, is based on the polarity of Action *And* Contemplation. It is in the same energetic field as the polarities named for this section: Doing *And* Being and this chapter: I–It *And* I–You.

This book has focused primarily on the Action pole of this living polarity. My hope is that it will be useful as you make your difference in the world. In the long arc of history, there is not much difference between my picking up a piece of paper littering the sidewalk and my writing this book over the past 18 years. Both are my effort to make a difference in the action pole of I–It. Both come from being loved and connected in the contemplative pole of I–You. The motivation is in loving our sidewalks and loving you as you read these words at this moment. The sidewalk with one less piece of litter is a difference. You reading these words is a difference, and I am a happy man imagining it.

May you find ways to regularly remind yourself and your community, as you move through the contemplation pole, that we are loved and connected. *And,* may this awareness support you and your community as you move through the action pole to make your difference.

New Realities in Chapter 34

Reality 120 Our efforts to make a difference are one pole of a polarity that is interdependent with, and supported by, the pole of universal unity and unconditional love. The richness, the energy, and the wonder of life and death is in the oscillation between these poles.

---

[111] Dad, we *see* you! Love, Kristin, Luke *And* Shalom

POSTSCRIPT ARTICLES
A Polarity Lens On the COVID-19 Pandemic

This book was completed and at the publisher when COVID-19 hit in early 2020. I wrote two articles identifying how a polarity lens could be helpful in addressing COVID-19 and its aftermath. They are included in the following pages as Postscripts to the book. I hope you find them useful.

~ Barry

Winning On Two Fronts – Health *And* Economy

Polarity Thinking can save lives, strengthen the economy, and speed the national recovery.

BARRY JOHNSON

IN THE BATTLE WITH COVID-19, we all feel a tension between our concerns for Public Health *And* our concerns for the Economy. We can't afford to have this battle on two fronts become a battle between two fronts. If it does, we all lose. Our leaders must leverage this tension to work for us. If they do, we all win.

Though the situation is very complicated, a fairly simple shift in thinking will help us save lives *And* accelerate our economic rebuild. The two battle fronts (Health, Economy) must be connected with *And* rather than *Or*. Health *And* Economy are an interdependent pair called a polarity. All polarities have two poles connected by *And* because they need each other. We need a Healthy Public to build a Strong Economy *And* we need a Strong Economy to care for a Healthy Public. *And*-thinking is required to leverage this polarity.

When dealing with polarities, *Or*-thinking makes things worse. It creates a false choice between Health *Or* Economy. If we focus on Health to the neglect of the Economy, we make the recession worse. If we focus on the Economy to the neglect of Public Health, we make the pandemic worse.

Paradoxically, a focus on Health alone will eventually undermine our health. And a focus on the Economy alone will eventually undermine our economy.

Polarities are unavoidable and indestructible. This means we have been living with the Health *And* Economy polarity, nationally and globally, long before COVID-19. And we will be living with it beyond the foreseeable future. As we enter a recovery phase, it would be easy for us to put all of our energy into rebuilding our economy. This is not a good idea. We must continue to give quality attention to public health both for the sake of public health and for the sake of the economy.

The process for leaders to optimize polarities for the benefit of everyone includes:

1. Recognizing Health *And* Economy as a polarity – embrace *And*-thinking.

2. Understanding the basics of how polarities work and how to leverage them.

3. Creating a dual strategy that supports both Health *And* Economy.

One half of the dual strategy must reflect the expertise of the economists. The other half must reflect the expertise of health-care professionals. Both halves must reflect the political judgement of the politicians. Creating the dual strategy together allows for each group to be informed by the other as it is being built.

This collaborative process is faster and delivers more sustainable results than if all sides create strategies separately and then try to combine them. It also provides a basis for political leaders to generate bipartisan legislation and financial support to implement the dual strategy. The wisdom in the room can be guided by and summarized on a one-page Polarity Map® like the one below.

Misdiagnosing Health *And* Economy as an *either/Or* problem will result in an unnecessary additional loss of life, a deeper economic recession, and a slower national recovery. Recognizing it as a polarity and

applying *And*-thinking will help us save lives, rebuild the economy, and accelerate a national recovery. We must win on both fronts – Health *And* Economy. A polarity lens will help.

There are other key polarities at play within this pandemic struggle. An expanded article on Individual Freedom *And* The Common Good is available on the Polarity Partnerships Resource Portal at www.PolarityResources.com/now

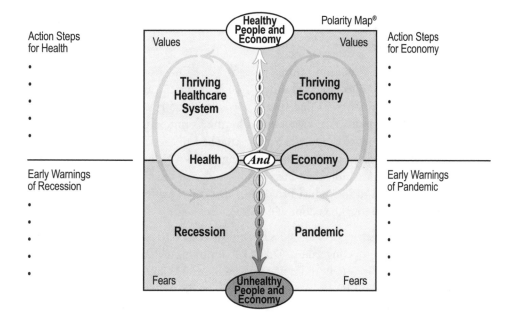

The Polarity Map is a wisdom organizer. It can help everyone understand and optimize polarities well. At its core are two interdependent poles: Health *And* Economy. If stakeholders leverage this polarity well, both sides will enjoy the benefits of the Greater Purpose at the top: Healthy People and Economy. If they don't, the entire system will descend into the Deeper Fear at the bottom: Unhealthy People and Economy. Polarity Map® is a registered trademark of Barry Johnson and Polarity Partnerships, LLC. Commercial use encouraged with permission. Visit PolarityPartnerships.com for more.

BARRY JOHNSON *is the author of* <u>And</u>: <u>Making a Difference by Leveraging Polarity, Paradox or Dilemma. Volume One – Foundations</u>. HRD Press, 2020 www.PolarityPartnerships.com

Individual Freedom *And* The Common Good

Both are essential in the fight against COVID-19 for our recovery and our future.

BARRY JOHNSON

O N THE ONE HAND, New York Governor Andrew Cuomo has expressed frustration over competing with every other state and with the federal government for ventilators, tests, and Personal Protection Equipment (PPE). In response to federal disorganization over resources, he has requested a centralized, nationally coordinated effort. Cuomo has a point. On the other hand, when pressed for national coordination, President Trump says he does not want to become a "socialist country." He decentralized by delegating many decisions to the states, including re-opening the economy, so they can respond to local realities. One size does not fit all. Trump also has a point.

Governor Cuomo *And* President Trump are each expressing a point of view shared by many supporters. The things expressed above, though important, are driven by a powerful value pair that is emotionally loaded. Each powerful value is attached to an equally powerful fear of losing that value. One value is for the Common Good, with centralized coordination as a means of support. The fear attached to the Common Good is that decentralization will lead to a disorganized government in which the Common Good is lost. A second value is for Individual Freedom, with decentralization as a means of support. The fear attached to Individual Freedom is that centralization will lead to big government in which Individual Freedom will be lost.

The tension over these strongly-held values has historically led to polarization between the groups holding those competing values. COVID-19 is shining a bright light on this tension today. Fighting over who is right did not serve us well before COVID-19. It is not serving us well in addressing COVID-19. And, it will not serve us well after COVID-19. What feeds the polarization is the assumption that we must choose between Individual Freedom "*Or*" the Common Good. When we divide these two powerful values with "*Or*", we allow COVID-19 to kill many more friends and family members; to deepen its damage to our economy and to slow our recovery. We also undermine our potential to thrive long after the virus is gone.

We Can Move From Polarized To Optimized

These two powerful values are both essential and they need each other. They are an interdependent pair called a polarity for which "*And*-thinking" is required. We need to maximize the benefits of decentralizing to protect Individual Freedom *And*[89] maximize the benefits

---

[89] I use an italic *And* only when connecting two poles of an interdependent pair and an italic *Or* as a mistaken connection between two poles of an interdependent pair.

of centralizing for the Common Good. We can and must do both. Effectively combining these two powerful values will reduce our deaths, minimize the damage to our economy, accelerate our recovery, and improve our potential to thrive long after the virus is gone.

Four things that will help:

1. Recognize the bigger picture – put both points of view on a Polarity Map

2. Appreciate the power and wisdom within each point of view (2a and 2b)

3. Understand how power works with polarities

4. Use a dual strategy to maximize the gifts of each point of view and minimize its liabilities.

1. Recognize the Bigger Picture – Put Both Points of View on a Polarity Map®[90]

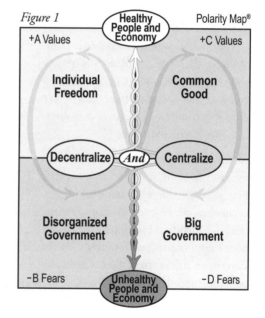

Figure 1 is a picture of a Polarity Map. The two points of view are represented in the diagonal quadrants. President Trump's point of view (light gray) has a strong value for Individual Freedom (+A) tied to an equally strong fear of losing that value to Big Government (-D). In support of that point of view, it is helpful to Decentralize (Left Pole).

Governor Cuomo's point of view (dark gray) has a strong value for the Common Good (+C) tied to an equally strong fear of losing that value to Disorganized Government (-B). In support of that point of view, it is helpful to Centralize (Right Pole).

We must leverage the tension between these two points of view to achieve the goal at the top of the map (white): Healthy People and Economy. The infinity loop represents the perpetual movement of energy through the system over time. The loop going high into each upside represents the intent to maximize the benefits of both Individual Freedom *And* the Common Good. The infinity loop going only slightly into each downside represents the intent to minimize the limits of Disorganized Government or Big Government.

2a. The Power and Wisdom in Preserving Individual Freedom

We value individual freedom and we decentralize and deregulate to support it. There are many values we, as a country, associate with **Individual Freedom**: "…life, liberty and the pursuit of happiness,"[91] entrepreneurship, individual expression/creativity/initiative, "Give me liberty or give me death."[92] "All for one…". Many have died for the values of Individual Freedom. There is a deep desire within our culture to hold on to them and we should.

The stronger we value Individual Freedom, the stronger our fear of losing it to "Big Government". There are many negative labels or fears that get associated with **Big Government**: "Socialism", "China", excessive centralized control, over-regulation, loss of freedom, "Welfare State" and "The Swamp" – to name a few.

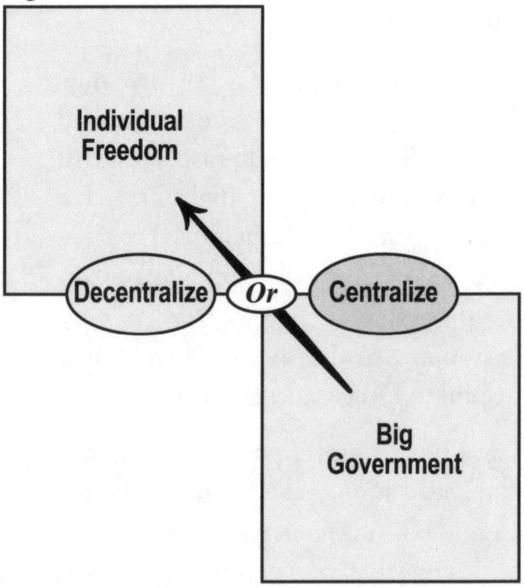

The emotional power within these values and fears is difficult to overstate. *Figure 2* highlights this point of view, with "*Or*" connecting the values and fears. When this point of view becomes the only point of view, the "*Or*" increases the power and certainty of a clear choice: "Am I going to choose Individual Freedom *Or* Big Government?" The answer is obvious: just follow the arrow.

At some level, we all value Individual Freedom and resist efforts to limit that Freedom. We don't like to be told, "Stay at home," or "Stop all non-essential work." Individual Freedom is valued by both Republicans and Democrats. At the same time, this point of view is generally held most tightly by Republicans. This is one of the gifts Republicans bring to our country. We need Individual Freedom and to limit Big Government.

Figure 2

There is wisdom in this point of view including its values and fears. It shows up in President Trump and most Republican Governors being hesitant to impose stay-at-home orders even when it is recommended by medical experts. It shows up in their taking the lead on opening things up as soon as possible. It also shows up in the energy behind the many protests at state capitals by citizens demanding an end to stay-at-home regulations. This point of view is historical in its origins, powerful in its conviction, and essential to preserve. *And,* it needs an equally valuable point of view to keep this gift from becoming a liability.

---

[91] US Declaration of Independence, 1776
[92] Patrick Henry, 1775

2b. The Power and Wisdom in Pursuing the Common Good

We value the Common Good. This requires Centralized coordination for the benefit of everyone. There are many values we, as a country, associate with the **Common Good**: we are all "...created equal,"[93] we are all in this together as a community, we must attend to the well-being of the marginalized as well as the dominant culture, no one left behind, the team is more than the sum of its individual members, "United we stand," "...One for all." Many have died for the values of the Common Good. There is a deep desire in our culture to hold on to them and we should.

The stronger the value for the Common Good, the stronger the fear of its loss: Freedom without Equality leads to gross inequality, including the creation and neglect of marginalized groups. Decentralization without Centralized coordination leads to polarization, selfishness, fighting over basic needs, redundancy, and **Disorganized Government**.

The emotional power within these values and fears is difficult to overstate. *Figure 3* highlights this point of view, with "*Or*" connecting the values and fears. When this point of view becomes the only point of view, the "*Or*" increases the power and certainty of a clear choice, "Am I going to choose the Common Good *Or* Disorganized Government?" The answer is obvious: just follow the arrow.

Figure 3

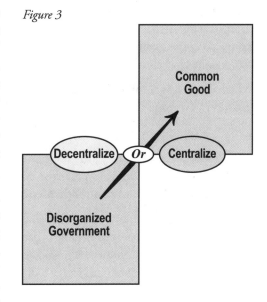

At some level, we all value the Common Good and basic equality. We value working in unity with everyone lending a hand. This value generates concern about inequality and Disorganized Government. The Common Good is valued by both Democrats and Republicans. At the same time, this point of view is generally held most tightly by Democrats. This is one of the gifts Democrats bring to our country. We need equitable treatment and centralized coordination in order to bring together "...one nation, under God, indivisible with Liberty and Justice for all."[94]

There is wisdom in this point of view, including its set of values and fears. It shows up when governors collaborate in sharing ventilators, PPE, and medical staff on a rolling, as-needed basis. It shows up when medical staff travel across the country to risk their lives in the hot zones where COVID-19 is most lethal. It shows up when Governors give stay-at-home mandates based on recommendations from medical experts while knowing it will

---

[93] US Declaration of Independence, 1776
[94] US Pledge of Allegiance

be hard on everyone and the economy. It shows up when Governors are hesitant to open things up too fast for fear of giving COVID-19 another foothold. This point of view is historical in its origins, powerful in its conviction, and is essential to preserve. *And,* it needs an equally valuable point of view to keep this gift from becoming a liability.

This returns us back to the power and wisdom of protecting Individual Freedom!

Respecting these two points of view is about understanding without blaming or condoning. Each brings a gift and each, without the other, becomes a liability. This brings us to power issues.

3. Understand How Power Works with Polarities

It is easy to see how the natural tension between these two points of view can become a power struggle in which each side sees their value as the solution to a problem. Focusing on Individual Freedom seems to be a "solution" to the many "problems" with Big Government. Conversely, focusing on the Common Good seems to be a "solution" to the many "problems" with Disorganized Government. Though understandable, neither solution alone is sustainable.

When any polarity is misdiagnosed as a problem to solve, with one pole perceived as the "solution", everyone pays three times:

1. We first pay by wasting energy in a power struggle over which pole to choose.

2. We pay a second time when the more powerful "win" because everyone gets the downside of the winners' preferred pole. If Individual Freedom wins, we all get Disorganized Government. If the Common Good wins, we all get Big Government.

3. We pay a third time when we find ourselves in the downside of both poles. Disorganized Government is vulnerable to getting bigger in response to its Disorganization. Big Government is vulnerable to being increasingly bureaucratic and disorganized. The result undermines both Individual Freedom *And* the Common Good.

4. Use A Dual Strategy to Maximize the Gifts of Each Point of View and Minimize Its Liabilities

Since there are two points of view to be respected and empowered in every polarity, the strategy for leveraging the tension within it must be a dual strategy involving advocates for both points of view.

A Polarity Map can help as a wisdom organizer. Advocates for each point of view need to create the content of the polarity map together with each side identifying content for all parts of the map. Together, they all identify the many benefits of preserving Individual Freedom. Together, they all identify the many benefits of caring for the Common Good. This respects the reality that each point of view has benefits and values worth preserving. Advocates for each point of view have a place to stand within the map: the upside of their preferred pole. The process continues as they, together, identify the liabilities of focusing on the Common Good to the neglect of preserving Individual Freedom. Together, they also identify the liabilities of focusing on Individual Freedom to the neglect of the Common Good. This respects the reality that each point of view has a potential liability worth avoiding. When filling out a polarity map, opposition becomes a resource as each point of view brings both values and fears that help fill out a rich map.

When the map is completed, the group can generate Action Steps to maximize the upsides identified in the two upper quadrants. They can then generate Early Warning signs to let them know early when they are getting into the downsides of either pole.

This fundamental polarity of Decentralizing for Individual Freedom *And* Centralizing for the Common Good applies to our global efforts to fight COVID-19 as well. We need centralized coordination internationally for the global common good *And* we need decentralized efforts that support each country in responding to its unique needs.

Whether we are addressing COVID-19 at the local, state, national or international level, making the false choice between Individual Freedom "*Or*" the Common Good leaves us with the worst of both worlds – a pandemic and an economic recession. Misdiagnosing this "*both/And*" polarity as an "*either/Or*" problem gives the advantage to COVID-19. Recognizing it as the polarity of Individual Freedom *And* the Common Good will give us more than a fighting chance.

In Conclusion

The powerful value pair of Individual Freedom *And* the Common Good, when recognized as a polarity, is a great resource not just in fighting COVID-19. What we learn from leveraging this polarity with COVID-19 will serve us well in addressing Health *And* Economy issues when the pandemic is far behind us.

Polarization over chronic issues is often based on a polarity which is misdiagnosed as a problem to solve. The issue remains chronic not because we lack problem-solving skills, but because we fail to recognize underlying polarities, which are inherently unavoidable and unsolvable. With such issues, a polarity lens is essential.

Resources

Polarity Partnerships has developed a variety of resources available at our online Resource Portal. To access the Polarity Resources and the books, go to
www.PolarityResources.com/now

BARRY JOHNSON *is the author of* <u>And</u>: <u>Making a Difference by Leveraging Polarity, Paradox or Dilemma. Volume One - Foundations</u>. HRD Press, 2020
www.PolarityPartnerships.com

RESOURCES

We want to partner with you.

Our company name, **Polarity Partnerships**, was chosen because of our desire to partner with individuals and organizations whose work is congruent with our mission: "Enhance our quality of life on the planet by supplementing *Or*-thinking with *And*-thinking." The set of appendices and resources that follow are intended to support your work while helping to scale the positive impact and sustainability of our mission. For more information on these resources and how we might partner together, please visit us at www.PolarityPartnerships.com.

Appendix A
Our Polarity Assessment™ as a Resource

Important Acknowledgement
Leslie DePol, Co-founder and CEO of Polarity Partnerships LLC, has been the primary force and coordinator of our web-based assessment. Many others have contributed And I want to recognize her central contribution. She has led us in developing this assessment product/service of which all of us at Polarity Partnerships are very proud. Leslie has co-authored this appendix.

Underlying Principles of Conditional Respect *And* Unconditional Respect *(Ch. 19)*

Unconditional respect requires no assessment. It cannot be earned. It is the basic right to respect we are all entitled to as human beings. Our ability to give and receive unconditional respect is supported by a complementary ability to give and receive conditional respect. Conditional respect is based on some form of assessment that gives us a basis to celebrate what is working well and for acknowledging issues that can be improved. Traditional assessments can trigger resistance and fears that the results will expose areas where one is failing to measure up. The Polarity Assessment is uniquely designed to provide a more wholistic picture. It describes how frequently a person, team or organization is experiencing both positive and negative results associated with ever-present challenges and opportunities. The Polarity Assessment's foundational basis holds everyone in unconditional regard. This supports the discovery of deeper insights about the conditions that may be supporting or undermining our ability to reach our full potential.

Some Unique Characteristics of a Polarity Assessment™

1. The Polarity Assessment provides a more complete and accurate picture.

The intent of assessments for individuals, teams, and organizations is to get helpful information on how we are doing. Most assessments come from an *either/Or* mindset that sits on a single-line continuum. On one end sits the "problem" or undesirable result or characteristic. On the other end sits the "solution" or desired result or characteristic. This type of *either/Or* assessment measures where a person, team, or organization sits on this *either/Or* continuum. For example, as shown in *Figure 1*, a leader is assessed in terms of their ability to be *flexible* rather than *rigid*. The result affirms and rewards a leader's ability to be *flexible.*

Figure 1

Let's examine this approach and result more carefully by comparing the results of two hypothetical leaders: Trish Tight runs a tight ship and sets clear expectations and parameters for others to follow. Larry Loose, on the other hand, values his ability to be flexible in responding to rapid changes and emerging circumstances. On the *either/Or* single-line continuum of *Figure 1*, Larry Loose is likely to receive a more *positive* score than Trish Tight because of his tendency to respond flexibly. This result reinforces the notion that Larry is the more effective leader.

On the other hand, if both leaders were being assessed using *Figure 2*, it is likely that Trish Tight would receive a more positive score than Larry Loose because of her tendency to provide clear direction. The implication in this result is that Trish Tight is the more effective leader.

Figure 2

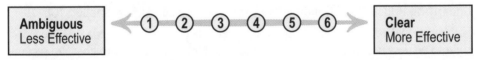

Upon closer examination, we can see how this *either/Or* approach to assessing a leader's effectiveness might not be helpful and could be outright misleading. *Figure 1* gives Larry Loose a misleadingly positive score while giving Trish Tight a misleadingly negative score. *Figure 2* gives Trish the misleading positive score while giving Larry the misleading negative score. In both cases, the leaders are mis-informed because each assessment item is measured on a single, *either/Or* continuum.

The following *Figure 3* shows the same characteristics being assessed on a Polarity-based, *both/And* continuum. The two characteristics of Clarity *And* Flexibility are measured as a pair of interdependent competencies that support each other and the ultimate goal of being an effective leader. This Polarity-based approach to assessing gives us a more accurate and complete picture of leader effectiveness: Larry Loose learns how his bias toward being flexible could make him seem wishy-washy and ineffective if he is unable to express himself with clarity. Trish Tight learns how her value around clarity could cause others to experience her as being rigid if her fears about being ambiguous keep her from developing complementary strengths related to flexibility.

Figure 3 highlights how an *either/Or,* single-line continuum approach to assessing can lead to misleading and distorted performance pictures. Polarity-based, *both/And* assessments help us to see the reality that an effective leader needs to be *both* Clear *And* Flexible, depending on the context. The Polarity Assessment is uniquely designed to assess the natural interdependency that exists among all leader competencies, cultural values, and strategic objectives. Whenever you are dealing with an interdependent pair, a Polarity-based assessment will give you a more complete and accurate picture to guide and support your learning and development.

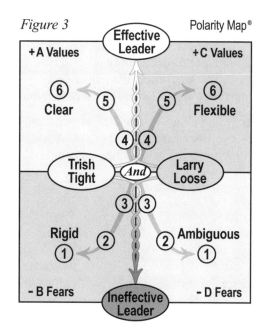

Figure 3 — Polarity Map®

2. **The Polarity Assessment helps you to achieve your greater purpose to support both People *And* Performance.**

In an easy-to-follow, 5-Step **S.M.A.L.L.** Process™, you can **See** your interdependent competencies, values, and objectives and **Map** your desired results associated with them. Your Polarity Map® then provides the basis to **Assess** how frequently key stakeholders are experiencing the upsides and downsides associated with your most strategic dilemmas. This feedback loop supports your ability to **Learn** what conditions are supporting and/or undermining your ability to **Leverage** these natural tensions to work *for* you, rather than *against* you. Polarity Assessment results inform the development of more effective and sustainable Action Steps to maximize upsides. Early Warnings signal the need to course correct in order to minimize your experience of downsides. This S.M.A.L.L. Process ultimately supports your achieving your greater purpose with more speed and sustainability.

3. **The Polarity Assessment helps you operationalize *And*-thinking more broadly and deeply.**

"You get what you measure." Periodically assess a few of your critical polarities and share the results and strategies informed by these results with key stakeholders. This will ensure ongoing demonstrable support and encouragement for everyone in their efforts to hold these natural and ongoing tensions more constructively, creatively and compassionately.

4. Polarity Assessments support the growing body of evidence-based research.

New research demonstrates that the ability to leverage interdependent pairs is essential to leader and organization effectiveness. Our assessment provides a solid basis for measuring the effectiveness of Polarity Thinking and its sustainable impact on your key performance indicators.

For more about The Polarity Assessment™, including its unique features and ability to measure custom and common competencies, values and strategic objectives, visit www.PolarityPartnerships.com/the-polarity-approach#the-polarity-assessment.

Appendix B
And: Volume Two *as a Resource*

Appendix B is a preview of the Table of Contents for the second book in this two-volume set:

And: Making a Difference by Leveraging Polarity, Paradox or Dilemma
Volume Two – Applications
by Polarity Practitioners

And: Volume Two is a resource for appreciating the variety of people and disciplines applying Polarity Thinking around the world. Each author or team of authors has contributed a chapter sharing how they have leveraged polarities to enhance our quality of life on the planet. Each chapter includes at least one author who is a graduate of our two-year Polarity Mastery Program. Our commitment to mastery students is to support them in becoming grounded in Polarity Thinking (Substance) *And* in becoming known as someone grounded in Polarity Thinking (Style). *And*: Volume Two is one reflection of that commitment.

Table of Contents

Forward

- *Introduction to* And: Volume Two *and Authors*
  Barry Johnson

Section One: Radical Possibilities for Equity

- *Reimagine Equity and Justice Through a Polarity Lens*
  Beth Applegate, MSOD

- *Black Survival: White Power and Privilege*
  Peter Whitt

- *Contributing to a Just and Equitable World: Why Is This So Hard?*
  Chandra Irvin, MDiv, MEd

- *Feminine And Masculine: For Health, Wealth and Happiness*
  Elaine Yarbrough, PhD
  Lindsay Y. Burr, MS

Section Two: Expanded Diversity of Applications

- *How Does Polarity Mapping Connect With Our Built-In Neurology?*
  Ann V. Deaton, PhD, PCC

- *Polarity Thinking and Creative Problem Solving*
  Elizabeth Monroe-Cook, PhD

- *Polarity Thinking and Vertical Development*
  Beena Sharma

- *Polarities and the Need for Vulnerability*
  Kelly Lewis, PCC

- *Sacred Union of Masculine And Feminine Principles: Applying the Master Polarity to Leadership and Culture*
  Allison Conte, MS

- *Polarity Thinking: The Foundation of Evolutionary Spirituality*
  Kelly Isola, MDiv

- *Navigating Transition With the Power of Polarity Thinking*
  Susan Walker-Morgan, GPCC, PCC, BCC, MPOD

- *Polarity Thinking as a Catalyst for Experiential Learning*
  Kay Peterson, MN, MBA, PCC

- *Interdependent Leadership: An Experiential Love Affair With the Earth!*
  Peter Dupre, BS, Med

- *Post-COVID-19 Planning for Sustained Benefit of Transition to Distant Learning Using PACT™*
  Cliff Kayser, MSHR, MSOD, PCC
  Samar A. Ahmed, Msc, MD, MHPE, (on behalf of ASU MENA FRI authors)

- *The Importance of Polarity Thinking in Healthcare*
  Bonnie Wesorick, MSN, RN, DPNAP, FAAN
  Tracy Christopherson, PhDc, MS, BAS, RRT
  Michelle Troseth, MSN, RN, FNAP, FAAN

- *Leveraging a Healthy Healing Organization (H2O) Framework Grounded in Polarity Thinking to Achieve Healthcare Transformation*
  Tracy Christopherson, PhDc, MS, BAS, RRT
  Michelle Troseth, MSN, RN, FNAP, FAAN
  Bonnie Wesorick, MSN, RN, DPNAP, FAAN

- *Applying Polarity Principles for a Healthcare IT Start-Up*
  Petra Platzer, PhD, NBC-HWC, PCC
  Cliff Kayser, MSHR, MSOD, PCC
  Dave Levin, MD

- *Applying Polarity Thinking to Increase Healthcare Leadership Capacity*
  Joy Goldman, MS, PCC
  Petra Platzer, PhD, NBC-HWC, PCC
  Cliff Kayser, MSHR, MSOD, PCC

- *Polarity Thinking to Alleviate Tensions in Community-Engaged Health Research*
  Melinda Butsch Kovacic, MPH, PhD
  Theresa Baker, MS

- *Polarity Thinking for Troubled Families and the People Who Work With Them in the Netherlands*
  Riet Portengen

- *Polarities and Homelessness*
  Tim Arnold

- *Managing Community Issues Through Polarity Thinking*
  Margaret Seidler, MPA

- *Polarity Thinking and Real Time Strategic Change*
  Robert "Jake" Jacobs

- *Polarities Are Generative Tensions at the Heart of Organization Evolution: A Living Systems Approach to Creating Conditions for Flourishing*
  Sally Parker

- *Polarity/Paradox Thinking in Business*
  Debbie Schroeder-Saulnier, DMgt

- *Key Polarities to Leverage for Successful IT Service Delivery in the Digital Era*
  Karen McCague

- *The Dynamic Engagement Model: Leveraging Polarities to Build Engagement at Work and at Home*
  Laura Mendelow, MAOD, PCC

- *Polarity Coaching™*
  Kathy Anderson, MBA, MAOD, CPCC

- *Institute for Polarities of Democracy: Leveraging Democratic Values and Advancing Social Change*
  William Benet, PhD
  Suzanne Rackl, MM, CFRE, CFRM
  Cliff Kayser, MSHR, MSOD, PCC

- *Demystifying Classic Assessments Through a Polarity Lens*
  Sandy Carter, PhD, MSW, PCC
  John Fraser, MBA, ACC
  Cliff Kayser, MSHR, MSOD, PCC

- *Polarity Thinking and Oshry's Organic Systems Framework*
  Cliff Kayser, MSHR, MSOD, PCC

- *Competing Visions: How Opposing, Underlying Feelings About Human.*
  Nature Lead to Political Polarization
  Bert Parlee, PhD

- *Dungeons and Dragons: A Ten-Minute, Participatory Process for Identifying*
  Key Polarities Within a System
  Patrick Masterson, MSOD
  Ann M. Caton, MSOD, ACC

- *Build Your Inspired Authentic Leadership Style*
  Lindsay Y. Burr, MS

- *Alleviating the Suffering of Paradox by Mapping Polarities*
  Brian Emerson, PhD

- *Polarity-Based Inquiry*
  Cliff Kayser, MSHR, MSOD, PCC

- *You Can't Leverage a Polarity Without Either/Or-Thinking*
  Leslie DePol, MSHROD

- *Multarities: Interdependencies of More Than Two*
  Cliff Kayser, MSHR, MSOD, PCC

- *Shifting From Drama To Empowerment: Using the Empowerment*
  Dynamic* and Polarity Thinking to Engage Key Stakeholders
  Cliff Kayser, MSHR, MSOD, PCC
  Bert Parlee, PhD
  Ann V. Deaton, PhD, PCC, CTPC

- *Values Come in Pairs at Natura*
  Beena Sharma
  Barry Johnson

Resources

- *Appendix A: The Polarity Assessment*

- *Appendix B: Realities of All Polarities*

- *Annotated Bibliography*

- *Blank Maps for Your Duplication and Use*

Appendix C
Realities of All Polarities

New Realities in Chapter 1

Reality 1   *Or*-thinking is essential for learning and for solving problems.

Reality 2   *And*-thinking is a supplement to *Or*-thinking, not a replacement.

Reality 3   Polarities are also known as interdependent pairs, Paradoxes, Dilemmas, Tensions, or Positive Opposites.

Reality 4   No matter what they are called, Polarities are unavoidable because we live in them and they live in us.

Reality 5   Polarities are inherently unsolvable in that you cannot choose one pole of the pair as a "solution" to the neglect of the other pole and be successful over time.

Reality 6   There is a natural tension between the two poles of a polarity.

Reality 7   If you treat a polarity as if it were a problem to solve, the natural tension between the poles becomes a negative, self-reinforcing loop or "vicious cycle" leading to unnecessary dysfunction, pain, and suffering.

Reality 8   If you can see a polarity within an issue, you can leverage the natural tension between the poles so it becomes a positive, self-reinforcing loop or "virtuous cycle" lifting you and your organization to goals unattainable with *Or*-thinking alone.

Reality 9   Individuals and organizations that leverage polarities well outperform those that don't. See bibliography of books supporting this point.

Reality 10   Polarity principles are scalable. What applies to a polarity at the family level of system, applies at the "family of nations" level of system.

Reality 11   The greater the complexity, the more useful it is to see underlying, predictable patterns. Polarities are just such a set of underlying, predictable patterns.

Reality 12   Leveraging polarities will increase the attainability, speed, and sustainability of change.

Reality 13   The natural tension within all polarities is often experienced as resistance. Polarity Thinking helps us leverage the wisdom within this resistance. It helps us convert resistance to change into a resource for Stability *And* Change.

Reality 14   Because polarities are unavoidable and unsolvable, we often experience them as chronic conflicts between polarized groups. If the polarization is over a polarity, not only are both sides "right," they both need each other's wisdom to be successful over time.

Reality 15   Polarity Thinking helps us see ourselves and our world more completely, thus increasing our capacity to love. This is built on Jack Gibb's insight that "Seeing is loving."

Reality 16   The phenomenon of polarities (paradoxes, dilemmas), like gravity and sunshine, is a free gift to all of us. No one owns the phenomenon of polarities any more than we own gravity or sunshine.

Reality 17   Since you have been living within polarities and polarities have been living within you for your whole life, you already have some tacit wisdom about them.

Reality 18   Your tacit wisdom is already helping you get along in the world. What we bring to your tacit wisdom are: A Polarity Map®; Polarity Realities; and a polarity approach.

Reality 19   Our Polarity Map®, principles, and approach have been evolving since the first Polarity Map and set of realities were created in 1975. We assume they will continue to evolve with your help.

New Realities in Chapter 2

Reality 20   Polarities are interdependent pairs that need each other over time.

Reality 21   They are energy systems we can leverage.

Reality 22   They are indestructible. If there is life, polarities will be at play.

Reality 23   They are unstoppable. The only way to stop the flow of energy in any polarity is to destroy the system in which it is flowing.

Reality 24   Each pole of a polarity has a benefit or "upside" which it brings to its relationship with the other pole. They are the positive results from focusing on that pole. Each pole also has its own limits or "downside."

Reality 25   The energy flow within a polarity crosses in the middle between the poles, keeping them separate. It also wraps around the outside of the two poles, holding them together as an interdependent pair. The poles never become one *And* they never separate into one without the other. They exist in nature as an interdependent pair.

Reality 26   There is a natural flow of energy within a polarity that goes from the downside of one pole to the upside of the other followed by anticipating or experiencing the downside of the new pole, which drives the system back to the upside of the original pole.

Reality 27   If we over-focus on one pole to the neglect of its pole partner (the other pole), we will find ourselves in the downside of the pole on which we over-focus.

Reality 28   When we find ourselves in the downside of one pole, the upside of the other pole is the natural, self-correction needed.

Reality 29   When in the downside of one pole, it is easy to see that downside as a "problem" and the self-correcting upside of the other pole as the "solution." Though the upside of the other pole is the necessary self-correction, it is not a sustainable "solution."

Reality 30   The longer we focus on one pole to the neglect of the other, the more problematic it will become.

Reality 31   The shorter the cycle time through the infinity loop the more obvious it is that you are in a polarity. The longer the cycle time, the more likely the polarity will be seen as a problem to solve.

Reality 32   Since we live in polarities and they live in our brain, there is no place we can go to step outside of the polarity and decide <u>if</u> we want to engage it.

New Realities in Chapter 3

Reality 33   SMALL: Seeing, Mapping, Assessing, Learning, and Leveraging, is our process for leveraging (making a difference with) any polarity. This process is influenced significantly by Robert "Jake" Jacob's work on Real Time Strategic Change (RTSC).[95]

Reality 34   The Polarity Map® is a wisdom organizer. The wisdom about the content often lies within the experience of the person or group creating the map.

Reality 35   The distorted infinity loop going high into the two upper quadrants and dipping only slightly into the two lower quadrants reflects the desire to maximize both upsides and minimize both downsides.

Reality 36   When leveraged well, the natural tension between the two poles becomes a virtuous cycle, symbolized by the upward, spiraling arrows on the Polarity Map. The original idea of synergy arrows pointing upward came from Bob DeWit and Ron Meyer.[96]

---

[95] Jacobs, Robert. *Real Time Strategic Change. How to Involve an Entire Organization in Fast and Far Reaching Change.* Berrett-Koehler, 1994.
[96] DeWit, Bob; Meyer, Ron. *Strategy Synthesis: Resolving Strategy Paradoxes to Create Competitive Advantage.* Thomson, 1999.

Reality 37   The upward spiraling synergy arrows represent lifting the person or system toward the Greater Purpose Statement (GPS) at the top of the map. The Greater Purpose Statement answers the question, "Why bother to leverage this polarity?" John Scherer identified the need for a Greater Purpose and suggested using GPS to play on the familiar Global Positioning System.[97]

Reality 38   When not leveraged well, the natural tension between the two poles becomes a vicious cycle symbolized by the downward spiraling synergy arrows on the Polarity Map.

Reality 39   The downward spiraling synergy arrows represent dragging the person or system toward the Deeper Fear at the bottom of the map. The Deeper Fear is the opposite of the Greater Purpose Statement. The stronger one's desire to gain their Greater Purpose, the stronger the desire to avoid the Deeper Fear.

Reality 40   There are Action Steps alongside each upside of the map. These steps are to proactively gain or maintain the upside they are next to.

Reality 41   There are Early Warnings alongside each downside of the map. These are early indicators that you are getting into a downside so that you can self-correct as early as possible. While Action Steps are proactive, Early Warnings are responsive. Todd Johnson contributed the idea of Early Warnings out of the need to have something measurable relating to the two downside quadrants.

Reality 42   A persistent over-focus on one pole to the neglect of the other gets you into the downside of both poles. The fear of getting into the downside of the opposite pole leads to sustained over-focus on your preferred pole. This sustained over-focus leads first to the downside of the preferred pole, then to the downside of the very pole you were attempting to avoid. Paradoxically, you get what you are afraid of through your efforts to avoid it.

New Realities in Chapter 4

Reality 43   Each of us is unique and all of us are connected.

Reality 44   High Leverage Action Steps are valuable because they simultaneously support both upsides of a polarity. You get double the benefit from one action. They are shown by just putting the same action step alongside both upsides. You can put an (HL) after the action step to remind yourself and others that it is High Leverage.

Reality 45   Polarities are about energy and power. In order to create a virtuous cycle with the tension within any polarity, you must empower both poles.

---

[97] Scherer, John. *Work And The Human Spirit*. John Scherer and Associates,1993.

Reality 46   With a polarity, it is possible to empower both poles in a way that the polarity becomes a power generator with both poles being increasingly powerful *And* the system in which the polarity sits will increase in power.

New Realities in Chapter 5

Reality 47   Values come in pairs. They show up in the two upsides or the two poles of a Polarity Map®.

Reality 48   Building a Polarity Map is always a values and language clarification process.

Reality 49   Both poles need to be either neutral or positive.

Reality 50   The downside of one pole represents the fear of losing the value in the upside of the other pole. The stronger the value, the stronger the fear and the reverse.

Reality 51   A powerful value/fear diagonal when combined with *Or*-thinking gets us "hooked" by a false choice between the poles. We become blind to the other value/fear diagonal and over-tolerate the downside of our valued pole. We then get "stuck" there – unable to access the upside of the pole that is feared. Cliff Kayser was the first to describe this process as getting "hooked" leading to getting "stuck."

Reality 52   When we get into trouble with polarities, the reason is not that our problem-solving perceptions are inaccurate; it is that they are incomplete.

Reality 53   The real opposites in a Polarity Map are the diagonals. The poles are interdependent but not always what we might call opposites.

Reality 54   It is helpful to engage key stakeholders in each step of the SMALL process. Based on Robert 'Jake' Jacob's, <u>Real Time Strategic Change</u> (RTSC).

Reality 55   Our paradoxical orientation toward change – that if you want people holding on to the present pole to support movement toward the other pole, first guarantee support, with Action Steps, for the upside of the present pole. Based on Gestalt psychology described by Arnold R. Beisser in <u>Gestalt Therapy Now</u>.[98]

Reality 56   It is helpful to acknowledge with Early Warnings the legitimate fears of the downside of the pole we are moving toward before creating Early Warnings for the downside of the pole we are moving from. This is based on the same paradoxical orientation in Reality 55.

---

[98] Shepherd, Irma Lee; Fagen, Joan. *Gestalt Therapy Now*. Gestalt Journal Press, 2008.

New Realities in Chapter 6

Reality 57   When the Whole becomes a Part, or the reverse, the Value focus shifts while the generic polarity remains the same.

Reality 58   It is always in the long-term interest of each pole to take care of both poles.

New Realities in Chapter 7

Reality 59   Within all polarities, there are two equally valid, essential, and inter-dependent points of view. They show up as the value/fear diagonal quadrants of a Polarity Map®. (+A/-D) and (-B\+C). The wisdom in each point of view is a combination of the value being affirmed (up-side) and the fear of losing that value (diagonal downside).

Reality 60   The stronger and more absolutely one advocates for the value in their point of view (+A) or (+C), the greater the fear that will be generated in those with the alternate point of view (-D) or (-B).

Reality 61   The longer and more painfully we experience the downside of one pole, the stronger the fear of that pole and the more we idealize the upside value of the opposite pole.

Reality 62   When we experience the downsides of the original "solution," it gets identified as a "mistake." It was not a mistake. It was the natural and necessary self-correction in an ongoing polarity. The effort to shift poles gets called a mistake because it was misdiagnosed as a solution in the first place.

Reality 63   Whenever there is a distribution issue with goods and services, such as food, education, healthcare, jobs, shelter, safety, and opportuni-ties, the Part *And* Whole polarity is at play.

New Realities in Chapter 8

Reality 64   There are times when we have an *either/Or* choice to make which is a problem to solve, like voting for or against a proposal. Even in these times in which we have a problem to solve, it can be helpful to see the choice in the context of an underlying polarity. If the vote empowers one pole of a polarity, we can know that, over time, future votes will need to empower the other pole as well.

New Realities in Chapter 9

Reality 65   Normative ethics bring the upside of the Whole pole within cultures emphasizing Individualism (U.S.A.) that lean toward the Part pole. Contextual ethics brings the upside of the Part pole within cultures emphasizing Collectivism (China) that lean toward the Whole pole.

New Realities in Chapter 10

Reality 66   A chain (Whole) is as strong as its weakest link (Part). Attending to the weakest Part (link) is in service to the Whole (chain).

Reality 67   Every level of system is a potential source of energy to be leveraged in service of its internal Parts *And* its external Wholes.

Reality 68   Nested polarities – The Greater Purpose of one polarity can be a pole of a larger polarity in which it is "nested."

New Realities in Chapter 11

Reality 69   The Left *And* Right hemispheres of our brain are a polarity.

New Realities in Chapter 12

Reality 70   One way to empower a pole is by adding someone to the team or organization who has a strong preference for that pole and an ability to gain the upsides of that pole.

New Realities in Chapter 13

Reality 71   When we treat the upside of one pole as a "solution" to a problem, the clearer the communication, the greater the resistance to that "solution".

Reality 72   There is a 5-step process for getting unstuck.

1. Understand and respect the values of those "holding on."
2. Understand and respect the fears of those "holding on."
3. Ask, "How can we gain what we are 'going after'…
4. …without letting go of the values of those 'holding on'…
5. …in order to move toward a Greater Purpose that works for both groups?"

New Realities in Chapter 14

Reality 73   If it seems relatively easy to identify a Greater Purpose Statement (GPS) that those present can agree to, having that GPS as a "True North" while filling out the rest of the map can be very useful. It becomes a constant reminder as to why we are investing in leveraging this polarity in the first place.

Reality 74   If it appears like it will be difficult to agree on a Greater Purpose Statement until those present have a chance to talk about their values and fears, you can start by filling in the 4 quadrants first. The agreed-upon quadrants will then provide a richer context in which to create, together, a Greater Purpose Statement.

Reality 75   When filling out the 4 quadrants, as a general rule, it is useful to fill out the content of the two upsides first. That allows people supporting either pole to have their pole affirmed for what it brings.

Realty 76   Once you have a Polarity Map®, you can do a "Trend Arrow" assess-
             ment in which you are asking, "At this point in time, are we or should
             we be moving toward the upper left quadrant (+A) or toward the upper
             right quadrant (+C)?"

New Realities in Chapter 15

Reality 77   Sometimes the names of the poles either show up or are changed in
             the process of building a map. It is helpful to hold the content lightly,
             including the pole, when building a map. As new stakeholders
             get involved, you may want to change them again.

Reality 78   There is an inherent fairness in mapping a polarity which allows some-
             one to facilitate the mapping even if they have a pole preference.

New Realities in Chapter 16

Reality 79   Naming the poles often provides a bridge between the downside and
             upside of a pole.

New Realities in Chapter 17

Reality 80   The realities we experience with all polarities regardless of system
             size is not just happening in the team, organization, or nation; it is
             happening within the brain of all the stakeholders involved.

New Realities in Chapter 18

Reality 81   The more our ability to love someone is contingent upon them doing
             something different, the more we have shifted the power to them in
             controlling our capacity to love.

Reality 82   Anger floats on a sea of fear. This means that an angry person is more
             than an angry person. They are also afraid. The fear is of losing some-
             thing valued. Thus, an angry person or nation is afraid of losing
             something valued. This fear/value combination can be seen as a
             "point of view" made up of two diagonal quadrants in a Polarity Map®.

Reality 83   Life is richer, more complicated and nuanced than the Polarity Map
             and set of polarity "realities" implies. Granting their limits, the ques-
             tion is whether they might be useful in dealing more effectively with
             our rich, complicated, and nuanced lives.

New Realities in Chapter 19

Reality 84   There are two kinds of "Respect," both of which are essential:

             1. Conditional Respect that you earn by doing good work for which
                you can be proud. Measurement is necessary.

             2. Unconditional Respect which is a birthright. It cannot be earned
                and need not be earned. Attempting to earn it is, at best, a waste
                of time. Measurement is irrelevant.

New Realities in Chapter 20

Reality 85   Intrinsic polarities are always a "false choice."

Reality 86   There are such things as "chosen polarities" which are different than "intrinsic polarities."

New Realities in Chapter 21

Reality 87   "Good" comes in pairs that show up in a Polarity Map® as the two upsides. "Evil" also comes in pairs that show up in a Polarity Map as the two downsides. Paradoxically, the pursuit of one "Good" without also pursuing its interdependent partner, a second "Good," leads to an unanticipated "Evil."

Reality 88   The greater the pursuit of Justice to the neglect of Mercy, the greater the number of laws and the harsher the consequences. This decreases our ability to own our shortcomings and increases the need to project them onto an "other" who is convenient and obviously "not me."

New Realities in Chapter 22

Reality 89   Claiming Power without Sharing Power causes an abuse of power, while Sharing Power without Claiming Power allows an abuse of power. This is a fundamental source and perpetuator of sexism, racism, and poverty.

Reality 90   Power Within – There is a power within each of us to make meaning for ourselves in whatever situation we find ourselves.

Reality 91   Power Beyond – This is the power within all religious traditions. It is the awareness that there is a power beyond us individually and beyond us collectively. This power is not dependent upon us to figure it out or do it right. This power is the gift of universal, unconditional love.

New Realities in Chapter 23

Reality 92   One of the results of mapping is that both points of view (+A/-D) and (-B\+C) are identified and respected, providing a "place to stand" for those valuing each pole.

Reality 93   To help think of measurable indicators, consider what might be increasing or decreasing that would indicate early that they are getting into the downside of that pole.

New Realities in Chapter 24

Reality 94   Fearing something does not make it true. It is important to recognize that our fears located in each downside of a Polarity Map® can be very powerful and significantly influence our actions regardless of how grounded they are in reality.

Reality 95   We are all accountable. Whether we are not preventing suffering by our inactions, causing suffering by our actions, or allowing suffering to continue by our inactions, we are accountable for the suffering.

Reality 96   A polarity lens can help us understand how we can become so cruel to each other at times. This understanding is not condoning. It just provides a more solid ground from which to reduce the cruelty and increase our compassion.

New Realities in Chapter 26

Reality 97   The rejection of *Or*-thinking is an example of *Or*-thinking.

Reality 98   *Or*-thinking and solving problems is one pole of a polarity. The other pole is *And*-thinking and leveraging polarities. They are an interdependent pair.

Reality 99   Through the process of education and acculturation, we all develop an unconscious bias for *Or*-thinking. This unconscious bias does not serve us well when addressing a Polarity/Paradox/Dilemma because a polarity is different than a problem to solve.

Reality 100   If you have an interdependent pair, connecting the two poles with "versus" can be as misleading as connecting them with *Or*.

Reality 101   *And*-thinking includes and transcends *Or*-thinking while *Or*-thinking cannot include *And*-thinking. I learned of this reality from Charles Hampden-Turner.

New Realities in Chapter 27

Reality 102   There are six, primary ways polarities show up:

1. As a value or set of values.
2. As resistance based on a fear of something that could happen.
3. As one or more Action Steps.
4. As a complaint or a complaint combined with a solution.
5. As a vision or dream for a preferred future.
6. As a conflict.

New Realities in Chapter 28

Reality 103   There are four questions that help us decide whether an issue is a polarity or a problem:

1. Is the issue ongoing, like breathing?
2. Is there an interdependence between two alternatives such that if we choose one alternative for the moment, we will be required to include the other alternative at some point in the future?
3. Is it necessary, over time, to have both identified upsides?

4. Will focusing on one upside to the neglect of the other eventually undermine efforts to move toward your Greater Purpose?

Reality 104   Polarities always contain problems to solve.

Reality 105   Problems to solve can be a part of a polarity and they can have polarities within them.

New Realities in Chapter 29

Reality 106   The vicious cycle caused by poorly leveraging one polarity becomes a hyper-vicious cycle when combined with a number of other poorly-leveraged polarities.

Reality 107   Supplementing *Or* with *And* creates a virtuous cycle in each of the polarities in a stack. This results in a hyper-virtuous cycle in which the benefits are multiplied, providing equity in quality of life for all.

Reality 108   An alternative to an "evil intent" or "evil source" as a root cause for chronic issues like poverty, racism, and sexism, can be found in a stack of polarities in which *Or*-thinking is used when *And*-thinking is required.

Reality 109   The stronger the need to project on Them, the stronger the unconscious need for power over Them.

Reality 110   The degree of inhumanness we employ to gain and maintain power over Them will be matched by the degree of inhumanness We need to project on Them. They become less than human so We can live with being less than human to Them.

Reality 111   *And*-thinking is not a solution to poverty, racism, or sexism, but it is a process requirement. Without supplementing *Or*-thinking with *And*-thinking, our most sincere efforts will be radically undermined, and no amount of money, commitment, or alignment will compensate.

New Realities in Chapter 30

Reality 112   *And*-thinking is a framework for addressing climate change. Without supplementing *Or*-thinking with *And*-thinking, efforts to reverse the climate crisis in time to protect future generations are undermined radically. The survival of future generations is dependent, in part, upon supplementing *Or*-thinking with *And*-thinking.

New Realities in Chapter 31

Reality 113   A group that has decision-making power over others is more insulated from experiencing a polarity's tension because decision makers have the power to choose one pole *Or* the other. They can override those supporting the alternate pole. Those with less decision-making power have richer, more direct experiences with the power differential and with the tension between one pole *And* the other. This gives them an experiential advantage in seeing polarities, valuing their potential, and in learning to leverage them.

Reality 114 Those with decision-making power can claim the upsides of their preferred pole for themselves and assign the downsides of both poles to those over whom they have power. This is why those with less decision-making power dislike being differentiated by and from those with more power. The differentiation itself is disempowering. The power differential is painfully reasserted as they often become identified with the downsides of both poles of any polarity which is the focus of attention.

New Realities in Chapter 32

Reality 115 Whenever we stack polarities, it is helpful to think of an organizing principle or common theme for all the left poles and all the right poles.

Reality 116 One of our most universal, inclusive, and ancient polarities is Yang *And* Yin energy. These two energies are an interdependent pair that are available to all of us *And* in all of us.

Reality 117 Within a Polarity Map®, the names of the two poles are completely interchangeable, so either name can go first to identify the left pole. When the pole names are switched, their upsides and downsides move with them.

Reality 118 From a polarity perspective, the alternative point of view is always a resource to seeing and experiencing the whole picture of the Polarity Map.

Reality 119 From a power perspective, the powerful need to listen to the less powerful because, in a polarity disagreement, they bring the alternate pole that is needed to leverage the polarity well. The greater the power differential, the greater the need for those with more power to listen to those with less power.

New Realities in Chapter 34

Reality 120 Our efforts to make a difference are one pole of a polarity that is interdependent with, and supported by, the pole of universal unity and unconditional love. The richness, the energy, and the wonder of life and death is in the oscillation between these poles.

Annotated Bibliography

Several books indicate that those leaders and organizations that leverage polarity, paradox, or dilemma well outperform those that don't. Below is a short, annotated list of 29 key books that emphasize this point.

Anderson, Kathy	*Polarity Coaching: Coaching People and Managing Polarities* (HRD Press, 2010). Anderson uses seven case studies where polarity coaching was useful.
Arnold, Tim	*The Power of Healthy Tension: Overcome Chronic Issues and Conflicting Values* (HRD Press, 2017). Arnold helps leaders address chronic tensions by seeing underlying polarities and leveraging them.
Collins, James C. Porras, Jerry I.	*Built to Last: Successful Habits of Visionary Companies* (HarperCollins, 1994). Authors identify the "Genius of the *'And'*" as a central variable that distinguished the "Gold" companies from the "Silver" companies. The whole book is based on managing the polarity of "Preserve the Core *And* Stimulate Progress." This could also be seen as the generic Stability *And* Change polarity.
Collins, Jim	*Good to Great: Why Some Companies Make the Leap...and Others Don't* (HarperCollins, 2001). The "Genius of the *'And'*" continues as an important variable in this book and is identified as a key characteristic of leaders moving companies from Good to Great. There are ten polarities identified as central to becoming a level 5 leader.
Deaton, Ann V.	*VUCA Tools for a VUCA World: Developing Leaders and Teams for Sustainable Results* (DaVinci Resources, 2018) Deaton identifies Polarity Thinking as one of her VUCA tools.
Dodd, Dominic Favaro, Ken	*The Three Tensions: Winning the Struggle to Perform Without Compromise* (John Wiley and Sons, 2007). Authors interview executives from 200 companies and identify three important

tensions (polarities) central to their organization's effectiveness: Profitability *And* Growth; Today *And* Tomorrow; and, The Whole *And* Its Parts.

de Wit, Bob Meyer, Ron	*Strategy Synthesis: Resolving Strategy Paradoxes to Create Competitive Advantage* (Thomson, 1999). De Wit and Meyer identify ten paradoxes (polarities) which are at the heart of strategic management.
Elsner, Richard Farrands, Bridget	*Lost in Transition: How Business Leaders Can Successfully Take Charge In New Roles* (Cavendish, 2006). Authors identify eight tensions (polarities) which, when managed well, contribute significantly to being successful in new jobs.
Emerson, Brian Lewis, Kelly	*Navigating Polarities, Using Both/And Thinking to Lead Transformation* (Paradoxical Press, 2019). Emerson and Lewis identify a number of leadership and organizational polarities and valuable steps for navigating them.
Fletcher, Jerry Olwyler, Kelle	*Paradoxical Thinking: How to Profit from Your Contradictions* (Berrett-Koehler, 1997). As their own book states, "After more than fifteen years of studying thousands of detailed examples of people performing at their best, Fletcher and Olwyler have found that individuals are always paradoxical when performing optimally and that each person has a particular combination of contradictory and paradoxical [polarity] qualities that work together to produce that person's best work."
Hammett, Peter	*Unbalanced Influence: Recognizing and Resolving the Impact of Myth and Paradox in Executive Performance* (Davies-Black Publishing, 2007). Ten years of executive research indicates the importance of paradox in executive performance.
Hampden-Turner, Charles	*Charting the Corporate Mind: Graphic Solutions to Business Conflicts* (The Free Press, 1990). Charles Hampden-Turner has written several books on the advantage of managing dilemmas in which his research shows that those companies that manage key dilemmas well outperform those that don't.
Hampden-Turner, Charles Trompenaars, Alfons	*The Seven Cultures of Capitalism: Value Systems for Creating Wealth in the United States, Japan, Germany, France, Britain, Sweden, and The Netherlands* (Doubleday, 1993). *Building Cross-Cultural Competence: How to Create Wealth from Conflicting Values* (John Wiley & Sons, 2000). Hampden-Turner and Trompenaars identify six dilemmas (polarities) which must be managed to support cross-cultural competence.

Handy, Charles — *The Age of Paradox* (Harvard Business School Press, 1994). Handy builds on his earlier work, *The Age of Unreason*, to assert the balancing of paradoxes (polarities) at the heart, not just of effective personal and organizational life, but of our survival as a world community.

Hickman, Craig R. — *Mind of a Manager Soul of a Leader* (John Wylie & Sons, 1990). Support for the benefits of paradoxical thinking also show up in Hickman's book title that, in and of itself, is a fundamental polarity in leadership.

Hofstede, Geert — *Culture's Consequences: Comparing Values, Behaviors, Institutions, and Organizations Across Nations* (Sage Publications, 2001). Hofstede identifies five dimensions (polarities) of national culture to help us tap national differences as a resource.

Johnson, Barry — *Polarity Management: Identifying and Managing Unsolvable Problems* (HRD Press, 1992). Johnson shares a number of case examples in which the shift – from seeing an issue as a problem to solve to managing it as a polarity – added real value for individual leaders and for organizations.

Johnston, Charles M. — *Necessary Wisdom: Meeting the Challenge of a New Cultural Maturity* (ICD Press, 1991). Johnston identifies five key polarity domains within culture and asserts the importance of understanding and bridging polarities. Managing polarities are at the heart of wisdom and cultural maturity and how we "must learn to think and act if our future is to be a healthy one."

Kise, Jane — *Unleashing the Positive Power of Differences* (Corwin, 2013). Kise identifies polarities in both school administration and classroom teaching.

Oswald, Roy M. Barry Johnson — *Managing Polarities in Congregations: Eight Keys for Thriving Faith Communities* (Alban Books, 2009). Oswald and Johnson identify eight polarities faced by all congregations regardless of denomination.

Pascale, Richard Tanner — *Managing on the Edge: How the Smartest Companies Use Conflict to Stay Ahead* (Simon & Schuster, 1991). Pascale identifies "managing contention better" as the key variable that separated the 14 companies that kept their "excellent" rating from the 29 that did not, when looking at the 43 companies identified in the book *In Search of Excellence*. What he means by "managing contention" is managing polarities/dilemmas/paradoxes of which he identifies seven, giving examples of each.

Quinn, Robert E.   *Beyond Rational Management: Mastering the Paradoxes and Competing Demands of High Performance* (Jossey-Bass, 1988). Quinn asserts that mastering paradox (polarity) is central to high performance.

Building The Bridge As You Walk On It: A Guide for Leading Change (Jossey-Bass, 2004). Quinn identifies 8 polarities as "The fundamental state of leadership."

Schroeder-Saulnier, *The Power of Paradox: Harness the Energy of Competing Ideas*
Deborah   *to Uncover Radically Innovative Solutions* (Career Press, 2014). Schroeder-Saulnier focuses on a number of business applications to paradoxical situations.

Seidler, Margaret   *Power Surge: A Conduit for Enlightened Leadership* (HRD Press, 2008). Seidler has the most extensive list of values pairs available. This book provides the "how to" in helping leaders supplement their strengths and keep them from becoming vulnerabilities.

Sisodia, Raj   *Firms of Endearment: How World Class Companies Profit from*
Sheth, Jag   *Passion And Purpose* (Wharton School Publishing, 2007).
Wolfe, David B.   The authors discovered that the key indicator for whether a company is a great investment is the degree to which it manages the polarity of taking care of the stockholders *And* the stakeholders. In other words, attending to company interests *And* the interests of the larger community in which the company exists.

Smith, Wendy K.   *The Oxford Handbook of Organizational Paradox* (Oxford
Lewis, Marianne W.   University Press, 2017) The editors have assembled a variety
Jarzabkowski,   of applications of paradox in organizational settings.
Paula
Langly, Ann

Tochluk, Shelly   *Living in the Tension: The Quest for a Spiritualized Racial Justice* (Crandall, Dostie & Douglass Books, 2016) Tochluk shares six tensions to be addressed in the interface between spiritual practice and social action.

Wesorick, Bonnie   *Polarity Thinking, The Missing Logic to Achieve Healthcare Transformation* (HRD Press, 2015). Wesorick identifies key polarities in healthcare, how to leverage them, and the benefits gained by those who give and receive healthcare.

*More Praise for **And***

"*... more Polarity Thinking could explain and alleviate some of our world's most pressing challenges and in-equities.*"

"Barry Johnson's new book on *And*..., is an eminently practical, clearly written and illustrated book. It offers an accessible thorough dive into using his ground-breaking polarity management approach across different subjects and scales. It includes his deep and heart-felt engagement and crystallization of years of exploring how more Polarity Thinking could explain and alleviate some of our world's most pressing challenges and inequities. This book may well be the culmination of a life well lived by a wise and caring master of all-embracing *both/And*-thinking."

Dr. Susanne Cook-Greuter
Chief Knowledge Officer, Vertical Development Associates

"*... I have experienced Polarity Thinking overcome in-tercultural differences.*"

"'Values come in pairs,' cultural values in particular. As an intercultural and international team leader and consultant, I have experienced Polarity Thinking overcome intercultural differences. Leveraging polarities has turned them into international win-win-solutions."

Michael A. Buchmann Dr rer oec
International Team Consultant, Germany

> *"Polarity Thinking ... can move teams, organizations and communities from levels of languishing to thriving ... "*

"The Polarity Thinking framework is a proven tool for leaders and teams using a powerful paradigm shift of supplementing *Or*-thinking with *And*-thinking. *Or*-thinking is alive and doing well in our chaotic and ever-changing workplaces. We constantly find ourselves searching for solutions to the most intractable problems that, over time, can be exhausting and limiting. This book provides a way of expanding our thinking that can move teams, organizations and communities from levels of languishing to thriving. We use Barry Johnson's Polarity Thinking framework extensively at our center and the university to help people reach their full potential while transforming their lives and the lives of others. Individual and organizational well-being is uplifted when we start to think in terms of possibilities (*And*-thinking). These two volumes are complete with real examples of strategies to help you accomplish this and more."

Nance Lucas, PhD
Executive Director/Chief Well-Being Officer, Center for the
Advancement of Well-Being, George Mason University

> *"... the Polarity approach in South Africa ... has em-powered many executives and managers to address complex issues ... in Mozambique, Zambia, Uganda, Rwanda, Kenia."*

"Working with Polarity Thinking in South Africa and other African countries has enabled M.B.A. students with invaluable insights and a methodology to understand the basics of leading and managing change. Polarity Thinking has empowered many executives and managers to address complex issues, including long standing nutritional issues in countries such as Mozambique, Zambia, Uganda, Rwanda, Kenia.

This is the best way I know of – and have experienced – to assist individual, team, and system-wide endeavors to enhance the quality of life of individuals and the effectiveness and survival of teams and organizations."

Leon Coetsee MA DPhil
Retired Professor of Organizational Behavior and Change,
Potchefstroom Business School, North West University,
South Africa Extraordinary Professor, Centre for Excellence for
Nutrition, North West University, Potchefstroom Campus

> *"The value and relevance of _And_ make it a significant contribution to the field. Highly recommended."*

"Barry Johnson presents unique opportunities to learn about polarity, paradox, and dilemma and experience deeper levels of understanding and knowledge about complex issues. The book is useful in various helpful and transformative ways and for a variety of purposes by individuals, groups, and organizations. It challenges the interested reader to start 'with the chapter that interests you most.' The goal (and title) of the book is to supplement *Or*-thinking with *And*-thinking. The desired result is to enhance our quality of life and Barry demonstrates many ways that can be accomplished. The dense and thoughtful content is accessible and organized and includes helpful models throughout. The value and relevance of _And_ make it a significant contribution to the field. Highly recommended."

> *Brenda B. Jones*
> *Former President and CEO of The NTL Institute,*
> *Co-Leader, NTL Global Leadership Development and*
> *Organization Development Group,*
> *Co-Editor, Gestalt Practice: Working and Living in Pursuit of wHolism*

> *"Barry outlines a both/And alternative to the either/Or mindset that too often drives our politics today..."*

"In his brilliant new book _And_, Barry Johnson gives us a fresh and timely way of understanding and addressing a wide range of polarities in society today. It certainly applies to our deep political divisions. Barry outlines a *both/And* alternative to the *either/Or* mindset that too often drives our politics today and deteriorates into *win/lose* warfare. He shows how even our most 'principled' perceptions are likely to be both accurate and incomplete. He invites us to apply the same lens to the perceptions of those too easily dismissed as opponents. Our mutual capacity to do this is a necessary component of any substantive realinement around a shared sense of the common good.

And is a rare and profoundly important book. It should be required reading for thought leaders of every party and stripe."

> *John Otterbacher, PhD*
> *Former State Senator*

> *"... one of the most significant contributions to change leadership and conflict utilization in recent history."*

"In the first few minutes of the first Polarity Thinking workshop I participated in back in 1995, I knew this powerful model would likely be embedded in every piece of work we did going forward. And it has! We use it in leadership development intensives, large-scale change initiatives, and in conflict utilization, equipping leaders and their people from 55 countries. Frankly, I can't imagine planning any kind of change or development initiative without embedding Polarity Thinking in it.

Polarity Thinking – and the processes that make it so useful in the real world – are, in my opinion, one of the most significant contributions to change leadership and conflict utilization in recent history."

> *John Scherer PhD*
> *Founding Director, Scherer Leadership Center*

> *"And teaches us how to move from polarization to a common purpose ..."*

"In *And*, Barry Johnson shares valuable wisdom and insight on polarities and how they assist in managing complex issues with no simple solutions. Through real world illustrations, he combines theory and practical application that allows readers to examine issues completely. And teaches us how to move from polarization to a common purpose and gain the benefits that come from *both/And*-thinking."

> *Gregory G. Mullen*
> *Former Chief of Police, Charleston, SC*

> *"Barry... gives us tangible and practical tools..."*

"Barry Johnson's work is critical for moving our world to a better place. He surfaces the critical and complex polarities in the world and gives us tangible and practical tools to effectively address those insights. This book is a must read for anyone who wants to make a difference in the world."

> *Wendy K. Smith*
> *Deutsch Family Fellow / Professor, University of Delaware,*
> *Co-Director, Women's Leadership Initiative at Lerner*
> *Associate Editor, Academy of Management Journal*

Barry was raised in Rice Lake, Wisconsin and graduated from the University of Wisconsin – Eau Claire in 1965. That same year he wrote an unpublished book called <u>All</u> from his awareness that "all are saved," a very elementary glimpse into Richard Rohr's comprehensive <u>Universal Christ</u>. Barry enrolled at Union Theological Seminary in New York City and began a one-year "Secular Internship Program" in East Harlem where he lived for five years. While there, he witnessed some of the impact of his dominant, white culture on those marginalized by that dominant culture. It's dehumanizing for both cultures. There was and

is plenty of injustice to protest and he found himself doing a lot of it. By 1970 Barry realized he wanted to understand how to develop organizations, communities, and nations that functioned well for all, rather than just protest when they became oppressive for many. Protest is important and Barry continues to do it. *And*, there is a need for prevention and development.

Barry decided to start with his own development and work up to larger systems. In 1975, while in the final weeks of a two-year program with the Gestalt Institute of Cleveland, he had a breakthrough session with a client. In an effort to get "unstuck" when encountering resistance, they walked around two chairs and discovered a predictable flow to the energy in the system. The first polarity map emerged. This powerful session impacted both the client and Barry. It was clear to Barry that the polarity map and principles were applicable to any system regardless of size. Since then he has been learning with people all over the world from a variety of disciplines, how to apply the Polarity Map® and principles to their situations.

In 1992 Barry wrote his first book on polarities, <u>Polarity Management, Identifying and Managing Unsolvable Problems</u>. In 1994 he founded Polarity Management Associates. In 1995 he began developing the current online Polarity Assessment™ tool. The first Two-year Mastery Program in Polarity Thinking began in 2005. In 2009 he coauthored a second book with Roy Oswald, <u>Managing Polarities in Congregations</u>. In 2011 Barry joined Leslie DePol and Robert 'Jake' Jacobs to found Polarity Partnerships, LLC.

The culmination of his work is a community of polarity practitioners authoring several polarity-related books. The two volumes of <u>*And*</u> represent what Barry and his colleagues have learned about *And*-thinking since his first book in 1992.

In 2015 Barry received the Lifetime Achievement Award from the Organization Development Network, Advancing the Practice and Theory of OD. Barry continues to learn with clients and colleagues how *And*-thinking can be useful for enhancing our quality of life with our families, organizations, communities, countries, and on our planet. <u>All</u> from '65 has led to <u>*And*</u> in '20.

Barry and his wife Dana have five children and eleven grandchildren. They both love kayaking and walking together anywhere.

Making a difference *And* enjoying life.

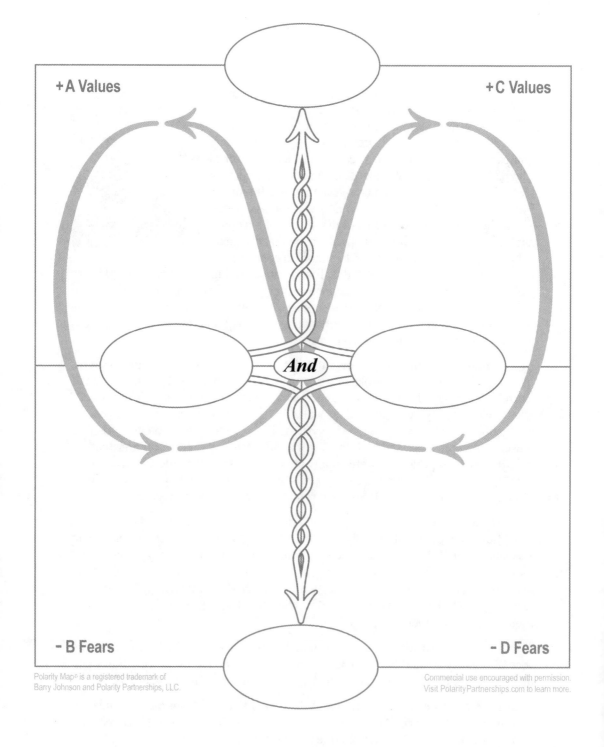

+A Values

+C Values

And

- B Fears

- D Fears

Action Steps + C

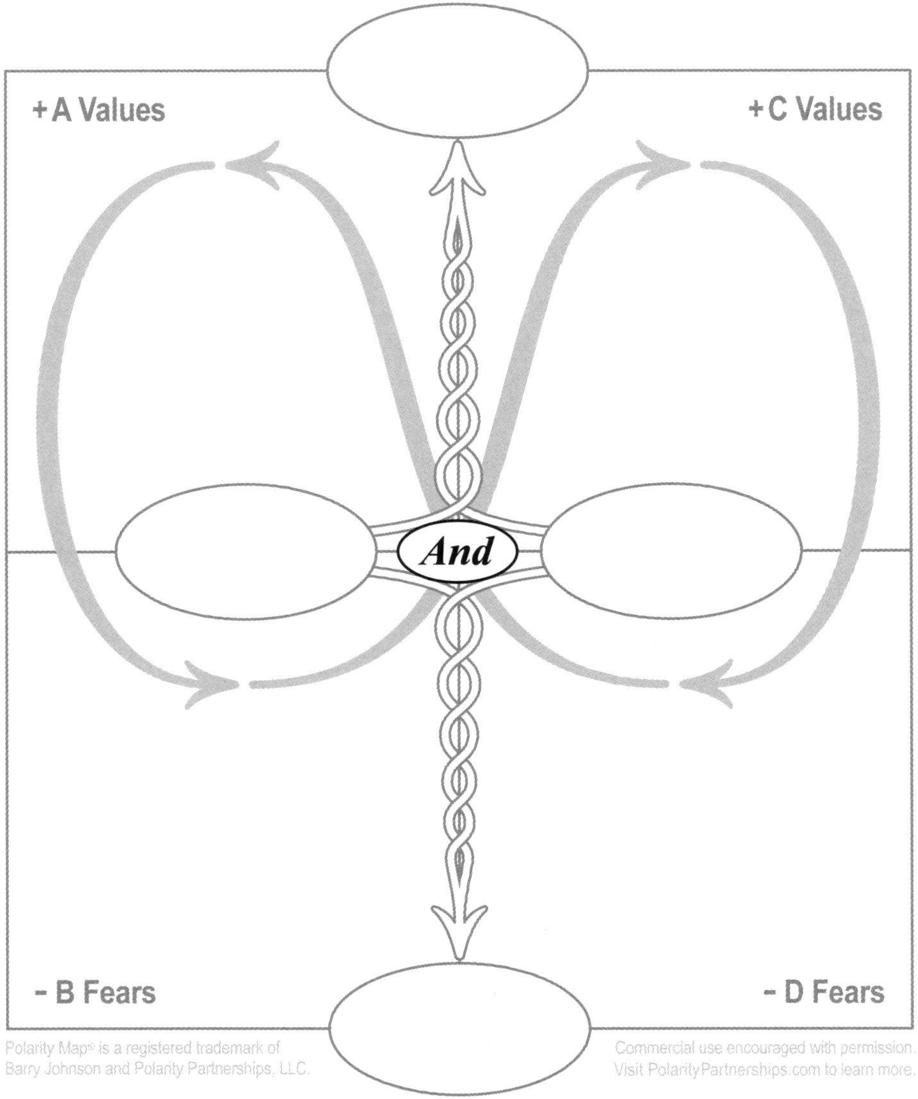

Action Steps + A

+ C Values

+ A Values

And

- D Fears

- B Fears

Early Warnings – D

Early Warnings – B

Action Steps +A

Early Warnings - B

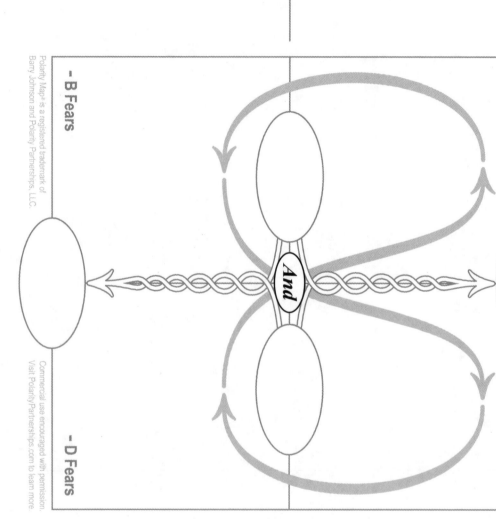

+A Values

- B Fears

And

+C Values

- D Fears

Action Steps +C

Early Warnings - D